RECORD OF SERVICES

OF THE

HONOURABLE EAST INDIA COMPANY'S
CIVIL SERVANTS

IN THE

MADRAS PRESIDENCY.

FROM 1741 TO 1858

RECORD OF SERVICES

OF THE

HONOURABLE EAST INDIA COMPANY'S
CIVIL SERVANTS
IN THE

MADRAS PRESIDENCY.

FROM 1741 TO 1858.

Including Chronological Lists of

GOVERNORS, COMMANDERS-IN-CHIEF, CHIEF JUSTICES AND JUDGES, OF THE MADRAS PRESIDENCY, BETWEEN 1652 AND 1858.

BY

CHARLES C. PRINSEP

GYAN

Published by

GYAN

Gyan Publishing House
5, Ansari Road
Daryaganj, New Delhi-110002
Phone: 011-47034999, 9811692060
E-mail: books@gyanbooks.com

Distribution Network
gyanbooks.com
India, USA, Canada, UK, Australia

ISBN: 978-81-212-6999-5 (PB)
First Published, 1885

2nd Impression 2024

Printed at: Gyan Press, Delhi.

RECORD OF SERVICES OF THE HONOURABLE EAST INDIA COMPANY'S CIVIL SERVANTS IN THE MADRAS PRESIDENCY FROM 1741 TO 1858
Author: CHARLES C. PRINSEP

RECORD OF SERVICES

OF THE

HONOURABLE EAST INDIA COMPANY'S CIVIL SERVANTS

IN THE

MADRAS PRESIDENCY.

FROM 1741 TO 1858.

Including Chronological Lists of

GOVERNORS, COMMANDERS-IN-CHIEF, CHIEF JUSTICES AND JUDGES, OF THE MADRAS PRESIDENCY, BETWEEN 1652 AND 1858.

AS WELL AS

LISTS OF THE DIRECTORS OF THE EAST INDIA COMPANY; CHAIRMEN AND DEPUTY CHAIRMEN OF THE DIRECTION; AND PRESIDENTS OF THE BOARD OF CONTROL.

Compiled and Edited, from Records in the Possession of the Secretary of State for India,

BY

CHARLES C. PRINSEP,

STATISTICAL REPORTER, AND LATE SUPERINTENDENT OF RECORDS, INDIA OFFICE.

LONDON:
TRÜBNER & CO., LUDGATE HILL.
1885.

CONTENTS.

PREFACE.

THE past History of the Old East India Company's service is too well known to require any description in this place; suffice it to remark, that it has produced a class of public servants not to be equalled by any other nation. No reader of Indian History can pronounce this eulogy as undeserved, for whether in peace or in war, rebellion or famine, its truth has been amply demonstrated.

The Indian Civil Service may be said to have commenced from the time when the Right Hon. Warren Hastings, who had previously served on the Council of the Government of Madras, was appointed Governor of Bengal in 1772, and subsequently became the first Governor-General under an Act passed (13 Geo. III., cap. 63) in 1773, when the East India Company first determined to take the country's revenues into their own hands. It was also resolved that the Presidencies of Madras and Bombay should be subject to the Governor-General in political matters. At this date the stupendous fabric of the Indian Civil Service fairly began, although from that time to the present day each Presidency has had its distinctive functions.

The first English Company for the purpose of trading with India was incorporated by Queen Elizabeth on 31st December

1599 under the title of "*The Governor and Company of Merchants of London trading to the East Indies.*" Courten's Association, *the Assada Merchants*, established in 1635, united with the *London Company* in 1650. The "*Merchant Adventurers*," chartered in 1654–55, united with the *London Company* in 1656–57. The "*English Company*" (or "*the General Society*") trading to the East Indies was incorporated in 1698. The aforesaid Company of Merchants of London, and the English Company, were finally incorporated under the title of "*The United Company of Merchants of England trading to the East Indies*" in 1708, and thus was founded the East India Company, which title it maintained until 1858 (an unbroken period of one hundred and fifty years), when the transfer of Indian affairs to the Crown was effected.

Fort St. George, Madras, was erected in the year 1640, and in 1653 the possessions of the East India Company along the Coromandel Coast, comprising the settlements (as they were then termed) of Fort St. George, Fort St. David, Vizagapatam, and Mechlipatam (Masulipatam), were raised to the rank of a Presidency.

In offering to the public a record of the services of the Madras Covenanted Civilians the compiler has no desire to credit himself with being the first to have initiated such a work, for Messrs. Dodwell and Miles prepared a similar register (now out of print and unobtainable), commencing with civilians who were in the service in 1780 and ending with the year 1839, the date of publication; but notwithstanding its excellence, there is a want of completeness as a work of reference at the present time to the general reader, thus rendering further work necessary, which it has been the object of the compiler herein to achieve.

The present register will be found to contain the names and services of all Civil servants who were on the Madras establishment of the East India Company in 1766 (which is the earliest date of the Indian Registers), and of all those who subsequently entered the service up to, and were in the service in, 1858, when the change of Government took place. In the case of those officers who continued in the service after that date, the appointments held by them up to retirement or death have also been included. It is to be regretted that the present work is still not so complete as it might have been made, for since going to press manuscript lists of services of civilians from 1700 have been discovered to exist, too late however for insertion in the present volume; but it may be hoped that these new sources of information will be placed before the public at some future time.

In all cases the dates of death have been given where the information has been accessible.

The services of civilians not recorded in this work will be found in a "History of Services of all Gazetted Officers in the Civil Department," covenanted, uncovenanted, and military officers in civil employ, annually published by each administration or province in India.

Further information of a varied character, extracted from the Old Court Books of the East India Company, public consultations of the respective Governments in India, and other valuable records in the India Office, has been appended, so as to render the work a more useful one for general reference, and to increase the interest of officers still living, as well as of relatives of deceased persons, in those who have played their parts so prominently, and added lustre to a record of services performed by civil servants, in India.

In conclusion, the compiler desires to express his sense of the valuable and willing assistance rendered by Colonel Laurie, of the Royal (late Madras) Artillery, in the laborious searches that had to be made in following up each individual name through nearly 200 volumes of registers and other books of reference, and without whose practical experience of India, and of Madras in particular, the publication of this record of services would have been much retarded.

INDIA OFFICE, *19th February* 1885.

ALPHABETICAL LIST

OF

DIRECTORS OF THE UNITED COMPANY OF MERCHANTS OF ENGLAND TRADING TO THE EAST INDIES

(*Incorporated under Act, Queen Anne, in* 1708),

OTHERWISE ENTITLED THE EAST INDIA COMPANY,

FROM 1708 TO 1858.

NOTE.—Previous to the year 1773, the twenty-four Directors were elected every year, and the day of election was in the month of April. In 1773 (Act 13 Geo. III. cap. 63) the system of election was changed. It was then provided that six Directors should be chosen for 4 years, six for 3 years, six for 2 years, and six for 1 year, and at every Annual Election six new Directors were to be chosen for the term of 4 years, and no longer. Subsequently, Act 17 Geo. III. cap. 8, of 1777, fixed the second Wednesday in April as the date of the Annual Election. The qualification of a Director was £2000 East India stock. In the event of a vacancy by death or otherwise, another Director had to be chosen within 40 days of the declaration of such vacancy, the new Director succeeding to the unexpired portion of his predecessor's term of office. The salaries of Directors were regulated by the Bye-laws. In earlier years each Director received £150 per annum, in 1794 the amount was increased to £300, and in 1854 to £500, a year.

Names.	Period of Service as Director.
ADAMS, ROBERT . . .	1736; 1737.
Addams, Abraham . . .	1721 to 1739.
Agnew, Patrick Vans (C.B.) .	1833; 1835 to 1842 (Lt.-Col. in 1840). Died in June 1842.
Aislabie, William . . .	1719 to 1726.
Alexander, Josias du Pré .	(M.P., Old Sarum); 1820 to 1839. Died in Sept. 1839.
Alexander, Henry . . .	(M.P., Barnstaple) 1826 to 1853. Died in Jan. 1861.
Allan, Alexander . . .	(M.P., Berwick); 1814 to 1819 (Bart. in 1819). Died in Oct. 1820.
Allen, Edward . . .	(Director of English Company) 1709.
Amyard, George . . .	1760; 1763.
Andrews, Sir Jonathan (Knt.) .	(Director of English Company) 1709; 1711; and 1712 to 1716.

Names.	Period of Service as Director.
Astell, William	(1807 to 1845 (M.P., Bridgewater, 1809). Died March 1847.
Astell, John Harvey . .	1851 to 1858.
BAKER, WILLIAM . . .	(Alderman) 1741 to 1752.
Baillie, Colonel John . .	(M.P., Hedon) 1823 to 1833. Died in May 1833.
Bance, John	1722 to 1730.
Bannerman, John Alexander .	1807 to 1816. Disqualified in 1817.
Baring, Francis . . .	1779 to 1810 (Bart. in 1799). Died in Oct. 1810.
Barne, Miles	1733; and 1736 to 1739.
Baron, Christopher . . .	1759; and 1761 to 1767.
Barrington, Fitzwilliam . .	1759 to 1767.
Barwell, William . . .	1753 to 1766.
Bateman, Sir James (Knt.) .	(Director of English Company) 1709; 1710, Alderman.
Bayley, William Butterworth .	1834 to 1858. Died in May 1860.
Baylis, Sir Robert (Knt.) .	(Alderman) 1731; 1732.
Beake, Abraham . . .	(Director of London Company) 1709.
Bebb, John	1805 to 1829. Disqualified in 1830.
Becher, Richard	1775 to 1783.
Beck, Justus	1714.
Bensley, William . . .	1786 to 1810 (Bart. in 1801). Died in Jan. 1810.
Benyon, Richard	1745 to 1748.
Betts, William	1709 to 1711.
Billers, William	(Alderman) 1724 to 1742 (Knight in 1727) (Lord Mayor in 1734).
Bisse, Stephen	1732; 1735 to 1741.
Blount, Richard	1730 to 1743.
Blunt, John	1709.
Boddam, Charles . . .	1769; 1772 to 1782.
Boehm, Edmund . . .	1784 to 1787.
Boone, Charles	1729 to 1735.
Booth, Benjamin . . .	1767 to 1783.
Bootle, Capt. Robert . .	1741 to 1749; 1752; 1753; 1755.
Bosanquet, Jacob (1) . . .	1759.
Bosanquet, Jacob (2) . . .	1790 to 1827. Disqualified in 1827.
Bosanquet, Richard . . .	1768 to 1772.
Bosanquet, Joseph . . .	1785 to 1788.
Boulton, Capt. Richard . .	1718 to 1736.
Boulton, Henry Crabb . .	1753 to 1773. Died in Sept. 1773.
Boyd, John	1753 to 1764.
Braddyll, Dodding . . .	1728 to 1748.
Baund, William	1745 to 1753.
Brisco, Robert	1712 to 1720.
Bristow, Robert	1716; 1717.
Browne, Capt. John . . .	1714 to 1720.
Browne, John	1757 to 1763.

Names.	Period of Service as Director.
Bryant, Maj.-Gen. Sir Jeremiah (C.B.)	1841 to 1845. Died in June 1845.
Burgess, John Smith	1791 to 1802 (Bart. in 1801). Died in 1803.
Burrow, Christopher	1735 to 1761.
Burrow, Robert	1762 to 1764.
Burton, Richard	1741 to 1746.
CAMPBELL, ROBERT	1817 to 1852 (Bart. in 1832). Died in 1858.
Carnac, James Rivett	1827 to 1839 (Bart. in 1836). Appointed Governor of Bombay in 1839.
Caulfield, Maj.-Gen. James, C.B.	1848 to 1851. Died in Nov. 1852.
Chambers, Charles (senr.)	1755 to 1757; 1763 to 1768.
Chambers, Charles (junr.)	1770; 1773.
Chauncey, Richard	1737 to 1754.
Cheap, Thomas	1780 to 1793.
Child, Robert	1709 to 1720 (Alderman in 1714) (Knight in 1715).
Child, Francis	1718; 1722 (Alderman); 1732 (Lord Mayor); 1733 (Knight).
Clarke, William Stanley	1815 to 1843. Died in Jan. 1844.
Clerk, Robert	1812 to 1815. Died in Aug. 1815.
Cock, Peter	1725 to 1730.
Cockburn, Sir James (Bart.)	1767 to 1772.
Cooke, Richard	(Director of London Company) 1709 to 1711.
Colborne, Charles	1734 to 1737.
Colebrooke, Sir George (Bart.)	1767 to 1772.
Cooke, John	(Director of London Company) 1709 to 1734.
Cornelison, William Henry	1713 to 1715.
Cotesworth, William	Director of English Company) 1710 to 1713.
Cotesworth, Dr. Caleb	1721 to 1734.
Cotton, Joseph	1795 to 1823. Disqualified in 1823.
Cotton, John	1833 to 1853. Died in July 1860.
Coupland, John	1713.
Coulson, Thomas	(Director of English Company) 1709 to 1712.
Creed, Sir James (Bart.)	1749; 1755 to 1758; 1761.
Creswicke, Joseph	1765 to 1768.
Cruttenden, Edward Holden	1765 to 1771.
Cuming, George	1764 to 1782, and 1785 to 1788.
Currie, Sir Frederick (Bart.)	1854 to 1858. Died in Sept. 1875.
Cust, Peregrine	1767 to 1769.
Cutts, Charles	1749 to 1754; 1758 to 1766.
DANIEL, JAMES	1810 to 1824.

Names.	Period of Service as Director.
Darell, Lionel	1780 to 1803 (Bart. in 1800). Died in 1803.
Davis, Samuel . . .	1810 to 1819. Died in July 1819.
Dawsonne, William . .	(Director of English Company) 1710 to 1722.
Decker, Matthew . . .	1714 to 1732 (Bart. in 1717).
Dempster, George . . .	1769; 1772.
Dent, William . . .	1851 to 1853. Died in Dec. 1877.
Dethick, Thomas . . .	1772.
Devaynes, William . . .	1770 to 1805 (1802, M.P., Barnstaple).
Dorrien, John	1755 to 1763.
Drake, Roger	1738 to 1758.
Drummond, John . . .	1722 to 1733.
Ducane, Peter (senr.) . .	1750 to 1753.
Ducane, Peter (junr.) . .	1764 to 1773.
Dudley, George . . .	1757 to 1767; 1770 and 1771.
Du Pré, Josias . . .	1765; 1766.
Dutry, Sir Dennis (Bart.) .	1724 to 1727.
Eastwick, Captain William Joseph	1849 to 1858.
Ecclestone, John . . .	1721 to 1735.
Edmonstone, Neil Benjamin .	1820 to 1840.
Ellice, Russell . . .	1832 to 1858.
Elphinstone, Hon. William Fullarton	1791 to 1824.
Elwick, John	1713 to 1720.
Emmerson, John . . .	1735 to 1745.
Ewer, Walter	1792 to 1795.
Eyles, Francis	(Director of English Company) 1709.
Eyles, John	1710 to 1713; and 1717 to 1720 (Bart. in 1717).
Eyles, Joseph	1714 to 1716; and 1721.
Farquhar, Sir Robert Townsend (Bart.) . . .	M.P., Hythe, 1826 to 1828.
Feake, Samuel . . .	1733 to 1751.
Fergusson, Robert Cutlar .	1830 to 1834 (1832, M.P., Kirkcudbright).
Fitzhugh, Thomas . . .	1787 to 1800. Died in 1800.
Fleet, Sir John (Knt.) . .	(Director of London Company and Alderman) 1709 and 1711. Died in July 1712.
Fletcher, Henry . . .	1769 to 1774; and 1777 to 1785 (Bart. in 1783.
Forbes, John	(M.P., Malmesbury) 1831 to 1839.
Fonnereau, Abel . . .	1749 to 1752.
Fonnereau, Zachary Philip .	1753 and 1754.
Fraser, Simon	1793 to 1807.
Freeman, William George .	1769; and 1774 to 1781.
Fryer, Sir John, Bart. . .	1719 (Alderman).

Names.	Period of Service as Director.
GALLOWAY, Maj.-Genl. ARCHIBALD, C.B.	1842 to 1849 (K.C.B. in 1849). Died in April 1850.
Gibbon, Edward	(Director of London Company) 1709 to 1711.
Gildart, Richard	1759.
Gill, Leonard	1724 to 1732.
Godfrey, Peter	1710 to 1717 and 1734 to 1760.
Gosselin, William	1714 to 1743.
Gough, Richard	(Director of English Company) 1713 to 1720 (Knight in 1715).
Gough, Capt. Harry (senr.)	1730 to 1733 and 1736 to 1751.
Gough, Harry (junr.)	1735 to 1751.
Gough, Charles	1749 to 1762.
Gould, John (senr.)	1710 to 1712 and 1715 to 1735.
Gould, Nathaniel	(Director of English Company) 1714.
Gould, John (junr.)	1724 to 1735.
Grant, Charles	1797 to 1823 (M.P., Inverness-shire in 1802). Died in November 1823.
Gregory, Robert	1769 to 1772 and 1775 to 1783.
HADLEY, HENRY	1757 to 1765.
Hall, Richard	1773 to 1789.
Hall, Urban	(Director of London Company) 1709.
Harrison, Sir Edmond (Knt.)	(Director of English Company) 1710, 1711.
Harrison, Edward	1718 to 1731.
Harrison, John	1758 to 1771 and 1774 to 1782.
Harrison, Samuel	1759; 1761; and 1762.
Hawkesworth, John	1773.
Heath, Thomas	1713 to 1715 and 1719 to 1721.
Heathcote, John	1716 to 1724 and 1728 to 1731.
Heathcote, Henry	1725 to 1727.
Herne, Joseph	1719 to 1722.
Herne, Frederick	1709 to 1713.
Herne, Nathaniel	(Director of London Company) 1710 to 1718.
Hewer, William	(Director of London Company) 1709 to 1712.
Hodges, Joseph	1714 to 1716 (Baronet in 1715).
Hodges, Sir William (Bart.)	1712.
Hogg, James Weir	(M.P., Beverley) 1839 to 1858 (1846, Baronet), (1850, M.P., Honiton). Died in May 1876.
Hope, John	1738 to 1741 and 1744 to 1752.
Hudlestone, John	1803 to 1826 (1805, M.P., Bridgewater). Disqualified in 1826.
Hudson, Capt. Robert	1721 to 1729; 1732 to 1734; and 1745 to 1748.
Hume, Alexander	1737 to 1748.
Humphreys, Sir William (Knt.)	(Alderman) 1711 to 1714.
Hunter, John	1781 to 1802.

Names.	Period of Service as Director.
Hurlock, Joseph	1768; and 1770 to 1773.
Hyde, Samuel	1734 to 1747.
IMPLY, MICHAEL . . .	1736 to 1757.
Inglis, Hugh	1784 to 1812 (Baronet in 1801) (M.P., Ashburton in 1802).
Inglis, John	1803 to 1821.
Irwin, James	1797 to 1800.
JACKSON, WILLIAM ADAIR .	1803; and 1804.
Jackson, John	1807 to 1820 (1808, M.P., Dover) (Baronet in 1815). Died in June 1820.
James, William . . .	1768 to 1786 (1779, Baronet).
Janssen, Abraham . . .	1725 to 1728.
Jenkins, Richard . . .	1833 to 1853 (M.P., Shrewsbury in 1837) (G.C.B. in 1839). Died 30th Dec. 1853.
KELSEY, HENRY	1709 to 1712; and 1715 to 1727.
LASCELLES, HENRY . .	1737 to 1745.
Lascelles, Peter . . .	1770 to 1775.
Law, Stephen	1746 to 1756.
Lethieullier, Benjamin . .	1730 to 1733.
Lemesurier, Paul . . .	(Alderman) 1784 to 1802; and 1805 (Lord Mayor in 1794). Died in 1806.
Lindsay, Honble. Hugh . .	1814 to 1844 (1826, M.P., Forfar). Died in May 1844.
Linwood, Nicholas . . .	1749 to 1754.
Loch, John	1821 to 1853.
Lock, Sir John (Knt.) . .	1733.
Loribond, Edward . . .	1736; and 1737.
Lumsden, John . . .	1817; and 1818. Died in Dec. 1818.
Lushington, Stephen . .	1782 to 1802. (Bart. in 1792); (M.P. for Penrhyn in 1802). Died in 1807.
Lushington, James Law . .	(M.P., Carlisle), 1827 to 1853; (C.B. in 1830); (1837, Major-Gen. and K.C.B.); (1847, G.C.B.) Died in 1859.
Lyall, George	1830 to 1850; (1842, M.P., London). Disqualified in 1851.
Lyell, Henry	(Director of English Company), 1710 to 1730.
Lyell, Baltzar	1723 to 1740.
MABBOTT, CAPTAIN WILLIAM .	1741 to 1756.
Macnaghten, Elliot . . .	1842 to 1858.
Mangles, Ross Donnelly . .	(M.P., Guildford), 1847 to 1858. Died in Aug. 1877.

Names.	Period of Service as Director.
Manship, John	1755 to 1758; 1762 to 1809. Disqualified in 1809.
Marjoribanks, Campbell	1807 to 1840. Died in Sept. 1840.
Marjoribanks, Dudley Coutts	1853.
Martin, Matthew	1722 to 1729; and 1732 to 1740.
Masterman, John	1824 to 1853; (1842, M.P., London).
Mathew, Sir George (Knt.)	1710 to 1713.
Mead, Richard	1709; and 1712.
Melville, Hon. William Henry Leslie	1845 to 1855.
Metcalfe, Thomas Theophilus	1789 to 1812; (1802, M.P., Abingdon); (1803, Bart.) Died in 1813.
Michell, Robert	1712 to 1718.
Michie, John	1770 to 1780; and 1783 to 1791.
Millett, George	1806 to 1812.
Mills, William	1778 to 1785. Disqualified in 1785.
Mills, Charles (senr.)	1778 to 1781; 1793 to 1815 (1802, M.P., Warwick). Disqualified in 1815.
Mills, Charles (junr.)	1823 to 1858 (Bart. in 1868). Died in 1872.
Moffat, James	1774 to 1782; and 1787 to 1790.
Money, William	1789 to 1797.
Money, William Taylor	(M.P., Wotton Basset), 1818 to 1825. Disqualified in 1826.
Moore, Arthur	(Director of London Company) 1709.
Moore, Major James Arthur	1850 to 1853. Died in July 1860.
Morris, John	1814 to 1837. Disqualified in 1838.
Motteux, John	1769; and 1784 to 1787.
Muspratt, John Petty	1824 to 1853. Died in Aug. 1855.
Newnham, Nathaniel	1738 to 1758.
Nightingale, Robert	1712 to 1722 (Bart. in 1715).
Oliphant, Major James	1844 to 1856 (Lieut.-Col. in 1856). Died in June 1881.
Owen, Edward	1722 to 1729.
Page, Ambrose	1714.
Page, Gregory (senr.)	(Director of London Company), 1709 to 1722; (Knt. in 1715).
Page, Gregory, junr.	1719 to 1722.
Page, John	1730 to 1732.
Paggen, Captain Peter	1709.
Pardoe, John	1765 to 1768.
Parry, Thomas	1783 to 1806.
Parry, Edward	1800 to 1826. Died in July 1827.
Parry, Richard	1815 to 1816. Died in July 1817.
Pattison, James	1806 to 1829. Disqualified in 1830.
Pattle, Thomas	1787 to 1795.
Payne, John	1741 to 1757.

Names.	Period of Service as Director.
Peach, Samuel	1773 to 1784.
Peers, Sir Charles (Knt.) .	(Director of English Company and Alderman) 1712 to 1714.
Phipps, Thomas . . .	1742 to 1758.
Pigou, Frederick . . .	1758 to 1776.
Plaut, Henry	1745 to 1758.
Plowden, Richard Chicheley .	1803 to 1829. Died in Feb. 1830.
Plowden, Wm. Henry Chicheley	1841 to 1853. Died in March 1880.
Pollock, Lieut.-Gen. Sir George, G.C.B.	1854 to 1858. Died in Oct. 1872.
Pomeroy, William . . .	1736 to 1744.
Prescott, Charles Elton . .	1820 to 1832. Died in June 1832.
Prinsep, Henry Thoby . .	1850 to 1858. Died in Feb. 1878.
Purling, John	1763 to 1771; and 1777 to 1780.
RAIKES, GEORGE . . .	1817 to 1836. Disqualified in 1836.
Ravenshaw, John Goldsborough	1819 to 1839. Died in June 1840.
Rawlinson, Lieut.-Col. Sir Henry Creswicke, K.C.B. .	1856 to 1858.
Raymond, Jones . . .	1734 to 1757.
Raymond, John . . .	1757 to 1760.
Reid, Thomas	1805 to 1824. (Baronet in 1824.) Died in March 1824.
Rider, William . . .	1738 to 1754.
Robarts, Abraham . . .	1788 to 1814 (1802, M.P., Worcester.) Disqualified in 1815.
Roberts, John	1764 to 1772; 1775 to 1778; 1784 to 1787; and 1790 to 1808.
Robertson, Major-Gen. Archibald	1841 and 1844 to 1847. Died in June 1847.
Robinson, George Abercrombie	1808 to 1829 (M.P., Honiton in 1813) (Baronet in 1825). Disqualified in 1829.
Rokeby, Benjamin . . .	1720.
Rooke, Giles	1758 to 1764.
Rous, William	1733 to 1741 (Knight and Alderman in 1738).
Rous, Thomas	1745 to 1771.
Rous, Thomas Bates . .	1773 to 1779.
Rumbold, Thomas . . .	1772 to 1778.
SATTER, JOHN	Alderman 1734 to 1744; (Knight in 1736); (Lord Mayor in 1740).
Saunders, Thomas . . .	1757; and 1765 to 1767.
Savage, Charles . . .	1725 to 1728; and 1731 (Disqualified for transferring part of his stock).
Savage, John	1733.
Savage, Henry	1755 to 1762; 1765 to 1767; and 1770 to 1782.
Scawen, Sir William (Knt.) .	(Director of English Company) 1710 to 1711.

Names.	Period of Service as Director.
Scott, David	1793 to 1801; 1814 to 1819 (Baronet in 1819). Disqualified in 1820.
Scrafton, Luke	1765 to 1768.
Seward, Richard	1759 to 1763.
Shank, Henry	1831 to 1853.
Shepheard, Samuel (1)	(Director of English Company) 1709 to 1710.
Shepheard, Francis	1712 to 1714.
Shepheard, Samuel (2)	1717 to 1719.
Shepherd, John	1836 to 1858. Died in January 1859.
Smith, Richard	1759 to 1764.
Smith, Joshua	1771; 1772.
Smith, John	1773 to 1789.
Smith, Nathaniel	1774 to 1795.
Smith, Samuel	1783 to 1786.
Smith, George	1797 to 1832 (M.P., Midhurst in 1802). Disqualified in 1833.
Smith, Martin Tucker	1840 to 1858 (M.P., Wycombe in 1848). Died in October 1880.
Snell, William	1742 to 1764; 1767 to 1769.
Sparkes, Joseph	1773 to 1789.
Stables, John	1774 to 1781.
Steele, William	1742 to 1748.
Steevens, George	1757 to 1763.
Stephenson, John	1765 to 1768.
Stewart, Sir William (Knt.)	(Alderman) 1716 to 1719.
Stuart, James	(M.P., Huntingdon) 1826 to 1833. Died in April 1833.
Styleman, John	1716 to 1718.
Sulivan, Laurence	1755 to 1758; 1760 to 1764; 1769 to 1772; 1778 to 1781; 1783.
Sykes, Lieut.-Col. William Henry	1840 to 1858 (Colonel in 1857). Died in June 1872.
Tatem, George	1772 to 1784; 1788 to 1801.
Taylor, John Bladen	1810 to 1819.
Thellusson, George Woodford	1799 to 1807.
Theunemans, Simon	1720 to 1732.
Thompson, St. Quentin	1732 to 1736.
Thornhill, John	1816 to 1840. Died in February 1841.
Thornton, John	1749; 1750.
Thornton, William (1)	1759 to 1764.
Thornton, Robert	1790 to 1813 (1802, M.P., Colchester)
Thornton, William (2)	1800 to 1805.
Toone, Sweny	1800 to 1830. Disqualified in 1831.
Tourton, Nicholas	(Director of London Company) 1710 to 1712.
Townson, John	1785 to 1798.
Travers, John	1786 to 1809. Died in October 1809.
Trenchfield, Elihu	1723.
Tucker, Henry St. George	1826 to 1851. Died in June 1851.

Names.	Period of Service as Director.
Tullie, Timothy	1750 to 1763.
Turner, Edward	1717; 1718; and 1721 to 1723.
Turner, Whichcott	1742 to 1755.
Twining, Richard	1810 to 1816. Disqualified in 1817.
VAN NECK, GERRARD . .	1729 to 1731.
Vansittart, Henry	1769.
Verelst, Harry	1771.
Vivian, Maj.-Gen. Sir John Hussey (K.C.B.) . .	1856 to 1858.
WALKER, JOHN	1732.
Wallis, James	1714 to 1716.
Walpole, Thomas	1753; and 1754.
Walton, Bourchier	1759 to 1762.
Ward, John (Senr.)	(Alderman, and Director of English Company) 1709 to 1711; and 1718.
Ward, John (Junr.)	1712 to 1715; and 1718 to 1726.
Ward, Edward	1762.
Warden, Francis	1838 to 1851. Disqualified in 1851.
Warner, Richard	1760 to 1763.
Waters, Thomas	1759 to 1762.
Webber, William	1762 to 1765.
Webster, Sir Thomas (Bart.) .	1715; 1716.
Webster, Sir Godfrey (Knt.) .	1717 to 1719.
Western, Maximilian . .	1755 to 1757.
Wheler, Edward	1765 to 1777.
Whiteman, John Clarmont .	1844 to 1852. Died in Aug. 1866.
Wier, Daniel	1768 to 1776.
Wigram, William	1809 to 1812 (1810, M.P., New Ross); 1815 to 1853 (M.P., Wexford, in 1825).
Wilberforce, William . .	1753; and 1754.
Wilkinson, Jacob	1782 to 1785.
Williams, Stephen	1791 to 1804. Died in 1805.
Williams, Robert	1809 to 1812. Died in July 1812.
Willock, Sir Henry (K.L.S.) .	1838 to 1858.
Willoughby, John Pollard .	1854 to 1858 (1857, M.P., Leominster). Died Sept. 1866.
Willy, William	1746 to 1754.
Winter, Capt. James . .	1737 to 1754.
Withers, Sir William . .	1709.
Wombwell, George . . .	1766 to 1768; and 1775 to 1783 (Bart. in 1780).
Woodhouse, John	1768 to 1781; and 1788 to 1791.
Wordsworth, Josias (Senr.) .	1712 to 1739.
Wordsworth, Josias (Junr.) .	1721 to 1736.
YOUNG, Sir WILLIAM (Bart.) .	1829 to 1846.

LIST OF

CHAIRMEN AND DEPUTY CHAIRMEN

OF THE

UNITED COMPANY OF MERCHANTS OF ENGLAND TRADING TO THE EAST INDIES.

1714 TO 1858.

[NOTE.—The Chairman and Deputy Chairman were first elected by the Directors permanently for a whole year in 1714. Previous to this date a Chairman was appointed on each occasion of a meeting of the Court. The salaries of the Chairman and Deputy Chairman in earlier years were under the Bye-laws £200 a year each. In 1794 they were increased to £500, and in 1854 to £1000 a year each.]

Years Elected.	Chairman.	Deputy Chairman.
1714	Sir Charles Peers (Knt.).	Robert Child (Alderman).
1715	Sir Robert Child (Knt.)	Josias Wordsworth.
1716	Sir Gregory Page (Bart.)	Henry Lyell.
1717	Josias Wordsworth.	Henry Lyell.
1718	Henry Lyell.	Sir Robert Nightingale (Bart.)
1719	Sir Robert Nightingale (Bart.)	William Dawsonne.
1720	William Dawsonne.	Sir Mathew Decker (Bart.)
1721	Henry Lyell.	Thomas Heath.
1722	Josias Wordsworth.	Joseph Herne.
1723	Josias Wordsworth.	Edward Harrison.
1724	Edward Harrison.	Abraham Addams.
1725	Sir Mathew Decker (Bart.)	Henry Lyell.
1726	Henry Lyell.	John Gould.
1727	John Gould.	Josias Wordsworth.
1728	Josias Wordsworth.	Edward Harrison.
1729	Edward Harrison.	Sir Mathew Decker (Bart.)
1730	Sir Mathew Decker (Bart.)	Josias Wordsworth.
1731	Sir Mathew Decker (Bart.)	Edward Harrison.
1732	Sir Mathew Decker (Bart.)	Josias Wordsworth.
1733	Josias Wordsworth.	John Gould.
1734	Josias Wordsworth.	Abraham Addams.
1735	Josias Wordsworth.	Sir William Billers (Knt. and Alderman).

Years Elected.	Chairman.	Deputy Chairman.
1736	Sir William Billers (Knt.)	Harry Gough.
1737	Harry Gough.	Josias Wordsworth.
1738	Josias Wordsworth.	Sir William Rous (Knt. and Alderman).
1739	Sir William Rous (Knt.)	Samuel Feake.
1740	Samuel Feake.	Harry Gough.
1741	Harry Gough.	Sir John Salter (Knt. and Alderman).
1742	Sir John Salter (Knt.)	Harry Gough.
1743	Harry Gough.	Samuel Feake.
1744	Samuel Feake.	Dodding Braddyll.
1745	Dodding Braddyll.	Harry Gough.
1746	Harry Gough.	Samuel Feake.
1747	Harry Gough.	Richard Chauncey.
1748	Richard Chauncey.	Dodding Braddyll. (Died in Jan. 1748–9.)
1749	William Baker.	Richard Chauncey.
1750	Richard Chauncey.	Harry Gough.
1751	Roger Drake.	William Baker.
1752	William Baker.	Richard Chauncey.
1753	Richard Chauncey.	Roger Drake.
1754	Roger Drake.	Richard Chauncey.
1755	Roger Drake.	Peter Godfrey.
1756	Peter Godfrey.	John Payne.
1757	John Payne.	Laurence Sulivan.
1758	Laurence Sulivan.	Roger Drake.
1759	Peter Godfrey.	John Boyd.
1760	Laurence Sulivan.	Thomas Rous.
1761	Laurence Sulivan.	Thomas Rous.
1762	Thomas Rous.	John Dorrien.
1763	John Dorrien.	Laurence Sulivan.
1764	Thomas Rous.	Henry Crabb Boulton.
1765	Henry Crabb Boulton.	George Dudley.
1766	George Dudley.	Thomas Rous.
1767	Thomas Rous.	Thomas Saunders.
1768	Henry Crabb Boulton.	Sir George Colebrooke (Bart.)
1769	Sir George Colebrooke (Bart.)	Peregrine Cust.
1770	Sir George Colebrooke (Bart.)	John Purling.
1771	John Purling.	George Dudley.
1772	Sir George Colebrooke (Bart.)	Laurence Sulivan.
1773	Henry Crabb Boulton. (Died in October 1773.)	Edward Wheler.
	Edward Wheler.	John Harrison.
1774	Edward Wheler.	John Harrison.
1775	John Harrison.	John Roberts.
1776	John Roberts.	William James.
1777	George Wombwell.	William Devaynes.
1778	George Wombwell.	William James.
1779	Sir William James (Bart.)	William Devaynes.
1780	William Devaynes.	Laurence Sulivan.

Years Elected.	Chairman.	Deputy Chairman.
1781	Laurence Sulivan.	Sir William James (Bart.)
1782	Robert Gregory.	Henry Fletcher.
1783	Sir Henry Fletcher (Bart.)	Nathaniel Smith.
1784	Nathaniel Smith.	William Devaynes.
1785	William Devaynes.	Nathaniel Smith.
1786	John Michie.	John Motteux.
1787	John Motteux.	Nathaniel Smith.
1788	Nathaniel Smith.	John Michie.
1789	William Devaynes.	Stephen Lushington.
1790	Stephen Lushington.	William Devaynes.
1791	John Smith Burges.	Francis Baring.
1792	Francis Baring.	John Smith Burges.
1793	William Devaynes.	Thomas Cheap.
1794	William Devaynes.	John Hunter.
1795	Sir Stephen Lushington (Bart).	David Scott.
1796	David Scott.	Hugh Inglis.
1797	Hugh Inglis.	Jacob Bosanquet.
1798	Jacob Bosanquet.	Sir Stephen Lushington (Bart.)
1799	Sir Stephen Lushington (Bart.)	Hugh Inglis.
1800	Hugh Inglis.	David Scott.
1801	David Scott.	Charles Mills.
1802	John Roberts.	Jacob Bosanquet.
1803	Jacob Bosanquet.	John Roberts.
1804	Hon. Wm. Fullarton Elphinstone.	Charles Grant.
1805	Charles Grant.	George Smith.
1806	Hon. Wm. Fullarton Elphinstone.	Edward Parry.
1807	Edward Parry.	Charles Grant.
1808	Edward Parry.	Charles Grant.
1809	Charles Grant, M.P.	William Astell, M.P.
1810	William Astell, M.P.	Jacob Bosanquet.
1811	Jacob Bosanquet.	Sir Hugh Inglis (Bart.)
1812	Jacob Bosanquet.	Sir Hugh Inglis (Bart.)
1813	Robert Thornton.	Hon. Wm. Fullarton Elphinstone.
1814	Hon. Wm. Fullarton Elphinstone.	John Inglis.
1815	Charles Grant, M.P.	Thomas Reid.
1816	Thomas Reid.	John Bebb.
1817	John Bebb.	James Pattison.
1818	James Pattison.	Campbell Marjoribanks.
1819	Campbell Marjoribanks.	George Abercrombie Robinson.
1820	George Abercrombie Robinson.	Thomas Reid.
1821	Thomas Reid.	James Pattison.
1822	James Pattison.	William Wigram.
1823	William Wigram, M.P.	William Astell, M.P.
1824	William Astell, M.P.	Campbell Marjoribanks.
1825	Campbell Marjoribanks.	Sir George Abercrombie Robinson (Bart.)

Years Elected.	Chairman.	Deputy Chairman.
1826	Sir George Abercrombie Robinson, (Bart.)	Hon. Hugh Lindsay, M.P.
1827	Hon. Hugh Lindsay, M.P. (Bart.)	James Pattison.
1828	William Astell, M.P.	John Loch.
1829	John Loch.	William Astell, M.P.
1830	William Astell, M.P.	Robert Campbell.
1831	Robert Campbell.	John Goldsborough Ravenshaw.
1832	John Goldsborough Ravenshaw.	Campbell Marjoribanks.
1833	Campbell Marjoribanks.	William Wigram.
1834	Henry St. George Tucker.	William Stanley Clarke.
1835	William Stanley Clarke.	James Rivett Carnac.
1836	Sir James Rivett Carnac, (Bart.)	John Loch.
1837	Sir James Rivett Carnac, (Bart.)	Major-Gen. Sir James Law Lushington, K.C.B.
1838	Major-Gen. Sir James Law Lushington, K.C.B.	Richard Jenkins, M.P.
1839	Sir Richard Jenkins, G.C.B., M.P.	William Butterworth Bayley.
1840	William Butterworth Bayley.	George Lyall.
1841	George Lyall.	Major-Gen. Sir James Law Lushington, G.C.B.
1842	Major-Gen. Sir James Law Lushington, G.C.B.	John Cotton.
1843	John Cotton.	John Shepherd.
1844	John Shepherd.	Sir Henry Willock, K.L.S.
1845	Sir Henry Willock, K.L.S.	James Weir Hogg, M.P.
1846	Sir James Weir Hogg, Bart., M.P.	Henry St. George Tucker.
1847	Henry St. George Tucker.	Lieut.-Gen. Sir James Law Lushington, G.C.B.
1848	Lieut.-Gen. Sir James Law Lushington, G.C.B.	Major-Gen. Archibald Galloway, C.B.
1849	Major-Gen. Sir Archibald Galloway, K.C.B.	John Shepherd.
1850	John Shepherd.	Sir James Weir Hogg, (Bart.), M.P.
1851	John Shepherd.	Sir James Weir Hogg, (Bart.), M.P.
1852	Sir James Weir Hogg, (Bart.), M.P.	Russell Ellice.
1853	Russell Elice.	Major James Oliphant.
1854	Major James Oliphant.	Elliot Macnaghten.
1855	Elliot Macnaghten.	Lieut.-Col. Wm. Henry Sykes.
1856	Colonel Wm. Henry Sykes.	Ross Donnelly Mangles, M.P.
1857	Ross Donnelly Mangles, M.P.	Sir Frederick Currie, (Bart.)
1858	Sir Frederick Currie, (Bart.)	Capt. Wm. Joseph Eastwick.

LIST

OF

PRESIDENTS OF THE BOARD OF CONTROL.

[The Board of Control was established by Law on the 13th August 1784, and abolished with the East India Company in 1858.]

Date of assuming charge of Office.	Names of Presidents of the Board of Control.
September 5, 1784 .	Right Hon. Henry Dundas (afterwards Viscount Melville).
April 25, 1801 . .	Viscount Lewisham (afterwards Earl Dartmouth).
July 12, 1802 . .	Viscount Castlereagh.
February 11, 1806 .	The Earl of Minto.
July 15, 1806 . .	Right Hon. Thomas Grenville.
September 30, 1806 .	Right Hon. George Tierney.
April 4, 1807 . .	Right Hon. Robert Dundas.
July 11, 1809 . .	Earl of Harrowby.
November 7, 1809 .	Right Hon. Robert Dundas (afterwards Viscount Melville).
April 4, 1812 . .	The Earl of Buckinghamshire.
June 4, 1816 . .	Right Hon. George Canning.
January 12, 1821 .	Right Hon. Charles Bathurst.
February 5, 1822 .	Right Hon. Charles Watkins Williams Wynn.
February 4, 1828 .	Viscount Melville.
September 17, 1828 .	The Earl of Ellenborough.
November 22, 1830 .	Right Hon. Charles Grant (afterwards Lord Glenelg).
December 15, 1834 .	The Earl of Ellenborough.
April 23, 1835 . .	Right Hon. Sir John Cam Hobhouse, Bart. (afterwards Lord Broughton).
September 4, 1841 .	The Earl of Ellenborough (became Governor-General of India).
October 23, 1841 .	Lord Fitzgerald and Vesey (died 11th May 1843).
May 17, 1843 . .	The Earl of Ripon.
July 6, 1846 . .	Lord Broughton.
February 5, 1852 .	Right Hon. Fox Maule.
February 27, 1852 .	Right Hon. John Charles Herries.
December 28, 1852 .	Right Hon. Sir Charles Wood, Bart. (afterwards Viscount Halifax).
February 28, 1855 .	Right Hon. Robert Vernon Smith.
February 26, 1858 .	The Earl of Ellenborough.
May 31, 1858 . .	Lord Stanley (became First Secretary of State for India).

CHRONOLOGICAL LIST

OF

GOVERNORS OF THE MADRAS PRESIDENCY

FROM 1652 TO 1858,

When the Affairs of the East India Company were transferred to the Imperial Government.

Date of Arrival at Madras.	Date of Assuming Charge of Office.	Names.
...	1652	AARON BAKER. At first Agent for the settlement of Madras, which was under the jurisdiction of the Presidency of Bantam in Java, from its foundation in 1639 till it was created a Presidency in 1653.
...	1659	Sir THOMAS CHAMBERS.
...	1661	Sir EDWARD WINTER. Made over charge 22d Aug. 1668, and embarked for England 19th Jan. 1672.
June — 1665	Aug. 22, 1668	GEORGE FOXCRAFT. Three months after his arrival with a commission to supersede Sir E. Winter, Mr. Foxcraft was, on a charge of disloyalty, placed in confinement by Sir E. Winter, who resumed the Governorship and retained it until Mr. Foxcraft was released and reinstated by commissioners from England. Mr. Foxcraft made over charge in 1670, and embarked for England the same year.
—— 1668	1670	Sir WILLIAM LANGHORN, Bart. Made over charge 27th Jan. 1678, and embarked for England.
July 7, 1676	Jan. 27, 1678	STREYNSHAM MASTER. Made over charge 3d July 1681.
July 3, 1681	July 3, 1681	WILLIAM GYFFORD. By the East India Company's commission dated 14th Nov. 1681, received 17th July 1682. The Bengal Agency, hitherto attached to Madras, became a separate Government.

Date of Arrival at Madras.	Date of Assuming Charge of Office.	Names.
June 23, 1672	July 25, 1687	ELIHU YALE. Also Acting Governor in Mr. Gyfford's absence in Bengal, 8th Aug. 1684 to 26th Jan. 1685.
Mar. 19, 1684	Oct. 3, 1692	NATHANIEL HIGGINSON. Made over charge 7th July 1698, and embarked for England 25th Feb. 1700.
July 7, 1698	July 7, 1698	THOMAS PITT. Made over charge 18th Sept. 1709, and embarked for England 26th Oct. 1709.
Feb. 3, 1693	Sept. 18, 1709	GULSTON ADDISON. Died at Madras 17th Oct. 1709.
—— 1684	Oct. 17, 1709	EDMUND MONTAGUE. Acting Governor; made over charge 3d Nov. 1709.
May 31, 1685	Nov. 3, 1709	WILLIAM FRASER. Acting Governor; made over charge and embarked for England 11th July 1711.
July 11, 1711	July 11, 1711	EDWARD HARRISON. Made over charge on 8th Jan. 1717, and embarked for England.
Aug. 28, 1716	Jan. 8, 1717	JOSEPH COLLET. Made over charge on 18th Jan. 1720, and embarked for England.
July 16, 1701	Jan. 18, 1720	FRANCIS HASTINGS. Acting Governor; made over charge and embarked for England 15th Oct. 1721.
Feb. 25, 1719	Oct. 15, 1721	NATHANIEL ELWICK. Made over charge 15th Jan. 1725, and embarked for England 17th Jan. 1725.
Aug. 30, 1724	Jan. 15, 1725	JAMES MACRAE. Made over charge 14th May 1730; embarked for England 21st Jan. 1731.
Dec. 26, 1724	May 14, 1730	GEORGE MORTON PITT. Made over charge 23d Jan. 1735, and embarked for England.
June 28, 1733	Jan. 23, 1735	RICHARD BENYON. Made over charge 17th Jan. 1744, and embarked for England.
June 25, 1718	Jan. 17, 1744	NICHOLAS MORSE. Taken prisoner on the capture of Fort St. George by the French in 1746. The Government devolved on Mr. Hinde, Deputy Governor of Fort St. David.
Aug. 22, 1743	Sept. 10, 1746	JOHN HINDE. Deputy Governor at Fort St. David, where he died on 14th April 1747, previous to receipt of Court's despatch, dated 24th Jan. 1747, creating Fort St. David the head settlement, and appointing him Governor and President.

Date of Arrival at Madras.	Date of Assuming Charge of Office.	Names.
May 23, 1730	April 16, 1747	CHARLES FLOYER. Dismissed from service under Court's despatch received 6th July 1750.
July 14, 1732.	Sept. 19, 1750	THOMAS SAUNDERS. Made over charge and embarked for England 14th Jan. 1755. (The seat of government was re-established at Fort St. George on 5th April 1752, four years after its restoration under the Treaty of Aix la Chapelle.)
July 26, 1737	Jan. 14, 1755	GEORGE PIGOTT. Made over charge and embarked for England 14th Nov. 1763. Became Lord Pigot (see below).
Oct. 2, 1761	Nov. 14, 1763	ROBERT PALK. Made over charge and embarked for England 25th Jan. 1767.
Dec. 30, 1741	Jan. 25, 1767	CHARLES BOURCHIER. Made over charge 31st Jan. 1770, and embarked for England 8th Feb. 1770.
June 10, 1752	Jan. 31, 1770	JOSIAS DU PRÉ. Made over charge and embarked for England 2d Feb. 1773.
July 12, 1768	Feb. 2, 1773	ALEXANDER WYNCH. Made over charge 11th Dec. 1775, and embarked for England 15th Feb. 1776.
Dec. 9, 1775	Dec. 11, 1775	Right Hon. Lord PIGOT. Governor for second time. Placed under arrest by order of Mr. Geo. Stratton and the majority of the Council, and detained at St. Thomas' Mount on 24th Aug. 1776; allowed to return to Garden House for change of air on 24th April 1777, and there died on 20th May 1777.
June 17, 1751	Aug. 23, 1776	GEORGE STRATTON. Suspended from service 31st Aug. 1777.
Aug. 3, 1752	Aug. 31, 1777	JOHN WHITEHILL. Acting Governor. Made over charge 8th Feb. 1778.
Feb. 8, 1778	Feb. 8, 1778	Sir THOMAS RUMBOLD, Bart. Was second in Council under Mr. Warren Hastings in Bengal. Made over charge, and embarked for England 6th April 1780.
(See above)	April 6, 1780	JOHN WHITEHILL. Acting Governor for second time, but suspended by order of the Governor-General of Bengal and his Council under sec. ix of the Regulations. Made over charge 8th Nov. 1780.

Date of Arrival at Madras.	Date of Assuming Charge of Office.	Names.
July 10, 1753	Nov. 8, 1780	CHARLES SMITH. Acting Governor. Made over charge 22d June 1781, and embarked for England.
June 22, 1781	June 22, 1781	Lord MACARTNEY, K.B. Embarked for the Northern Ports and Bengal 4th June 1785, and resigned 8th June by letter from Vizagapatam.
Sept. 8, 1760.	June 18, 1785	ALEXANDER DAVIDSON. Acting Governor. Made over charge 6th April 1786. Died in Madras 1791.
...	April 6, 1786	Major-Gen. Sir ARCHIBALD CAMPBELL, K.B. Made over charge, and embarked for England 7th Feb. 1789.
July 26, 1760	Feb. 7, 1789	JOHN HOLLAND. Acting Governor. Made over charge and embarked for England 13th Feb. 1790.
June 5, 1769	Feb. 13, 1790	EDWARD HOLLAND. Acting Governor. Made over charge 20th Feb. 1790.
Feb. 20, 1790	Feb. 20, 1790	Major-General WILLIAM MEDOWS. Made over charge and embarked for England 1st Aug. 1792.
Oct. 15, 1790	Aug. 1, 1792	Sir CHARLES OAKELEY, Bart. Date of arrival as writer in Madras 6th June 1767. Resigned Governorship 7th Sept. 1794, and embarked for England 29th Sept. 1794.
Sept. 7, 1794	Sept. 7, 1794	Lord HOBART. Made over charge and embarked for England 20th Feb. 1798.
Mar. — 1797	Feb. 21, 1798	Lieutenant-General GEORGE HARRIS. Commander-in-chief and Acting Governor. Made over charge 21st Aug. 1798.
Aug. 21, 1798	Aug. 21, 1798	Lord CLIVE (The Second). Made over charge 30th Aug. 1803, and embarked for England 12th Sept. 1803.
Aug. 30, 1803	Aug. 30, 1803	Lord WILLIAM CAVENDISH BENTINCK. Made over charge 11th Sept. 1807, and embarked for England 27th Sept. 1807. Died 17th June 1839.
Jan. 23, 1765	Sept. 11, 1807	WILLIAM PETRIE. Acting Governor. Made over charge 24th Dec. 1807. Died 27th Oct. 1816 at Prince of Wales Island.
Dec. 24, 1807	Dec. 24, 1807	Sir GEORGE HILARO BARLOW, Bart., K.C.B. Made over charge 21st May 1813, and embarked for England 26th Aug. 1813.

Date of Arrival at Madras.	Date of Assuming Charge of Office.	Names.
March 6, 1813	May 21, 1813	Lieutenant-General the Hon. JOHN ABERCROMBY. Commander-in-chief and Acting Governor. Made over charge 16th Sept. 1814, and embarked for England 20th Oct. 1814.
Sept. 16, 1814	Sept. 16, 1814	Right Hon. HUGH ELLIOT. Made over charge 10th June, and embarked for England 16th June 1820.
June 10, 1820	June 10, 1820	Major-General Sir THOMAS MUNRO, Bart., K.C.B. Died at Pattikonda, in the Kurnul district, 6th July 1827.
Feb. 3, 1798	July 10, 1827	HENRY SULLIVAN GRÆME. Acting Governor. Made over charge 18th Oct. 1827. Died 14th July 1850.
Oct. 18, 1827	Oct. 18, 1827	STEPHEN RUMBOLD LUSHINGTON. Made over charge and embarked for England 25th Oct. 1832.
Oct. 25, 1832	Oct. 25, 1832	Lieutenant-General Sir FREDERICK ADAM, K.C.B. Made over charge and embarked for England 4th March 1837.
Aug. 29, 1803	March 4, 1837	GEORGE EDWARD RUSSELL. Acting Governor. Made over charge 6th March 1837. Died 20th Oct. 1863.
March 6, 1837	March 6, 1837	Lord ELPHINSTONE, G.C.H. Made over charge 24th Sept. 1842, and left the Presidency on the 29th Sept. for Bangalore and Nilgiri Hills *en route* to Europe. Died 19th July 1860.
Sept. 24, 1842	Sept. 24, 1842	Lieutenant-General the Most Honourable the Marquis of TWEEDDALE, K.T. and C.B. Also Commander-in-chief. Made over charge and embarked for England 23d Feb. 1848. Died 10th Oct. 1876.
July 5, 1809	Feb. 23, 1848	Major-General HENRY DICKINSON. Acting Governor. Made over charge 7th April 1848.
April 7, 1848	April 7, 1848	Right Hon. Sir HENRY POTTINGER, Bart., G.C.B. Made over charge and embarked for England 24th April 1854. Died 18th March 1856.
Aug. 3, 1817	April 24, 1854	DANIELL ELIOTT. Acting Governor. Made over charge 28th April 1854. Died 30th Oct. 1872.
April 28, 1854	April 28, 1854	Lord HARRIS. Made over charge 28th March and embarked for England 31st March 1859. Died 23d November 1872.

CHRONOLOGICAL LIST

OF

COMMANDERS-IN-CHIEF IN THE MADRAS PRESIDENCY

FROM 1697 TO 1858,

When the Affairs of the East India Company were transferred to the Imperial Government.

[In the earlier years the Commissions of Governors also bore the title of Commanders-in-Chief.]

Date of Commission.	Date of Assuming Command.	Names.
Jan. 5, 1697	July 7, 1698	THOMAS PITT. Also Governor. Embarked for England 20th Oct. 1709.
Jan. 20, 1708	Sept. 18, 1709	GULSTON ADDISON. Also Governor. Died at Madras 17th Oct. 1709.
Dec. 22, 1710	July 11, 1711	EDWARD HARRISON. Also Governor. Embarked for England 8th Jan. 1717.
Dec. 19, 1719	Jan. 18, 1720	FRANCIS HASTINGS. Also Governor. Embarked for England 15th Oct. 1721.
April 14, 1721	Oct. 15, 1721	NATHANIEL ELWICK. Also Governor. Embarked for England 17th Jan. 1725.
Jan. 27, 1724	Jan. 15, 1725	JAMES MACRAE. Also Governor. Embarked for England 21st Jan. 1731.
Dec. 5, 1729	May 14, 1730	GEORGE MORTON PITT. Also Governor. Embarked for England 23d Jan. 1735.
Jan. 29, 1735	Jan. 23, 1735	RICHARD BENYON. Also Governor. Embarked for England 17th Jan. 1744.
July 24, 1747	Sept. 10, 1746	JOHN HINDE. Also Governor at Fort St. David, where he died 14th April 1747, previous to receipt of commission and the orders creating Fort St. David the head settlement, in consequence of the capture of Fort St. George by the French.

Date of Commission.	Date of Assuming Command.	Names.
Dec. 24, 1747	April 16, 1747	CHARLES FLOYER. Also Governor. Dismissed the service 6th July 1750.
Aug. 21, 1751	Sept. 19, 1750	THOMAS SAUNDERS. Also Governor. Embarked for England 14th Jan. 1755.
Feb. 15, 1754	Jan. 14, 1755	GEORGE PIGOT. Also Governor. Embarked for England 14th Nov. 1763. (See below.)
Nov. 14, 1764	...	Brigadier-General JOHN CAILLAND. Commander of the Forces on the Coromandel Coast.
Jan. 4, 1765	Nov. 14, 1763	ROBERT PALK. Also Governor. Embarked for England 25th Jan. 1767.
Jan. 12, 1768	Jan. 25, 1767	CHARLES BOURCHIER. Also Governor. Embarked for England 8th Feb. 1770.
Mar. 17, 1769	Jan. 31, 1770	JOSIAS DU PRÉ. Also Governor. Embarked for England 2d Feb. 1773.
April 12, 1774	Feb. 2, 1773	ALEXANDER WYNCH. Also Governor. Embarked for England 15th Feb. 1776.
April 12, 1774	...	Brigadier-General JOSEPH SMITH. Commander of the Forces on the Coromandel Coast.
April 4, 1775	Dec. 11, 1775	Right Hon. Lord PIGOT. Also Governor. Placed under arrest by the majority of his Council. Died 20th May 1777. (See under Governors.)
June 25, 1777	...	Major-General HECTOR MUNRO. Commander of the Forces on the Coromandel Coast.
Jan. 5, 1781	June 22, 1781	Lord MACARTNEY, K.B. Also Governor. Resigned 8th June 1785.
Nov. 24, 1784	June — 1785	Lieutenant-General Sir ROBERT SLOPER, K.B. Died 13th August 1802 at West Green, Hants.
Sept. 21, 1784	July 21, 1785	Lieutenant-General Sir JOHN DALLING, Bart., K.B. Commander of the Forces at Madras. Commission revoked 21st April 1786.
Sept. 7, 1785	April 6, 1786	Lieutenant-General Sir ARCHIBALD CAMPBELL, K.B. Also Governor. Embarked for England 7th Feb. 1789. Died March 1791 in London.
Nov. 25, 1789.	Feb. 20, 1790	Major-Gen. Sir WILLIAM MEDOWS, K.B. Also Governor. Was Commander-in-Chief in Bombay. Quitted command and embarked for England 1st Aug. 1792. Died 14th Nov. 1813 in England.

Date of Commission.	Date of Assuming Command.	Names.
June 3, 1790	Aug. 1, 1792	Sir CHARLES OAKELEY, Bart. Also Governor. Embarked for England 29th Sept. 1794.
Feb. 12, 1794	Sept. 7, 1794	Right Hon. Lord HOBART. Also Governor. Embarked for England 20th Feb. 1798.
May 1, 1795	Jan. 15, 1796	Major-Gen. Sir ALURED CLARKE, K.B. Commander of the Forces Madras. Governor of Bengal 6th Aug. 1796. Governor-General of Bengal and Commander-in-Chief of India 17th May 1798. Died Sept. 1832 in England.
Oct. 11, 1797	Mar. 27, 1797	Major-Gen. GEORGE (afterwards Lord) HARRIS, G.C.B. Commander of the Forces; also Governor 21st Feb. 1798. Quitted command 21st Aug. 1798. Died 31st May 1829 at Belmont, Kent.
Dec. 10, 1800	Aug. 1, 1801	Lieut.-Gen. JOHN STUART. Quitted command 17th Oct. 1804.
Mar. 16, 1803	Aug. 30, 1803	Lord WILLIAM CAVENDISH BENTINCK. Also Governor. Embarked for England 29th Sept. 1807. Died 17th June 1839.
May 7, 1804	Oct. 17, 1804	Major-Gen. Sir JOHN FRANCIS CRADOCK, G.C.B., K.H. (afterwards Lord HOWDEN). Commander of the Forces. Quitted command 17th Sept. 1807. Died July 1839 in England.
June 3, 1807	Sept. 17, 1807	Lieut.-Gen. Sir HAY M'DOWALL. Commander of the Forces. Quitted command 10th April 1810.
Jan. 6, 1807	April 10, 1810	Lieut.-Gen. Sir GEORGE HEWITT, G.C.B. Quitted command 27th Sept. 1810.
Mar. 23, 1810	Sept. 27, 1810	Major-Gen. Sir SAMUEL AUCHMUTY, G.C.B. Commander of the Forces. Governor and Commander-in-Chief 15th Oct. 1811. Quitted command 21st May 1813. Died 31st Aug. 1822 while in command at Dublin.
May 3, 1809	May 21, 1813	Lieut.-Gen. the Hon. JOHN ABERCROMBY, G.C.B. Also Governor. Was Commander-in-Chief at Bombay. Quitted command 25th May, and embarked 20th Oct. 1814. Died Feb. 1819 in England.
Dec. 21, 1813	May 25, 1814	Lieut.-Gen. Sir THOMAS HISLOP, G.C.B. Was Commander-in-Chief at Bombay. Captured on his voyage to

Date of Commission.	Date of Assuming Command.	Names.
		Madras. Governor and Commander-in-Chief, Fort St. George, 2d July 1817. Quitted command 15th June 1821. Died 3d May 1843 at Charlton, Kent.
Dec. 6, 1819	June 10, 1820	Major-Gen. Sir THOMAS MUNRO, Bart., K.C.B. Also Governor. Died at Pattikonda in Kurnul district 6th July 1827.
Feb. 12, 1821	June 15, 1821	Lieut.-Gen. Sir ALEXANDER CAMPBELL, Bart., K.C.B. Commander of the Forces. Died 11th December 1824.
Dec. 11, 1824	Dec. 11, 1824	General BOWSER. Assumed command as senior officer.
May 25, 1825	Mar. 3, 1826	Lieut.-Gen. Sir GEORGE TOWNSEND WALKER, Bart., G.C.B. Quitted command 11th May 1831. Died Governor of Chelsea Hospital 15th Nov. 1842.
Oct. 17, 1830	May 11, 1831	Lieut.-Gen. Sir ROBERT WILLIAM O'CALLAGHAN, G.C.B., K.C.H. Quitted command 11th Oct. 1836. Died 9th June 1840 in London.
April 17, 1836	Oct. 11, 1836	Lieut.-Gen. Sir PEREGRINE MAITLAND, K.C.B. Quitted command 21st Sept. 1838. Governor at the Cape of Good Hope 19th Dec. 1843. Died 30th May 1854 in London.
July 4, 1838	Dec. 21, 1838	Lieut.-Gen. Sir JASPER NICOLLS, K.C.B. Quitted command 7th Dec. 1839, and became Commander-in-Chief of India. Died 4th May 1849 at Goodrist, Reading.
Sept. 18, 1839	Aug. 1, 1840	Lieutenant-General Sir SAMUEL FORD WHITTINGHAM, K.C.B., K.C.H. Died 19th Jan. 1841 at Madras.
July 3, 1841	Jan. — 1841	Major-General Sir HUGH GOUGH (afterwards Lord GOUGH), G.C.B. Appointed temporarily, but did not assume command. Became Commander-in-chief of India 11th Aug. 1843. Died 2d March 1869 at Dublin.
Jan. 20, 1841	Jan. 20, 1841	Major-General Sir JAMES ALLEN, K.C.B. Temporary command. Died 17th Feb. 1853 at Cheltenham.
Feb. 11, 1841	Feb. 11, 1841	Major-General Sir ROBERT HENRY DICK, K.C.B., K.C.H. Temporary command. Killed at Sobraon 10th Feb. 1846.

Date of Commission.	Date of Assuming Command.	Names.
April 20, 1842	Sept. 20, 1842	Lieutenant-General the Marquis of TWEEDDALE, K.T., G.C.B., G.C.H. Also Governor. Embarked for England 23d Feb. 1848. Died 10th Oct. 1876.
Sept. 29, 1847	Mar. 13, 1848	Lieutenant-General Sir GEORGE HENRY FREDERICK BERKELEY, K.C.B. Quitted command 29th Sept. 1851. Died 12th Feb. 1863.
May 20, 1851	Sept. 29, 1851	Lieutenant-General Sir RICHARD ARMSTRONG, K.C.B., K.T., and S. Quitted command 27th Oct. 1853. Died 3d March 1854 on his voyage home on board the "Barham."
Sept. 7, 1853	Oct. 27, 1853	Lieutenant - General Sir WILLIAM STAVELEY, K.C.B. Died at Ootacamund 4th April 1854.
Sept. 23, 1854	Sept. 23, 1854	Lieutenant-General the Hon. GEORGE ANSON. Removed to Bengal. Commander-in-chief of India 23d Jan. 1856. Died of cholera 27th May 1857.
Jan. 23, 1856	Jan. 23, 1856	Major-General MARCUS BERESFORD. Temporary command. Died 16th March 1876 at Leamington.
April 24, 1856	June 10, 1856	Lieutenant - General Sir PATRICK GRANT, K.C.B.

LIST

OF

CHIEF JUSTICES AND PUISNE JUDGES OF THE MADRAS PRESIDENCY.

FROM 1800 TO 1858.

[The Mayor's Court, which existed at Madras for many years, was abolished in 1797, and in its place was established a Recorder's Court, under Act 37 of George III., cap. 142. In 1800 a Supreme Court of Judicature was established, under 39 and 40 of George III., cap. 79, to consist of a Chief Justice and two Puisne Judges. Letters Patent granting a Charter of Justice were issued on the 26th December 1801.]

Date of Appointment.	Names.
	CHIEF JUSTICES.
Dec. 26, 1800	Sir THOMAS A. STRANGE, Knt. Resigned 4th June 1817.
Sept. 6, 1815	Sir JOHN H. NEWBOLT, Knt. Resigned 31st Aug. 1820. Died March 1823.
May 17, 1820	Sir EDMUND STANLEY, Knt. Resigned 28th Jan. 1825.
Jan. 28, 1825	Sir RALPH PALMER, Knt. Resigned 25th Oct. 1835 Died 25th Jan. 1838.
Dec. 31, 1831	Sir ROBERT BUCKLEY COMYN, Knt. Resigned 17th Jan. 1842. Died 23d May 1853.
May 22, 1842	Sir EDWARD J. GAMBIER, Knt. Resigned — June 1848. Died 31st May 1879.
April 15, 1850	Sir CHRISTOPHER RAWLINSON, Knt. Resigned 14th Feb. 1859.
Mar. 11, 1859	Sir HENRY DAVIDSON. Died at Ootacamund, 4th Nov. 1860.
	PUISNE JUDGES.
Dec. 26, 1800	Sir HENRY GWILLIM, Knt. Resigned 28th Oct. 1808. Died 12th Sept. 1837.
Dec. 26, 1800	Sir BENJAMIN SULLIVAN, Knt. Resigned 7th May 1809. Died — Nov. 1810.

Date of Appointment.	Names.
May 7, 1809	Sir FRANCIS M'NAUGHTEN, Knt. (Baronet in 1836). Removed to Bengal 3d July 1815. Resigned 2d March 1825. Died in 1876.
May 30, 1810	Sir JOHN H. NEWBOLT, Knt. Chief Justice 6th Sept. 1815.
July 3, 1815	Sir EDMUND STANLEY, Knt. Chief Justice 17th May 1820.
Sept. 6, 1815	Sir ANTHONY BULLER, Knight. Removed to Bengal 10th April 1816. Resigned 1st Jan. 1827. Died in June 1866.
April 15, 1817	Sir ANDREW GEORGE COOPER, Knt. Died 30th Aug. 1821.
May 17, 1820	Sir CHARLES E. GREY, Knt. Removed to Bengal 18th Aug. 1824. Chief Justice 29th June 1825. Resigned 2d July 1832. Died June 1865.
April 12, 1822	Sir WILLINGHAM FRANKLIN, Knt. Died May 1824.
Aug. 18, 1824	Sir RALPH PALMER, Knt. Chief Justice 28th Jan. 1825. Resigned 25th Oct. 1835.
Jan. 28, 1825	Sir ROBERT BUCKLEY COMYN, Knt. Chief Justice 31st Dec. 1831. Resigned 17th Jan. 1842.
Mar. 7, 1825	Sir GEORGE W. RICKETTS, Knt. Died at Sea 14th July 1832.
Nov. 28, 1836.	Sir EDWARD J. GAMBIER, Knt. Chief Justice 22d May 1842. Resigned June 1848. Died 31st May 1879.
April 5, 1842	Sir JOHN DAVID NORTON, Knt. Died at sea 24th Sept. 1843.
Aug. 29, 1844	Sir WILLIAM WESTBROOKE BURTON, Knt. Resigned 15th March 1857.
Mar. 16, 1857	Sir HENRY DAVIDSON, Knt. Chief Justice 11th March, 1859.
July 26, 1858	Sir ADAM BITTLESTON, Knt. Pensioned 3d April 1870.

RECORD OF SERVICES

OF

CIVIL SERVANTS IN THE MADRAS PRESIDENCY.

FROM THE YEAR 1740 TO THE YEAR 1858.

N.B.—See also Supplementary List, page 161, and Addendum, page 209.

ABERCROMBY, ROBERT.—1802: Writer; Acting Assistant to Secretary to the Special Commission. 1803: Assistant to the Collector of the Northern Division of Canara. 1805: Register of Canara. 1806: Register of the Zillah of the Southern Division of Canara. 1808: *At home.* 1809: *Resigned, 8th November, in England.* (*Annuitant,* 1836.) *Died, 6th July* 1855.

ADAMSON, WILLIAM DAVID.—1813: Writer. 1816: Second Assistant to Collector and Magistrate of Nellore. 1817: Register of the Zillah of Guntoor. 1819: Head Assistant to Collector and Magistrate of Guntoor. *Died,* 5*th June,* 1820, *at Guntoor.*

AGNEW, JOHN VANS.—1801: Writer. 1802: Assistant to Chief Secretary in Secret, Political, and Foreign Departments. 1803: Secretary and Accountant to the Commissioners of the Sinking Fund. 1804: *At home.* 1808: *Out of the service.*

ALCOCK, DAVID.—1766: Writer. 1771: Factor and Assistant at Masulipatam. ;1774: Junior Merchant. *No trace after this date.*

ALEXANDER, ROBERT.—1790: Writer; Assistant to the Secretary to the Board of Revenue. 1791: Assistant at Vizagapatam. 1794: Assistant and Accountant under Mr. Chamier in the Vizianagram Zemindary. 1796: Assistant to the Collector in the Northern Division of Vizianagram. 1797: Assistant to the Resident at Ceylon. 1798: Assistant to the Collector in the Second Division of Vizagapatam District. 1800: Sub-Secretary to the

Public Commercial and Revenue Departments; Collector in the First Division of the Vizagapatam Districts. 1803: Judge of the Zillah of Vizagapatam. 1806: Collector in the Zillah of Ganjam. 1808: Second Member of the Board of Revenue. 1812: Senior Member of the Board of Revenue. 1814: Member of Council and President of the Board of Revenue. 1818: *At home.* 1821: *Resigned, 21st December, in England.* (*Annuitant,* 1819.) *Died, 15th July* 1861.

ALEXANDER, JOSIAS DU PRE.—1796: Writer. 1798: Assistant under the Secretary to the Board of Trade. 1799: Deputy Commercial Resident at Colombo. 1801: Assistant to the Collector of Government Customs. 1803: *Leave to Bengal.* 1818: *At home. Out of the service in* 1820, *and elected a Director of the East India Company, 16th August* 1820. (*Annuitant,* 1822.) *Died, 20th August* 1839.

ALEXANDER, HENRY STEWART.—1854: Writer. 1856: Assistant to Collector and Magistrate, Coimbatore. 1857: Third Assistant to Accountant-General. 1858: *Proceeded on furlough; died, 6th April, in England.*

ANDERSON, ROBERT.—1807: Writer. 1810: Assistant to Secretary in the Revenue and Judicial Department. 1811: Fixed Examiner in the Office of Register of the Sudder and Foujdarry Adawlut. 1813: Persian Translator to the Carnatic Commissioners. 1816: Assistant Register to the Sudder and Foujdarry Adawlut, and Deputy Persian Translator to Government. 1818: *At home.* 1821: *Resigned, 28th December, in England.* (*Annuitant,* 1843.) *Died, 22d March* 1843.

ANDERSON, WILLIAM BENSLEY.—1815: Writer. 1818: Assistant to the Accountant-General. 1821: Register of the Provincial Court, Western Division. 1826: *At home on absentee allowance.* 1828: *Returned to India per "Lyndoch."* 1829: Sheriff of Madras, &c., and Acting Senior Deputy Register of the Sudder Court. 1830: Judge and Criminal Judge of Canara. 1832: Acting Judge of the Provincial Court, Western Division; Third Judge of the Provincial Court, Western Division. 1838: Second Judge of the Provincial Court, Western Division. 1842: *Resigned the service. Died, 16th July* 1863.

ANDERSON, FINDLAY.—1825: Writer. 1827: Assistant to the Principal Collector of Malabar. 1829: Head Assistant to the Principal Collector of Malabar. 1832: Additional Sub-Collector and Joint Magistrate of Canara. 1834: Sub-Collector and Joint

Magistrate of Canara. 1835: Acting Sub-Collector of Canara. 1836: Sub-Collector and Joint Magistrate of Canara. 1837: *At home on absentee allowance.* 1841: *Returned to India.* 1842: Judge and Criminal Judge, Canara. 1844: Civil and Sessions Judge, Mangalore. 1856: Civil and Sessions Judge, Calicut. 1857: *Resigned the service, 28th April.* (*Annuitant on Company's Fund.*)

ANDERSON, Stuart Murray.—1851: Writer. 1853: *Proceeded on furlough; Died, 9th December in England.*

ANDREWS, John.—1768: Member of the Council of the Governor. 1774: *Out of the service.*

ANDREWS, Robert.—1778: Writer. 1790: Senior Merchant. 1791: Second in Council at Cuddalore. 1792: Collector in the Trichinopoly District. 1804: *At home.* 1808: *Returned to India.* 1810: Acting Judge of the Provincial Court of Appeal and Circuit for the Southern Division. 1813: Postmaster-General. 1815: First Judge of the Provincial Court of Appeal, Southern Division. *Died, 13th November* 1821, *at Trichinopoly.*

ANGELO, Anthony Edward.—1815: Writer. 1819: Assistant to the Collector of Madras. 1822: Assistant to the Collector of Sea Customs at Madras. 1825: *At home.* 1829: *Returned to India.* 1832: Assistant Judge and Joint Criminal Judge of Guntoor. 1834: Judge and Criminal Judge of Chicacole. 1836: Judge and Criminal Judge of Bellary; Acting Judge and Criminal Judge of Cuddapah. 1837: Judge and Criminal Judge of Cuddapah; Judge and Criminal Judge, Bellary. 1840: Judge and Criminal Judge, Chittoor. 1843: *Resigned the service, 1st January. Died, 28th July* 1855.

ANSTEY, Thomas.—1789: Writer. 1790: Assistant under the Military Secretary. 1791: Assistant under the Secretary to the Board of Assumed Revenue. 1793: Assistant Commercial Resident at Ganjam. 1794: Assistant Export Warehouse-keeper. 1796: Deputy Commercial Resident at the Presidency. 1800: Head Assistant to the Collector of Salem. 1801: Malabar Translator to Government. 1802: Third Judge of Court of Circuit and Appeal, Southern Division. 1806: Commercial Resident at Tinnevelly. 1811: Commercial Resident at Ingeram. 1813: *At home.* 1815: *Resigned, 1st December, in England.*

ANSTEY, John Thomas.—1812: Writer. 1816: Assistant to the Magistrate of Guntoor. 1817: Head Assistant to the Collector of Guntoor. 1819: Head Assistant to the Collector and Magistrate of Bellary. 1821: *At home.* 1824: *Returned to India;* Sub-

Collector and Assistant Magistrate of Ganjam. 1827: Collector and Magistrate of Rajahmundry. 1830: *At home.* (*Retired on the Annuity Fund in* 1839.)

ANSTRUTHER, THOMAS ANDREW.—1828: Writer. 1831: Second Assistant to Principal Collector and Magistrate of Southern Division of Arcot. 1832: Head Assistant to Principal Collector and Magistrate of Northern Division of Arcot; Acting Head Assistant to the Principal Collector and Magistrate of Madura. 1835: Acting Sub-Collector of Coimbatore. 1837: Sub-Collector and Joint Magistrate of the Southern Division of Arcot; Sub-Collector and Joint Magistrate of Coimbatore; Acting Assistant Judge and Joint Criminal Judge of Salem. 1838: Acting Judge and Criminal Judge of Madura. 1839: *At home on absentee allowance.* 1841: *Returned to India.* 1842: Judge and Criminal Judge, Rajahmundry. 1844: Civil and Sessions Judge, Honore. 1845: Civil and Sessions Judge, Rajahmundry. 1855: *On furlough.* 1856: *Resigned the service, 2d April in England. Died, 14th April* 1876.

ANTROBUS, THOMAS.—1781: Writer. 1783: Assistant to the Secretary to the Select Committee; *Leave to China for health. Not traced after* 1784.

ARBUTHNOT, WILLIAM URQUHART.—1825: Writer; Temporary Sub-Collector of Vizagapatam. 1827: Assistant to the Principal Collector of South Arcot. 1828: Head Assistant to the Principal Collector of South Arcot. 1833: Temporary Sub-Collector of Vizagapatam. 1836: Acting Judge and Criminal Judge of Chicacole. 1837: Acting Collector and Magistrate of Vizagapatam. 1838: Collector and Magistrate of Vizagapatam. 1840: Collector and Magistrate, Vizagapatam, and Agent to Governor. 1846: *Resigned the service, 16th April.* 1858: Member of Council of the Secretary of State for India. *Died, 11th December* 1874, *in England.*

ARBUTHNOT, COUTTS TROTTER.—1837: Writer. 1840: Assistant to Collector and Magistrate, Coimbatore. 1843: Head Assistant to Collector and Magistrate, Arcot. 1847: *On furlough.* 1850: *Returned to India.* 1852: Head Assistant to Collector and Magistrate, Nellore. 1853: *On furlough.* 1855: *Resigned the service, 19th December.*

ARDLEY, SAMUEL.—1749: Writer. 1768: Member of the Council of the Governor. 1774: *Out of the service.*

ASHTON, WILLIAM.—1816: Writer. 1818: *At Home.* 1822: *Returned to India.* 1823: Assistant to the Collector and Magistrate of Masulipatam. 1824: *At home.* 1827: *Returned to India;* Subordinate Collector and Joint Magistrate of Tanjore. 1828: Deputy Collector of Sea Customs at Madras, and Acting Superintendent of Civil Pensions. 1830: Joint Magistrate on the Beach. 1832: Collector of Sea Customs at Madras; Member of the Marine Board. 1836: Acting Principal Collector and Magistrate of the Southern Division of Arcot. 1838: Collector and Magistrate, afterwards Principal Collector and Magistrate of the Southern Division of Arcot. 1842: Principal Collector and Magistrate, Cuddapah. 1845: *On furlough; resigned the service, 5th December.*

ATKINSON, EDWARD.—1783: Writer. 1785: Assistant to the Secretary of the Select Committee. 1786: Assistant to the Secretary in the Military Department. 1787: Clerk to the Court of Requests, and under the Secretary in the Secret Department. 1788: Secretary to the Hospital Board. 1789: Muster-Master of the Troops on the Guntoor Sircar. 1790: Muster-Master of the Troops with the Centre Army. 1791: Assistant to the Collector of Trichinopoly. 1793: *Out of employ.* 1794: Assistant under Mr. Gregory in the Vizianagram Zemindary. 1796: Commissary of Provisions, with Expedition under General Stewart. 1798: Commissary of Provisions at Colombo. 1800: *At home. Not traced after* 1808.

AUFRERE, THOMAS NORRIS.—1792: Writer. 1793: Assistant under the Accountant-General. 1794: Assistant under the Secretary to the Board of Revenue. 1796: Assistant under the Collector in the 4th Division of Masulipatam. 1799: *At home for health.* 1800: *Returned to India;* Assistant under the Collector of Ganjam. 1803: Judge of the Zillah of Salem. 1810: *At home.* 1814: *Out of the service.*

AYLMER, HENRY.—1773: Writer. 1780: Promoted to Factor. *Not traceable after this date.*

BABINGTON, JOHN.—1804: Writer. 1805: Assistant under the Secretary in the Revenue and Judicial Departments. 1807: Malabar Translator to Government; Assistant to the General Agent for the Salt Monopoly. 1810: Cashier to the Government Bank. 1815: Deputy Collector, afterwards Collector of Sea Customs at Malabar and Canara. 1823: Collector and Magistrate of Chingleput. 1824: Principal Collector and Magistrate of Canara. 1829: *At home on absentee allowance.* (*Retired on the Annuity Fund from 1st May* 1833.)

BABINGTON, Benjamin G.—1812: Writer. 1814: Assistant to the Secretary to the Board of Revenue. 1815: *At home.* 1817: *Returned to India;* Assistant to the Secretary to the Board of Revenue. 1819: *At home.* 1822: *Out of the service.*

BABINGTON, William Henry.—1821: Writer. 1824: Assistant to the Principal Collector and Magistrate of Canara. 1827: *At home on absentee allowance.* 1831: *Returned to India;* Sub-Collector and Joint Magistrate of the Northern Division of Arcot. 1834: Member of the Committee to Report upon the Export, Import, and Transit Duties of the three Presidencies. 1836: Sub-Collector and Joint Magistrate of Cuddapah. 1838: Placed temporarily under the Board of Revenue; Acting Principal Collector and Magistrate of Coimbatore. 1839: Sub-Collector and Joint Magistrate of Cuddapah; Sub-Collector and Joint Magistrate of Malabar. 1841: Judge and Criminal Judge, Madura. 1842: Third Judge of the Provincial Court of Appeal and Circuits, Centre Division. 1844: Civil and Session Judge, Cuddalore. 1849: *Resigned the service, 30th June, in India.* (*Annuitant on the Fund,* 1849.) *Died,* 17*th September* 1867.

BAINE, Duncan Andrew.—1771: Writer. 1776: Factor. 1780: Junior Merchant. 1782: Senior Merchant. *No trace after this date.*

BAKER, Charles.—1783: Writer; Assistant in the Civil Department. 1785: One of the Company's Solicitors. 1791: Assistant to the Senior Member of the Board of Revenue in the Management of the Beetle Farm. 1792: Manager of the Company's Exclusive Privilege for Supplying Beetle Tobacco and Ganja. 1801: Collector of Revenue on the Sale of Arrack, Toddy, and other Spirituous Liquors. 1803: *At home.* 1807: *Out of the service.*

BAKER, Joseph.—1771: Writer. 1776: Factor and Assistant at Masulipatam. 1780: Junior Merchant; *In England; No trace after this date.*

BALFOUR, James.—1793: Writer. 1796: Assistant under the Secretary in the Public Commercial and Revenue Department. 1797: Assistant under the Collector of Polygar Peishcush. 1799: *Out of employ.* 1800: Deputy Commercial Resident at the Presidency; *Suspended the service; Ordered to proceed home.* 1802: *Returned to India.* 1812: *At home.* 1815: *Out of the service.*

BALFOUR, John.—1772: Writer. 1778: Factor. 1780:

Junior Merchant. 1790: Senior Merchant; *At home.* 1795: *Out of the service.*

BALFOUR, WALTER.—1777: Writer. 1782: Factor. 1790: Senior Merchant and Paymaster at Chingleput and Permacoil. 1792: Collector in the Southern Division of the Jaghir. 1800: Civil Paymaster-General. 1801: Collector of Government Customs. 1809: *At home.* 1811: *Out of the service.*

BALFOUR, WILLIAM.—1778: Writer. 1790: Senior Merchant. 1791: Secretary to Board of Revenue, and Agent for Clothing Troops. 1792: Member of the Board of Revenue. 1795: *Out of the service.*

BALMAIN, GEORGE.—1789: Writer. 1790: Assistant under the Secretary in the Military, Political, and Secret Departments. 1793: Assistant under the Collector of the Peishcush in the Southern Polygars. 1796: Collector in the Mannargoody Districts of the Tanjore Country. 1799: Collector at Peddapore, in the 1st Division of Masulipatam. 1803: *At home.* 1805: *Returned to India. Died, 16th January 1807, at Fort St. George.*

BANNERMAN, DAVID.—1815: Writer. 1818: Assistant to the Secretary to Government. 1819: Register of the Zillah of Masulipatam. 1821: *Leave to the Cape of Good Hope.* 1822: Register to the Zillah of Madura. 1824: Sub-Collector and Assistant Magistrate of Madura. 1826: *At home on absentee allowance.* 1829: *Returned to India, per "Brunswick."* 1830: Judge and Criminal Judge of Chicacole. *Died, 1st September 1832, at Guntoor.*

BANNERMAN, EDWARD.—1816: Writer. 1819: Second Assistant afterwards Head Assistant to Collector and Magistrate of Masulipatam. 1821: Head Assistant to Collector and Magistrate of Tinnevelly. 1825: Acting Deputy Persian Translator to Government. 1826: Assistant to the Chief Secretary to Government. 1828: Senior Deputy Register of the Sudder Court. 1830: Judge and Criminal Judge of Madura. 1833: Judge and Criminal Judge of Salem. 1835: *Out of employ.* 1836: Acting Judge and Criminal Judge of Cuddapah; Acting Judge and Criminal Judge of Salem. 1837: Judge and Criminal Judge of Salem. 1840: *Out of employ.* (*Retired on the Annuity Fund,* 1843.) 1844: *Died on his passage to England.*

BANNERMAN, ROBERT ALEXANDER.—1821: Writer. 1824: Assistant to the Principal Collector of Tanjore. 1826: Head Assistant to the Collector and Magistrate of Tinnevelly. 1828:

Junior Deputy Secretary to the Board of Revenue. 1830: Senior Deputy Secretary to the Board of Revenue. 1832: Secretary to the Commissioners for the Government of Mysore; Acting Secretary to the Board of Revenue; Joint Magistrate and Deputy Collector of Salem. 1834: *At home on absentee allowance.* 1837: *Returned to India, via Egypt.* 1838: Collector and Magistrate of Ganjam and Commissioner of Goomsoor. 1840: Agent to Governor, and Collector and Magistrate of Ganjam, and Commissioner of Goomsoor. 1849: *Resigned the service, 6th June. (Annuitant on the Fund,* 1849.) *Died, 29th June* 1851.

BARCLAY, ANDREW.—1796: Writer. 1799: Assistant in the Military Secret and Political Departments. 1800: Assistant to the Import Warehouse-Keeper; Head Assistant under the Collector of Dindigul. *Died, 29th March* 1801, *at Dindigul.*

BARCLAY, ROBERT.—1763: Writer. 1776: Senior Merchant and Paymaster at Chicacole. *No trace after this date.*

BARKER, WILLIAM.—1755: Writer. 1768: Senior Merchant and third in Council at Vizagapatam. 1771: *Out of the service.*

BARLOW, NATHANIEL.—1763: Writer. 1776: Senior Merchant. 1790: *Out of the service.*

BARNARD, THOMAS.—1765: Writer. 1776: Senior Merchant. 1790: *Out of the service.*

BARNETT, CHARLES JAMES.—1817: Writer. *Appointed but never joined the service; Resigned in England, 7th January* 1820.

BARRINGTON, FITZWILLIAM.—1771: Writer. 1776: Factor, and Assistant at Ganjam. 1780: Junior Merchant. 1782: *Out of the service.*

BASKERVILLE, HARRY.—*See* VIVEASH, HARRY.

BAYARD, ROBERT.—1807: Writer. 1808: Deputy Commercial Resident at Maddepollam; Assistant to the Register of the Zillah of Ganjam. 1811: Register of the Zillah of Ganjam. 1819: Sub-Collector in charge of the Hill Zemindaries in Ganjam. 1824: Collector and Magistrate of Vizagapatam. 1827: Collector and Magistrate of Ganjam. 1830: *At home on absentee allowance. (Annuitant on the Fund, 1st May* 1833.)

BAYLEY, EDWARD THOMAS.—1775: Writer. 1780: Factor. 1790: Senior Merchant and Assistant at Tanjore. *Died in* 1790.

BAYLEY, WILLIAM HENRY.—1831: Writer. 1834: Assistant to the Principal Collector and Magistrate of South Arcot. 1837: Acting Head Assistant to the Principal Collector and Magistrate of

South Arcot. 1838: Acting Head Assistant to the Principal Collector and Magistrate of Salem. 1839: Deputy Secretary to Government under the Chief Secretary's Department; Commissioner for Drawing Government Lotteries. 1843: Commissioner in Kurnool. 1844: *Proceeded on furlough.* 1848: *Returned to India.* 1849: Sub-Collector and Joint Magistrate of the North Division of Arcot. 1850: Secretary to the Board of Revenue; Tamil Translator to Government; Member of the College Board. 1851: Secretary to the Board of Revenue; Tamil Translator to Government; Member of the Mint Committee. 1855: Secretary to the Board of Revenue; Tamil Translator to Government; Member of the College Board; Third Member of the Board of Revenue. 1856: Third Member of the Board of Revenue; Member of Mint Committee; *Proceeded on furlough.* 1857: *Returned to India;* Third Member of the Board of Revenue; Member of Mint Committee. 1860: *Proceeded on furlough.* 1861: *Resigned the service, 10th June.* (*Annuitant on the Fund,* 1861.)

BAYNES, CHARLES ROBERT.—1828: Writer. 1831: Assistant to the Collector of Rajahmundry. 1832: Assistant in the Accountant-General's Office; Commissioner for Drawing Government Lotteries; Second Assistant in the Accountant-General's Office; Acting Head Assistant to the Accountant-General. 1834: Head Assistant in the Accountant-General's Office. 1835: Acting Sub-Collector of Nellore. 1836: Acting Sub-Collector and Joint Magistrate of Cuddapah. 1837: Acting Assistant Judge and Joint Criminal Judge of Chingleput. 1838: Assistant Judge and Joint Criminal Judge of Chingleput. 1842: *Proceeded on furlough.* 1844: *Returned to India.* 1845: Subordinate Judge, Calicut. 1846: Assistant Judge, Calicut. 1847: Civil and Session Judge, Madura. 1856: *Proceeded on furlough.* 1857: *Returned to India;* Civil and Session Judge, Madura. 1858: Puisne Judge of the Sudder Dewannee and Sudder Foujdarry Adawlut. 1859: *Resigned the service in January.* (*Annuitant on the Fund,* 1859.)

BEAUCHAMP, GEORGE THOMAS.—1830: Writer. 1833: Assistant under Principal Collector, Nellore; Assistant to Principal Collector, North Arcot. 1834: Second Assistant to the Accountant-General, and Commissioner for Government Lotteries. 1836: Register of the Provincial Court, Northern Division. 1838: Acting Assistant Judge and Joint Criminal Judge, Rajahmundry; Acting Head Assistant to the Accountant General; and Commissioner for Government Lotteries. 1840: Acting Assistant Judge and Joint Criminal Judge, Guntoor. 1843: Acting Assistant Judge and Joint Criminal Judge, Trichinopoly; Extra Assistant to Collector, and Magistrate at Trichinopoly; Acting Sub-Judge, and afterwards Civil and Sessions Judge, Combaconum. 1844: Sub-Judge at Combaconum. 1845: Acting Civil and Sessions Judge at Combaconum. 1849: Register to the Court of Sudder and Foujdaree Adawlut. 1851: Member of the College Board. 1852: Acting, afterwards Civil and Sessions Judge, Tinnevelly. 1855: Civil and Sessions Judge, Combaconum. 1859: Officiating Assistant Judge of the Sudder and Foujdaree Adawlut. 1861: Officiating Puisne Judge of same Court. 1862: *Resigned the service, 1st May.* (*Annuitant on the Fund,* 1862.)

BELL, WILLIAM.—1807: Writer. 1808: Assistant to the Chief Secretary in the Secret, Political, and Foreign Departments. 1810: Assistant to the Collector of Salem; Assistant to the Collector of Coimbatore. 1811: Persian Translator to the Carnatic Commissioners. 1812: *At home.* 1814: *Returned to India;* Head Assistant to the Collector of Trichinopoly. 1816: Head Assistant to the Collector of Chingleput; Assistant to the Magistrate of Chingleput. *Died 30th July 1817, at St. Thomas's Mount.*

BELL, JAMES HAMILTON.—1829: Writer. 1832: *At home on absentee allowance.* 1834: *Returned to India, per "Duke of Buccleuch."* 1835: Assistant to the Collector and Magistrate of Rajahmundry. 1836: Acting Head Assistant to the Collector and Magistrate of Guntoor; Head Assistant to the Collector and Magistrate of Rajahmundry. 1837: Charge of the Zillah of Rajahmundry. 1838: Acting Deputy Collector of Sea Customs at Madras; Commissioner for Drawing Government Lotteries. 1840: Assistant Judge and Joint Criminal Judge, Malabar. 1842: Assistant Judge and Joint Criminal Judge, Chingleput. 1844: Subordinate Judge, Chittoor. 1850: Civil and Sessions Judge, Guntoor. *Died at Guntoor, in India, 25th August* 1851.

BENFIELD, PAUL.—1765: Writer. 1776: Senior Merchant. *Recalled,* 1776. *Suspended,* 1790. 1792: *Out of the service.*

BIGSBY, THOMAS.—1797: Writer. 1798: Assistant in the Military, Secret, and Political Departments. *Died at sea in* 1798.

BINNING, ROBERT BLAIR MONRO.—1833: Writer. 1835: Assistant to the Collector and Magistrate of Masulipatam. 1837: Acting Head Assistant to the Collector and Magistrate of Rajahmundry. 1839: *At home on absentee allowance.* 1842: *Returned to India.* 1843: Assistant, afterwards Head Assistant, to Collector and

Magistrate, Northern Division of Arcot. 1850: Sub-Collector and Joint Magistrate, Northern Division of Arcot. 1856: *Proceeded on furlough.* 1861: *Resigned the service in England. (Annuitant on the Fund,* 1860.) *Died in England.*

BINNY, Edward Dyer.—1852: Writer. 1855: Assistant to Collector and Magistrate, Canara. 1858: Head Assistant to Collector and Magistrate, Canara. 1860: *Proceeded on furlough; Died,* 13*th January, at Cheltenham.*

BIRCH, Richard.—1779: Writer. 1782: *Out of the service.*

BIRCH, Sylvester Douglas.—1830: Writer. 1833: Doing duty under the Collector of Chingleput. 1834: Assistant to Collector and Magistrate, Chingleput. 1835: Assistant to Principal Collector and Magistrate, Tanjore. 1838: Acting Cashier at Government Bank, and Assistant to Sub-Treasurer. 1839: Cashier at Government Bank, and Assistant to Sub-Treasurer. 1841: Commissioner for Government Lotteries, and Acting Sub-Treasurer and Superintendent and Treasurer of Government Bank. 1843: Secretary and Treasurer of the Bank of Madras. 1845: Acting Sub-Treasurer, Director of the Bank of Madras, and Acting Member and Secretary to the Mint Committee. 1847: Head and Special Assistant to the Accountant-General. 1848: Sub-Collector and Joint Magistrate, North Arcot. 1849: Sub-Treasurer and Member of the Mint Committee; and Director of the Incorporated Bank of Madras. 1859: Accountant-General at Bombay; President of the Mint Committee; and Government Director of the Bank of Bombay. 1865: *Resigned the service,* 28*th February. (Annuitant on the Fund,* 1865.) *Died* 4*th February* 1881, *in England.*

BIRD, John.—1801: Writer. 1805: Assistant under the Principal Collector of Tanjore. 1806: Assistant under the Principal Collector of the Ceded Districts; Register of the Zillah of the Western Division of Ceded Districts. 1814: Secretary to the Board of Trade and Reporter of External Commerce; Assistant Judge of Zillah of Coimbatore. 1815: Judge and Magistrate of the Zillah of Canara. 1816: Judge and Criminal Judge of Zillah of Salem. 1824: Third Judge of Provincial Court in the Southern Division. 1828: Second Judge of Provincial Court in the Southern Division. 1830: First Judge of Provincial Court in the Southern Division. 1831: Acting Third Puisne Judge of the Sudder and Foujdarry Adawlut. 1832: Second Puisne Judge of the Sudder and Foujdarry Adawlut. 1838: First Puisne Judge of the Sudder and Foujdarry Adawlut, and Provincial Member of Council. 1842:

Member of Council, and Chief Judge of the Sudder Dewannee and Sudder Foujdarry Adawlut. 1845: *Resigned the service, 30th June, in India.* (*Annuitant on the Fund,* 1845.) *Died, in* 1850, *at Cheltenham.*

BIRD, CHARLES.—1806: Writer. 1809: Register to the Zillah of Bareilly. 1812: Register to the Zillah of Cuddapah. 1815: Register to the Zillah of Vizagapatam. 1818: Head Assistant to the Collector, and Assistant Magistrate, of Ganjam. *Died, 23d August* 1819, *near Ganjam.*

BIRD, GEORGE.—1821: Writer. 1824: Employed at Dharwar under the Bombay Government. 1829: *At home on absentee allowance.* 1832: *Returned to India;* Sub-Collector and Joint Magistrate of Bellary. 1833: Acting Assistant Judge of Chingleput. 1834: Assistant Judge of Guntoor; Judge and Criminal Judge of Combaconum. 1835: Judge and Criminal Judge of Canara. 1838: Acting Judge of the Provincial Court, Western Division. 1839: Judge and Criminal Judge of Canara. 1842: Third Judge, afterwards Second Judge, of the Provincial Court of Appeal and Circuit, West Division. 1844: Civil and Session Judge, Coimbatore. 1847: *Proceeded on furlough.* 1849: *Returned to India.* 1850: Civil and Session Judge, Coimbatore; *Proceeded on furlough.* 1851: *Resigned the service, 25th February, in India. Died, 20th July* 1880, *in England.*

BIRD, CHARLES JAMES.—1830: Writer. 1832: Assistant to the Commissioners for the Government of Mysore. 1833: Assistant to Principal Collector of North Arcot. 1835: Head Assistant to the Collector and Magistrate of Tinnevelly. 1836: Acting Joint Criminal Judge at Madura. 1838: Sub-Collector and Joint Magistrate of Tinnevelly. 1839: Sub-Collector and Magistrate of Tinnevelly. 1842: *Proceeded on Furlough.* 1844: *Returned to India.* 1845: Sub-Collector and Magistrate of Coimbatore. 1850: Collector and Magistrate of Southern Division of Arcot. 1851: Collector and Magistrate of Tinnevelly. 1856: *Proceeded on Furlough.* 1859: *Resigned the service, 8th February.* (*Annuitant on the Fund,* 1860.) *Died, 21st April* 1879, *in England.*

BIRD, JOHN.—1830: Writer. 1832: Second Assistant to the Collector and Magistrate of Chingleput. 1835: Head Assistant to the Collector and Magistrate of Chingleput. 1838: Acting Sub-Collector and Joint Magistrate of Nellore; Acting Sub-Collector and Joint Magistrate of Coimbatore; Sub-Collector and Joint Magistrate of Coimbatore. 1839: Sub-Collector and Magistrate of

Coimbatore. 1845: *Proceeded on furlough.* 1848: *Returned to India;* Sub-Collector and Joint Magistrate, Tanjore. 1851: Collector and Magistrate, Trichinopoly. 1860: *Resigned the service 30th April, in India.* (*Annuitant on the Fund,* 1860.) *Died, 16th April* 1877, *in England.*

BISHOP, JOHN FITZ-SIMMONS.—1827: Writer. 1829: Assistant to the Collector of Trichinopoly. 1830: Head Assistant to the Collector of Trichinopoly. 1831: Head Assistant to the Collector of Tinnevelly. 1832: Acting Head Assistant to Principal Collector and Magistrate of Coimbatore. 1835: Sub-Collector and Joint Magistrate of Tinnevelly. 1838: *At home on absentee allowance.* 1841: *Returned to India.* 1842: *Out of employ.* 1843: Sub-Collector and Joint Magistrate, Tanjore. 1845: Collector and Magistrate, Nellore. 1847: Collector and Magistrate, Tanjore. 1854: *Proceeded on furlough.* 1856: *Resigned the service, 13th November, in England.* (*Annuitant on the Fund,* 1858.)

BLACKBURN, JOHN.—1815: Writer. 1818: Second Assistant to the Collector and Magistrate of Tanjore. 1823: Assistant to the Principal Collector and Magistrate, and Head Assistant to Principal Collector, Tanjore. 1826: *At home on absentee allowance.* 1830: *Returned to India.* 1831: Acting Resident at Tanjore. 1832: Acting Collector and Magistrate, afterwards Collector and Magistrate of Tinnevelly; Collector and Magistrate of Guntoor. 1834: Principal Collector and Magistrate of Madura. 1847: *Resigned the service.* (*Annuitant on the Fund,* 1847.) *Died, 17th June* 1850, *Sloane Street, Chelsea.*

BLACKETT, ROBERT STEWART.—1848: Writer. 1852: *Name removed in England.*

BLAIR, WILLIAM THOMAS.—1808: Writer. 1811: Assistant to the Accountant-General. 1814: Deputy Accountant-General in the Military Department. 1817: *At home.* 1818: *Returned to India;* Assistant to the Accountant-General. 1819: Sheriff of Madras. 1822: Deputy Accountant-General in the Military Department of Accounts. 1826: *At home on absentee allowance.* (*Retired on the Civil Service Annuity Fund from 1st January* 1828.)

BLAIR, HENRY MARTIN.—1818: Writer. 1823: Assistant to the Collector and Magistrate of Chingleput. 1825: Register of the Zillah of Canara. 1826: Head Assistant to the Principal Collector and Magistrate of Malabar. 1829: *At home on absentee allowance.* 1831: *Returned to India, "La Belle Alliance."* 1832: Acting Secretary to the College of Public Instruction; Collector and Magistrate of

Trichinopoly. 1838: Acting Principal Collector and Magistrate of Canara. 1839: Principal Collector and Magistrate of Canara. 1846: *Proceeded on furlough.* 1847: *Resigned the service.* (*Annuitant on the Fund*, 1847.) *Died, 16th October* 1880.

BLAKE, ARTHUR GARLAND.—1796: Writer. 1799: Assistant in the Public Department at Colombo. 1800: Assistant to the Collector at Guntoor; Assistant under the Collector at Chicacole. 1802: Register to the Judge of the Zillah of Guntoor. 1803: Register to the Judge of the Provincial Court, Northern Division. 1806: *At home.* 1808: *Returned to India.* 1809: Assistant Judge at Masulipatam. 1812: Collector of Rajahmundry. *Died, 30th November* 1812, *at Rajahmundry.*

BLAKE, EDWARD PARKER.—1797: Writer. 1799: Assistant under the Commercial Resident at Cuddalore. 1800: Assistant under the Commercial Resident at Maddepollam. 1802: Deputy Commercial Resident in the Ceded District. 1804: *Out of employ.* 1805: Register of the Zillah of Guntoor. 1808: *Out of employ.* 1809: Assistant Judge at Combaconum. 1811: Collector of Sea Customs at Malabar and Canara. 1816: *At home.* 1821: *Out of the service.*

BLANE, THOMAS LAW.—1826: Writer. 1828: Assistant to the Collector of Chingleput. 1830: Acting Head Assistant to the Collector of Tanjore; Head Assistant to the Principal Collector of Tanjore. 1832: Additional Sub-Collector and Joint Magistrate of Tanjore. 1835: Sub-Collector and Joint Magistrate of Bellary. 1837: Charge of Office of Principal Collector and Magistrate of Cuddapah. 1838: Acting Collector and Magistrate of Masulipatam; Acting Collector and Magistrate, afterwards Collector and Magistrate of Cuddapah. 1842: Collector and Magistrate of Southern Division, Arcot. 1843: *Proceeded on furlough.* 1845: *Returned to India.* 1846: Principal Collector and Magistrate, Canara. 1851: Third Member of Board of Revenue. 1854: *Resigned the service, 1st May.* (*Annuitant on the Fund*, 1854.)

BLANSHARD, JOHN.—1830: Writer. 1833: Placed under the Principal Collector of North Arcot. *Died, 6th September* 1833, *at Chittoor.*

BOILEAU, JOHN PETER.—1765: Writer. 1776: Senior Merchant and Paymaster at Ishapore. 1790: *Out of the service.*

BOILEAU, THOMAS EBENEZER JOHN.—1815: Writer. 1818: Assistant Register of Provincial Court, Southern Division, and Acting Register. 1819: Acting Register of the Zillah of Trichinopoly. 1820: Acting Register of the Zillah of Salem. 1821: Register of the Zillah of Chingleput. 1824: Acting Judge of Chingleput. 1827: Assistant Judge and Joint Criminal Judge of the Zillah of Canara. 1832: Judge and Criminal Judge of Bellary. 1833: Acting Third Judge of Centre Circuit Provincial Court. 1835: Acting Third Judge of Northern Circuit Provincial Court. 1836: Third Judge of Northern Circuit Provincial Court, and Acting Second Judge. 1838: Third Judge of Western Circuit Provincial Court. 1841: Second Judge of the Provincial Court of Appeal and Circuit, Northern Division. 1842: First Judge of the Provincial Court of Appeal and Circuit, Northern Division. 1844: Civil and Session Judge, Masulipatam. 1846: Third Judge of the Court of Sudder Dewannee and Sudder Foujdarry Adawlut. 1847: Civil and Session Judge, Chingleput. 1848: *Proceeded on furlough.* 1850: *Returned to India.* 1851: Civil and Sessions Judge, Guntoor; *Resigned the service, 15th April, in India.*

BOLDERO, CHARLES.—1777: Writer. 1782: Factor. 1790: *Out of the service.*

BOURCHIER, CHARLES.—1741: Writer. 1768: Became Governor of the Madras Presidency. *Out of the service prior to* 1771.

BOURCHIER, JAMES.—1751: Writer. 1768: Member of the Council of the Governor. 1771: *Out of the service.*

BOURDILLON, JAMES DEWAR.—1829: Writer. 1831: Second Assistant to the Collector of Trichinopoly. 1833: Head Assistant to the Collector of Trichinopoly. 1835: Acting Assistant Judge of Salem. 1836: Head Assistant to the Collector and Magistrate of Trichinopoly. 1837: Acting Sub-Collector and Joint Magistrate of Nellore. 1838: Sub-Collector and Joint Magistrate of Northern Division of Arcot. 1843: Secretary to the Board of Revenue. 1845: *Proceeded on furlough.* 1848: *Returned to India;* Sub-Collector and Joint Magistrate, Nellore. 1849: Collector and Magistrate of the Northern Division of Arcot. 1855: Third Member of the Board of Revenue; Secretary to Government Revenue and Judicial Departments. 1857: *Proceeded on furlough.* 1859: *Returned to India;* Secretary to Government Revenue Department. 1860: Secretary to Government Revenue and Public Works Departments. 1861: *Resigned the service in England.* (*Annuitant on the Fund*, 1860.)

BOUTFLOWER, SAMUEL.—1796: Writer. 1798: Assistant under the Collector in the First Division of Vizagapatam District. 1802: *At home.* 1804: *Returned to India;* Register to the

Zillah Judge of Ganjam. 1806: Register to the Zillah Judge of Vizagapatam. 1810: Assistant Judge at Canara. 1812: *Out of employ.* 1823: *Out of the service.*

BRANFILL, Benjamin.—1781: Writer. 1783: Assistant to the Secretary to the Select Committee; Assistant to the Secretary to the Committee of Circuit. 1789: *Out of employ.* 1790: Sheriff; Land Customer Deputy Commissary-General and Register of the Choultry Court. 1791: Assistant to the Collector of Nellore. 1793: Second Member of the Committee of Investigation at Nuzeed. 1794: Superintendent of the Nuzeed Zemindary; Collector in the Third Division of Masulipatam District. 1802: *Out of employ.* 1804: *At home.* 1807: *Out of the service.*

BREEKS, Richard.—1848: Writer. *Died, at Trichinopoly, 19th February* 1852.

BRETT, Harry Augustus.—1831: Writer. 1832: Assistant in Chief Secretary's Office. 1833: Assistant to Principal Collector, Madura. 1834: Assistant to Principal Collector and Magistrate, North Arcot. 1836: Acting Register of the Zillah Court of Salem; and Acting Register of the Provincial Court, Centre Division. 1837: Register of the Provincial Court, Centre Division. 1839: Register of the Zillah Court of Bellary; Acting Head Assistant to the Collector and Magistrate, Chingleput, and to the Principal Collector and Magistrate, Salem. 1840: Assistant to the Principal Collector and Magistrate, Salem. 1842: Acting Sub-Collector and Joint Magistrate, Salem. 1843: Sub-Collector and Joint Magistrate, Salem. 1844: In charge of the Salem Sub-Court. 1846: *Proceeded on furlough.* 1849: Acting Sub-Collector and Joint Magistrate, Madura; Acting, afterwards Sub-Judge, Chittoor. 1852: Acting Collector and Magistrate, North Arcot. 1853: Acting Collector and Magistrate, and afterwards Collector and Magistrate, Salem. 1858: *On medical leave to Europe for* 21 *months.* 1860: Collector of Salem. 1862: Member of the Board of Revenue, and President of the Income Tax Commission. 1865: President of the Income Tax Commission. 1867: *Resigned the service, 27th May.* (*Annuitant on the Fund,* 1867.) *Died, 20th December* 1867.

BRICKENDEN, Richard.—1752: Writer. 1768: Senior Merchant. 1771: Member of the Council of the Governor. 1774: *Out of the service.*

BRODIE, James.—1789: Writer. 1790: Assistant under the Secretary in the Public and Revenue Departments. 1793: Acting

Secretary to the Military Board. 1796: Garrison Store-keeper and Import Warehouse-keeper. *No trace after* 1801.

BRODIE, Alexander.—1773: Writer. 1780: Factor. 1782: Junior Merchant. 1790: *Out of the service.*

BROOKE, Henry.—1751: Writer. 1768: Chief of Cuddalore. 1771: Member of the Council of the Governor. 1774: Chief of Masulipatam. 1776: *Recalled.* 1780: *Suspended.* 1782: *Out of the service.*

BROOKE, Arthur.—1793: Writer. 1796: Assistant under the Secretary in the Military, Political, and Secret Departments. 1797: Land Customer. 1799: Assistant to the Military Paymaster-General. 1800: Assistant to the Collector of Government Customs. 1802: Head Assistant to the Commercial Resident at Cuddalore. 1803: *At home.* 1808: *Returned to India;* Deputy Commercial Resident at Salem. 1811: Commercial Resident at Cuddalore. 1815: *Out of employ.* 1817: Commercial Resident at Nagore. 1826: *At home on absentee allowance.* 1829: *Returned to India.* 1830: Deputy Warehouse-keeper. 1832: Officiating Superintendent of Stationery. 1836: Superintendent of Government Lotteries; Acting Cashier to the Government Bank, and Assistant to the Sub-Treasurer. 1837: Superintendent of the Government Lotteries. 1845: *Out of employ. Died, 11th January* 1850, *in Madras.*

BROWN, William.—1783: Writer; Assistant to the Secretary to the Select Committee. 1786: Assistant at Masulipatam. 1787: Under the Secretary in the Secret Department. 1790: Paymaster to the Detachment serving with the Nizam. 1793: *Out of employ.* 1794: Assistant in the Vizianagram Zemindary. 1796: Collector in the Southern Division of the Vizianagram Zemindary. 1797: Collector in the Cashimcottah Havelly, the resumed Pergunnahs of Vizianagram and Vizagapatam Farms. 1798: Collector in the First Division of the Vizagapatam District. 1800: Collector in the First Division of the Ganjam. 1802: Third Judge of the Court of Circuit and Appeal, Northern Division. 1806: Second Judge of the Court of Circuit and Appeal, Northern Division. 1810: *At home.* 1816: *Returned to India;* Sheriff of Madraspatam. 1817: Commissioner at Rajahmundry. 1819: Acting Third Judge of the Provincial Court, Northern Division. 1820: Commercial Resident and Collector of Sea Customs, Vizagapatam and Ganjam. 1821: *Out of employ.* 1822: Second Judge of the Provincial Court, Centre Division. 1824: Senior Judge of the

Provincial Court, Centre Division. 1828: Additional Government Commissioner for Carnatic Claims. 1831: Telugoo Translator to Government. 1832: *Out of employ.* 1835: Persian Translator to Government. *Died, 27th June* 1837, *at St Thome.*

BROWN, HENRY.—1789: Writer. 1790: Assistant under the Secretary in the Public and Revenue Departments. 1792: Acting Deputy Export Warehouse-keeper. 1793: Deputy Warehouse-keeper. 1794: Export Warehouse-keeper. 1796: Commercial Resident at the Presidency. 1801: Commercial Resident at Ramnad. *Died, 29th December* 1808, *at Madura.*

BROWN, CHARLES PHILIP.—1816: Writer. 1820: Assistant to the Collector and Magistrate of Cuddapah. 1822: Register of the Zillah of Masulipatam. 1824: Head Assistant to the Collector and Magistrate of Rajahmundry. 1826: Register of the Zillah of Cuddapah. 1829: Register to the Provincial Court, Southern Division. 1830: Assistant Judge and Joint-Criminal Judge of Rajahmundry. 1835: *At home on absentee allowance.* 1837: *Returned to India, per "Mary Ann."* 1838: Persian Translator to Government; Acting Secretary to the College Board, and to the Native Education Committee; and Member of the College Board. 1839: Acting Register to the Sudder and Foujdarry Adawlut; Persian Translator to Government; Member of the College Board. 1847: Persian, Tamul, and Telugoo Translator to Government; Postmaster-General. 1854: *Resigned the service, 1st May, in India.* (*Annuitant on the Fund*, 1854.)

BROWN, CHRISTIAN JAMES.—1824: Writer. 1825: Assistant to the Principal Collector and Magistrate of Cuddapah. 1828: Head Assistant to the Accountant-General. *Died, 10th April* 1831, *on his passage to England.*

BRUCE, PETER.—1796: Writer. 1799: Assistant to the Accountant-General. 1801: Assistant under the Principal Collector in the Ceded District. 1803: Subordinate Collector in the Ceded Districts. 1806: Judge and Magistrate of Bellary. 1820: Third Judge of the Provincial Court, Southern Division; Second Judge of the Provincial Court, Centre Division. *Died, 2d September* 1821, *at Gooty.*

BRUCE, FREDERICK HERVEY.—1808: Writer; Assistant to Secretary in Judicial and Revenue Department. 1809: Assistant to the Collector of Vizagapatam. 1811: Assistant to the Register of the Provincial Court, Northern Division. 1813: Deputy Commercial Resident at Maddepollam and Masulipatam. 1815:

Register of the Zillah of Cuddapah. *Died, 10th September 1817, at Cuddapah.*

BRUCE, ALEXANDER FAIRLIE.—1817: Writer. 1820: Assistant to the Collector and Magistrate of Tanjore. 1824: Register of the Zillah of Salem. 1825: Head Assistant to the Principal Collector of the Northern Division of Arcot; *At home.* 1829: *Returned to India;* Acting Sub-Collector of Nellore. 1830: Sub-Collector and Joint-Magistrate of Nellore. 1834: Acting Secretary to the Board of Revenue. 1835: Mint Master. 1836: Acting Collector, afterwards Collector and Magistrate of Guntoor. 1837: Acting Police Magistrate at the Presidency; Acting Civil Auditor; Acting Superintendent of Stamps; Member of Mint Committee. 1838: Collector and Magistrate of Guntoor (resumed); Acting Collector and Magistrate of Chingleput; Collector and Magistrate of Cuddapah; Postmaster-General. 1847: Civil Auditor, and Superintendent of Stamps. 1852: *Resigned the service, 1st July, in India.* (*Annuitant on the Fund,* 1852.) *Died, 26th June 1875, in England.*

BRUERE, JAMES GRAHAM SADLEIR.—1826: Writer. 1828: Register of the Zillah of Chittoor. 1832: Acting Assistant Judge and Joint Criminal Judge at Salem; Acting Deputy Collector of Madras. 1833: Secretary to the Marine Board. 1834: Assistant Judge and Joint Criminal Judge of Rajahmundry. 1836: Assistant Judge and Joint Criminal Judge of Chingleput. 1837: *At home.* 1840: *Returned to India.* 1841: *Out of employ.* 1842: Deputy Collector of Sea Customs, Madras; Judge and Joint Criminal Judge of Salem. 1844: Civil and Session Judge, Salem. 1852: Civil and Session Judge, Cuddalore. 1854: *Resigned the service, 1st May.* (*Annuitant on the Fund,* 1854.) *Died, 27th September 1865, in England.*

BUCHAN, GEORGE.—1792: Writer. 1794: Assistant under the Secretary in the Military, Political, and Secret Department, and French Translator. 1795: Assistant Manager for Supplying Beetle Tobacco and Ganja. 1796: Paymaster to the Expedition against Malacca. 1799: Sub-Secretary in the Military, Political, and Secret Department. 1801: Secretary in the Public and Commercial Department; Secretary in the Military Department. 1803: Chief Secretary to Government. 1809: Private Secretary to the Governor. 1810: *At home.* 1814: *Out of the service.*

BURLTON, JOHN PHILIP.—1777: Writer. 1780: *At home.* 1790: Senior Merchant and Muster-Master of the Calcroon. 1795:

Resident at Negapatam. 1800: Paymaster at Kistnagherry. 1801: *Out of the service.*

BURY, John Fuller.—1834: Writer. 1836: Assistant to the Principal Collector and Magistrate of Malabar; Assistant to the Principal Collector and Magistrate of North Arcot. 1840: Assistant to Agent to Governor; Collector and Magistrate, Vizagapatam. 1845: *Proceeded on furlough.* 1848: *Returned to India. Died, 11th May* 1848, *in India (Waltair).*

BUSHBY, Henry Turner.—1811: Writer. 1817: Assistant to the Register of the Sudder and Foujdarry Adawlut. 1818: Register of the Zillah of Chittoor. 1823: Register to the Provincial Court, Centre Division. 1827: Assistant Judge and Joint Criminal Judge of Cuddapah. 1829: Judge and Criminal Judge of Bellary. 1832: Third Judge of the Provincial Court, Northern Division; Third Judge of the Provincial Court, Nellore. 1834: Third Judge of the Provincial Court, Rajahmundry; *Out of employ.* 1836: Acting Judge and Criminal Judge of Bellary; Acting Judge and Criminal Judge of Salem. 1837: Judge and Criminal Judge of Bellary; Acting Judge of Provincial Court, Centre Division. *Died, 17th May* 1838, *at Cuddapah.*

BUSHBY, Charles Maitland.—1817: Writer. 1820: Assistant to the Collector and Magistrate of Salem. 1823: Register of the Zillah of Chittoor. 1827: Register to the Provincial Court, Western Division. 1832: Assistant Judge and Joint Criminal Judge of Canara. *Died, 30th January* 1835, *at Mangalore.*

BYNG, John.—1796: Writer. 1797: Assistant under the Secretary in the Public, Revenue, and Commercial Departments. 1798: Deputy Postmaster-General; Paymaster at Malacca. 1805: Acting Register and Assistant Magistrate to Act in the Zillah of Masulipatam. 1806: Judge and Magistrate of the Zillah of Guntoor. 1807: Judge and Magistrate of the Zillah of Ganjam. 1810: Judge and Magistrate of the Zillah of Trichinopoly. *Died, 23d November* 1811, *at Trichinopoly.*

BYRNE, Patrick.—1789: Writer. 1790: Assistant under the Military Secretary. 1791: *At home. No trace after* 1791.

CADOGAN, Hon. George.—1771: Writer. 1776: Factor. 1780: Junior Merchant. *No trace after* 1780.

CALL, John.—1751: Writer. 1768: Member of the Council of the Governor. 1771: *Out of the service.*

CALL, James.—1766: Writer. 1771: Factor. 1774: Junior

Merchant. 1778: Senior Merchant, and Provisional Member of Board of Revenue. 1792: Sea Customer. 1800: *Out of the service.*

CALL, JEWEL.—1771: Writer. 1776: Factor. 1780: Junior Merchant. 1782: Senior Merchant. 1790: *Out of the service.*

CALLAND, JOHN.—1751: Writer. 1768: Senior Merchant; *Suspended from service.*

CAMERON, N. S.—1813: Writer. 1816: Head Assistant to the Collector, afterwards Assistant Magistrate, Canara. 1823: Sub-Collector and Assistant Magistrate of Canara. 1825: *At home.* 1828: *Returned to India;* Collector and Magistrate of Trichinopoly. 1831: Principal Collector and Magistrate of Canara. 1833: Principal Collector and Magistrate of Madura. *Died, 12th December* 1833, *at the Cape of Good Hope.*

CAMPBELL, FREDERICK.—1781: Writer. 1782: Assistant to the Secretary in the Select Committee. 1783: Assistant to the Secretary in the Civil Department. 1784: Secretary to General Campbell. 1786: Deputy Import Warehouse-keeper; Assistant to the Committee of Circuit. 1789: Muster-Master of the Centre Division. 1790: *Out of employ. Died, 26th March* 1791, *at Chingleput.*

CAMPBELL, WILLIAM.—1806: Writer. 1808: Assistant in the Secret, Political, and Foreign Departments. 1809: Assistant to the Collector of Canara. 1816: *Suspended. Dismissed, 16th December* 1818, *in England.*

CAMPBELL, ALEXANDER DUNCAN.—1807: Writer. 1809: Assistant under the Collector of Bellary; Fixed Assistant under the Secretary to the Board of Revenue, and Assistant to the Superintendent of Stamps. 1811: Secretary to the Board of Superintendence for the College of Fort St. George. 1812: Deputy Secretary to the Board of Revenue. 1817: Secretary to the Board of Revenue. 1820: Collector and Magistrate of Bellary. 1824: Third Judge of the Provincial Court, Centre Division. 1826: Third Member of the Board of Revenue. 1827: Principal Collector and Magistrate of Tanjore. 1828: *Out of employ;* Register to the Sudder and Foujdarry Adawlut. 1830: Telugoo Translator to Government. 1831: *At home on absentee allowance.* 1833: *Returned to India per "Alfred."* 1834: Acting Judge of

*

the Sudder and Foujdarry Adawlut. 1835: Superintendent of Stamps and Civil Auditor; Acting Judge of the Sudder Adawlut. 1837: Member of the Mint Committee; Persian Translator to Government; Acting Third Judge of the Sudder Foujdarry Adawlut. 1838: Third Puisne Judge of the Sudder Foujdarry Adawlut, and Member of the College Board. 1840: Second Puisne Judge of the Court of Sudder Dewannee and Sudder Foujdarry Adawlut, and Member of the College Board. 1842: First Puisne Judge of the Court of Sudder Dewannee and Sudder Foujdarry Adawlut, and Member of the College Board; *Resigned the service, 6th May, in India.* (*Annuitant on the Fund,* 1842.) *Died, 23d April* 1857, *in England.*

CAMPBELL, E. C.—1856: Writer. 1859: *Proceeded on furlough.* 1861: *Resigned the service, 24th July, in England.*

CAPPER, JAMES.—1770: Writer. 1776: Factor. *Died, 31st August* 1776, *at Calcutta.*

CARPENTER, CHARLES.—1789: Writer; Assistant under the Secretary in the Secret Department. 1790: Assistant under the Secretary in the Military Department. 1791: Assistant under the Collector of Coimbatore. 1792: *Out of employ.* 1793: Assistant under the Resident at Maddepollam. 1794: Commercial Resident at Salem. *Died, 4th June* 1818, *at Salem.*

CASAMAJOR, JAMES HENRY.—1762: Writer. 1776: Senior Merchant; Paymaster at Vellore. *No trace after* 1782. *Died, 23d January* 1815, *in England.*

CASAMAIJOR, JOHN.—1792: Writer; Assistant under the Secretary in the Political, Secret, and Military Departments. 1794: Assistant under the Commercial Resident at Tinnevelly. 1796: Deputy Commercial Resident at Ramnad and Tinnevelly. 1800: Commercial Resident at Tinnevelly. 1806: Third Judge of the Court of Circuit and Appeal, Southern Division. 1809: Third Member of the Board of Trade. 1813: Acting General Superintendent of Investments. 1816: Senior Member of the Board of Trade. *Died, 1st February* 1821, *at Singapore.*

CASAMAIJOR, JAMES ARCHIBALD.—1802: Writer. 1803: Assistant to the Secretary to the Board of Trade. 1804: Secretary and Accountant to the Sinking Fund. 1806: Deputy Secretary to the Board of Revenue. 1809: Register of Seringapatam; Judge, Magistrate, and Collector of Seringapatam. 1811: Military Paymaster at the Presidency and of Extraordinaries. 1813:

Judge, Magistrate, and Collector of Seringapatam. 1818: Assistant to the Resident at Mysore. 1827: Resident at Mysore. 1832: Occasional Member of Council, and Officiating President of the Revenue and Marine Board. 1834: Resident at Travancore and Cochin. 1836: *At home on absentee allowance.* (*Annuitant on the Fund from 1st May* 1837.)

CASAMAIJOR, George James.—1812: Writer. 1816: Assistant to the Secretary in the Military Department. 1819: *At home.* 1823: *Returned to India;* Assistant to the Chief Secretary to Government. 1826: Register to the Sudder and Foujdarry Adawlut. 1828: Judge and Criminal Judge of Nellore. 1832: Second Judge of the Provincial Court, Northern Division. 1834: Second Judge of the Provincial Court, Centre Division. 1836: Acting Principal Collector and Magistrate of Cuddapah. 1838: Acting First Judge of the Provincial Court, Centre Division. 1839: Second Judge of the Provincial Court of Appeal and Circuit, Centre Division. 1840: First Judge of the Provincial Court of Appeal and Circuit, Centre Division. 1842: Third Judge, afterwards Second Judge, of the Sudder Dewannee and Sudder Foujdarry Adawlut. 1844: *Resigned the service, 3d December, in India.* (*Annuitant on the Fund,* 1845.) *Died, 31st May* 1849, *at Ootacamund.*

CATOR, Frederick Sawbridge Wright.—1843: Writer. 1846: Assistant to Collector and Magistrate, Tinnevelly. 1847: Assistant to Collector and Magistrate, Madura. 1852: Head Assistant to Collector and Magistrate, Madura; Head Assistant to Collector and Magistrate, Guntoor. *Died, 11th February* 1854, *at Cape Town.*

CATHCART, Robert.—1826: Writer. 1827: Assistant to the Principal Collector of Tanjore. 1829: Employed under the Bombay Government. 1832: Acting Additional Sub-Collector and Joint Magistrate of Salem. 1833: Special Assistant to the Collector and Magistrate of Chingleput. 1834: Acting Sub-Collector of Ganjam. *Died, 26th May* 1834, *at Ganjam.*

CAZALET, Peter Reade.—1796: Writer. 1798: Assistant under the Accountant-General. 1799: Assistant under the Collector of the Fourth Division of Masulipatam. 1802: Assistant under the Collector of the Third Division of Masulipatam. 1803; Collector of the Zillah of Masulipatam. 1806: Collector of the Zillah of Carangoody. 1809: Judge and Magistrate of the Zillah of Rajahmundry. 1813: *At home.* 1816: *Returned to India.*

1817: Acting Collector and Magistrate of Ganjam. 1819: Collector and Magistrate of Ganjam. (*Annuitant on the Fund in* 1827.) *Died, 27th January* 1839, *at Bath.*

CHAMBERS, WILLIAM.—1765: Writer. 1776: Senior Merchant. 1780: *In Bengal.* 1790: Interpreter to Supreme Court of Judicature in Bengal. *No trace after* 1792.

CHAMIER (DESCHAMPS), JOHN. — 1772: Writer. 1778: Factor. 1780: Junior Merchant. 1782: *At home.* 1790: Senior Merchant; Secretary to the Military, Political, and Secret Departments, and Judge-Advocate-General. 1792: Collector at Muglatore. 1795: Chief of Vizagapatam. 1801: Chief Secretary to Government. 1802: Chief Secretary to Government, and Provisional Member of Council. 1803: Full Member of Council. 1804: President of the Board of Trade. 1806: *At home.* 1809: *Out of the service.*

CHAMIER, HENRY.—1812: Writer. 1816: Persian Translator to the Carnatic Commissioners. 1817: Second Deputy Secretary to the Board of Revenue. 1818: Temporary Assistant to the Chief Secretary to Government. 1820: Assistant to the Chief Secretary to Government. 1821: Sub-Collector and Assistant Magistrate of Chittoor. 1825: Sub-Collector and Assistant Magistrate of South Arcot. 1827: Secretary in the Public Department. 1828: Secretary in the Military Department. 1829: Acting Secretary in the Revenue and Judicial Department; Acting Secretary in the Military Department. 1831: Secretary in the Revenue and Judicial Department; Chief Secretary to Government. 1832: Acting Persian Translator to Government; Occasional Member of Council under the Provisions of the Act, 33 George III., cap. 52; Trustee for St. George's Church. 1837: Chief Secretary to Government. 1842: Chief Secretary to Government, and Provisional Member of Council. 1843: Member of Council, and President of the Revenue, Marine, and College Boards. 1848: President of the Revenue, Marine, and College Boards; *Resigned the service, 14th January. Died, 4th February* 1867, *in England.*

CHAPLIN, WILLIAM.—1799: Writer. 1804: Register in the Ceded Districts. 1806: Subordinate Collector in the Ceded Districts. 1807: Collector in the Zillah of Cuddapah. 1809: Collector in the Zillah of Bellary. 1818: Employed in the late Peishwah's Dominions. 1823: Commissioner in the Deccan. 1827: *Out of the service.*

CHAPMAN, ROBERT.—1791: Writer; Assistant under the

Secretary to the Board of Revenue. 1792: Assistant under the Resident at Ingeram. *Died, 15th December 1792, at Ingeram.*

CHARLTON, JASPER.—1778: Writer. 1790: Senior Merchant. 1791: *Absent. No trace after 1792.*

CHASE, THOMAS.—1781: Writer. 1783: Assistant to the Secretary to the Select Committee. 1784: Clerk to the Justices, and French Translator. 1786: Assistant to the Secretary in the Military Department, and Clerk to the Committee of Stores. 1788: Examiner to the Mayor's Court. 1790: Secretary to the Board of Trade. 1796: *Out of employ.* 1799: *At home.* 1801: *Returned to India. Died, 5th February 1808, at Vizagapatam.*

CHASE, THOMAS CURTIS.—1808: Writer. 1809: Second Assistant to the Collector of Nellore. 1812: Head Assistant to the Collector of Nellore. 1817: *At home. Died, 19th May 1818, at Kensington.*

CHATFIELD, JAMES.—1806: Writer; Assistant under the Secretary to the Board of Revenue. 1808: *At home.* 1813: *Out of the service.*

CHATFIELD, ROWLEY WINSLEY.—1832: Writer. 1834: Doing Duty under the Principal Collector and Magistrate, Madura. 1835: Second Assistant to Principal Collector and Magistrate, Madura. 1836: Assistant to Principal Collector and Magistrate, Canara. 1837: Acting Register of the Zillah Court of Canara; Acting Head Assistant to Principal Collector and Magistrate, Canara; afterwards Register of the Zillah Court of Malabar. 1839: Acting Assistant Judge and Joint Criminal Judge of Cochin; Resumed charge of the Office of Register of the Zillah Court of Cochin. 1842: Acting Senior Deputy Register to the Court of Sudder and Foujdarry Adawlut. 1843: Commissioner for Government Lotteries; Extra Assistant to Collector and Magistrate, Malabar. 1844: Acting Additional Sub-Collector and Joint Magistrate of Canara. 1845: Acting Additional Sub-Collector and Joint Magistrate of Malabar; Special Assistant to Collector and Magistrate, Tinnevelly. 1846: Sub-Collector and Joint Magistrate, Malabar. 1850: Acting Civil and Sessions Judge, Tellicherry. 1851: Acting Civil and Sessions Judge, Calicut. 1852: Acting Civil and Sessions Judge, Mangalore. 1853: *Proceeded to England on furlough.* 1856: Acting Civil and Sessions Judge, Guntoor. 1857: Civil and Sessions Judge, Mangalore. 1863: *Resigned the service, 1st May. (Annuitant.)*

CHEAPE, ANSTRUTHER.—1819: Writer. 1824: Assistant to

the Collector and Magistrate of Bellary; Register of the Zillah of Bellary. 1829: Register of the Zillah of Cuddapah; Assistant Judge of Cumbum. 1830: Assistant Judge and Joint Criminal Judge of Malabar. *Died, 16th June 1831, at Tellicherry.*

CHERRY, PETER.—1789: Writer. 1790: Assistant under the Secretary in the Public and Revenue Department. 1791: Assistant under the Collector of the Ganjam Havelly. 1796: Assistant under the Collector in the Northern Division of the Vizianagram Zemindary. 1798: Paymaster to Detachment under Lieutenant-Colonel Roberts. 1799: Paymaster to the Army. 1800: Collector of the Third Division of the Vizagapatam District. 1804: Judge of the Zillah of Ganjam. 1806: Judge of the Zillah of Combaconum. 1807: *At home.* 1811: *Returned to India.* 1813: Paymaster at the Presidency and of Extraordinaries. 1815: Third Judge, afterwards Second Judge of the Provincial Court, Northern Division. 1821: Senior Judge of the Provincial Court, Centre Division. *Died, 26th November 1823, at the Cape of Good Hope.*

CHERRY, GEORGE FREDERICK.—1804: Writer. 1807: Assistant under the Chief Secretary to Government in the Secret, Political, and Foreign Department; Assistant to the Register of the Zillah of Tinnevelly. 1809: Register of the Zillah of Madura. 1821: Judge and Criminal Judge of Masulipatam. 1824: Judge and Criminal Judge of Combaconum. *Died, 10th February 1827, at Combaconum.*

CHERRY, ALEXANDER INGLIS.—1824: Writer. 1825: Assistant to the Principal Collector and Magistrate of Tanjore. 1827: Head Assistant to the Secretary to the Board of Revenue. 1828: Deputy Tamil Translator to Government; Assistant to the Collector of Sea Customs at Madras. 1829: *At home.* 1834: *Returned to India;* Deputy Secretary in the Chief Secretary's Department. 1836: Acting Secretary to Government. 1837: Cashier to the Government Bank, and Assistant to the Sub-Treasurer; Commissioner for Drawing Government Lotteries. 1838: Acting Sub-Treasurer and Superintendent Treasurer of Government Bank. 1839: Sub-Treasurer and Superintendent Treasurer of Government Bank. 1840: Superintendent and Treasurer to the Government Bank, and Sub-Treasurer to Government. 1844: Sub-Treasurer to Government, and Member of the Mint Committee. *Died, 26th October 1850, at the Cape of Good Hope.*

CHERRY, JOHN WILLIAM.—1839: Writer. 1840: Assistant to Principal Collector and Magistrate, South Arcot. 1841: Assistant to Chief Secretary to Government. 1842: Acting Head Assistant to Collector and Magistrate, Chingleput, and Assistant to Accountant-General. 1843: Second Assistant to Accountant-General. 1844: Commissioner for Government Lotteries. 1847: Head Assistant to Accountant-General. 1849: *Proceeded to Europe on furlough.* 1853: Acting Sub-Collector and Joint Magistrate, Salem; Acting Deputy Collector of Sea Customs, Madras; Sub-Collector and Joint Magistrate, Salem. 1855: Acting Civil and Sessions Judge, Salem. 1856: Acting Collector and Magistrate, Tanjore. 1857: Acting Collector and Magistrate, Acting Civil and Sessions Judge, and Sub-Judge, Salem. 1858: Acting Collector and Magistrate, Coimbatore. 1859: At first Acting, afterwards Civil and Sessions Judge, Salem. 1859: *On medical certificate to Europe for* 24 *months.* 1861: Assumed Charge of the Office of Civil Court of Salem. 1864: *Six months special leave, extended to sick leave to Europe.* 1865: Civil and Sessions Judge, Ootacamund. *Died,* 3d *December* 1866, *in India.*

CHESTER, John E.—1848: Writer. 1850: Assistant to Collector and Magistrate, Malabar. *Died,* 28*th April* 1850, *at Calicut.*

CHINNERY, John.—1792: Writer; Assistant under the Secretary in the Secret, Political, and Military Department. 1793: Assistant under the Resident at Cuddalore. 1796: Deputy Commercial Resident at Cuddalore. 1799: *Out of employ.* 1812: Commercial Resident in the Northern Division of Arcot. 1813: *Out of employ. Died,* 15*th November* 1817, *at Madras.*

CHURCHILL, Charles Henry.—1789: Writer. 1790: Assistant under the Export Warehouse-keeper. 1791: Assistant under the Export Warehouse-keeper at Masulipatam. 1796: Assistant to the Commercial Resident at Ingeram. 1797: Assistant to the Collector at Guntoor. 1800: *Out of employ.* 1801: Assistant under the Collector of the Third Division of Masulipatam. 1802: Assistant under the Collector of the First Division of Masulipatam. 1803: Collector of the Zillah of Rajahmundry. 1805: Collector of the Zillah of Vizagapatam. *Died,* 16*th April* 1811, *at Vizagapatam.*

CLARKE, Richard.—1804: Writer. 1807: Assistant under the Collector of Customs at Madras. 1808: *Proceeded to England on private affairs.* 1813: *Returned to India;* Assistant to the Secretary to Government, and to Revenue and Judicial Department. 1814: Secretary to the Police Committee; Register of Chingleput. 1815: Junior Deputy Register of the Sudder and Foujdarry Adawlut; Tamil Translator to Government. 1817: Acting Register of the Sudder and Foujdarry Adawlut. 1819: Secretary to the Board for Revising the Regulations. 1820: Secretary to the Board of Revenue. 1824: Third Member of the Board of Revenue. 1826: *At home on absentee allowance.* (*Annuitant on the Fund from 1st January* 1828.)

CLARKE, Sydenham Charles.—1818: Writer. 1820: Assistant to the Collector and Magistrate of Malabar. 1824: *At home.* 1827: *Returned to India;* Register of the Zillah of Nellore. *Died, 26th August* 1828, *at Madras.*

CLARKE, Thomas.—1833: Writer. 1835: Assistant to Collector and Magistrate, Trichinopoly. 1838: Acting Head Assistant and afterwards Head Assistant to Register of the Sudder and Foujdarry Adawlut; also Commissioner for Government Lotteries. 1839: Acting Senior Deputy Register of the Sudder and Foujdarry Adawlut. 1840: Acting Tamil Translator to Government, Commissioner for Lotteries, and Acting Deputy Register of the Sudder and Foujdarry Adawlut. 1842: Senior Deputy Register of the Sudder and Foujdarry Adawlut. 1845: Acting Tamil Translator to Government. 1847: Acting Sub-Collector and Joint Magistrate, Madura. 1848: Acting Sub-Collector and Joint Magistrate, Tanjore. 1849: Sub-Collector and Joint Magistrate, Madura. 1851: Acting Civil and Sessions Judge, Tinnevelly. 1853: Acting Collector and Magistrate, Madura. 1855: Acting Civil and Sessions Judge, Madura, and Collector and Magistrate, Malabar. 1856: *On medical certificate to Europe for 21 months.* 1858: Collector and Magistrate, Madura. 1860: Member of the Board of Revenue. 1863: Member of the Board of Examiners, and of the Central Committee for the Examination of Assistants. 1867: Additional Member of the Council of Fort St. George for Making Laws and Regulations, and First Member of the Board of Revenue; also President of the Committee for the Examination of Assistants. 1868: On Special Duty in the Famine Districts. 1869: *Resigned the service, 3d September.* (*Annuitant.*)

CLARKE, Richard Gwatkin.—1839: Writer. 1840: Acting Head Assistant to Register of the Court of Sudder and Foujdarry Adawlut. 1841: Assistant to Collector and Magistrate, Chingleput, Acting Cashier to the Government Bank, and Assistant to Sub-Treasurer. 1842: Head Assistant to Register of the Court of

Sudder and Foujdarry Adawlut, and Commissioner for Government Lotteries. 1845: Deputy Secretary to Government. 1848: Private Secretary to the Governor of the Presidency. 1851: Acting Deputy Collector of Sea Customs, Madras; Acting Sub-Judge, and afterwards Sub-Judge, Bellary. 1857: Acting Civil and Session Judge, Tinnevelly. 1858: Subordinate Judge, Combaconum; Acting Civil and Sessions Judge at Salem, and afterwards at Trichinopoly. 1860: At first Acting Civil and Sessions Judge at Combaconum; afterwards Civil and Sessions Judge, Negapatam. 1861: *On medical certificate to Europe for* 21 *months.* 1863: *Returned to India.* 1867: Acting Civil and Sessions Judge, Ootacamund. 1871: Civil and Sessions Judge, Tranquebar; *On furlough; Resigned the service,* 17*th May, in England.* (*Annuitant.*)

CLEMENTSON, Frederick Fenby.—1817: Writer. 1820: Assistant to the Principal Collector and Magistrate of Coimbatore. 1825: Head Assistant to the Principal Collector and Magistrate of Coimbatore. 1827: Sub-Collector and Joint Magistrate of Coimbatore. 1828: Deputy Accountant-General, and Commercial Accountant and Auditor. 1831: Acting Mint Master. 1832: Principal Collector and Magistrate of Malabar. 1842: *On furlough.* 1846: *Resigned the service, 24th February.* (*Annuitant on the Fund,* 1846.) *Died, 9th March* 1881, *in England.*

CLERK, John.—1778: Writer. 1790: Senior Merchant, and one of the Collectors of the Jaghire Revenue. 1793: *At home.* 1795: *Out of the service.*

CLERK, Robert.—1780: Writer. 1790: Junior Merchant, Deputy Secretary to Public and Revenue Department, Sea Gate, and Register and Clerk of the Peace. 1793: *At home.* 1800: Senior Merchant, and Junior Member of the Board of Trade. 1801: *At home.* 1806: *Out of the service.*

CLERK, Robert (1st).—1781: Writer. 1782: Assistant to the Secretary in the Civil Department. 1783: Under Searcher of the Sea Gate. 1786: Deputy Sea Customer, and Deputy Secretary Commercial and Revenue Departments, Sea Gate Register, and Clerk of the Peace. 1793: Secretary in the Public, Revenue, and Commercial Department, Clerk of Appeals, and Clerk to the Committee of Treasury. 1796: *At home.* 1799: *Returned to India;* Junior Member to the Board of Trade. 1800: Second Member to the Board of Trade; *At home.* 1805: *Out of the service.*

CLERK, Robert (2d).—1816: Writer. 1819: Assistant to the Sub-Treasurer. 1820: Assistant to the Principal Collector and Magistrate of Tanjore. 1822: *At home.* 1824: *Returned to India;* Second Assistant to the Principal Collector and Magistrate of Tanjore. 1826: Assistant to the Secretary in the Military Department. 1829: Acting Secretary in the Military Department, and Secretary to the Civil Fund. 1831: Secretary to Government in the Military Department. 1832: Acting Chief Secretary to Government, and Acting Director of the Government Bank; Trustee for St. George's Church. 1835: Secretary to Government in the Civil Department. 1836: Secretary to Government in the Secret, Political, and Public Departments. 1837: Secretary to Government in the Civil Department. 1844: *Resigned the service, 22d February, in India.* (*Annuitant on the Fund,* 1843.) *Died, 3d April* 1873, *in England.*

CLIVE, Richard.—1808: Writer. 1814: Assistant to the Chief Secretary to Government. 1816: Secretary to the Mint Committee. 1820: Secretary in the Military Department. 1824: Paymaster of Carnatic Stipends. 1828: Chief Secretary to Government. 1829: Acting Secretary in the Revenue and Judicial Department. 1831: Chief Secretary to Government. *Died, 6th August* 1831, *at Coimbatore.*

CLIVE, Robert Herbert.—1816: Writer. 1819: Assistant to the Secretary in the Military Department. 1820: Assistant to the Secretary in the Civil Department; Assistant to the Collector and Magistrate of Madura. 1822: Head Assistant to the Collector and Magistrate of Coimbatore. 1825: Sub-Collector and Assistant Magistrate of Coimbatore. 1827: *At home on absentee allowance.* 1829: *Returned to India per "David Scott;"* Acting Secretary in the Public Department. 1831: Collector of Sea Customs at Madras. 1832: *At home.* 1838: *Out of the service.*

CLUBLEY, Thomas.—1796: Writer. 1798: Assistant to the Secretary to the Board of Revenue. 1799: Assistant under the Collector of Vizianagram. 1802: Assistant to the Collector in the First Division of Vizagapatam. 1803: Register of the Zillah of Vizagapatam. *Died, 17th May* 1805, *at St Thomé.*

CLULOW, Joseph.—1816: Writer. 1818: Second Assistant to the Collector and Magistrate of Rajahmundry. 1821: Head Assistant to the Collector and Magistrate of Guntoor. 1826:

Head Assistant to the Collector and Magistrate of Bellary. 1828: *At home on absentee allowance.* 1830: *Returned to India per "Neptune."* 1831: Acting Superintendent of Police. 1832: Acting Treasurer and Secretary to the Government Bank; Acting Sub-Treasurer. 1834: *At home.* 1840: *Absent from India five years.*

COCHRANE, HON. BASIL.—1769: Writer. 1776: Factor. 1778: Junior Merchant. 1780: Senior Merchant. 1792: Agent for the Management and Distribution of Liquors for the Use of the Army. 1795: Agent for the Management and Distribution of Liquors for the Use of the Army, and Civil Paymaster. 1808: *At home.* 1810: *Out of the service.*

COCHRANE, JAMES.—1794: Writer. 1796: Assistant under the Secretary in the Public, Commercial, and Revenue Department. 1797: Assistant under the Sea Customer. 1798: Deputy Persian Translator. 1799: Senior Assistant under the Resident at Mysore, and Postmaster. 1800: Subordinate Collector in the Ceded Districts. 1803: Collector of Ramnad and Tinnevelly. 1806: Judge and Magistrate of the Northern Division of Canara. 1807: *At home.* 1811: *Returned to India;* Sub-Treasurer. 1812: Superintendent of Government Lotteries. 1814: Second Member of the Board of Revenue. 1819: Senior Member of the Board of Revenue. 1824: Acting Member of Council and President of the Board of Revenue. 1825: Second Puisne Judge of the Sudder and Foujdarry Adawlut. 1830: *At home on absentee allowance. Died, 8th August* 1830, *at Cheltenham.*

COCHRANE, JOHN HENRY.—1829: Writer. 1831: Assistant to the Principal Collector of Tanjore. 1832: Acting Head Assistant, afterwards Head Assistant, to the Principal Collector and Magistrate of North Arcot. 1837: Acting Sub-Collector and Joint Magistrate of Cuddapah. 1839: Sub-Collector and Joint Magistrate of Cuddapah. 1841: *Proceeded on furlough.* 1844: *Returned to India.* 1845: Sub-Collector and Joint Magistrate of Bellary. 1848: Collector and Magistrate, Cuddapah. 1851: Collector and Magistrate, Chingleput. *Died, 28th August* 1854, *in Europe (Homburg).*

COCHRANE, WILLIAM EDWARD.—1838: Writer. 1842: Assistant to Collector and Magistrate, Nellore. 1843: Head Assistant to Collector and Magistrate, Nellore. 1847: *Proceeded on furlough.* 1850: *Returned to India;* Head Assistant to Collector and Magistrate, Madura. 1852: *Out of employ.* 1853:

Sub-Collector and Joint Magistrate, Salem. 1854: *Out of employ.* 1855: Deputy Collector of Sea Customs, Madras. 1859: *Proceeded on furlough.* 1860: *Returned to India;* Deputy Collector of Sea Customs, Madras. 1861: Collector of Sea Customs, Madras. *Died, 7th May* 1861, *at Madras.*

COCKBURN, THOMAS.—1779: Writer. 1790: Senior Merchant; Commissary-General of Grain and Provisions; Accountant to Board of Revenue; Register and Transfer Accountant of Debts of the Nabob and Rajah of Tanjore; Bullock Contractor. 1795: Member of the Board of Revenue. 1800: Second Member of the Board of Revenue. 1801: Senior Member of the Board of Revenue. 1803: *At home.* 1807: *Out of the service.*

COCKBURN, DAVID.—1796: Writer. 1798: Assistant under the Accountant to the Board of Revenue. 1799: Second Assistant under the Collector of Salem. 1801: Collector of Baramahl with District of Salem Kishnagherry, and conquered Territory lately under Major Graham's charge. 1803: Collector of the Western Polygar Pieshcush and of Arcot, north of the River Patar. 1804: Judge of the Zillah of the North Division of Arcot. 1805: Judge of the Zillah of Dindigul. 1806: Judge of the Zillah of the Southern Division of Arcot. 1814: *At home.* 1817: *Out of the service.*

COCKBURN, MONTAGUE DUNDAS.—1807: Writer. 1808: Assistant under the Judge of Verdochellam. 1809: Head Assistant to the Collector of the Southern Division of Arcot. 1816: Assistant Magistrate of the Southern Division of Arcot. 1820: Collector and Magistrate of Salem. 1829: *Out of employ.* 1836: Judge and Criminal Judge of Malabar. 1842: Judge and Criminal Judge of Madura. 1843: *Out of employ.* 1850: *Resigned the service, 16th February.* (*Annuitant on the Fund,* 1850.) *Died, 28th September* 1869, *at Kotagherry* (*Neilgherries*).

COLE, THE HON. ARTHUR HENRY.—1801: Writer. 1806: Secretary to the Resident at Mysore. 1809: Acting Resident at Mysore. 1812: Resident at Mysore. 1818: Superintendent of the Government Lotteries. 1827: *At home on absentee allowance.* (*Annuitant on the Fund from 1st May* 1829.)

COLE, ARTHUR.—1831: Writer. 1834: Assistant to the Principal Collector and Magistrate of Madura. *Died, 1st April* 1835, *at Madura.*

COLEMAN, GEORGE.—1790; Writer. 1791: Assistant under

the Accountant-General. 1792: Assistant under the Accountant-General to the Board of Trade. 1794: Deputy-Accountant to the Board of Trade. 1797: Assistant in the Export Warehouse. 1798: Deputy Accountant to the Board of Trade. 1800: Deputy Commercial Resident at Masulipatam. 1805: Commercial Resident at Masulipatam. 1806: Judge of the Zillah of Chingleput. 1816: *At home.* 1818: *Out of the service.*

COLLINS, John.—1793: Writer. 1796: Assistant under the Commercial Resident at Salem. 1800: Deputy Commercial Resident at Salem. 1808: Commercial Resident at Maddepollam. 1809: *Out of employ.* *Died, 8th February* 1811, *at St Thomé.*

COLT, Oliver.—1779: Writer. 1790: Senior Merchant and Postmaster-General. 1794: *At home.* *No trace after* 1795.

COMBE, Harvey.—1804: Writer. 1807: Assistant to the Principal Collector of Coimbatore. 1809: Head Assistant in the Secret and Political Department. 1810: *At home.* 1814: *Out of the service.*

CONOLLY, Henry Valentine.—1824: Writer. 1826: Assistant to the Principal Collector and Magistrate of Bellary. 1828: Head Assistant to the Principal Collector of Tanjore; Deputy Secretary in the Military Department. 1831: Canarese Translator to Government. 1834: Cashier to the Government Bank. 1835: Assistant to the Sub-Treasurer. 1836: Acting Additional Government Commissioner for Carnatic Claims. 1837: Cashier to the Government Bank and Assistant to Sub-Treasurer, and Canarese Translator. 1838: *Proceeded on furlough.* 1840: *Returned to India.* 1841: Collector and Magistrate, Malabar. *Assassinated, 11th September* 1855, *at Calicut.*

CONWAY, Thomas Barlow A.—1831: Writer. 1834: Assistant to the Principal Collector and Magistrate of Nellore. 1835: Assistant to the Collector and Magistrate of Ganjam. 1837: Head Assistant to the Collector and Magistrate of Ganjam. 1840: Head Assistant to Agent, Collector, and Magistrate, Vizagapatam. 1841: Head Assistant to Agent, Principal Collector, and Magistrate, Vizagapatam. 1845: Private Secretary to Governor. 1847: *Proceeded on furlough.* 1850: *Returned to India.* 1851: Sub-Collector and Joint Magistrate, Salem. 1852: Agent to the Governor, Kurnool. 1856: *Out of employ.* 1859: *Resigned the service, 1st August, in India.* (*Annuitant on the Fund,* 1861.)

COOK, William.—1797: Writer. 1800: Assistant under the Secretary in the Military, Secret, and Political Department. 1802: Assistant under the Collector of Government Customs. 1803: Assistant to the Reporter of External Commerce at Fort St. George. 1808: Acting Collector and Reporter of External Commerce; Collector of Sea Customs and Reporter of External Commerce and in Charge of Government Grain. 1815: Collector of Chingleput. 1820: Collector and Magistrate of Chittoor. 1821: Principal Collector and Magistrate of Chittoor. 1826: *At home.* 1829: *Out of the service.*

COOK, Henry David.—1835: Writer. 1836: Assistant to Principal Collector and Magistrate, Malabar. 1839: Acting Head Assistant to Principal Collector and Magistrate, Tanjore. 1840: Head Assistant to Principal Collector and Magistrate, Tanjore. 1843: Head Assistant to Principal Collector and Magistrate, Malabar. 1847: Acting Sub-Judge, Mangalore. 1848: *Proceeded to Europe on furlough.* 1851: Acting Sub-Judge, Calicut; Head Assistant to Collector and Magistrate, Madura; subsequently Sub-Judge, Calicut. 1855: Acting Civil and Sessions Judge, Salem; later, at Madura. 1856; Acting Civil and Sessions Judge, Calicut. 1857; Civil and Sessions Judge, Calicut. 1866: Civil and Sessions Judge, Coimbatore. 1868: *On furlough to Europe for two years.* 1870: *Resigned the service, 18th September.* (*Annuitant.*) *Died, 16th June 1882, in England.*

COOPER, Thomas.—1767: Writer. 1776: Junior Merchant. 1778: Senior Merchant. 1790: *At home.* 1791: *Returned to India.* 1795: Paymaster at Ganjam and Aska. 1800: *Out of the service.*

COPLESTON, Francis.—1831: Writer. 1833: Assistant to Principal Collector, Nellore. 1834: Assistant to Principal Collector and Magistrate, Nellore. 1835: Acting Register of the Zillah of Cuddapah. 1836: Acting Head Assistant to Principal Collector and Magistrate, Cuddapah. 1837: Head Assistant to Principal Collector and Magistrate, Cuddapah. 1838: Acting Head Assistant to Principal Collector and Magistrate, Guntoor. 1839: Head Assistant to Principal Collector and Magistrate, Guntoor. 1840: Acting Head Assistant to Principal Collector and Magistrate, Coimbatore: Acting Assistant Judge and Joint Criminal Judge, Salem. 1841: Acting Register of the Zillah Court of Madura; Acting Judge and Criminal Judge, Madura; Acting Assistant Judge and Joint Criminal Judge, Trichinopoly. 1843: Acting Assistant

Judge and Joint Criminal Judge, afterwards Sub-Judge, Rajahmundry. 1845: *Proceeded to Europe on furlough.* 1847: Sub-Judge, Mangalore. 1851: Acting Civil and Sessions Judge, Honore. 1852: Acting Civil and Sessions Judge, Mangalore. 1854: Acting Civil and Sessions Judge, Honore, subsequently Civil and Sessions Judge, Rajahmundry. 1856: *On medical leave to Europe for 20 months.* 1857: *Returned to India.* 1858: Resumed Charge of the Civil Court of Rajahmundry. 1862: *On sick leave for 12 months, forfeiting appointment; Resigned the service, 1st December.* (*Annuitant.*) *Died, 28th March* 1869.

CORBETT, THEODORE.—1769: Writer. 1776: Factor. 1778: Junior Merchant. 1780: Senior Merchant. 1790: *At home.* 1793: *Returned to India.* 1795: Civil Storekeeper and one of the Justices. *Died in* 1795.

CORBETT, VINCENTIO.—1771: Writer. 1776: Factor. 1782: Senior Merchant. 1791: Mayor of Madraspatnam. 1792: Collector at Coimbatore. 1795: Resident at Masulipatam. 1806: Commercial Resident at Vizagapatam. *Died, 17th December* 1808, *at Vizagapatam.*

COTSFORD, EDWARD.—1756: Writer. 1776: Member of Council of the Governor and Chief of Masulipatam. 1780: *Came home.* 1790: *Out of the service.*

COTTON, JOHN.—1801: Writer. 1802: Head Assistant to the Collector of Tanjore. 1805: Sub-Collector of Tanjore. 1808: *Out of employ;* Senior Assistant to the Collector of Tanjore. 1813: Collector and Magistrate of Tinnevelly. 1820: Collector and Magistrate of Tanjore. 1821: Principal Magistrate of Tanjore. 1827: *At home on absentee allowance.* (*Annuitant on the Fund, 1st May* 1830.) 1833: *Elected a Director of the East India Company, 30th April.* 1842: Deputy Chairman of the Court of Directors. 1843: Chairman of the Court of Directors. 1845: *Went out of the Direction by Rotation. Died, 16th July* 1860, *in England.*

COTTON, CHARLES ROBERT.—1815: Writer. 1818: Second Assistant to the Collector and Magistrate of Canara. 1823: Head Assistant to the Principal Collector and Magistrate of Canara. 1825: Sub-Collector and Assistant Magistrate of Canara. 1826: *At home on absentee allowance.* 1829: *Returned to India per "David Scott."* 1830: Collector and Magistrate of Chingleput. 1832: Acting Collector of Madras; Member of the Police Committee; Third Judge of the Provincial Court, Southern Division.

1835: Principal Collector and Magistrate of Canara. 1836: Temporary Member of the Board of Revenue; Member of the Marine Board and Commercial Committee. 1838: Acting Second Member of the Board of Revenue. 1839: Second Member of the Board of Revenue. 1842: *On furlough.* 1843: *Resigned the service, 24th February.* (*Annuitant on the Fund,* 1843.) *Died, 19th May* 1873, *in England.*

COTTON, Joseph John.—1831: Writer. 1833: Assistant to the Principal Collector, Malabar. 1834: Assistant to the Principal Collector and Magistrate, Tanjore. 1836: Assistant to the Principal Collector and Magistrate, Bellary and Tanjore. 1837: Register of the Zillah of Combaconum. 1839: Acting Assistant Judge and Joint Criminal Judge, Trichinopoly. 1841: Acting Judge and Criminal Judge, Combaconum; Sub-Collector and Joint Magistrate, Cuddapah. 1843: Acting Sub-Collector and Joint Magistrate, Tanjore. 1845: Sub-Collector and Joint Magistrate, Tanjore. 1848: *Proceeded to Europe on furlough.* 1851: Acting Sub-Judge, Combaconum, afterwards Sub-Judge, Rajahmundry. 1853: Acting Civil and Sessions Judge, Masulipatam. 1854: Civil and Sessions Judge, Masulipatam. 1859: *Six months' leave in India.* 1860: *On medical leave to Europe for* 21 *months.* 1862: *Resigned the service,* 13*th April, in England.* (*Annuitant.*)

COTTON, Robert Rolland.—1836: Writer. 1838: Under the Principal Collector of Tanjore. 1839: Doing Duty as Assistant to the Principal Collector at Tanjore and at Trichinopoly, and Assistant to the Principal Collector at Tinnevelly. 1840: Register of the Zillah Court of Cuddapah. 1841: Acting Head Assistant to Collector and Magistrate, Trichinopoly. 1843: Assistant to Principal Collector and Magistrate, Cuddapah. 1844: Extra Assistant to Collector and Magistrate, Chingleput. 1845: Acting Head Assistant to Collector and Magistrate, Chingleput; Acting Sub-Judge of the Zillah of Combaconum; Acting Sub-Collector and Joint Magistrate, North Arcot. 1849: Acting Sub-Judge, Salem. 1850: Head Assistant to Collector and Magistrate, Chingleput. 1851: Sub-Judge, afterwards Acting Civil and Sessions Judge, Salem. 1853: *Proceeded to Europe on furlough.* 1856: Acting Civil and Sessions Judge, Rajahmundry. 1857: Acting Collector and Magistrate, Guntoor. 1858: Sub-Judge, Bellary, and Acting Civil and Sessions Judge, Madura. 1859: Civil and Sessions Judge, Madura. 1864: *On medical leave to*

Europe for 19 *months.* 1867: *Resigned the service,* 27*th May.* (*Annuitant.*)

COURT, Mathew.—1769: Writer. 1776: Factor. 1768: Junior Merchant. 1780: Senior Merchant. *No trace after* 1782.

COURT, David.—1797: Writer. 1799: Assistant in the Office of the Secretary to the Board of Trade. 1800: Assistant under the Collector in the Jaghire. 1802: Register to the Judge of the Zillah of Chingleput. *Died,* 12*th July* 1804, *at the Mount.*

COXE, Edward.—1796: Writer. 1798: Assistant in the Military, Political, and Secret Departments; Acting Dutch Translator; Assistant under the Commercial Resident at the Presidency. 1800: Deputy Commercial Resident at the Presidency. 1802: Deputy to the Superintendent of the Quality of Investment. 1806: Assistant to the Superintendent of the Salt Monopoly. 1810: Commercial Resident at Masulipatam. 1813: *Out of employ.* 1814: Commercial Resident at Ramnad. *Died,* 17*th July* 1818, *at Fort St. George.*

CRAIG, Hew Alexander.—1771: Writer. 1776: Factor. 1780: Junior Merchant. 1782: Senior Merchant. 1791: Chief of Cuddalore. 1795: *Out of the service.*

CRAIG, Alexander Cobham.—1794: Writer. 1797: Assistant under the Secretary in the Public, Revenue, and Commercial Departments. 1798: Assistant under the Commercial Resident at Amboyna. 1799: Deputy Commercial Resident at Banda. *No trace after* 1800.

CRAUFORD, Quintin.—1761: Writer. 1776: Senior Merchant. 1780: Member of Council. 1782: *At home.* 1790: *Out of the service.*

CRAWFORD, Henry.—1763: Writer. 1776: Senior Merchant. 1791: Senior Merchant and Manager of the Havallies under Vizagapatam. 1792: Chief of Ganjam. 1795: *At home.* 1800: *Out of the service.*

CRAWFORD, Daniel.—1789: Writer. 1790: Assistant under the Accountant. 1791: Assistant under the Collector of Ongole and Palnaud. 1792: Assistant under the Accountant to the Board of Revenue. 1793: Assistant to the Superintendent of the Noozeed Zemindary. 1794: Assistant under the Military Paymaster-General. 1796: *At home.* 1801: *Returned to India;* Agent for Public Property at Tranquebar. 1802: Secretary to the Board of Trade. 1803: Collector of the Zillah of Guntoor and of

Palnaud. 1805 : Acting Zillah Judge of Guntoor. 1806 : Judge of the Zillah of Rajahmundry. 1807 : Judge and Magistrate of the Zillah of Guntoor. 1808 : *At home. Lost in the ship "Lady Jane Dundas," 14th March* 1809.

CRAWFORD, STEWART.—1824 : Writer. 1826 : Assistant to the Principal Collector and Magistrate of the Southern Division of Arcot. 1827 : Register of the Zillah of Chingleput. 1828 : Assistant to the Accountant-General. 1830 : Head Assistant to the Accountant-General. 1832 : Acting Deputy Accountant-General, afterwards Deputy Accountant-General and Commercial Accountant and Auditor. 1835 : Superintendent of the Government Lotteries. 1837 : Deputy Accountant-General. 1840 : Accountant-General. 1843 : *Out of employ.* 1848 : Secretary to the College Board. 1852 : *Proceeded on furlough.* 1853 : *Resigned the service, 13th July, in India. (Annuitant on the Fund,* 1853.) *Died, 5th June* 1876, *in England.*

CRAWLEY, AMBROSE.—1812 : Writer. 1817 : Assistant to the Collector of Chingleput. 1820 : Head Assistant to the Collector and Magistrate of Chingleput. 1826 : Sub-Collector and Assistant Magistrate of Salem. 1830 : Collector and Magistrate of Rajahmundry. 1835 : Judge and Criminal Judge of Chicacole. 1837 : *At home on absentee allowance.* 1840 : *Resigned the service, 1st December. (Annuitant on the Fund,* 1841.) *Died, in* 1849, *at Chepstow.*

CROZIER, FRANCIS HENRY.—1831 : Writer. 1833 : Assistant to Collector, Vizagapatam. 1834 : Assistant to Collector and Magistrate, Vizagapatam. 1835 : Acting Head Assistant to Collector and Magistrate, Masulipatam. 1837 : Head Assistant to Collector and Magistrate, Ganjam. 1838 : Head Assistant to Register of the Sudder and Foujdarry Adawlut ; *Proceeded to Europe on furlough.* 1841 : Acting Sub-Collector and Magistrate, and Acting Register to Zillah Court of Malabar. 1842 : Sub-Collector and Joint Magistrate, Malabar. 1846 : *Proceeded to Europe.* 1848 : Acting Deputy Secretary to Government. 1849 : Special Agent for the Management of the Vizianagram Zemindary, and to exercise within the Zemindary the Powers of Assistant to the Agent of the Governor of Madras in the Departments of Criminal Justice and Police. 1853 : Sub-Collector and Joint Magistrate, Tanjore ; Civil and Sessions Judge, Nellore. 1859 : *On medical leave to England for* 33 *months.* 1861 : *Resigned the service, 14th November, in England. (Annuitant.)*

CRUTTENDEN, Edward Holden.—1806: Writer; Assistant to the Principal Collector of the Southern Division of Arcot. 1809: Register of the Zillah of Trichinopoly. 1820: Judge and Criminal Judge of the Zillah of Trichinopoly. *Died, 30th March 1822, at Neilgherry Hills.*

CUMING, William.—1760: Writer. 1768: Junior Merchant. 1771: Senior Merchant. 1782: *Out of the service.*

CUNINGHAME, Alexander.—1791: Writer; Assistant under the Secretary in the Public and Revenue Department. 1792: Assistant to Resident at Maddepollam. 1796: Commercial Resident at Maddepollam. 1797: Commissary and Paymaster at Amboyna and Patna. *Died, 3d April* 1797.

CUNLIFFE, Ellis W.—1806: Writer. 1808: Assistant to the Register, afterwards Fixed Register in the Sudder and Foujdarry Adawlut. 1810: First Assistant to the Register in the Sudder and Foujdarry Adawlut. 1811: Deputy Register in the Sudder and Foujdarry Adawlut. 1813: *At home.* 1817: *Out of the service.*

CUNLIFFE, Brooke, Sen.—1808: Writer. 1809: Assistant to the Secretary in the Revenue and Judicial Department. 1810: Fixed Examiner in the Revenue and Judicial Department. 1811: Assistant to the Collector of Salem. 1812: Head Assistant to the Collector of Salem. 1814: Register of the Zillah of Verdachellum. 1821: Sub-Collector and Assistant Magistrate of the Southern Division of Arcot. 1825: Collector and Magistrate of Chingleput. 1826: Principal Collector and Magistrate of the Southern Division of Arcot. 1832: *At home on absentee allowance.* (*Retired on the Annuity Fund from 19th May* 1835.)

CUNLIFFE, Brooke, Jun.—1833: Writer. 1835: Assistant to Principal Collector and Magistrate, South Arcot. 1836: Assistant to Collector and Magistrate, Guntoor; Acting Assistant to the Principal Collector and Magistrate, South Arcot. 1839: Acting Head Assistant to the Principal Collector and Magistrate at Salem, and afterwards in South Arcot. 1841: Assistant, and subsequently Head Assistant to Principal Collector and Magistrate, South Arcot. 1842: Deputy Secretary to Government. 1844: Commissioner for Government Lotteries. 1845: *Proceeded to Europe on furlough.* 1849: Acting Sub-Collector and Joint Magistrate, Coimbatore. 1850: At first Acting, then Sub-Secretary to the Board of Revenue. 1853: Acting Secretary to the Board of Revenue. 1854: Acting Secretary to the Board of Revenue; Acting Tamil Translator to Government; Member of the Board of Examiners. 1855:

Secretary to the Revenue Board, and Acting Collector, Madras. 1856: Collector, Madras; Member of the Board of Examiners. 1860: Collector of the United Districts of Madras and Chingleput, and Magistrate of Chingleput. 1863: *Resigned the service, 14th May.* (*Annuitant.*)

CUNLIFFE, FOSTER.—1845: Writer; *Died, 17th November, at Secunderabad.*

DACRE, JOSEPH.—1802: Writer. 1803: Assistant to the Collector of Tanjore. 1804: *Out of employ.* 1805: Register under the Judge of the Zillah of Dindigul. 1806: Register under the Judge of the Zillah of Madura. 1808: Acting Register of the Southern Circuit Court; Register of the Provincial Court, Centre Division. 1816: Assistant Judge at Chittoor. 1818: Judge and Criminal Judge of Chittoor. 1826: Third Judge of the Provincial Court, Centre Division. *Died, 22d February* 1828, *at Chittoor.*

DALLAS, DAVID.—1819: Writer. 1822: *At home.* 1827: *Out of the service.*

DALRYMPLE, ALEXANDER.—1775: Member of Council. 1777: *At home.* (*Recalled by order of the General Court of Proprietors, 9th May.*) 1782: *Out of the service.*

DALZELL, JOHN ALLEN.—1811: Writer. 1815: Register of the Zillah of Guntoor. 1816: Register of the Zillah of Bellary. 1819: *At home.* 1821: *Returned to India;* Assistant to the Secretary in the Civil Department, and to the Secretary in the Military Department. 1822: Postmaster-General. 1824: Secretary to the Native Pension Fund. 1828: Principal Collector and Magistrate of Cuddapah. 1831: *At home on absentee allowance.* (*Retired on the Annuity Fund in* 1839.)

DANCE, CHARLES WHITWORTH ALLEN.—1839: Writer. *Died, 11th February* 1840, *at Cuddalore.*

DANIEL, JAMES.—1761: Writer. 1768: Factor. 1771: Junior Merchant and Paymaster of the Circars. 1774: Senior Merchant. 1776: Senior Merchant and Paymaster at Madura. 1782: Member of Council. 1790: *Out of the service.*

DANIEL, THOMAS.—1797: Writer. 1798: Assistant in the Public, Commercial, and Revenue Department. 1799: Assistant under the Collector of Mannargoody. 1800: Assistant in the Public and Commercial Department. 1801: Deputy Secretary to the Board of Trade. 1803: Commercial Agent at Ceylon. 1808: *At home.* 1811: *Returned to India;* Commissioner at Tranquebar. 1815: *Out of employ.* 1817: Police Magistrate and Commissioner for Recovery of Small Debts. 1820: Secretary to the Board of Trade. 1822: Superintendent of Government Lotteries. 1824: Secretary to the Marine Board, and Deputy Warehouse-keeper. 1826: Third Commissioner for the Recovery of Small Debts, and Police Magistrate. 1827: Joint Officiating Magistrate on the Beach. 1830: Commercial Superintendent and Warehouse-keeper, &c. 1831: *Out of employ.* 1832: Acting Cashier to the Government Bank; Acting Collector of Madras. 1833: Additional Government Commissioner for Carnatic Claims. 1835: *At home on absentee allowance. (Retired on the Annuity Fund from 1st May* 1837.)

DANIELL, MURRAY PATTISON.—1832: Writer. 1833: Assistant under the Principal Collector of South Arcot. 1834: Assistant to the Principal Collector and Magistrate of Coimbatore. 1837: Acting Register of the Zillah of Cuddapah; Acting Head Assistant to the Collector and Magistrate of Masulipatam. 1838: Acting Head Assistant to the Principal Collector and Magistrate of Coimbatore. 1840: Head Assistant to Collector and Magistrate of Coimbatore. 1843: Head Assistant to Collector and Magistrate of Chingleput. 1845: *Proceeded on furlough.* 1848: *Returned to India. Died, 24th February* 1849, *at Madras.*

DANIELL, LINDSAY.—1835: Writer. 1838: Assistant to the Principal Collector and Magistrate of Nellore. 1841: Register of the Zillah Court, Nellore. 1844: Extra Assistant to Collector and Magistrate, South Division of Arcot. 1845: Head Extra Assistant to Collector and Magistrate, South Division of Masulipatam. 1847: Head Assistant to Collector and Magistrate, South Division of Masulipatam. 1848: Sub-Collector and Joint Magistrate, Bellary. 1855: Agent to the Governor, Kurnool. *Died, 7th March* 1856, *at Kurnool.*

DARVALL, ROGER.—1772: Writer. 1776: Writer and Assistant at Masulipatam. 1778: Factor. 1780: Junior Merchant. 1790: Senior Merchant and Paymaster of the Sibbendies at Masulipatam. 1795: Collector of the Northern Division of the Jaghire. 1800: *At home.* 1804: *Returned to India.* 1806: Second Member of the Board of Trade. 1808: *At home.* 1810: *Out of the service.*

DASHWOOD, ROBERT.—1781: Writer. 1790: Junior Merchant, and Third in Council at Cuddalore. 1792: Assistant at Cuddalore. 1795: Commercial Resident in the Salem Country. 1800: *Out of the service.*

DAVIDSON, JOHN.—1753: Writer. 1768: Senior Merchant, and Second in Council at Vizagapatam. 1776: *Out of the service.*

DAVIDSON, ALEXANDER.—1760: Writer. 1768: Junior Merchant. 1771: Senior Merchant, and Second in Council at Cuddalore. 1776: Senior Merchant, and Second in Council at Masulipatam. 1782: Member of Council of the Governor. 1791: Chief of Vizagapatam. *Died in* 1791.

DAVIDSON, ROBERT.—1827: Writer. 1831: Second Assistant to the Principal Collector and Magistrate of Nellore. 1833: Head Assistant to the Collector of Ganjam. 1834: Head Assistant to the Collector and Magistrate of Masulipatam. 1836: Acting Sub-Collector and Joint Magistrate of Madura. 1837: Acting Assistant Judge and Joint Criminal Judge of Rajahmundry. 1838: Sub-Collector and Joint Magistrate of Madura. *Died, 20th October* 1841, *at Madura.*

DAVIDSON, THOMAS HARDWICK.—1831: Writer. 1833: Acting Assistant, afterwards Head Assistant to the Register of the Sudder and Foujdarry Adawlut. 1836: Commissioner for Drawing Lotteries. 1838: Senior Deputy Register of the Sudder and Foujdarry Adawlut, and Commissioner for Drawing Government Lotteries. 1839: Acting Register of the Sudder and Foujdarry Adawlut. 1840: Senior Deputy Register of the Court of Sudder and Foujdarry Adawlut. 1842: *Proceeded on furlough.* 1845: *Returned to India.* 1846: *Out of employ.* 1847: Member of College Board, and Tamil Translator to Government. 1848: Register of the Sudder Dewannee and Sudder Foujdarry Adawlut, Member of the College Board, and Tamil Translator to Government. 1850: Subordinate Judge, Combaconum. *Died, 11th May* 1852, *at Salem.*

DAVIS, WILLIAM DONE.—1815: Writer. 1818: Second Assistant to the Collector and Magistrate of the Southern Division of Arcot. 1822: Head Assistant to the Collector and Magistrate of Salem. 1826: Sub-Collector and Assistant Magistrate of the Northern Division of Arcot. 1828: Sub-Collector and Assistant Magistrate of the Southern Division of Arcot. 1832: Acting Collector and Magistrate of Chingleput; afterwards Collector and Magistrate of Chingleput. 1833: Third Judge of the Provincial Court, Centre Division. 1837: Third Judge of the Provincial Court of Appeal and Circuit for the Centre Division. 1842: *Out of employ.* 1844: Collector and Magistrate, Southern Division of Arcot. 1850: *Proceeded on furlough.* 1853: *Resigned the service,*

1st May, in India. (*Annuitant on the Fund,* 1853.) *Died,* 17*th November* 1865, *in England.*

DAVISON, WILLIAM.—1817: Writer. 1828: *Out of the service.*

DAWES, HENRY.—1779: Writer. 1790: Senior Merchant. *Died in* 1790.

DAWSON, GEORGE.—1751: Writer. 1768: Member of Council of the Governor. 1771: Member of Council of the Governor and Chief of Cuddalore. 1776: *At home.* 1778: *Out of the service.*

DAY, CHARLES.—1807: *Transferred from the Bencoolen Establishment.* 1811: *At home.* 1816: *Out of the service.*

DAYRELL, FRANCIS B. V.—1796: Writer. 1798: Assistant under the Secretary to the Board of Revenue. 1803: Register to the Adawlut in the Zillah of Masulipatam. *Died,* 26*th August* 1805, *at Madras.*

DE MIERRE, FERDINAND.—1812: Writer. 1817: Second Assistant to the Collector and Magistrate of Bellary. 1818: Head Assistant to the Collector and Assistant to the Magistrate of Cuddapah. 1819: Employed in the late Peishwah's Dominions. *Died,* 21*st March* 1821.

DENT, COTTON BOWERBANK.—1763: Writer. 1768: Factor. 1771: Junior Merchant. 1774: Senior Merchant. 1791: Senior Merchant and Civil Storekeeper. 1792: Senior Merchant and Civil Storekeeper; Member of the Board of Trade. 1795: Senior Merchant and Civil Storekeeper; Senior Member of the Board of Trade. 1804: *At home.* 1806: *In India.* 1808: Paymaster and Garrison Storekeeper at Vellore. *Died,* 11*th August* 1817, *at Vellore.*

DENT, JOHN.—1812: Writer. 1815: Second Assistant to the Collector of Malabar. 1816: Assistant to the Collector of Sea Customs. 1820: Malayalum Translator to Government; Secretary to the Mint Committee. 1821: Deputy Collector of Government Sea Customs at Madras. 1824: Secretary to the Board of Trade. 1827: Collector and Magistrate of Masulipatam and in Charge of the Treasury there. 1831: Principal Collector and Magistrate of the Southern Division of Arcot. 1838: First Member of the Board of Revenue. 1842: First Member of the Board of Revenue; Commissioner in Southern Division of Arcot. 1843: Member of the Board of Revenue, and appointed Provisional Member of Council. *Died,* 17*th January* 1845, *at Calcutta.*

DESCHAMPS, JOHN.—*See* CHAMIER.

DESVŒUX, CHARLES.—1763: Writer. 1768: Factor. 1771: Junior Merchant. 1774: Senior Merchant. 1776: Senior Merchant, and Third in Council at Masulipatam. 1778: *At home.* 1790: *Out of the service.*

DICK, MUNGO.—1771: Writer. 1776: Factor and Assistant at Maddepollam. 1780: Junior Merchant. 1782: Senior Merchant. 1791: Senior Merchant and Resident at Maddepollam. 1795: Commercial Resident at Vizagapatam. 1800: Member of the Board of Trade. 1801: Member of Council of the Governor. 1803: Superintendent of Investments, and to have a Seat at the Board of Trade. 1809: *At home.* 1813: *Out of the service.*

DICKENSON, HENRY.—1806: Writer. 1810: Assistant to the Register of the Provincial Court, Centre Division; Assistant to the Register of the Provincial Court of Chittoor. 1813: Register of the Zillah of Verdachellum; Register of the Zillah of Chittoor. 1816: Register of the Provincial Court, Centre Division. 1819: *At home.* 1821: *Returned to India;* Secretary in the Public Department. 1823: Judge and Criminal Judge of the Zillah of Nellore. 1826: Collector and Magistrate of Trichinopoly. 1828: Principal Collector and Magistrate of Canara. 1831: Second Judge of the Provincial Court, Southern Division. 1836: Acting First Judge of the Provincial Court, Southern Division. 1838: First Judge of the Provincial Court, Southern Division. 1839: Acting Puisne Judge of the Sudder and Foujdarry Adawlut. 1840: First Judge of the Provincial Court of Appeal and Circuit for the Southern Division; Third Puisne Judge of the Court of Sudder Dewannee and Sudder Foujdarry Adawlut. 1842: Second Puisne Judge of the Court of Sudder Dewannee and Sudder Foujdarry Adawlut; afterwards First Puisne Judge of the Court of Sudder Dewannee and Sudder Foujdarry Adawlut. 1845: First Puisne Judge of the Court of Sudder Dewannee and Sudder Foujdarry Adawlut, and appointed Provisional Member of Council. 1846: Member of Council, and Chief Judge of the Sudder Dewannee and Sudder Foujdarry Adawlut. 1850: *Resigned the service,* 16*th February.* (*Annuitant on the Fund,* 1850.) *Died,* 29*th November* 1859.

DIGBY, KENELM.—1772: Writer. 1778: Factor. 1780: Junior Merchant. *No trace after* 1780.

DIGHTON, RICHARD.—1771: Writer. 1776: Factor. 1780: Junior Merchant. 1782: Senior Merchant. 1791: Senior Merchant, and one of the Collectors of the Jaghire Revenue. 1792: Collector in the Nellore District. 1795: *At home.* 1799: *Out of the service.*

DILLON, RICHARD.—1781: Writer. 1783: Assistant to the Secretary to the Select Committee. 1784: Assistant to the Secretary at Vizagapatam. 1787: Assistant to the Secretary at Ingeram. 1789: Muster-Master of the Troops in the Itchapore and Chicacole Districts. 1794: Assistant to the Commercial Resident at Vizagapatam. 1796: Deputy Commercial Resident at Masulipatam, and in Charge of the Factory of Maddepollam. 1800: Commercial Resident at Maddepollam. 1806: *At home.* 1811: *Out of the service.*

DOBBYN, WILLIAM AUGUSTUS.—1767: Writer. 1774: Factor and Assistant at Madura. 1776: Junior Merchant and Assistant at Masulipatam. 1778: Senior Merchant. 1791: In Council at Masulipatam, and Salt Farmer there. *No trace after* 1791.

DODWELL, WILLIAM.—1797: Writer. 1798: Assistant in the Military, Political, and Secret Department. 1799: Assistant under the Resident at Mysore. 1801: Head Assistant under the Collector in the Jaghire. 1802: Assistant to the Resident at Mysore. 1804: Assistant to the Secretary to the Board of Trade and to the Superintendent of the Quality of Investments. 1806: *At home.* 1808: *Returned to India;* Deputy Commercial Resident at Maddepollam. 1810: Commercial Resident at Maddepollam. 1813: Commercial Resident at Maddepollam and Masulipatam. 1818: Commercial Resident at Vizagapatam. 1820: *At home.* (*Annuitant on the Fund in* 1824.)

DOLBEN, GEORGE.—1752: Writer. 1768: Senior Merchant, and First in Council at Ingeram. 1771: *Out of the service.*

DOUGLAS, ROBERT.—1800: Writer. 1802: Assistant to the Secretary in the Public and Commercial Department; Deputy Commercial Resident at Tinnevelly. 1808: Commercial Resident at Ingeram. 1811: Commercial Resident at Tinnevelly. *Died, 17th September* 1814, *at Tuticorin.*

DOUGLAS, WILLIAM.—1824: Writer. 1827: *At home on absentee allowance.* 1828: *Returned to India, per "Fairlie."* 1829: Senior Assistant to the Register of the Sudder Court. 1830: Senior Deputy Register to the Sudder and Foujdarry Adawlut. 1832: *At home.* 1833: *Returned to India;* Acting Senior Deputy Register of the Sudder and Foujdarry Adawlut. 1834: Additional Government Commissioner for Carnatic Claims. 1835:

Register of the Sudder and Foujdarry Adawlut. 1843: Judge and Criminal Judge, Madura. 1844: Civil and Sessions Judge, Tinnevelly. 1853: Civil Auditor and Superintendent of Stamps; *Resigned the service, 1st July, in India.* (*Annuitant on the Fund,* 1853.)

DOWDESWELL, William.—1826: Writer. 1829: *At home on absentee allowance.* 1831: *Returned to India, per "Minerva;"* Head Assistant to the Collector, Guntoor. 1832: Head Assistant to the Collector, Chingleput. 1833: Acting Register of the Zillah Court of Chingleput. 1834: Register of the Zillah Court of Chingleput; Acting Sub-Collector and Joint Magistrate, Nellore. 1835: Acting Assistant Judge and Joint Criminal Judge, Rajahmundry. 1836: Register of the Zillah Court of Madura; Acting Register of the Zillah Court of Nellore; Acting Assistant Judge and Joint Criminal Judge, Guntoor; Register to the Provincial Court for the Centre Division. 1837: Acting Assistant Judge and Joint Criminal Judge, afterwards Assistant Judge and Joint Criminal Judge, subsequently Acting Judge and Joint Criminal Judge, Rajahmundry; Acting Judge and Joint Criminal Judge, Chingleput. 1838: Assistant Judge and Joint Criminal Judge, Chicacole. 1839: Acting Judge and Joint Criminal Judge, Rajahmundry. 1840: Assistant Judge and Joint Criminal Judge, Madura. 1841: Acting Judge and Criminal Judge, Nellore. 1843: *Proceeded to Europe on furlough.* 1845: Acting Civil and Sessions Judge, Coimbatore; Acting Civil and Sessions Judge, Madura; Civil and Sessions Judge, Masulipatam. 1846: Commissioner for the Northern Division. 1854: Civil and Sessions Judge, Chingleput; *Absent on medical certificate.* 1860: Collector and Magistrate, Trichinopoly; *Absent on medical certificate for* 21 *months.* 1861: *Resigned the service, December, in England.* (*Annuitant.*) *Died,* 12*th December* 1870.

DOWSETT, Robert.—1754: Writer. 1768: Senior Merchant, and Second in Council at Cuddalore. 1776: *Out of the service.*

DRAKE, Dawsonne.—1742: Writer. 1768: Member of the Council of the Governor. 1771: *Out of the service.*

DRAKE, Francis Henry.—1777: Writer. 1782: Factor. 1790: Senior Merchant; *At home.* 1795: *Out of the service.*

DROZ, Benjamin.—1813: Writer. 1817: Second Assistant to the Collector and Magistrate of the Northern Division of Arcot. 1818: Acting Register of the Zillah of Vizagapatam. 1820: *Out* *of employ;* Head Assistant to the Collector and Magistrate of Guntoor. *Died, 7th May 1821, at Guntoor.*

DRUMMOND, ANDREW J.—1807: Writer. 1808: Assistant to the Chief Secretary in the Secret, Political, and Foreign Department; Assistant under the Collector of Coimbatore. 1813: *Out of employ.* 1814: Head Assistant to the Collector of Tinnevelly. 1817: Deputy Commercial Resident at Ramnad. 1819: *Out of employ.* 1823: Assistant to the Collector of Madras; Deputy Collector of Madras, and Superintendent of the Custody and Issue of Stationery. 1828: Judge and Criminal Judge of Bellary. 1829: *Out of employ. Died, 1st May 1834, at Cuddalore.*

DRURY, GEORGE DOMINICO.—1812: Writer. 1815: Head Assistant to the Collector of Madura. 1816: Assistant Magistrate of Madura. 1823: Sub-Collector and Assistant Magistrate of Salem. 1826: Sub-Collector and Assistant Magistrate, Southern Division of Arcot. 1828: Collector and Magistrate of Tinnevelly. 1832: Commissioner for the Government of Mysore; Acting Member of the Board of Revenue; Principal Collector and Magistrate of Coimbatore. 1842: Second Member of the Board of Revenue. 1843: Chief Secretary to Government. 1845: Member of the Board of Revenue. 1847: First Member of the Board of Revenue. 1850: *Resigned the servive, 1st July, in India. (Annuitant on the Fund, 1850.) Died, 5th August 1870.*

DUFF, WILLIAM.—1767: Writer. 1774: Factor and Assistant at Maddepollam. 1776: Junior Merchant and Factor and Assistant at Maddepollam. 1778: Senior Merchant. 1790: *Out of the service.*

DUMERGUE, HENRY FRANCIS.—1824: Writer. 1827: *At home on absentee allowance.* 1828: *Returned to India per "Wellington."* 1829: Register of the Zillah of Madura; Assistant to the Collector of Sea Customs at Madras. 1831: Cashier to the Government Bank. 1835: Assistant Judge of the Adawlut in the Zillah of Canara. 1837: Acting Judge and Criminal Judge of Malabar and Canara. 1838: Acting Judge and Criminal Judge of Canara. 1839: Assistant Judge of the Zillah of Canara. *Died at sea, 8th April 1840, on board "Reliance."*

DUMERGUE, CHARLES.—1829: Writer. 1832: Second Assistant to the Collector of Chingleput; Head Assistant to the Collector of Guntoor. 1833: Head Assistant to the Collector and Magistrate of Rajahmundry. *Died at sea, 22d May 1837.*

DUMERGUE, GEORGE PENRICE.—1832: Writer. 1834: Assistant

to the Principal Collector and Magistrate of North Arcot. 1836: Acting Second Assistant to the Accountant-General; Assistant to the Principal Collector and Magistrate of Canara. 1837: Commissioner for Drawing Government Lotteries. 1838: Second Assistant to the Accountant-General. *Died, January* 1839, *at the Cape of Good Hope.*

DUNDAS, WILLIAM.—1778: Writer. 1782: *At home. No trace after* 1782.

DU PRÉ, JOSIAS.—1768: Appointed Member of the Council of the Governor. 1771: Became Governor of the Presidency. *Retired before* 1774.

DUTTON, JOHN.—1770: Writer. 1776: Factor. *Died, 8th November* 1776.

DYNELEY, THOMAS.—1763: Writer. 1768: Factor. 1771: Junior Merchant. 1774: Senior Merchant and Assistant at Ganjam. 1776: Senior Merchant and Third in Council at Ganjam. 1780: *Out of the service.*

EDEN, HENRY.—1764: Writer. *No trace after* 1768.

EDEN, ROBERT.—1819: Writer. 1823: Employed under the Commissioner in the Deccan. 1826: *At home on absentee allowance.* 1830: *Returned to India, per "Duke of Roxburgh;"* Canarese Translator to Government; Sheriff of Madras. 1831: Collector and Magistrate of Ganjam. 1832: Collector and Magistrate of Tinnevelly; Acting Principal Collector and Magistrate, afterwards Principal Collector and Magistrate of Northern Arcot. 1837: Principal Collector and Magistrate of Tinnevelly. 1841: *Out of employ.* 1842: *Proceeded on furlough.* 1843: *Resigned the service, 20th September, in England. (Annuitant on the Fund,* 1847.) *Died, 23d April* 1879, *in England.*

ELLIOTT, HON. JOHN E.—1805: Writer. 1806: *Removed to the Bengal Establishment, 23d July.*

ELLIOTT, HUGH MAXIMILIAN. — 1814: Writer. 1816: *Resigned, 1st April, in India.*

ELLIOTT, DANIEL.—1817: Writer. 1819: Register of the Zillah of Chingleput. 1821: Register of the Provincial Court, Centre Division. 1822: Deputy Tamil Translator to Government. 1823: Junior Deputy Secretary to the Board of Revenue, and Mahratti Translator to Government. 1826: Mahratti Translator to the Tanjore Commissioners. 1827: Secretary to the Board of Revenue. 1832: Member of the Board for the College and for Public Instruction; Acting Member of the Board of Revenue;

Register to the Sudder and Foujdarry Adawlut; Temporary Member of the Board of Revenue. 1833: Mahratti Translator to Government. 1836: Third Member of the Board of Revenue. 1837: Second Member of the Board of Revenue. 1838: Member of the Indian Law Commission, Calcutta. 1839: Mahratti Translator to Government; Second Member of the Board of Revenue; Member of the College Board; Member of the Indian Law Commission. 1847: Member of the Indian Law Commission, and Provisional Member of Council. 1848: Member of Council, and President of the Revenue, Marine, and College Boards. 1855: Member of the Legislative Council of India. 1858: *Proceeded on furlough; Resigned the service,* 1st *May, in India.* (*Annuitant on the Fund,* 1859.)

ELLIOTT, WALTER.—1821: Writer. 1824: Employed under the Commissioner in the Deccan. 1833: *At home.* 1837: *Returned to India;* Private Secretary to the Governor; Canarese Translator to Government; Member of the College Board; Acting Persian Translator to Government; and Third Member of the Board of Revenue. 1844: Third Member of the Board of Revenue; Member of the College Board and Mint Committee; and Canarese Translator to Government. 1848: Second Member of Board of Revenue, Member of College Board, and Canarese Translator to Government. 1851: First Member of Board of Revenue. 1855: Member of Council and President of the Revenue and Marine Boards. 1856: *Proceeded on furlough.* 1857: *Returned to India;* Member of Council, and President of the Revenue and Marine Boards. 1859: *Resigned the service, 27th December, in India.* (*Annuitant on the Fund,* 1860.) *Knight Commander of the Star of India, 25th May* 1866.

ELLIOT, WILLIAM. — 1828: Writer. 1831: Assistant to Secretary in Revenue Department. 1832: Commissioner for Government Lotteries, and Acting Canarese Translator. 1833: Acting Head Assistant to Principal Collector and Magistrate, Nellore; Assistant and Acting Head Assistant to Principal Collector and Magistrate, North Arcot; Acting Register to the Zillah Court, and Acting First Assistant to the Principal Collector, of Nellore. 1834: Head Assistant to Principal Collector and Magistrate, Salem. 1837: Acting Sub-Collector and Joint Magistrate, Salem. 1838: Acting Sub-Collector and Joint Magistrate at Nellore; Acting Sub-Collector and Joint Magistrate at Salem; and Acting Judge and Criminal Judge, Madura. 1840:

Acting Sub-Collector and Joint Magistrate, Salem. 1841: Sub-Collector and Joint Magistrate, Madura. 1842: Acting Judge and Criminal Judge, Madura. 1847: Acting Collector and Magistrate, Trichinopoly. 1849: Civil and Sessions Judge, Cuddapah. 1860: Civil and Sessions Judge, Tinnevelly; (*Proceeded to Europe on medical certificate.*) 1861: Civil and Sessions Judge, Honore. 1862: Civil and Sessions Judge, Cuddapah, and at Guntoor. 1865: *Resigned the service, 24th January.* (*Annuitant.*) *Died, 19th March 1872.*

ELLIS, FRANCIS W.—1796: Writer. 1798: Assistant under the Secretary to the Board of Revenue. 1801: Deputy Secretary to the Board of Revenue. 1802: Secretary to the Board of Revenue. 1806: Judge and Magistrate of the Zillah of Masulipatam. 1809: Collector of Land Customs. 1810: Collector of Madras. *Died, 10th March 1819, at Ramnad.*

ELLIS, CHARLES JOHN ROBERT.—1801: Writer. 1802: Assistant to the Secretary in the Revenue and Judicial Department; Assistant to the Collector of Dindigul. 1803: Assistant to the Collector of the Northern Division of Arcot. 1807: Assistant to the Register of the Court of Appeal and Circuit, Northern Division. 1811: Register to the Provincial Court, Northern Division. 1816: Judge and Criminal Judge of the Zillah of Canara. 1819: *Suspended.* 1820: *At home.* 1822: *Dismissed the service, 4th December.*

ELLIS, GEORGE HENRY.—1839: Writer. 1841: Assistant to Chief Secretary to Government, and Assistant to Collector and Magistrate, South Arcot. 1842: Acting Head Assistant to Collector and Magistrate, Trichinopoly. 1843: Head Assistant to Collector and Magistrate, Trichinopoly. 1844: Head Assistant to Collector and Magistrate, Tanjore. 1847: Acting Sub-Collector and Joint Magistrate, Tanjore. 1850: Acting Sub-Judge, Madura. 1851: *Proceeded to Europe on furlough.* 1854: Acting Collector and Magistrate, Chingleput; Additional Sub-Collector and Joint Magistrate, Canara; Sub-Judge, Mangalore; and Acting Civil and Sessions Judge, Combaconum. 1855: Register to the Court of Sudder and Foujdarry Adawlut. 1857: Acting Civil and Sessions Judge, Cuddalore. 1859; Civil and Sessions Judge, Cuddalore. 1863: Collector of Sea Customs, Madras. 1866: Acting Judge of the High Court of Judicature, Madras. 1867: Acting Commissioner for Inquiring into the Debts of Prince Azeem Jah Bahadoor; also Acting Judge of the High Court. 1869: Acting

Civil and Sessions Judge, Coimbatore, and Acting Collector and Magistrate and Agent to the Governor in Ganjam. 1870 : Civil and Sessions Judge, Cuddalore, and at Coimbatore. 1873 : District and Sessions Judge, Coimbatore. 1874 : *Resigned the service, 15th August.* (*Annuitant.*)

ELTON, Frederick Bayard.—1830 : Writer. 1832 : Register of the Zillah of Bellary. 1838 : *At home on absentee allowance.* 1840 : *Returned to India.* 1841 : *Out of employ.* 1844 : Special Assistant to Collector and Magistrate, Tinnevelly. 1845 : Sub-Collector and Joint Magistrate, Tinnevelly. 1850 : *Proceeded on furlough.* 1853 : *Returned to India.* 1854 : Collector and Magistrate, Nellore. 1860 : *Proceeded on furlough ; Resigned the service, 30th April, in India.* (*Annuitant on the Fund*, 1860.) *Died, 4th October* 1878, *in England.*

ERSKINE, John.—1779 : Writer. 1790 : Senior Merchant. 1792 : Senior Merchant and Collector in the Ongole and Palnaud Districts. *Died in* 1793.

FALCONER, Alexander.—1789 : Writer. 1790 : Assistant under the Secretary in the Public and Revenue Department, and Deputy Persian Translator. 1792 : Examiner and Head Assistant to the Secretary in the Public, Commercial, and Revenue Department. 1794 : Gentoo Translator to the Board of Revenue, Deputy Secretary in the Public, Commercial, and Revenue Department, and Persian Translator to Government. 1800 : Junior Member of the Board of Revenue. 1803 : Second Member of the Board of Revenue. 1806 : Senior Member of the Board of Revenue. 1809 : Acting Chief Secretary to Government. 1811 : *Out of the service.*

FALLOFIELD, Ernest William. — 1767 : Writer. 1774 : Factor and Assistant at Cuddalore. 1776 : Junior Merchant, and Fifth in Council at Cuddalore. 1778 : Senior Merchant. 1791 : Resident at Nagore. 1792 : Collector at Tanjore. 1793 : Member of Council of the Governor. 1800 : Member of Council of the Governor, and President of the Board of Trade. 1806 : President of the Court of Judicature at Pondicherry, and Collector of Revenues there and of Cuddalore. 1807 : Senior Member of the Board of Revenue. 1808 : Third Member of the Board of Revenue. 1809 : Third Member of the Board of Revenue, and Acting Judge of Court of Judicature, Pondicherry. 1810 : *Without employ. Died, 5th June* 1816, *at Pondicherry.*

FANE, EDWARD GEORGE ROBERT.—1839: Writer. 1840: Assistant to Collector and Magistrate, Tinnevelly. 1842: Acting Head Assistant to Principal Collector and Magistrate, Madura. 1843: Head Assistant to Principal Collector and Magistrate, Madura. 1845: Senior Assistant to Collector and Magistrate, and Agent to the Governor, in Vizagapatam. 1846: Acting Principal Assistant to Collector and Magistrate, and Agent to the Governor, in Vizagapatam. 1850: Acting Sub-Collector and Joint Magistrate, Rajahmundry. 1851: Acting, afterwards Principal Assistant to the Collector and Magistrate, and Agent to the Governor, in Vizagapatam. 1855: *Proceeded to England.* 1858: *Without employ for* 6 *months.* 1859: Acting Postmaster-General; Collector and Magistrate, and Agent to the Governor, in Vizagapatam. 1862: *On medical leave for* 15 *months, extended to* 24 *months.* 1864: Collector and Magistrate of the Madras District. 1866: Acting Member of the Board of Revenue. 1867: *On* 6 *months' special leave to Europe.* 1868: *On medical leave to the Cape of Good Hope.* 1869: Acting Third Member of the Board of Revenue. 1870: Collector and Magistrate, Madras District; *Resigned the service, 20th March.* (*Annuitant.*)

FARQUHAR, SIR ROBERT TOWNSEND, Bart.—1793: Writer. 1796: Assistant under the Accountant to the Board of Revenue. 1797: Assistant under the Resident at Amboyna and Banda, and Dutch Translator to the Expedition under Admiral Rainier. 1798: Deputy Commercial Resident at Amboyna and Banda, and Dutch Interpreter; afterwards Commercial Resident at Amboyna and Banda. 1802: *Out of employ.* 1804: Lieutenant-Governor of Prince of Wales' Island. 1806: *At home.* 1810: *Returned to India;* Employed on the Expedition to Bourbon; Appointed Governor of the Mauritius, Bourbon, and its Dependencies. 1823: *At home.* 1826: *Elected a Director of the East India Company, 1st March. Died, 16th March 1830, in London.*

FARQUHAR, M. W. T.—1857: Writer. 1860: *Proceeded on furlough.* 1861: *Resigned the service, 22d May, in England.*

FEATHERSTONE, HENRY.—1818: Writer. 1820: Assistant to the Collector and Magistrate of Chingleput. 1822: Assistant to the Collector and Magistrate of Trichinopoly. 1824: Register of the Zillah of Combaconum. 1826: Head Assistant to the Accountant-General. *Died, on his passage to England, 3d July 1826, on board the "Barossa."*

FIRTH, Gideon.—1766: Writer. 1771: Factor. 1774: Junior Merchant. 1780: Senior Merchant. *No trace after* 1780.

FISHER, William.—1836: Writer. 1838: Assistant to Principal Collector and Magistrate, North Arcot. 1839: Acting Head Assistant to Principal Collector and Magistrate, Bellary. 1842: Head Assistant to Collector and Magistrate, Bellary. 1844: Acting Sub-Judge of the Zillah of Bellary. 1845: *Proceeded to Europe.* 1848: Acting Sub-Judge of the Zillah of Chittoor; Acting Head Assistant to Collector and Magistrate, North Arcot; Acting Head Assistant to Collector and Magistrate, Canara. 1849: Head Assistant to Collector and Magistrate, and Acting Additional Sub-Collector and Joint Magistrate, Canara. 1851: Acting Sub-Judge, Mangalore. 1852: Sub-Judge, Combaconum. 1854: At first Additional, and subsequently Sub-Collector and Joint Magistrate, Canara. 1855: Acting Collector and Magistrate, Canara. 1856: Collector and Magistrate, Canara. 1859: Collector and Magistrate, South Canara. 1860: Collector and Magistrate, North Canara. 1862: Resident of Travancore and Cochin. 1864: *Resigned the service, 4th April. (Annuitant.)*

FITZHUGH, Valentine.—1774: Writer. 1782: Factor. *No trace after* 1782.

FLOYER, Charles (1st). — 1754: Writer. 1771: Senior Merchant. 1776: Member of the Council of the Governor. 1777: *Recalled by order of the General Court of Proprietors, 9th May, and suspended.* 1782: Appointed Chief of the Guntoor Circars. *No trace after* 1782.

FLOYER, Charles (2d).—1781: Writer. 1782: Assistant to the Secretary to the Select Committee. 1783: Clerk to the Committee of Stores; Assistant to the Committee of Circuit. 1786: Paymaster at Samalcottah. 1790: Collector in the Southern Division of Arcot. 1793: *Out of employ. Died, 1st May* 1794.

FORBES, Michie.—1796: Writer. 1799: Assistant in the Public, Commercial, and Revenue Department. 1800: Assistant to the Accountant in the Commercial and Revenue Department; Assistant under the Collector of the Polygar Peishcush. 1802: Deputy Revenue Accountant. 1804: *On leave to Bombay on private affairs.* 1813: *At home.* 1815: *Out of the service.*

FORBES, Sir John, Bart.—1802: Writer. 1804: Assistant to the Secretary in the Revenue and Judicial Department. 1805: Assistant under the Collector of Nellore and Ongole. 1806:

Register of the Zillah of the Southern Division of Arcot. 1813: Assistant Judge at Salem. 1818: Judge and Criminal Judge of South Malabar. 1823: Judge and Criminal Judge of the Zillah of Combaconum. 1824: *At home.* (*Annuitant on the Fund from 1st January,* 1827.)

FORBES, Charles Henry.—1827: Writer. 1830: Second Assistant to the Principal Collector and Magistrate of Madura. 1831: *At home.* 1837: *Out of the service.*

FORBES, Henry.—1830: Writer. 1832: Doing Duty in Secretary's Office, Revenue and Judicial Department. 1833: Assistant to the Principal Collector, Coimbatore. 1835: Acting Head Assistant to the Principal Collector, Coimbatore; Acting Head Assistant and afterwards Assistant to the Principal Collector, Tanjore. 1839: Acting Sub-Collector and Joint Magistrate, Tinnevelly and Tanjore. 1840: Sub-Collector and Joint Magistrate, Tanjore. 1842: *Proceeded to Europe on furlough.* 1845: Acting Civil and Sessions Judge, Chingleput; Officiating Civil and Sessions Judge, Masulipatam; Sub-Collector and Joint Magistrate, Rajahmundry. 1850: Commissioner to Inquire into the Post Office System of the Presidency. 1851: Collector and Magistrate, Cuddapah. 1853: Acting Collector and Magistrate, afterwards Resident, at Tanjore. 1856: Acting Member of the Board of Revenue. 1857: Acting Secretary to Government in Revenue and Public Works Department. 1858: Member of the Legislative Council of India. 1862: *Resigned the service,* 10*th May.* (*Annuitant.*)

FORBES, Alexander Penrose.—1837: Writer. 1838: Assistant to the Collector and Magistrate of Rajahmundry. 1839: Acting Head Assistant to the Sudder and Foujdarry Adawlut. 1840: Assistant to Collector and Magistrate, Rajahmundry; *Proceeded on furlough.* 1844: *Resigned the service,* 5*th June, in England.*

FORBES, Gordon Sullivan.—1838: Writer. 1839: Assistant to Principal Collector and Magistrate, Guntoor. 1840: Acting Head Assistant to Collector and Magistrate, Guntoor. 1841: Register of the Zillah Court of Combaconum. 1843: Extra Assistant to Collector and Magistrate, Tinnevelly. 1844: Acting Head Assistant to Collector and Magistrate, Canara. 1845: Acting Assistant Judge of the Zillah of Mangalore. 1846: Acting Head Assistant to Collector and Magistrate, Canara. 1847: Head Assistant to Collector and Magistrate, Canara. 1849: *Proceeded* *to Europe on furlough.* 1852: Acting Deputy Collector of Sea Customs, Madras; Acting Sub-Collector and Joint Magistrate, Malabar; Additional Acting Sub-Collector and Joint Magistrate, South Arcot. 1854: Acting Sub-Collector and Joint Magistrate, South Arcot. 1855: Acting Secretary to Board of Revenue; Sub-Collector and Magistrate, South Arcot, and at Nellore. 1856: Secretary to the Board of Revenue; *On medical leave to Europe for* 15 *months.* 1858: Collector and Magistrate, and Agent to the Governor of Madras, in Ganjam. 1864: *On special leave, extended to* 12 *months' medical leave to Europe.* 1867: Third Member of the Board of Revenue; Member of the Committee for the Examination of Assistants. 1869: Additional Member of the Governor-General of India in Council; Second Member of the Board of Revenue; and Acting Commissioner for the Uncovenanted Civil Service Examination. 1870: First Member of Board of Revenue, and Additional Member of Legislative Council of India. 1873: *Resigned the service,* 13*th December.* (*Annuitant.*)

FORSTER, GEORGE.—1770: Writer. 1776: Factor. 1778: Junior Merchant. 1782: Senior Merchant. 1790: *In Bengal, where he died.*

FORSYTH, WILLIAM ALEXANDER.—1826: Writer. 1829: Assistant to the Principal Collector of Coimbatore. 1830: Head Assistant to the Collector of Guntoor. 1831: Register of the Zillah of Malabar. 1835: Sub-Collector and Joint Magistrate of Nellore; Acting Assistant Judge of Malabar. 1836: Acting Assistant Judge and Joint Criminal Judge of Salem. 1837: Sub-Collector and Joint Magistrate of Canara; Re-appointed Acting Assistant Judge and Joint Criminal Judge of Salem; Assistant Judge and Joint Criminal Judge of Madura; Acting Assistant Judge and Joint Criminal Judge of Salem. 1838: *At home on absentee allowance.* 1841: *Returned to India.* 1842: Sub-Collector and Joint Magistrate of Canara. 1845: Civil and Sessions Judge, Tellicherry. 1852: Civil and Sessions Judge, Salem. 1854: Civil and Sessions Judge, Nellore; *Resigned the service,* 1*st May, in India.* (*Annuitant on the Fund,* 1854.) *Died,* 24*th October* 1867, *in London.*

FOSTER, HENRY.—1781: Writer. *No trace after* 1782.

FRASER, THOMAS.—1794: Writer. 1797: Assistant under the Secretary in the Public, Revenue, and Commercial Department. 1799: Accountant and Civil Auditor at Ceylon. 1802: *Out of employ.* 1803: Head Assistant to the Collector of Government

Customs; Deputy Accountant-General. 1806: Collector of the Zillah of Masulipatam. 1809: Accountant-General, and Accountant to the Supreme Court of Judicature; Collector of Nellore. *Died, 1st September 1823, at Madras.*

FRASER, WILLIAM A.—1806: Writer; Assistant under the Collector of Nellore and Ongole. 1810: *At home.* 1813: *Returned to India;* Head Assistant to the Collector of Malabar. 1815: Deputy Commercial Resident at Maddepollam and Masulipatam. 1823: *Out of the service.*

FRASER, JAMES.—1821: Writer. 1824: Assistant to the Principal Collector of the Southern Division of Arcot. 1826: *At home on absentee allowance.* 1828: *Returned to India, per "Wellington."* 1829: Additional Sub-Collector of Cuddapah. 1830: Sub-Collector of Ganjam. 1835: *At home. Died, 22d July 1835, at Lymington.*

FRASER, JAMES BURNETT.—1828: Writer. 1830: Head Assistant to the Collector of Ganjam. 1832: Commissioner for Drawing Government Lotteries; Acting Deputy Telugoo Translator to Government. *Died, 31st October 1832, at Madras.*

FREEMAN, CHARLES.—1771: Writer. 1776: Factor and Assistant at Ingeram. 1780: Junior Merchant. 1782: Senior Merchant. 1791: *At home.* 1792: *Out of the service.*

FREESE, ARTHUR.—1821: Writer. 1824: Employed under the Commissioner in the Deccan. 1826: Second Assistant to the Principal Collector in the Southern Mahratta Country. 1827: Third Assistant to the Principal Collector in the Southern Mahratta Dooab. 1828: Additional Sub-Collector and Joint Magistrate of Cuddapah. 1829: Sub-Collector and Joint Magistrate of Cuddapah. 1832: *At home on absentee allowance.* 1835: *Returned to India, per "Asia;"* Collector and Magistrate of Vizagapatam. 1837: Acting Judge and Criminal Judge of Chicacole. 1838: Judge and Criminal Judge of Chicacole; Acting Collector and Magistrate, afterwards Collector and Magistrate of Chingleput. 1839: Judge and Criminal Judge, Chicacole; Collector and Magistrate of Chingleput. 1851: Collector and Magistrate, Cuddapah. 1852: *Resigned the service, 30th June, in India. (Annuitant on the Fund, 1851.) Died, 3d January 1882, in England.*

FRENCH, WILLIAM.—1814: Writer. 1817: Second Assistant to the Collector at Madura. 1820: Head Assistant to the Collector and Magistrate of the Southern Division of Arcot. *Died, 1st April 1823, at Cuddalore.*

FRERE, Hatley.—1829: Writer. 1832: *At home on absentee allowance.* 1836: Assistant and Acting Head Assistant to Principal Collector and Magistrate, Malabar; Acting Head Assistant, afterwards Head Assistant to Principal Collector and Magistrate, Coimbatore. 1837: Officiating Assistant Judge and Joint Criminal Judge, Salem. 1838: Acting Sub-Collector and Joint Magistrate, Coimbatore; Acting Assistant Judge and Joint Criminal Judge, Salem. 1839: Acting Sub-Secretary to the Board of Revenue. 1840: Assistant Judge and Joint Criminal Judge, Salem. 1843: Sub-Judge, Salem. 1849: Acting Civil and Sessions Judge, Tinnevelly. 1851: Civil and Sessions Judge, Tellicherry. 1859: Officiating Judge of the Court of Sudder and Foujdarry Adawlut. 1860: Puisne Judge of the Court of Sudder and Foujdarry Adawlut. 1862: Judge of the High Court of Judicature at Madras. 1866: *Resigned the service, 30th January.* (*Annuitant.*)

FROUD, Edward.—1764: Writer. 1771: Factor. 1774: Junior Merchant. 1776: Senior Merchant and Paymaster at Vellore. *No trace after* 1780.

FULLERTON, Robert.—1789: Writer. 1790: Assistant under the Military Secretary. 1791: Assistant at Masulipatam. 1797: Assistant under the Commercial Resident at the Presidency. 1798: Deputy Commercial Resident at Ingeram. 1802: Commercial Resident at Ingeram. 1805: General Agent for Managing the Monopoly and Sale of Salt. 1806: Third Judge of the Provincial Court, Northern Division. 1809: Third Member of the Board of Trade, and General Superintendent of Investments. 1812: Superintendent of Government Lotteries. 1814: Second Member of Council, and President of the Board of Trade. *Died in* 1830.

FULLERTON, James.—1794: Writer. 1797: Assistant under the Secretary in the Military, Secret, and Political Department. 1799: Assistant under the Commercial Resident at Maddepollam. 1800: Deputy Commercial Resident at Maddepollam. *Died, 25th October* 1808, *at Maddepollam.*

FULLERTON, Charles.—1804: Writer. 1805: Assistant under the Collector of the Zillah of Rajahmundry. 1807: Register of the Zillah of Cuddapah. 1809: Register of the Zillah of Masulipatam. 1815: Assistant Judge of the Zillah of Madura; Assistant Judge of the Zillah of Chittoor. 1816: Judge and Criminal Judge of the Zillah of Chingleput. *Died, 17th September* 1824, *at Madras.*

FULLERTON, William Elphinstone.—1817: Writer. 1820:

At home. 1824: *Returned to India;* Assistant to the Secretary to the Board of Revenue. 1826: *Out of employ.* 1827: Employed under the Penang Government. 1831: *At home on absentee allowance.* 1835: *Out of the service.*

FULLERTON, GEORGE F.—1843: Writer. 1846: Assistant to Collector and Magistrate, Chingleput. 1852: Head Assistant to Collector and Magistrate, Chingleput. 1855: *Proceeded on furlough.* 1857: *Returned to India.* 1858: Subordinate Judge, Mangalore. 1859: Deputy Register of Court of Sudder and Foujdarry Adawlut. *Died, 5th July* 1861, *in London.*

GAHAGAN, FREDERICK.—1796: Writer. 1798: Assistant in the Public Revenue and Commercial Department; Assistant under the Commercial Resident at the Presidency. 1799: Assistant under the Governor of Ceylon. 1801: Head Assistant in the Revenue and Judicial Department. 1802: Deputy Postmaster-General. 1803: Subordinate Collector in the Ceded Districts. 1807: Collector of the Zillah of Bellary. 1809: Secretary in the Revenue and Judicial Department; French Translator to Government. 1810: Superintendent of Stamps. 1812: Third Judge of the Provincial Court, Centre Division. *Died, 19th May* 1815, *at Nellore.*

GAHAGAN, THOMAS.—1804: Writer. 1806: Assistant under the Secretary in the Revenue and Judicial Department. 1808: Assistant to the Register of the Zillah of Mangalore; Fixed Examiner under the Secretary to the Board of Revenue. 1809: Deputy Secretary to the Board of Revenue. 1812: Head Assistant to the Collector of Malabar. 1813: Register of the Zillah of Canara. 1815: Register of the Zillah of Masulipatam. 1816: Register to the Provincial Court, Northern Division. 1817: Head Assistant to the Collector and Assistant Magistrate of Chingleput. 1820: Judge and Criminal Judge of the Zillah of Nellore. 1823: *At home.* 1828: *Returned to India;* Judge and Criminal Judge of Malabar. 1830: Second Judge of the Provincial Court, Centre Division. *Died, 28th November* 1833, *at Chittoor.*

GAMBIER, CORNISH.—1779: Writer. 1790: Senior Merchant. 1795: Senior Merchant, and Collector at Muglatore. *No trace after* 1799.

GARDINER, ROBERT.—1767: Writer. 1771: Assistant at Vizagapatam. 1774: Factor and Assistant at Vizagapatam. 1776: Junior Merchant and Assistant, Vizagapatam. 1778: Senior Merchant. 1790: *At home.* 1795: Chief of Masulipatam. 1800: *At home.* 1801: *Out of the service.*

GARDINER, HENRY.—1811: Writer. 1814: Register and Assistant Collector of the Zillah of Seringapatam. 1821: *At home.* 1826: *Returned to India;* Acting Collector and Magistrate of Rajahmundry; Acting Collector and Magistrate of Vizagapatam. 1833: *At home.* (*Annuitant on the Fund from 1st January* 1836.)

GARDINER, RICHARD.—1824: Writer. 1827: Assistant to the Principal Collector and Magistrate of Tanjore. 1828: Head Assistant to the Principal Collector and Magistrate of North Arcot. 1829: Head Assistant to the Principal Collector and Magistrate of Salem. 1832: Acting Sub-Collector and Joint Magistrate, afterwards Sub-Collector and Joint Magistrate of South Arcot. 1835: *At home on absent allowance.* 1840: *Absent from India five years.*

GARRATT, ROBERT SUDLOW.—1840: Writer. 1843: Assistant to Principal Collector and Magistrate, Malabar. 1845: Assistant to Principal Collector and Magistrate, Canara. 1846: Assistant to Principal Collector and Magistrate, Tanjore. 1847: Head Assistant to Principal Collector and Magistrate, Tanjore. 1848: *Proceeded on furlough.* 1850: *Returned to India.* 1851: *Proceeded on furlough; Resigned the service, 3d September, in England.*

GARROW, EDWARD.—1769: Writer. 1771: Assistant at Cuddalore. 1774: Factor and Assistant at Cuddalore. 1778: Junior Merchant. 1780: Senior Merchant. 1792: Senior Merchant, and Paymaster and Storekeeper at Trichinopoly. 1795: *At home.* 1799: *Out of the service.*

GARROW, JOSEPH.—1779: Writer. 1790: Senior Merchant. *Died in* 1791.

GARROW, GEORGE.—1794: Writer. 1797: Assistant under the Secretary in the Public, Revenue, and Commercial Department. 1798: Assistant in the Revenue and Commercial Department at Ceylon. 1799: *Out of employ;* Deputy Secretary to the Board of Revenue. 1800: Superintendent of the Company's Land in Black Town. 1801: Secretary to the Board of Revenue. 1802: Collector in the Division of Arcot south of the River Palar. 1803: *Out of employ.* 1805: *At home.* 1807: *Returned to India;* Acting Superintendent of Police. 1808: Collector of Trichinopoly. 1809: Accountant-General, and Accountant-General to the Supreme Court. 1827: Judge and Criminal Judge of

Combaconum. 1829: First Judge of the Provincial Court, Northern Division. 1832: First Judge of the Provincial Court, Southern Division. 1836: Acting Civil Auditor and Superintendent of Stamps. *Died, 4th August 1838, at Trichinopoly.*

GARROW, William.—1796: Writer. 1799: Assistant under the Public, Commercial, and Revenue Department. 1800: Assistant to the Sea Customer, and Collector of Government Customs; Deputy Secretary to the Board of Trade. 1801: Head Assistant under the Collector of Dindigul. 1803: Collector of Coimbatore. 1805: Principal Collector of Coimbatore. *Died, 17th July 1815, at Fort St George.*

GIBBES, George S.—1830: Writer. *Died, 16th July 1833, at Kamptee.*

GLASS, Edward Binney.—1822: Writer. 1823: *At home.* 1826: *Returned to India;* Acting Head Assistant to the Collector and Magistrate of Masulipatam. 1828: Head Assistant to the Collector and Magistrate of Bellary. 1831: Sub-Collector and Joint Magistrate of Bellary. 1832: Assistant Judge and Joint Criminal Judge of Salem. 1833: *At home.* 1835: *Returned to India.* 1836: Acting Judge and Criminal Judge of Combaconum; Acting Judge and Criminal Judge of Cuddapah; Acting Collector and Magistrate of Guntoor. 1837: Assistant Judge and Joint Criminal Judge of Guntoor; Acting Judge and Criminal Judge of Madura. 1838: Acting Assistant Judge and Joint Criminal Judge of Chingleput; Acting Assistant Judge and Joint Criminal Judge of Chicacole; Judge and Criminal Judge of Chicacole. 1840: Judge and Criminal Judge, Vizagapatam. 1842: Third Judge of the Provincial Court of Appeal, Northern Division. 1844: Civil and Sessions Judge, Chicacole. 1859: *Proceeded on furlough; Returned to India the same year;* Civil and Sessions Judge, Chicacole. 1860: *Resigned the service in India.* (*Annuitant on the Fund,* 1860.) *Died, 17th December 1872.*

GLEIG, Jonathan Duncan.—1812: Writer. 1819: Head Assistant to the Collector and Magistrate of Cuddapah; (*At home.*) 1822: *Returned to India.* 1823: Register at Salem. 1824: Sub-Collector and Assistant Magistrate of Madura; (*At home.*) 1826: *Returned to India;* Sub-Collector of Madura. 1828: Sub-Collector and Magistrate of Madura. 1829: *At home on absentee allowance.* 1832: *Returned to India;* Acting Judge and Criminal Judge of Chittoor. 1833: Collector and Magistrate of Masulipatam, and in Charge of the Treasury there. 1835: Principal Collector and

Magistrate of Cuddapah. 1838: Principal Collector and Magistrate of Salem. 1844: *Resigned the service, 3d December, in India.* (*Annuitant on the Fund,* 1845.) *Died, 20th January* 1852.

GODDARD, WALTER.—1762: Writer. 1768: Factor and Assistant at Masulipatam. *No trace after* 1771.

GOLDIE, JOHN HENRY.—1839: Writer. 1841: Assistant to Principal Collector and Magistrate, Coimbatore. 1843: Acting Head Assistant to Collector and Magistrate, Malabar. 1844: Acting Head Assistant to Register of the Court of Sudder and Foujdarry Adawlut; Acting Head Assistant to Principal Collector and Magistrate, Coimbatore. 1845: Head Assistant to Collector and Magistrate, Bellary; (*Proceeded to Europe on furlough*). 1848: Assistant to Collector and Magistrate, North Arcot; Acting Head Assistant to Collector and Magistrate, Rajahmundry. 1849: Acting Sub-Judge, Rajahmundry. 1850: Head Assistant to Collector and Magistrate, Cuddapah; Head Assistant to Collector and Magistrate, Rajahmundry; Acting Sub-Collector and Magistrate, North Arcot. 1852: Acting Sub-Judge, Chittoor. 1853: Sub-Judge, Chittoor. 1857: Acting Civil and Sessions Judge, Chittoor. 1858: Acting Civil and Sessions Judge, Bellary. 1861: Civil and Sessions Judge, Tinnevelly. 1863: *On medical leave to Europe for* 18 *months.* 1865: *Resigned the service,* 13*th September.* (*Annuitant.*)

GOLDINGHAM, JOHN.—1820: Writer. 1821: Assistant to the Collector and Magistrate of Nellore. 1825: Assistant to the Secretary to the Board of Revenue. 1826: Deputy Tamil Translator to Government; Officiating Junior Deputy Secretary to the Board of Revenue. 1827: Junior Deputy Secretary to the Board of Revenue. 1828: Sub-Collector and Joint Magistrate of Tanjore. 1832: *At home on absentee allowance.* 1835: *Returned to India;* Acting Judge and Criminal Judge of Salem. 1836: Acting Collector and Magistrate of Masulipatam. 1837: Acting Judge and Criminal Judge of Nellore; Assistant Judge and Joint Criminal Judge of Chingleput; Acting Collector and Magistrate of Guntoor. 1838: Collector and Magistrate of Guntoor. 1843: Collector and Magistrate of Northern Division, Arcot. 1849: Third Member of the Board of Revenue. 1851: Second Member of the Board of Revenue. 1852: Second Member of the Board of Revenue, and Member of the College Board. 1855: First Member of the Board of Revenue. 1860: *Resigned the service in March, in India.* (*Annuitant on the Fund,* 1860.)

GOMONDE, Edward Thomas.—1806: Writer. 1807: Assistant to the Secretary in the Revenue and Judicial Department. 1809: Assistant to the Collector of Bellary. 1812: Student at the College of Fort St. George; Register of Seringapatam. *Died, 16th December 1813, at Seringapatam.*

GOODLAD, William Martin.—1762: Writer. 1768: Factor. 1771: Junior Merchant. *No trace after 1771.*

GOODWYN, Thomas W.—1831: Writer. 1832: Second Assistant to the Principal Collector of Tanjore. 1833: Register of the Zillah of Madura. 1834: Register of the Zillah of Rajahmundry. 1835: Acting Assistant to the Principal Collector of Madura. 1837: Head Assistant to the Principal Collector and Magistrate of Madura, and Acting Head Assistant to the Principal Collector and Magistrate of Malabar; Officiating Judge and Joint Criminal Judge of Malabar. 1838: Acting Head Assistant to the Principal Collector and Magistrate of Malabar; Acting Sub-Collector and Joint Magistrate of Malabar. 1839: Head Assistant to the Principal Collector and Magistrate of Madura. 1841: Sub-Collector and Joint Magistrate of Madura. 1842: *Proceeded on furlough.* 1845: *Returned to India;* Assistant Judge, Calicut. 1846: Subordinate Judge, Calicut. 1851: Sub-Collector and Joint Magistrate, Tanjore. 1854: Civil and Sessions Judge, Salem. 1855: *Proceeded on furlough.* 1856: *Returned to India.* 1857: Civil and Sessions Judge, Salem. 1859: *Proceeded on furlough.* 1861: *Resigned the service in England.* (*Annuitant on the Fund,* 1861.)

GORDON, William.—1778: Writer. 1790: Senior Merchant and Assistant, Vizagapatam. 1795: Senior Merchant and Assistant, Ganjam. 1800: Paymaster and Garrison Storekeeper at Masulipatam. 1803: First Judge of the Court of Circuit and Appeal for the Centre Division. 1806: *At home.* 1809: *Out of the service.*

GORDON, William Hesse.—1791: Writer; Assistant under the Secretary to the Board of Revenue. 1792: Under Searcher at the Sea Gate. 1796: *At home.* 1797: *Returned to India.* 1799: Paymaster and Garrison Storekeeper at Seringapatam. 1806: *At home.* 1809: *Returned to India.* 1810: *At home. Died, 30th June 1813, in England.*

GORDON, William Colin.—1816: Writer. *Died, 8th February 1820, at Coimbatore.*

GORDON, James Richard.—1847: Writer. 1849: Assistant

to Collector and Magistrate, Coimbatore. 1851: Assistant to Collector and Magistrate, Trichinopoly. 1854: Assistant to Collector and Magistrate, Guntoor. 1855: Head Assistant to Collector and Magistrate, Guntoor. *Died, 5th December 1857, at Vellore.*

GOSLING, GEORGE ROBERT.—1818: Writer. 1820: Assistant to the Collector and Magistrate of Bellary. 1821: Acting Head Assistant to the Collector and Magistrate of Bellary. *Died, 20th December 1825, at Anantapore.*

GOSTLING, CHARLES PHILIP.—1848: Writer. 1851: Assistant to Collector and Magistrate, Rajahmundry. 1854: Assistant to Collector and Magistrate, Chingleput. 1855: Head Assistant to Collector and Magistrate, Chingleput; Third Assistant to Accountant-General. 1857: *Proceeded on furlough. Died, 1st April 1857, at Exeter.*

GOWAN, GEORGE.—1796: Writer. 1798: Assistant under the Secretary in the Public, Revenue, and Commercial Department. 1800: Assistant under the Secretary in the Military, Political, and Secret Department; Assistant Collector of Canara. 1804: Register in the Northern Division of Arcot. 1805: Subordinate Collector of Canara. 1808: *At home.* 1814: *Returned to India;* Judge and Magistrate of the Zillah of Verdachellum. 1821: Second Judge of the Provincial Court, Southern Division. 1823: Second Puisne Judge of the Sudder and Foujdarry Adawlut. 1826: *At home.* 1827: *Out of the service.*

GRÆME, HENRY SULIVAN.—1796: Writer. 1798: Second Assistant under the Collector of the Polygar Peishcush. 1799: Head Assistant under the Collector of the Polygar Peishcush. 1800: Subordinate Collector in the Ceded Districts. 1803: Collector in the Southern Division of Coimbatore. 1804: Collector in the Northern Division of Arcot. 1818: Third Judge of the Provincial Court, Southern Division. 1820: Third Judge of the Provincial Court, Central Division; Third Member of the Board of Revenue. 1821: Second Puisne Judge of the Sudder and Foujdarry Adawlut. 1823: Member of Council and President of the Sudder Court and Board of Revenue. 1828: *Vacated Council agreeably to the Regulations.* 1830: Resident at Nagpore. 1834: *At home on absentee allowance.* (*Annuitant on the Fund from 1st May 1837.*)

GRAHAM, DAVID.—1773: Writer. 1778: Factor. 1782: Junior Merchant. *No trace after 1782.*

GRAHAM, John.—1818: Writer. 1820: *At home.* 1825: *Out of the service.*

GRANT, Alexander.—1789: Writer; Assistant under the Secretary in the Secret Department. *No trace after* 1789.

GRANT, Francis Alexander.—1789: Writer. 1790: Assistant to the Secretary to the Board of Revenue. 1791: Assistant under one of the Collectors of Tanjore. 1793: Assistant under the Resident at Nagpore. 1796: Collector in the Mayavaram Districts of the Tanjore Country. 1799: Resident at Nagpore. 1801: *At home.* 1806: *Returned to India.* 1809: Judge and Magistrate of the Zillah of Rajahmundry; Third Judge of the Provincial Court, Southern Division. 1811: Second Judge of the Provincial Court, Southern Division. 1821: Senior Judge of the Provincial Court, Southern Division. 1824: First Puisne Judge of the Sudder and Foujdarry Adawlut. (*Annuitant on the Fund from 1st May* 1832.)

GRANT, Patrick.—1817: Writer. 1819: Assistant to the Secretary to the Board of Revenue; Register of the Zillah of Nellore. 1820: Assistant to the Collector and Magistrate of the Northern Division of Arcot. 1823: Head Assistant to the Principal Collector and Magistrate of the Southern Division of Arcot. 1828: *At home on absentee allowance.* 1831: *Returned to India.* 1832: Sheriff of Madras. 1833: Judge and Criminal Judge of Canara. 1835: Collector and Magistrate of Guntoor, and Acting Collector of Rajahmundry. 1836: Collector and Magistrate of Rajahmundry. 1838: Collector and Magistrate of Masulipatam. *Died*, 25*th May* 1842, *at Masulipatam.*

GRANT, Robert.—1817: Writer. 1820: Assistant to the Collector and Magistrate of Guntoor. 1824: Head Assistant to the Collector and Magistrate of Trichinopoly. 1828: Sub-Collector and Joint Magistrate of the Northern Division of Arcot. 1831: *At home on absentee allowance.* 1834: *Returned to India, per "Amelia Thompson;"* Judge and Criminal Judge of Nellore. 1844: *Proceeded on furlough; Resigned the service, 4th June, in India.* (*Annuitant on the Fund*, 1844.) *Died, 1st December* 1870, *in England.*

GREENHILL, Joseph.—1781: Writer. 1783: Assistant to the Secretary to the Select Committee. 1784: Assistant to the Secretary in the Civil Department. 1786: Assistant to the Secretary in the Military Department, Deputy Garrison Storekeeper, Acting Secretary to the Committee for Revising, Correcting, and

Re-publishing the Book of Military Regulations, and Surveyor of the Company's Grounds. 1787: Assistant to the Board of Trade. 1788: Under Searcher at the Sea Gate. 1790: Upper Searcher at the Sea Gate; Deputy Sea Customer, and Deputy Controller-General. 1791: Garrison Storekeeper. 1796: Import Warehouse-keeper. 1797: Commercial Resident at Ceylon. 1801: *At home.* 1803: *Returned to India;* Commercial Resident in the Ceded Districts. 1805: Military Paymaster at the Presidency and of Extraordinaries. 1807: Garrison Storekeeper. 1811: Paymaster to the King's Troops. *Died,* 18*th June* 1811, *at Madras.*

GREENWAY, EDWARD CROFT.—1796: Writer. 1798: Assistant under the Secretary in Public, Revenue, and Commercial Department; Assistant to the Collector in the Jaghire. 1799: First Assistant to the Collector in the Jaghire. 1801: Collector in the Jaghire; Collector of the Pulicat and the District of Setwadoo. 1803: Secretary in the Revenue and Judicial Department. 1809: Acting Junior Puisne Judge of the Sudder Adawlut, and Sudder Foujdarry Adawlut. 1811: Junior Puisne Judge of the Sudder Adawlut and Sudder Foujdarry Adawlut. 1821: *At home.* 1826: *Returned to India;* Judge and Criminal Judge of the Zillah of Bellary. *Died,* 27*th March* 1828, *at Mangalore.*

GREENWAY, GEORGE S.—1829: Writer; Assistant to the Collector of Trichinopoly. 1831: Second Assistant, afterwards Head Assistant to the Collector and Magistrate of Chingleput. 1832: Junior Deputy Secretary to the Board of Revenue. 1833: Special Assistant to the Collector and Magistrate of Chingleput. 1835: Register of the Zillah of Malabar. 1837: Acting Assistant Judge and Joint Criminal Judge of Malabar; Assistant Judge and Joint Criminal Judge of Cochin. 1844: Assistant Judge and Joint Criminal Judge of Canara. 1844: Assistant Judge of Mangalore. 1846: Subordinate Judge of Mangalore. 1848: Civil and Sessions Judge, Trichinopoly. 1854: *Proceeded on furlough. Died,* 10*th March* 1857, *in London.*

GREGORY, ARTHUR WILLIAM.—1773: Writer. 1778: Factor. 1782: Junior Merchant. 1790: Senior Merchant. 1791: Senior Merchant and Paymaster at Chicacole. 1792: Second in Council at Vizagapatam. 1795: Second in Council at Vizagapatam, and Accountant; also Collector of a Division of the Vizianagram Zemindary. 1800: *At home.* 1802: *Out of the service.*

GREGORY, George.—1793: Writer. 1796: Assistant under the Export Warehouse-keeper, and Examiner in the Office of Commercial Accountant. 1797: Assistant under the Commercial Resident at Ceylon; Deputy Commercial Resident at Ceylon. 1801: Acting Commercial Agent at Ceylon. 1803: *Out of employ.* 1806: Judge and Magistrate of the Zillah of Ramnad. 1809: Collector of Cuddapah. 1810: Judge and Magistrate of the Zillah of Salem. 1816: Judge of the Zillah of Guntoor. 1818: Judge and Criminal Judge of the Zillah of Ganjam. 1821: Judge and Criminal Judge of the Zillah of Chicacole. 1824: *At home.* 1828: *Out of the service.*

GRENFELL, St. Leger Murray.—1850: Writer. 1853: Assistant to Collector and Magistrate, Chingleput. 1855: Head Assistant to Collector and Magistrate of the Northern Division of Arcot. 1856: Head Assistant to Collector and Magistrate, Tanjore. *Died, 22d February* 1860, *at Cuddapah.*

GUY, Richard. — 1769: Writer. 1774: Factor. 1776: Assistant at Cuddalore. 1778: Junior Merchant. 1780: Senior Merchant. *No trace after* 1782.

GWATKIN, John.—1806: Writer; Deputy Secretary to the Board of Trade. 1807: Acting Secretary to the Board of Trade. 1810: Secretary to the Board of Trade. 1812: Reporter of External Commerce. 1814: *At home.* 1815: *Returned to India;* Secretary to the Board of Trade. 1819: Superintendent of Investments, and in Charge of the Import Warehouse. 1820: Second Member of the Board of Trade. 1823: Export Warehouse-keeper. 1824: Commercial Superintendent and Warehouse-keeper. 1830: *At home on absentee allowance.* (*Annuitant on the Fund from 1st May* 1832.)

HADOW, George John.—1804: Writer. 1807: Assistant to the Chief Secretary in the Secret, Political, and Foreign Department. 1808: Assistant Collector of Government Sea Customs. 1821: Collector of Government Sea Customs. 1830: *Resigned the service, in May. Died, 5th March* 1869, *in England.*

HAIG, James.—1808: Writer. 1810: Assistant to the Superintendent of Stamps; Assistant to the Collector in the Northern Division. 1812: Student at the College of Fort St. George; Register of the Zillah of Salem. 1816: Register of the Zillah of Tinnevelly. 1822: Acting Register of the Zillah of Combaconum. 1824: Register of the Zillah of Combaconum; Judge and Criminal Judge of Cuddapah. 1832: Acting Third

Judge of the Provincial Court, Southern Division; (*At home on absentee allowance.*) 1834: *Returned to India, per "Abberton."* 1836: Second Judge of Provincial Court, Northern Division, and Acting Second Judge of Provincial Court, Southern Division. 1837: Acting First Judge of Provincial Court, Southern Division. 1840: First Judge of the Provincial Court of Appeal and Circuit for the Northern Division. (*Annuitant on the Fund,* 1840.) *Died,* 31*st May* 1854, *in England.*

HAGGARD, John.—1843: Writer. 1845: Assistant to Collector and Magistrate, Nellore. *Died,* 30*th June* 1849, *at Tranquebar.*

HALIBURTON, David.—1770: Writer. 1776: Factor. 1778: Junior Merchant. 1782: Senior Merchant. 1790: Senior Merchant, and Paymaster at Chandergherry. 1792: Member of the Board of Revenue. 1795: Member of the Board of Revenue and Persian Translator; (*At home.*) 1800: *Out of the service.*

HALL, Henry.—1796: Writer. 1798: Assistant under the Secret, Military, and Political Department, Dutch Translator, and Deputy Commercial Resident at Banda. *Died,* 1799, *at Malacca.*

HALL, Frederick.—1825: Writer. 1827: Assistant to the Collector and Magistrate of Madura. 1828: Head Assistant to the Collector of Tinnevelly. 1830: *At home on absentee allowance.* 1832: *Returned to India, per "Claudine." Died at sea,* 13*th May* 1834, *on board the "Hero of Malown."*

HALL, Arthur.—1831: Writer. 1834: Assistant to Principal Collector and Magistrate, Canara. 1836: Assistant to Principal Collector and Magistrate, North Arcot. 1837: Acting Head Assistant to Principal Collector and Magistrate, North Arcot. 1839: Head Assistant to Principal Collector and Magistrate, North Arcot. 1842: Acting Sub-Collector and Joint Magistrate, North Arcot. 1843: *Proceeded to Europe on furlough.* 1846: Acting Head Assistant to the Accountant-General, and Acting Tamil Translator to Government; Member of the College Board; and Acting Sub-Secretary to the Board of Revenue. 1847: Sub-Collector and Joint Magistrate, Canara. 1849: Acting Civil and Sessions Judge, Honore. 1854: Collector and Magistrate, South Arcot. 1857: *On medical leave to England for* 24 *months.* 1859: Member of the Board of Revenue. 1860: President of the Commissioners of Income Tax. 1862:

On medical leave for 12 *months; Resigned the service,* 25*th November. (Annuitant.)*

HALLETT, Charles Hughes.—1828: Writer. 1830: Assistant to the Accountant-General. 1832: Acting Head Assistant, afterwards Senior Assistant, to the Accountant-General. 1834: Register to the Provincial Court, Centre Division; Acting Sub-Collector and Joint Magistrate of North Arcot. 1836: Sub-Collector and Joint Magistrate of North Arcot. 1838: *At home on private affairs.* 1839: *Returned to India, per "Thomas Grenville."* 1840: *Out of employ.* 1842: Head Assistant to Accountant-General; Collector and Magistrate, Southern Division of Arcot. *Died,* 4*th November* 1843, *at the Cape of Good Hope.*

HAMILTON, William (of Edinburgh).—1766: Writer. 1771: Factor, and Assistant at Vizagapatam; Junior Merchant, and Assistant at Vizagapatam. 1778: Senior Merchant. 1790: *At home.* 1795: *Out of the service.*

HAMILTON, William (of Kinghorn).—1766: Writer. 1771: Factor. 1774: Junior Merchant. 1778: Senior Merchant. 1790: *Out of the service.*

HAMILTON, Thomas.—1768: Factor. *No trace after* 1768.

HAMILTON, Robert.—1789: Writer. 1791: Assistant under the Secretary in the Public and Revenue Department. 1792: Assistant under the Resident at Cuddalore. 1796: Assistant to the Collector of Baramahal. *Died,* 12*th April* 1797.

HAMILTON, John.—1792: Writer. *Died,* 1794, *at sea.*

HAMILTON, Sackville Robert.—1800: Writer; *Resigned,* 9*th August.*

HAMILTON, Terrick.—1800: Writer. 1804: Register of the Zillah of Chingleput. 1805: Register under the Collector of the Northern Division of Arcot. 1806: Register of the Court of Appeal and Circuit, Centre Division. 1808: *At home.* 1813: *Resigned,* 6*th August, in England.*

HAMILTON, Archibald.—1839: Writer. 1842: Assistant to Principal Collector and Magistrate of Salem. 1844: Head Assistant to Principal Collector and Magistrate of Salem. *Died,* 6*th June* 1846, *in India (Shevaroy Hills).*

HAMMOND, Anthony.—1771: Writer. 1776: Factor. 1778: *At home.* 1780: Junior Merchant. 1782: *Out of the service.*

HANBURY, John.—1804: Writer. 1806: Assistant under

the Secretary to the Board of Revenue; Assistant to the Collector in the Zillah of Tinnevelly. 1813: Secretary to the Board of Revenue. 1817: Collector and Magistrate of Cuddapah. 1824: Collector and Magistrate of Rajahmundry. 1827: *At home on absentee allowance.* 1832: *Returned to India;* Acting Cashier to the Government Bank, and Superintendent of Lotteries. *Died, 18th April* 1834, *at Madras.*

HANKEY, THOMSON.—1792: Writer. 1793: Assistant under the Commercial Resident at Salem. 1794: *At home.* 1795: *Returned to India.* 1797: Deputy Commercial Resident at Salem. 1800: *Resigned, 28th March, in India.*

HARDING, THOMAS.—1802: Writer. 1805: *Transferred from the Bencoolen Establishment;* Assistant to the Commercial Resident at Ramnad; First Assistant to the Collector in the Zillah of Dindigul. 1806: Register to the Zillah of the Southern Division of Tanjore. 1807: *At home.* 1812: *Out of the service.*

HARE, EDWARD.—1778: Writer. 1790: Senior Merchant, and Assistant at Ganjam. 1802: *Out of the service.*

HARGRAVE, EDWARD ROBERT.—1793: Writer. 1797: Assistant under the Secretary in the Secret, Military, and Political Department; Assistant to the Collector of Guntoor. 1799: Assistant under the Collector in the Mayavaram District of Tanjore. 1801: *At home.* 1803: *Returned to India;* Collector of the Zillah of Salem. 1823: *At home.* 1828: *Returned to India;* Cashier of the Government Bank. *Died, 1st March* 1830, *at Salem.*

HARINGTON, WILLIAM, Sen.—1783: Writer. 1785: Assistant to the Secretary to the Select Committee. 1786: Assistant to the Secretary in the Military Department, and Assistant at Tanjore. 1787: Under the Secretary in the Secret Department. 1789: Deputy Secretary to the Board of Revenue. 1790: Secretary to the Board of Revenue. 1796: Junior Member of the Board of Revenue. 1799: *Out of employ.* 1806: *At home.* 1813: *Restored to the service.* 1814: *Returned to India;* Acting Postmaster-General. 1815: Postmaster-General and Superintendent of Lotteries. 1818: Collector of Government Sea Customs. *Died, 14th December* 1821, *at Fort St George.*

HARINGTON, WILLIAM, Jun.—1815: Writer. 1817: Assistant to the Register of the Provincial Court, Centre Division. 1819: Assistant to the Secretary to the Board of Revenue. 1821:

Head Assistant to the Collector and Magistrate of Northern Division of Arcot. 1825: Sub-Collector and Assistant Magistrate of Northern Division of Arcot. 1827: *At home on absentee allowance.* 1829: *Returned to India, per "Neptune."* 1830: Senior Deputy Register of the Sudder Adawlut. 1831: Sub-Collector and Joint Magistrate of Salem; Assistant Judge and Joint Criminal Judge of Chingleput. 1832: Judge and Criminal Judge of Chicacole; Acting Judge and Criminal Judge of Salem. 1834: Acting Judge and Criminal Judge of Chittoor. 1835: Acting Judge and Criminal Judge of Salem; Acting Third Judge of the Provincial Court, Southern Division. 1836: Acting Second Judge of the Provincial Court, Southern Division. 1837: Third Judge of the Provincial Court, Southern Division; Acting First Judge of the Provincial Court, Southern Division; Acting Second Judge of the Provincial Court, Southern Division. 1838: Third Judge of the Provincial Court of Appeal and Circuit for the Southern Division. 1842: Second Judge, afterwards First Judge, of the Provincial Court of Appeal and Circuit for the Southern Division. 1844: Civil and Sessions Judge, Trichinopoly. 1848: Civil and Sessions Judge, Coimbatore. *Died, 28th June 1849, at Coimbatore.*

HARKER, Robert.—1776: Writer. 1782: Factor. *No trace after* 1782.

HARRIS, Charles.—1789: Writer. 1790: Assistant under the Military Secretary. 1791: Assistant under the Collector in the Centre Division of Arcot. 1793: Assistant under the Secretary to the Board of Revenue. 1794: Assistant under the Collector in the Southern Division of the Jaghire. 1796: *At home.* 1797: *Returned to India;* Senior Assistant to the Collector of the Polygar Peishcush. 1798: Second Member of the Tanjore Commission. 1799: *Out of employ.* 1800: Collector in the Tanjore Country. 1804: *Out of employ.* 1805: Sub-Director and Treasurer of the Government Bank. 1806: General Agent for the Salt Monopoly. 1807: Acting Member of the Board of Revenue; Second Judge of the Central Provincial Court. 1809: First Judge of the Central Provincial Court. 1821: First Puisne Judge of the Sudder and Foujdarry Adawlut. 1824: *At home.* 1827: *Returned to India.* 1828: First Judge of the Provincial Court, Centre Division. 1829: Member of Council and President of the Sudder Court. 1831: President of the Revenue and Marine Boards. 1834: Quitted Council agreeably to the Regulations, and appointed Senior Member of the Board of Revenue. (*Annuitant on the Fund*, 1835.)

HARRIS, STEPHEN.—1794: Writer. 1795: Assistant under the Accountant to the Board of Revenue. 1796: Assistant under the Accountant-General; Head Assistant under the Resident at Cuddalore. 1802: Assistant to the Military Paymaster-General; Second Assistant to the Manager for the Supply of Beetle, &c., and Collector of Revenues derived from the Sale of Arrack, &c. 1804: Assistant to the Collector of the Home Farms; (*At home.*) 1809: *Returned to India;* Commercial Resident at Cuddalore. 1812: *At home.* 1817: *Out of the service.*

HARRIS, HON. MICHAEL THOMAS.—1799: Writer. 1802: Assistant to the Collector of Ramnad and Tinnevelly. 1803: Assistant to the Collector of the Zillah of Ramnad. 1805: *At home.* 1807: *Returned to India;* Deputy Revenue Accountant. 1810: *Out of employ.* 1811: Deputy Collector of Madras. 1815: Superintendent of Police. 1816: Collector of Canara. 1822: Principal Collector and Magistrate of Canara. *Died, 17th May* 1824, *at Mangalore.*

HARRIS, GEORGE ANSTRUTHER.—1830: Writer. 1831: Assistant to the Chief Secretary. 1832: Second Assistant to Principal Collector and Magistrate, North Arcot; Acting Assistant to the Chief Secretary. 1833: Acting Register of the Zillah Court of Cuddapah; Second Assistant to the Collector and Magistrate, Vizagapatam; Officiating Assistant to Principal Collector and Magistrate, North Arcot. 1836: Acting Register of the Zillah Court of Bellary; Acting Head Assistant to Collector and Magistrate, Rajahmundry, and of Guntoor. 1838: Head Assistant to Collector and Magistrate, Bellary; Acting Assistant Judge and Joint Criminal Judge, Malabar. 1839: Acting Assistant Judge and Joint Criminal Judge, Cochin, and at Malabar. 1842: Assistant Judge and Joint Criminal Judge, Malabar. 1843: Sub-Judge, Mangalore. 1846: Assistant Judge at Mangalore. 1848: Officiating Civil and Sessions Judge, and Acting Sub-Judge, at Mangalore. 1849: *Proceeded to Europe on furlough.* 1852: Acting Register to the Court of Sudder and Foujdarry Adawlut. 1853: Acting Civil and Sessions Judge, Cuddalore; Civil and Sessions Judge, Calicut. 1856: Acting Civil and Sessions Judge, Mangalore; Acting Puisne Judge of the Court of Sudder and Foujdarry Adawlut. 1857: Civil and Sessions Judge, Chittoor. 1862: *On medical leave for* 15 *months.* 1863: Civil and Sessions

Judge, Ootacamund; Civil and Sessions Judge, Coimbatore. 1866: *Resigned the service, 25th July.* (*Annuitant.*)

HARRIS, Thomas Inglis Parish.—1830: Writer. 1833: Assistant under the Principal Collector of Tanjore; Assistant under the Principal Collector and Magistrate, Madura. 1835: Assistant under the Principal Collector and Magistrate, Coimbatore. 1837: Acting Head Assistant to Principal Collector and Magistrate, Madura. 1838: Register of the Provincial Court, Southern Division. 1839: Acting Assistant Judge and Joint Criminal Judge, and Acting Sub-Collector and Magistrate, Salem. 1840: Acting Assistant Judge, and Acting Register of the Zillah Court, Canara. 1842: Assistant Judge and Joint Criminal Judge, Cochin. 1843: Sub-Judge, Bellary. 1847: Acting Civil and Sessions Judge, Bellary. 1849: *Proceeded to Europe on furlough.* 1851: Acting Deputy Collector of Sea Customs, Madras. 1852: Acting Civil and Sessions Judge, Cuddalore. 1853: Civil and Sessions Judge, Trichinopoly. 1858: *On medical leave to Europe for 18 months.* 1860: Resumed Charge of Office. 1866: *Resigned the service, in February.* (*Annuitant.*)

HARRISON, John.—1808: Writer; Assistant under the Collector of Tinnevelly. 1811: Deputy Commercial Resident at Tinnevelly. *Died, 11th May 1812, at Tinnevelly.*

HARRISON, Benjamin, Sen.—1807: Writer. 1810: Assistant to the Secretary to the Board of Revenue. 1811: Assistant to the Collector of Malabar. 1813: Head Assistant to the Collector of Madura. 1814: *At home.* 1819: *Out of the service.*

HARRISON, Benjamin, Jun.—1845: Writer. 1847: Assistant to Collector and Magistrate, Guntoor. *Died, 25th December 1847, at Guntoor.*

HASLEWOOD, Thomas.—1778: Writer. *No trace after 1780.*

HATHWAY, Arthur.—1839: Writer. 1840: Assistant to Principal Collector and Magistrate, Nellore. 1841: Acting Head Assistant to Principal Collector and Magistrate, Guntoor. 1842: Head Assistant to Principal Collector and Magistrate, Masulipatam. 1845: *Proceeded to Europe on furlough.* 1847: Assistant to Collector and Magistrate, North Arcot. 1848: Head Assistant to Collector and Magistrate, Trichinopoly. 1850: Acting Sub-Collector and Joint Magistrate, Cuddapah. 1851: Acting Sub-Judge, afterwards Sub-Judge, Cuddapah. 1852: Acting Civil and Sessions Judge, Chittoor. 1857: Acting Civil and Sessions

Judge, Tinnevelly. 1858: Acting Collector and Magistrate, Madura; Additional Sub-Collector and Joint Magistrate, Canara; Acting Collector and Magistrate, Salem. 1859: Collector and Magistrate, Bellary. 1863: *On medical leave to England for 12 months. Died, 17th April 1866, in India.*

HAWKINS, WILLIAM.—1776: Writer. 1782: Factor. 1790: Senior Merchant, and Paymaster at Poonamallee. 1795: Paymaster at Trichinopoly. 1800: Paymaster at Trichinopoly, and Garrison Storekeeper. 1805: *At home.* 1808: *In India without employ.* 1810: Collector in the Zillah of Masulipatam. 1813: *No employ.* 1815: Third Judge of the Court of Appeal, Centre Division. 1819: Second Judge of the Court of Appeal, Centre Division. 1820: *At home.* 1823: Agent to the East India Company at the Cape of Good Hope. 1831: *Out of the service.*

HAWKINS, WILLIAM BROWN.—1832: Writer. 1834: Assistant under the Principal Collector of North Arcot. 1836: Assistant to the Principal Collector and Magistrate of Bellary. 1837: Acting Register, afterwards Register, of the Zillah of Bellary. 1838: Assistant to Principal Collector and Magistrate, Bellary; Register to the Zillah Court of Bellary. 1840: Register to the Court of Appeal and Circuit, Centre Division. 1844: Extra Assistant to Collector and Magistrate, Bellary. 1845: Subordinate Judge, Cuddapah. 1847: *Proceeded on furlough. Died, 3d July 1848, in London.*

HAY, JAMES.—1756: Writer. 1768: Senior Merchant. 1771: Senior Merchant, and Paymaster at Trichinopoly. 1774: *At home.* 1776: *Resigned the service.*

HEATH, JOSIAH MARSHALL.—1806: Writer. 1808: Assistant to the Secretary to the Board of Revenue. 1809: Fixed Examiner under the Secretary to the Board of Trade. 1811: Register to the Zillah of Chingleput. 1812: Deputy Commercial Resident at Salem. 1820: *Out of employ.* 1825: *At home. (Annuitant on the Fund from 1st January 1829.)*

HEPBURN, SAMUEL.—1792: Writer. *Died at sea in 1794.*

HEPBURN, JAMES.—1796: Writer. 1798: Assistant under the Secretary in the Public, Revenue, and Commercial Department; Head Assistant under the Collector in the Jaghire. 1801: Assistant to the Principal Collector in Coimbatore; Head Assistant to the Collector in the Jaghire. 1802: Collector in the Zillah Caragoody. 1806: Collector of Tinnevelly. 1813: Collector of Tanjore. 1820: *At home.* 1824: *Out of the service.*

HEYWOOD, Edmund Culling.—1838: Writer. *Died, 8th July 1839, at Madras.*

HICHENS, Robert.—1838: Writer. 1840: Assistant to Collector and Magistrate, Nellore; Assistant to Collector and Magistrate, Rajahmundry. 1841: Assistant to Collector and Magistrate, Masulipatam. *Died, 2d November 1841, at Rajahmundry.*

HIGGINSON, George Joseph.—1776: Junior Merchant and Sub-Accountant. 1790: *Out of the service.*

HIGGINSON, Charles H.—1799: Writer. 1803: Head Assistant to the Secretary in the General and Commercial Department. 1804: Deputy Revenue Accountant. 1807: Register to Provincial Court, Northern Division. 1811: Register to Provincial Court, Southern Division; Judge and Magistrate of the Zillah of Trichinopoly. 1821: Third Judge of the Provincial Court, Southern Division. 1824: First Judge of the Provincial Court, Southern Division. *Died, 18th July 1824, at Trichinopoly.*

HILL, David.—1804: Writer. 1806: Assistant to the Collector of the Zillah of Tinnevelly. 1807: Assistant to the Principal Collector of Malabar. 1809: Head Assistant to the Chief Secretary to Government; Deputy Postmaster. 1810: Sub-Secretary to Government. 1812: Acting Secretary in the Revenue and Judicial Department; Paymaster of Carnatic Stipends; Secretary to Government. 1820: Paymaster of Carnatic Stipends at the Presidency. 1824: Chief Secretary to Government. 1828: *At home.* 1829: *Returned to India;* Chief Secretary to Government. 1831: *At home on absentee allowance.* (*Annuitant on the Fund from 1st May 1832.*) 1832: Appointed (*27th July*) an Assistant in Examiner's Office of the Home Establishment of the East India Company. 1836: Assistant Examiner. (*Retired on pension, 28th March 1856.*) *Died, 16th October 1866, in England.*

HIPPESLEY, John Coxe.—1782: Writer. 1786: Paymaster at Tanjore. 1787: Member of the Committee of Inspection, Tanjore. *No trace after 1787.*

HOARE, George.—1771: Writer. 1776: Factor. 1780: Junior Merchant. 1782: Senior Merchant. 1792: Senior Merchant, and Paymaster to the Army. 1795: *At home.* 1800: *Out of the service.*

HODGES, James.—1764: Writer. 1771: Factor. 1774: Junior Merchant. 1776: Senior Merchant, and Fourth in Council at Masulipatam. 1791: Second in Council at Masulipatam. 1792: *At home.* 1795: *Out of the service.*

HODGSON, John.—1792: Writer. 1794: Assistant under the Secretary in the Public, Commercial, and Revenue Department, and Assistant to the Accountant to the Board of Revenue. 1796: Assistant under the Collector in the Jaghire. 1799: Collector in the Jaghire. 1800: Secretary in the Judicial and Revenue Department. 1802: Secretary to the Special Commission. 1803: Junior Member of the Board of Revenue. 1806: Second Member of the Board of Revenue. 1808: *At home.* 1812: *Returned to India;* Second Member of the Board of Revenue. 1813: Senior Member of the Board of Revenue. 1819: Fourth Member of Council and President of the Board of Revenue. 1821: *At home.* 1823: *Out of the service.*

HOISSARD, George Isaac.—1771: Writer. 1776: Factor. 1780: Junior Merchant. 1782: Senior Merchant. 1791: Senior Merchant, and Assistant to Resident at Nagore, but to reside at Negapatam. *Died in* 1791.

HOLLAND, Francis.—1806: Writer. 1810: Assistant to the Secretary in the Military Department; Assistant to the Collector in the Zillah of Salem. 1811: Fixed Examiner in the Revenue and Judicial Department. 1813: Register to the Circuit Court, Western Division. 1821: Sub-Collector and Assistant to the Magistrate of Malabar. 1824: Judge and Criminal Judge of Malabar. *Died on his passage to England, in 1828, on board the "Valleyfield."*

HOLLIER, Henry.—1773: Writer. 1778: Factor. 1782: Junior Merchant. *No trace after* 1782.

HOLLOND, John.—1761: Writer. 1768: Factor. 1771: Junior Merchant. 1774: Senior Merchant. 1782: Member of Council of the Governor. 1790: *Out of the service.*

HOLLOND, Edward John.—1769: Writer. 1774: Factor. 1778: Junior Merchant. 1780: Senior Merchant. 1790: *Suspended from the service.* 1792: *At home.* 1795: *Out of the service.*

HOLLOND, Edward.—1789: Writer. 1790: Assistant under the Secretary to the Board of Revenue. 1791: *Out of employ.* 1793: Assistant to the Secretary in the Public, Commercial, and Revenue Department; Assistant under the Secretary to the Board of Trade, and at the Import Warehouse. 1794: Deputy Secretary to the Board of Trade. 1797: Assistant to the Board of Trade. 1798: *At home.* 1801: *Returned to India.* 1802: *At home.* 1808: *Out of the service.*

HOME, Sir James, Bart., Sen.—1808: Writer. 1809: Assistant to the Secretary to the Board of Revenue. 1812: *At home.* 1815: *Resigned, 6th September, in England.*

HOME, Sir James, Bart., Jun. — 1819: Writer. 1820: Assistant to the Collector of Sea Customs in Malabar and Canara. 1824: Assistant to the Principal Collector and Magistrate of Malabar. 1825: Register of the Zillah of Salem. 1827: Deputy Accountant-General in the Military Department. 1828: Malyalum Translator to Government. 1830: Mint-Master. 1833: *At home.* 1836: *Returned to India, and died, 12th March, at Madras.*

HOME, William Gosset.—1828: Writer. 1831: *At home on absentee allowance. Died, 31st October 1831, at Madeira.*

HONEYMAN, Richard Bempde Johnstone.—1806: Writer. 1807: Assistant under the Chief Secretary in the Secret and Foreign Department; Assistant to the Collector of Coimbatore. 1809: Deputy Commercial Resident at Ramnad. 1811: *At home.* 1816: *Out of the service.*

HOOPER, George Stanley.—1817: Writer. 1819: *At home.* 1823: *Returned to India;* Assistant to the Collector and Magistrate of Tinnevelly. 1826: Register of the Zillah of Malabar. 1827: Head Assistant to the Principal Collector of Canara. 1828: Assistant Judge and Joint Criminal Judge of Salem. 1830: Judge and Joint Criminal Judge of Salem. 1832: Acting Collector and Magistrate of Masulipatam. 1833: Judge and Criminal Judge of Madura. 1836: Acting Third Judge of the Provincial Court, Southern Division. 1837: Judge and Criminal Judge of Madura. 1841: Third Judge of the Provincial Court of Appeal and Circuit, Western Division. 1842: Third Judge, afterwards Second Judge, of the Provincial Court of Appeal and Circuit, Southern Division. 1844: Civil and Sessions Judge, Madura. 1847: First Puisne Judge of the Sudder Dewannee and Sudder Foujdarry Adawlut. 1855: Puisne Judge of the Sudder Dewannee and Sudder Foujdarry Adawlut. 1860: *Resigned the service, May, in India.* (*Annuitant on the Fund*, 1860.)

HOOPER, Edward Pulteney Stanley.—1844: Writer. *Died, 26th July 1846, at Ramnad.*

HORNBY, John.—1789: Writer. 1790: Assistant under the Accountant and Import Warehouse-keeper. 1793: *At home; No trace after this date.*

HORNE, Benjamin.—1814: Writer. 1817: Second Assistant

to the Collector of Trichinopoly. *Died, 19th May 1819, near Trichinopoly.*

HORSLEY, JOHN.—1817: Writer. 1821: *At home.* 1824: *Returned to India;* Register to the Zillah of Madura. 1826: Head Assistant to the Principal Collector and Magistrate of Tanjore. 1828: Sub-Collector and Joint Magistrate of Tinnevelly. 1829: Assistant Judge and Joint Criminal Judge of Madura. 1832: Judge and Criminal Judge of Chingleput. 1842: Judge and Criminal Judge, Madura; Second Judge of the Provincial Court of Appeal and Circuit, Northern Division. 1844: Civil and Sessions Judge, Guntoor. 1850: Civil and Sessions Judge, Cuddalore. *Died, 12th June 1851, at Madras.*

HORSLEY, RALPH.—1851: Writer. 1853: Assistant to Collector and Magistrate, Bellary. *Died, 4th July 1856, at Bellary.*

HOUSTOUN, GEORGE.—1805: Writer. *Died, 16th September 1806.*

HOWDEN, ROBERT.—1781: Writer. 1783: Assistant to the Secretary to the Select Committee. 1784: Secretary to General Ogle. 1786: Assistant to the Secretary in the Military Department and Superintendent of Godown. 1787: Deputy Commercial Storekeeper. *Died, 26th June 1788.*

HUDDLESTON, JOHN.—1766: Writer. 1771: Factor. 1774: Junior Merchant. 1776: Junior Merchant, and Fifth in Council at Ganjam. 1778: Senior Merchant. 1790: *Out of the service.*

HUDDLESTON, ANDREW FLEMING.—1812: Writer. 1817: Assistant to the Collector of Sea Customs at Malabar and Canara. 1821: *At home.* 1825: *Returned to India;* Assistant to the Secretary in the Revenue and Judicial Department. 1826: Sub-Collector and Assistant Magistrate of Canara. 1831: Principal Collector and Magistrate of Malabar. 1832: Third Judge of the Provincial Court, Western Division. 1833: *At home on absentee allowance.* 1838: *Absent five years, and out of the service. (Annuitant on the Fund,* 1841.) *Died, 2d September 1861, in England.*

HUDLESTON, JOHN BURLAND.—1804: Writer. 1806: Acting Register of the Zillah of Tinnevelly. 1807: Register of the Zillah of Tinnevelly. 1812: Register of the Provincial Court, Southern Division. 1818: Justice of the Peace. 1820: Judge and Criminal Judge of the Zillah of Tinnevelly; Collector and Magistrate of Tinnevelly. *Died, 6th June 1823.*

HUDLESTON, WILLIAM. — 1808: Writer. 1814: First

Assistant to the Register of the Sudder and Foujdarry Adawlut. 1815: *Leave to the Cape, and eventually to Europe.* 1817: *Returned to India;* Assistant to the Register of the Sudder and Foujdarry Adawlut. 1818: First Assistant to the Register of the Sudder and Foujdarry Adawlut. 1819: Junior Deputy Register of the Sudder and Foujdarry Adawlut. 1821: Secretary to the Trustees of the Civil Fund. 1824: Register to the Sudder and Foujdarry Adawlut, and Persian Secretary to Government. 1826: *At home on absentee allowance.* 1830: *Returned to India, per "Minerva;"* Secretary to the Marine Board. 1831: Register to the Sudder and Foujdarry Adawlut. 1832: Third Judge, afterwards Officiating Second Judge, of the Sudder and Foujdarry Adawlut. 1838: Second Puisne Judge of the Sudder and Foujdarry Adawlut. (*Annuitant on the Fund,* 1840.) *Died, 29th June* 1855, *in England.*

HUDLESTON, Josiah Andrew. — 1817: Writer. 1820: Second Assistant to the Collector and Magistrate of Tinnevelly. 1824: Head Assistant to the Register of the Sudder and Foujdarry Adawlut. 1826: Acting Deputy Register of the Sudder Court. 1828: Deputy Collector of Madras. 1831: Superintendent of Stationery. 1836: Acting Collector of Madras. 1837: Deputy Collector of Madras and Superintendent of Stationery. 1844: Collector of Madras. 1855: *Resigned the service, 1st May, in India.* (*Annuitant on the Fund,* 1856.)

HUDSON, Mark Gilbert.—1796: Writer. 1798: *On leave to the Cape.* 1799: *Returned to India;* Assistant in the Public, Revenue, and Commercial Department. 1800: Assistant under the Collector of Guntoor. 1803: Deputy Postmaster at Guntoor. 1807: Deputy Commercial Resident at Ganjam. 1810: Commercial Resident at Ganjam. *Died, 19th July* 1812, *at Ganjam.*

HUGHES, Robert.—1766: Writer. 1771: Factor and Assistant at Masulipatam. 1774: Junior Merchant. 1776: Junior Merchant, and Fourth in Council at Ganjam. 1778: Senior Merchant. 1791: Senior Merchant, and Collector of Revenue in Guntoor Circar. 1795: Paymaster in the Burramehal and Salem. 1800: Paymaster and Garrison Storekeeper at Madura. *Died, 17th April* 1803, *in England.*

HUNTER, John Alexander.—1840: Writer. 1842: Assistant to Collector and Magistrate, Rajahmundry. 1846: Assistant to Collector and Magistrate, and Agent to the Governor, Vizagapatam. *Died, 9th July* 1848, *at Vizianagram.*

HURDIS, Thomas Bower.—1792: Writer; Assistant under the Accountant to the Board of Revenue. 1793: Assistant under the Secretary in the Secret, Political, and Military Department. 1794: Assistant to the Military Paymaster-General, and Assistant to the Collector in the Burramehal. 1796: Head Assistant under the Collector of Ramnad. 1798: Acting Collector of Dindigul. 1799: Collector of Dindigul. 1801: Collector of Madura and Dependent Polygars. 1803: Register of the Sudder and Foujdarry Adawlut. 1806: Puisne Judge of the Sudder and Foujdarry Adawlut. *Died, 16th November* 1808, *at Madras.*

HUTT, John.—1813: Writer. 1817: Register of the Zillah of Nellore. 1818: Register of the Provincial Court, Centre Division. 1821: *At home.* 1826: *Out of the service.*

HYDE, Charles.—1797: Writer. 1799: Assistant under the Secretary to the Board of Revenue. 1800: Assistant under the Commercial Resident at Salem. 1801: Assistant under the Collector of Burramehal and Salem. 1803: Assistant to the Collector of the Southern Division of Arcot. 1805: Subordinate Collector of the Northern Division of Arcot. 1808: Head Assistant to the Collector of the Northern Division of Arcot. 1809: Collector in the Zillah of Chingleput. 1811: Collector in the Zillah of Vizagapatam. 1813: Collector in the Southern Division of Arcot. 1821: Principal Collector and Magistrate in the Southern Division of Arcot. 1826: *At home on absentee allowance.* (*Annuitant on the Fund from 1st May* 1831.)

IBBETSON, Samuel.—1802: Writer. 1804: Assistant to the Collector of Tinnevelly. 1806: Register of the Zillah of the Northern Division of Malabar. 1808: Register of the Zillah of Tellicherry. 1810: Register of the Zillah of Rajahmundry. 1812: Register of the Zillah of Southern Malabar. 1815: *At home.* 1819: *Returned to India;* Sheriff of Madras. 1820: Judge and Criminal Judge of Bellary. *Died, 5th April* 1826, *at Bellary.*

INCE, Daniel.—1781: Writer. 1783: Assistant at Ganjam. 1787: Assistant to the Secretary in the Public and Revenue Department. 1788: Deputy Secretary in the Military Department. 1790: Secretary in the Military Department. 1793: Deputy Secretary in the Military, Political, and Secret Department. 1797: Collector in the First Division of the Masulipatam Districts. 1800: *Resigned, 8th April, in India.*

INGLIS, William Arthur David.—1827: Writer. 1828:

Assistant to the Principal Collector of Nellore. 1830: Head Assistant to the Principal Collector and Magistrate of Cuddapah. 1833: Head Assistant to the Principal Collector and Magistrate of Bellary. 1835: Sub-Collector of Ganjam. 1838: *At home on absentee allowance.* 1842: *Returned to India.* 1843: *Out of employ.* 1845: Civil and Sessions Judge, Cuddapah. 1848: Civil and Sessions Judge, Chingleput. 1853: Civil and Sessions Judge, Chingleput, and Member of the College Board. 1855: *Proceeded on furlough.* 1856: *Resigned the service, 1st May, in India.* (*Annuitant on the Fund,* 1857.)

IRVINE, Patrick.—1832: Writer. 1834: Assistant to Principal Collector of Salem. 1836: Assistant to Collector and Magistrate, Vizagapatam. 1837: Assistant to Principal Collector and Magistrate, Salem. 1838: Acting Head Assistant to Principal Collector and Magistrate, Madura. 1840: Head Assistant to Principal Collector and Magistrate, Madura; (*Proceeded to Europe on furlough.*) 1844: Acting Sub-Judge, Calicut. 1845: Acting Sub-Judge, Mangalore. 1846: Acting Assistant Judge, and Acting Sub-Judge, Mangalore; Head Assistant to Collector and Magistrate, Bellary. 1847: Sub-Judge, Rajahmundry. 1848: Acting Civil and Sessions Judge, Chicacole. 1849: Acting Civil and Sessions Judge, Masulipatam, and at Guntoor. 1850: Acting Civil and Sessions Judge, Masulipatam. 1851: *Proceeded to Europe on furlough.* 1853: Acting Civil and Sessions Judge, Nellore; and Acting Sub-Judge, Rajahmundry. 1854: Sub-Judge, Rajahmundry. 1855: Civil and Sessions Judge, Guntoor. 1856: Civil and Sessions Judge, Bellary. 1859: *On medical leave to Europe for* 24 *months.* 1862: *Resigned the service, 23d April.* (*Annuitant.*) *Died,* 13*th June* 1876, *in England.*

IRWIN, Eyles.—1767: Writer. 1774: Factor. 1776: Junior Merchant. 1778: Senior Merchant. 1780: *At home.* 1782: *In India. No trace after this date.*

IRWIN, William Robert.—1795: Writer. 1798: Assistant under the Secretary to the Board of Revenue; Assistant under the Resident at Tanjore; Assistant to the Collector at Tanjore. 1802: Register to the Court of Circuit and Appeal, Northern Division. 1806: Judge and Magistrate of Madura. *Died, 2d September* 1810, *at sea, near Malacca.*

JACKSON, William.—1770: Writer. 1776: Factor. 1778: Junior Merchant. 1782: Senior Merchant. 1790: *Out of the service.*

JACKSON, William Collins.—1781: Writer. 1783: Assistant to the Secretary to the Select Committee. 1785: Deputy Secretary to the Select Committee. 1786: Deputy Secretary in the Military and Political Department; Dutch, Spanish, and Portuguese Translator. 1790: Secretary in the Military, Political, and Secret Department, and Judge Advocate-General. 1797: Collector of the Southern Polygar Peishcush, and of Ramnad. 1799: *At home.* 1812: *Resigned, 18th March, in England.*

JACKSON, Thomas Scott.—1789: Writer. 1790: Assistant under the Secretary in the Political and Revenue Department. 1791: Assistant under Collector of Tinnevelly. 1793: Assistant under Manager for supplying Beetle Tobacco and Ganja. 1794: *At home.* 1797: *Returned to India.* 1798: Paymaster and Garrison Storekeeper at Kistnagherry and its Dependency. 1799: *Out of employ; At home.* 1806: *Returned to India.* 1807: Paymaster and Garrison Storekeeper at Vizagapatam. *Died, 7th June 1807, at Vizagapatam.*

JARRETT, Thomas.—1790: Writer on the Bencoolen Establishment. 1805: *Transferred to Madras Presidency.* 1806: Commercial Resident at Masulipatam. 1807: Collector in the Zillah of Guntoor. 1811: Collector in the Zillah of Chingleput. 1814: Sub-Treasurer. (*Annuitant on the Fund from December 1832.*) *Died, 11th September 1837, at Groombridge, near Tunbridge Wells.*

JELLICOE, William Edward.—1830: Writer. 1831: Doing Duty under the Principal Collector and Magistrate of Nellore. 1837: Acting Register of the Zillah Court of Rajahmundry. 1838: Assistant to the Principal Collector and Magistrate of Nellore; Acting Head Assistant to the Collector and Magistrate of Guntoor; Acting Register in the Provincial Court, Northern Division. 1839: Acting Register, afterwards Register of the Zillah of Rajahmundry; Acting Assistant Judge and Joint Criminal Judge of Guntoor. 1843: Register of the Zillah Court of Chittoor. 1844: *Proceeded on furlough.* 1846: *Resigned the service, 30th September.*

JERVIS, John.—1789: Writer; Assistant under the Secretary in the Secret Department. 1790: Assistant under the Accountant. 1791: Assistant under one of the Collectors of Ganjam. 1793: Assistant under the Sea Customer. 1796: Assistant under the Collector of Jaffnapatam. 1797: Assistant to the Resident at Ceylon. *Died, December 1797.*

JESSUP, George Kilby.—1807: Writer. 1809: Assistant to the Chief Secretary in the Secret, Political, and Foreign Department. 1812: Head Assistant to the Collector of Madura. *Died, 30th January* 1813.

JOHNSON, Samuel, Sen.—1754: Writer. 1768: Senior Merchant, and Second in Council at Masulipatam. 1774: Member of Council of the Governor. 1776: Member of Council of the Governor, and Chief of Vizagapatam. 1790: *Out of the service.*

JOHNSON, Samuel, Jun.—1781: Writer. 1782: Paymaster at Madura. 1787: Paymaster at Trichinopoly. 1790: *Suspended, and dismissed from the service.*

JONES, Charles Edward.—1767: Writer. 1774: Factor. 1776: Junior Merchant. 1778: Senior Merchant. 1782: *At home. No trace after* 1782.

JONES, William.—1779: Writer. 1790: Senior Merchant; Inspector of Godowns, and Deputy Civil Storekeeper; Postmaster-General. 1800: Commercial Resident at Amboyna and Banda. 1801: Sub-Treasurer and Mint-Master. 1806: *At home.* 1809: *Out of the service.*

JOURDAN, Francis.—1759: Writer. 1768: Junior Merchant. 1771: Senior Merchant. 1774: Senior Merchant, and Third in Council at Masulipatam. 1776: Member of Council of the Governor. 1777: *Recalled by order of the General Court, 9th May.* 1780: *Suspended from service.*

KAYE, Charles Turton.—1831: Writer. 1832: Assistant to the Principal Collector and Magistrate of Madura. 1834: Acting Register of the Zillah of Malabar. 1835: Acting Head Assistant to the Principal Collector. 1836: Second Assistant and Acting First Assistant to the Accountant-General. 1838: First Assistant to the Accountant-General, and Acting Assistant Judge and Joint Criminal Judge of Chingleput. 1839: First Assistant to the Accountant-General. 1841: Assistant Judge and Joint Criminal Judge, Chingleput. 1843: *Proceeded on furlough.* 1846: *Returned to India. Died, 24th August* 1846, *at Madras.*

KEATE, Charles Robert Henry.—1832: Writer. *Died, 5th January* 1835, *at Tanjore.*

KEATING, Michael.—1776: Writer. 1782: Factor. 1790: Senior Merchant; In Council at Vizagapatam, and Paymaster of the Troops. 1792: Manager of the Havellies, Vizagapatam. 1800: *At home.* 1805: *Out of the service.*

KEBLE, George Gilbert.—1794: Writer. 1796: Assistant under the Secretary in the Public, Commercial, and Revenue Department. 1798: Senior Assistant under the Superintendent of the Export Warehouse; Head Assistant in the Public Department, and French Translator. 1801: Secretary to Government in the Public and Commercial Department. 1809: Sub-Treasurer and Postmaster-General. *Died, 26th August* 1811, *at Cuddalore.*

KEENE, George Henry.—1801: Writer. 1804: Assistant to the Register to the Sudder and Foujdarry Adawlut. 1805: *At home.* 1809: *Returned to India;* Register of the Zillah of Rajahmundry. 1810: Second Assistant under the Register of the Sudder and Foujdarry Adawlut. 1811: *At home.* 1816: *Out of the service.*

KELSO, Alexander Hamilton.—1800: Writer. 1802: Assistant to the Collector of the Western Polygar Peishcush and of Arcot, North of the River Palar. 1805: Subordinate Collector of Coimbatore. 1807: Judge and Magistrate of the Zillah of Mangalore. 1808; Commissioner at Tranquebar. 1811: *At home; Out of the service.*

KENNAWAY, Richard.—1806: Writer. *Died, 30th May* 1807, *at Rewarri.*

KENSINGTON, Henry Warner.—1808: Writer. 1810: Assistant to the Secretary to the Board of Revenue. 1811: Assistant to the Collector of Cuddapah. 1814: Register of the Zillah of Vizagapatam. 1815: Register of the Zillah of Chingleput. 1819: Assistant to the Mint-Master. 1820: Assistant to the Collector and Magistrate of Malabar. 1822: Register to the Provincial Court, Southern Division. *Died, 12th May* 1825, *at Cuddalore.*

KENWORTHY, John.—1770: Writer. 1776: Factor. 1778: Junior Merchant. 1782: Senior Merchant. 1790: *At home.* 1795: Resident at Cuddalore. 1800: Commercial Resident at Tinnevelly and Ramnad. 1803: Garrison Storekeeper. 1806: Garrison Storekeeper and Postmaster-General. 1808: Postmaster-General. 1809: Postmaster-General and Sub-Treasurer. 1810: Second Member of the Board of Trade. *Died, 24th July* 1812, *at Fort St. George.*

KINCHANT, Richard.—1769: Writer. 1774: Factor and Assistant at Cuddalore. 1778: Junior Merchant. 1780: Senior Merchant. 1791: Senior Merchant and Resident at Ragapore. 1795: *At home.* 1800: Commercial Resident at Cuddalore. 1809: Commercial Resident at Cuddalore, and in Charge of the

Revenues of Pondicherry and Cuddalore. *Died, 24th August, 1809, at Cuddalore.*

KINDERSLEY, NATHANIEL EDWARD.—1779: Writer. 1790: Senior Merchant, and Member of the Board of Trade; also Assistant to Persian Translator. 1792: Collector in Southern Division of Arcot. 1800: *At home.* 1805: *Out of the service.*

KINDERSLEY, NATHANIEL WILLIAM.—1814: Writer. 1817: Second Assistant to the Collector and Magistrate of Coimbatore. 1818: *At home.* 1822: *Returned to India;* Head Assistant to the Collector and Magistrate of Nellore. 1824: Sub-Collector and Assistant Magistrate of Canara. 1825: Sub-Collector of Tinnevelly. 1828: Principal Collector and Magistrate of Tanjore. 1837: Principal Collector and Magistrate of Tanjore. 1843: Second Member of the Board of Revenue. 1844: *Proceeded on furlough; Resigned the service, 1st June, in India. (Annuitant on the Fund, 1843.) Died, 3d December 1844, in England.*

KINDERSLEY, EDWARD COCKBURN.—1815: Writer. 1817: *Resigned, 28th May, in England.*

KING, PHILIP STEVENS.—1781: Writer. *Lost on his passage to Bengal in 1783.*

KING, JAMES.—1807: Writer. 1809: Assistant to the Secretary in the Military Department. 1810: Fixed Examiner to the Military Department. 1812: Acting Register of the Zillah of Verdachellum. 1813: Register of the Zillah of Verdachellum. *Died, 10th May 1814, at Pondicherry.*

KINGSCOTE, THOMAS.—1773: Writer. 1778: Factor. 1782: Junior Merchant. 1790: Senior Merchant, and Agent for Clothing Company's Troops. 1792: Commissary of Grain and Provisions to the Army. 1793: *At home.* 1799: *Out of the service.*

KINLOCK, PEREGRINE.—1797: Writer. 1798: Assistant under the Secretary to the Board of Revenue. 1799: Assistant under the Collector of Ramnad. 1801: Assistant under the Collector of Trichinopoly. 1804: Acting Collector to the Register of Trichinopoly. 1805: Register of the Southern Division of Arcot. 1806: Collector of the Zillah of Ramnad. *Lost, 20th November 1808, in the ship "Lord Nelson," on his passage home.*

KNOX, WILLIAM.—1834: Writer. 1837: Assistant to Collector and Magistrate, Rajahmundry. 1838: Acting Head Assistant to Collector and Magistrate, Cuddapah. 1839: Head Assistant to Collector and Magistrate, Cuddapah. 1840: At first Acting

Assistant, afterwards Head Assistant to Collector and Magistrate, Rajahmundry. 1843: Acting Assistant Judge and Joint Criminal Judge, Vizagapatam; Acting Sub-Collector and Magistrate, Cuddapah. 1845: Sub-Collector and Joint Magistrate, Cuddapah; *Proceeded to Europe on furlough.* 1849: Acting Sub-Collector and Joint-Magistrate, Madura; also Head Assistant to Collector and Magistrate, Madura. 1850: Principal Assistant to Collector and Magistrate, and Agent to the Governor of Madras, Ganjam. 1854: Acting Collector and Magistrate, and Agent to the Governor in Ganjam. 1857: Collector and Magistrate, Masulipatam. 1859: Collector and Magistrate, Kistna. 1860: *On medical leave for* 15 *months.* 1861: *Resigned the service, 27th December, in England.* (*Annuitant.*) *Died, 27th October* 1867.

KNOX, THOMAS JOHN.—1839: Writer. 1840: Assistant to Collector and Magistrate, Rajahmundry. 1841: Acting Register of the Zillah Court of Rajahmundry. 1843: Register of the Zillah Court of Rajahmundry; Acting Head Assistant, afterwards Head Assistant, to the Collector and Magistrate, Rajahmundry. 1846: Acting Sub-Judge of the Zillah of Rajahmundry. 1848: *Proceeded to Europe on furlough.* 1853: Acting Deputy Collector of Sea Customs, Madras, and Sub-Collector and Joint Magistrate, Malabar. 1855: Principal Assistant to Collector and Magistrate, and Agent to the Governor of Madras, in Vizagapatam; Acting Civil and Sessions Judge, Masulipatam. 1857: Acting Collector and Magistrate, Masulipatam. 1858: Acting Collector and Magistrate, and Agent to the Governor of Madras, in Ganjam. 1859: Acting Collector and Magistrate, Masulipatam; Acting Collector and Magistrate at Salem. 1860: Civil and Sessions Judge, Chicacole. 1864: *On medical leave to Europe for* 15 *months.* 1865: *Resigned the service, 28th October, in England.* (*Annuitant.*) *Died, 3d October,* 1877.

LACON, HENRY.—1807: Writer. 1810: Assistant to the Register of the Sudder and Foujdarry Adawlut. 1811: Assistant to the Collector of Ganjam. 1813: Register of the Zillah of Northern Malabar. 1819: *At home.* 1823: *Returned to India;* Commissioner for Small Claims on the Carnatic Fund. 1827: Judge and Criminal Judge of the Zillah of Chicacole. 1830: Collector and Magistrate of Ganjam. 1831: Principal Collector and Magistrate of Cuddapah. (*Annuitant on the Fund from 1st January* 1835.) *Died, 1st February* 1864, *in England.*

LANDON, James.—1777: Writer. 1782: Factor. 1790: Senior Merchant; Upper Searcher at Sea Gate; Deputy Customer and Assay Master. 1792: Collector in the Centre Division of Arcot. *Died, 22d June* 1794.

LANE, Richard.—1777: Writer. *Died, August* 1777, *in Bengal.*

LANE, John Fraser.—1804: Writer. 1807: Assistant to the Collector of the Zillah of Chittoor. 1809: Head Assistant to the Collector of the Zillah of Bellary. 1814: Head Assistant to the Collector of the Zillah of Chingleput. 1815: French Translator to Government. 1816: Deputy Collector of Madras. 1820: Secretary to the Mint Committee; Superintendent of the Issue and Custody of Stationery. 1821: Collector and Magistrate of Masulipatam, and in Charge of the Treasury there. *Died, 2d January* 1824, *at Madras.*

LARKING, William Fleete.—1807: Writer. 1810: Assistant to the Chief Secretary in the Secret, Political, and Foreign Department. *Drowned, 30th April* 1812, *while bathing at Vizagapatam.*

LASCELLES, Francis.—1815: Writer. 1818: Second Assistant to the Collector and Magistrate of Cuddapah. 1820: Register of the Zillah of Cuddapah. 1826: Register of the Provincial Court, Centre Division. 1827: *At home on absentee allowance.* 1829: *Returned to India.* 1831: Acting Judge and Criminal Judge of Combaconum. 1832: Acting Third Judge of Provincial Court, Southern Division. 1833: Judge and Criminal Judge of Chittoor; *Out of employ for seven months.* 1835: Judge and Criminal Judge of Chittoor. 1839: Judge and Criminal Judge of Cuddapah. 1840: Judge and Criminal Judge of Rajahmundry. 1843: *Out of employ.* 1845: Civil and Sessions Judge, Second Class, Honore. 1856: *Proceeded on furlough; Resigned the service, 20th December, in India. (Annuitant on the Fund,* 1858.) *Died, 15th July* 1882, *at Brighton.*

LATHOM, Richard.—1756: Writer. 1768: Junior Merchant. 1771: Senior Merchant and Resident at Ingeram. 1776: Member of Council of the Governor. 1777: *Recalled by order of the General Court, 9th May.* 1780: Chief at Cuddalore. *No trace after* 1782.

LATHOM, Robert George.—1776: Writer. 1782: Factor. *Taken prisoner by Hyder Ally. No trace after* 1782.

LATHOM, Richard Henry.—1794: Writer. 1797: Assistant

under the Secretary to the Board of Revenue. 1798: Senior Assistant under the Accountant-General. 1799: *Out of employ.* 1800: Assistant under the Collector in the Third Division of Vizagapatam District. 1802: Register of the Court of Circuit and Appeal, Northern Division. 1803: Judge of the Zillah of Ramnad. 1807: Judge and Magistrate of Trichinopoly. *Died, 8th October* 1810, *at Trichinopoly.*

LAUTOUR, JAMES.—1806: Writer. 1808: *At home.* 1816: *Out of the service.*

LAVIE, WILLIAM.—1824: Writer; Assistant to the Collector and Magistrate of Madura. 1826: Register of the Zillah of Combaconum. 1828: Head Assistant to the Principal Collector of Canara. 1831: Sub-Collector and Joint Magistrate of Canara. 1832: Acting Assistant Judge and Joint Criminal Judge of Canara. 1834: Assistant Judge and Joint Criminal Judge of Guntoor. 1835: Sub-Collector and Joint Magistrate of Canara. 1836: *At home on absentee allowance.* 1839: *Returned to India.* 1840: *Out of employ.* 1841: Judge and Criminal Judge of Canara. 1842: Second Judge of the Provincial Court of Appeal and Circuit, Centre Division. 1844: Civil and Sessions Judge, Cuddapah; Civil and Sessions Judge, Chittoor. 1848: *Resigned the service, 15th April. (Annuitant on the Fund,* 1848.) *Died, 28th April* 1862, *in England.*

LENNOX, JOHN.—1778: Writer. 1782: *At home.* 1790: Senior Merchant and Assistant at Maddepollam. 1792: Paymaster at Aska and Ganjam. 1795: Paymaster at Ongole and in the Palnaud. 1800: *At home.* 1805: *Out of the service.*

LEVINGE, VERE HENRY.—1839: Writer. 1841: Assistant to Principal Collector and Magistrate, Madura, and at Tanjore. 1842: Acting Register of the Zillah Court of Madura. 1843: Acting Head Assistant to Collector and Magistrate, Tinnevelly. 1845: Head Assistant to Collector and Magistrate, Tinnevelly. 1851: Acting Sub-Collector and Joint Magistrate, Madura; *Proceeded to Europe on furlough.* 1854: Acting Sub-Judge, Combaconum; and Sub-Collector and Joint Magistrate, Tinnevelly. 1856: Acting Civil and Sessions Judge, Tinnevelly. 1858: Acting Collector and Magistrate, Tinnevelly. 1859: Collector and Magistrate, North Canara. 1860: Collector and Magistrate, Madura. 1867: *Resigned the service, 8th April. (Annuitant.)*

LEWIN, THOMAS.—1770: Writer. 1776: Factor. 1778:

Junior Merchant. 1782: Senior Merchant; *At home; Returned to India.* 1790: *At home.* 1792: *In India without employment.* 1800: *Out of the service.*

LEWIN, Malcolm.—1815: Writer. 1818: Third Assistant to the Collector and Magistrate of Malabar. 1819: Register of the Zillah of Malabar. 1824: Acting Register of the Zillah of Canara. 1825: Head Assistant to the Collector and Magistrate of Canara. 1826: Acting Additional Sub-Collector of Canara. 1828: Additional Sub-Collector of Canara. 1830: *At home on absentee allowance.* 1834: *Returned to India;* Collector and Magistrate of Guntoor. 1835: Collector and Magistrate of Rajahmundry, and Acting Second Judge of Provincial Court, Northern Division. 1836: Principal Collector and Magistrate of Canara. 1838: Acting Second Judge of the Provincial Court, Centre Division. 1839: Principal Collector and Magistrate of Bellary. 1840: Second Judge of the Provincial Court of Appeal and Circuit, Centre Division. 1842: Third Judge of the Sudder Dewannee and Sudder Foujdarry Adawlut. 1845: Judge of the Sudder Dewannee and Sudder Foujdarry Adawlut. 1846: Second Judge of the Sudder Dewannee and Sudder Foujdarry Adawlut, and appointed Provisional Member of Council of the Governor; *Resigned the service, 10th December.* (*Annuitant on the Fund,* 1848.) *Died,* 5*th March* 1869, *in England.*

LEWIN, Frederick Mortimer. — 1818: Writer. 1821: Assistant to the Collector and Magistrate of the Southern Division of Arcot. 1824: Register and Assistant Collector of Seringapatam. 1827: Assistant Judge and Joint Criminal Judge of Salem. 1828: Judge and Criminal Judge of Salem. 1831: *At home on absentee allowance.* 1833: *Returned to India, per "Horatio."* 1835: Acting Zillah Judge of Combaconum; afterwards Judge and Criminal Judge of Combaconum. 1844: Civil and Sessions Judge of Combaconum. 1847: *Resigned the service.* (*Annuitant on the Fund,* 1847.) *Died,* 17*th June* 1877, *in England.*

LEWIN, Richard Cotton. — 1846: Writer. Assistant to Collector and Magistrate, Canara. 1851: *Proceeded on furlough.* 1852: *Returned to India;* Assistant to Collector and Magistrate, Northern Division of Arcot. 1855: Assistant to Collector and Magistrate, Trichinopoly. 1857: Additional Sub-Collector and Joint Magistrate, Canara. *Died,* 28*th July* 1858, *at Bellary.*

LEWIS, John Walter.—1808: Writer. 1814: Acting Assistant to the Register of the Sudder and Foujdarry Adawlut. 1816: Register of the Zillah of Masulipatum. 1819: *At home.* 1823: *Returned to India;* Register of the Zillah of Carnatic. 1824: Deputy Collector of Government Sea Customs at Madras. 1827: *At home on absentee allowance.* (*Annuitant on the Fund from 1st January* 1829, *and died*, 20*th October* 1836, *at Foxdown, near Wellington, Somersetshire.*)

LIGHT, William.—1765: Writer. 1768: Assistant at Cuddalore. 1771: Factor. 1774: Junior Merchant. 1776: Senior Merchant. *No trace after* 1782.

LIMOND, David Rouse.—1831: Writer. 1833: Assistant to the Collector of Tinnevelly. 1836: Acting Register, afterwards Register of the Zillah of Madura. 1838: Acting Assistant Judge and Joint Criminal Judge of Madura; and in Charge of Auxiliary Court at Tinnevelly; also Register of the Zillah Court of Madura. 1844: Extra Assistant to Collector and Magistrate, Madura. 1845: Subordinate Judge, Madura. *Died*, 18*th November* 1846, *at Madura.*

LIND, Francis.—1771: Writer. 1776: Factor. 1780: Junior Merchant. 1782: Senior Merchant and Military Storekeeper. 1792: *At home.* 1800: *Out of the service.*

LINLEY, William. — 1790: Writer; Assistant under the Military Secretary. 1791: Assistant under the Collector of Madura and Dindigul. 1793: Deputy Secretary to the Military Board. 1796: *At home.* 1800: *Returned to India.* 1801: Paymaster and Garrison Storekeeper, at Nellore and Dependencies. 1805: Sub-Treasurer and Mint-Master. 1806: *At home.* 1810: *Out of the service.*

LLOYD, Hugh.—1795: Writer. *Not to be traced.*

LOCKART, Robert.—1781: Writer. 1783: Assistant to the Secretary of the Select Committee. *No trace after* 1786.

LOCKHART, Walter Elliott.—1826: Writer. 1829: Register to the Zillah of Nellore. 1832: Acting Judge and Criminal Judge of Chingleput; Junior Deputy Secretary to the Board of Revenue; Additional Sub-Collector and Joint Magistrate of Cuddapah. 1835: Sub-Collector and Joint Magistrate of Madura. 1837: Re-appointed Joint Magistrate of Madura. 1838: *At home on absentee allowance.* 1843: *Returned to India.* 1844: *Out of employ.* 1845: Collector and Magistrate, Salem. *Died*, 30*th January* 1850, *at Ossoor.*

LONG, John.—1796: Writer on the Bencoolen Establishment. 1803: *Transferred to Madras Presidency;* Assistant to the Register of the Sudder and Foujdarry Adawlut; Register of the Zillah of Guntoor. 1805: Collector in the Zillah of Rajahmundry. 1810: Judge and Magistrate of Madura. 1813: Judge and Criminal Judge of Rajahmundry. 1823: *Out of the service.*

LORD, Hugh.—1796: Writer. 1797: Assistant under the Secretary in the Public, Revenue, and Commercial Department; Assistant under the Commercial Resident at Amboyna. 1801: Paymaster and Garrison Storekeeper at Amboyna. 1802: Acting Commercial Resident at Amboyna. 1804: *Out of employ.* 1806: Register to the Court of Appeal and Circuit, Northern Division; Acting Judge and Magistrate of Nellore. 1807: Judge and Magistrate of the Zillah of Nellore. 1820: Third Judge of Provincial Court, Northern Division. 1821: Second Judge of Provincial Court, Northern Division. 1825: Acting Judge of the Sudder and Foujdarry Adawlut. 1828: First Judge of the Provincial Court, Northern Division. *Died, 9th April* 1829, *at Mysore.*

LOVELL, Edmund Charles.—1827: Writer. 1829: Assistant to the Secretary in the Military Department. 1832: Acting Malayalum Translator, and First Assistant to the Secretary to Government in the Revenue and Judicial Department; First Assistant to the Chief Secretary to Government; Acting Deputy Secretary in the Military Department. 1833: Head Assistant to the Collector and Magistrate of Rajahmundry; Head Assistant to the Principal Collector and Magistrate of Cuddapah. 1837: Sub-Collector and Joint Magistrate of the Northern Division of Arcot. 1838: *At home on absentee allowance.* 1842: *Returned to India.* 1843: Sub-Collector and Joint Magistrate, Northern Division of Arcot. 1848: Civil and Sessions Judge, Chittoor. *Died, 1st September* 1851, *at Madras.*

LUSHINGTON, Stephen Rumbold.—1790: Writer. 1792: Assistant under the Secretary in the Military, Political, and Secret Department. 1793: Assistant under the Translator to the Board of Revenue. 1794: Deputy Persian Translator to Government, and Persian Translator to the Board of Revenue. 1796: Deputy Secretary to the Board of Revenue; Under Searcher at the Sea Gate. 1798: Secretary and Persian Translator to the Board of Revenue. 1799: Collector of the Southern Polygar Peishcush at Ramnad. 1801: Collector of Tinnevelly. 1803: Register of the Sudder and Foujdarry Adawlut; *At home.* 1807: *Out of the service.*

LUSHINGTON, Charles May.—1801: Writer. 1803: Assistant to the Register of the Sudder and Foujdarry Adawlut. 1804: Register of the Zillah of Rajahmundry. 1808: *Out of employ.* 1809: Second Assistant to the Register of the Sudder and Foujdarry Adawlut; Assistant Judge of Rajahmundry. 1813: Assistant Judge of Combaconum. 1815: Collector and Magistrate of Trichinopoly. 1823: Third Judge of the Provincial Court, Southern Division. 1824: Second Judge of the Provincial Court, Southern Division. 1828: First Judge of the Provincial Court, Southern Division. 1830: Third Puisne Judge of the Sudder and Foujdarry Adawlut. 1831: Second Puisne Judge of the Sudder and Foujdarry Adawlut. 1832: First Puisne Judge of the Sudder and Foujdarry Adawlut. 1838: Chief Puisne Judge of the Sudder and Foujdarry Adawlut, and Member of Council of the Governor. 1841: Member of Council, and President of the Revenue, Marine, and College Boards. 1843: *Resigned the service, 24th January, in India. (Annuitant on the Fund,* 1843.) *Died, 8th March* 1844, *in England.*

LUSHINGTON, Thomas Davies.—1832: Writer; Doing Duty as Assistant in the Chief Secretary's Office. 1834: Assistant under the Principal Collector and Magistrate of Malabar. 1836: Acting Head Assistant to the Principal Collector and Magistrate of Canara. 1837: Head Assistant to the Principal Collector and Magistrate of Canara. 1842: Additional Sub-Collector and Magistrate of Canara. 1845: *Proceeded on furlough.* 1849: *Returned to India.* 1850: Principal Assistant to Collector and Magistrate, Ganjam; Sub-Collector and Joint Magistrate, Salem. 1851: Agent to the Governor at Kurnool. 1852: Collector and Magistrate, Masulipatam. 1857: *Proceeded on furlough.* 1858: *Returned to India;* Collector, Magistrate, and Agent to Governor, Ganjam. *Died at sea, 17th June* 1858, *on board the "Hydaspes."*

LUSHINGTON, Franklyn.—1838: Writer. 1839: Under the Principal Collector, Malabar; Assistant to Collector and Magistrate, Chingleput. 1841: Acting Second Assistant to the Accountant-General. 1842: Second Assistant to the Accountant-General. 1843: *Proceeded to Europe on furlough.* 1845: Assistant to Collector and Magistrate, South Arcot. 1846: Head Assistant to Collector and Magistrate, South Arcot. 1847: Acting Senior Deputy Register to the Court of Sudder and Foujdarry Adawlut. 1849: Senior Deputy Register to the Court of Sudder and Foujdarry Adawlut. 1852: At first Acting Register, afterwards

Register, to the Court of Sudder and Foujdarry Adawlut. 1855: Civil Auditor, and Superintendent of Stamps. 1859: Accountant, North-Western Provinces; and Accountant to the Government of Bengal. 1860: Officiating Accountant-General, Madras. 1861: Officiating Deputy Auditor and Accountant-General to the Governor of Fort St. George. 1862: *On medical leave for 12 months.* 1863: Deputy Auditor and Accountant-General, Madras. 1871: *On furlough.* 1873: Accountant-General, Madras; *Resigned the service, 16th August. (Annuitant.)*

MACDONALD, CHARLES EDWARD.—1826: Writer. 1828: Assistant to the Principal Collector of South Arcot. 1829: Head Assistant to the Principal Collector of North Arcot. 1832: Additional Sub-Collector and Joint Magistrate of Cuddapah. *Died, 15th June 1832, at Cuddapah.*

MACDONELL, ÆNEAS R.—1807: Writer. 1808: Assistant to the Secretary in the Revenue and Judicial Department; Assistant under the Register of the Sudder and Foujdarry Adawlut. 1809: Assistant under the Assay Master; Head Assistant to the Collector of Cuddapah. 1816: Head Assistant to the Magistrate at Cuddapah. 1818: Secretary to the Honourable Mountstuart Elphinstone, Sole Commissioner for the Settlement of the Peishwah Territories. 1820: Private Secretary to Sir Thomas Munro, the Governor of Madras. 1822: Third Member of the Board of Revenue. 1824: Second Member of the Board of Revenue. 1832: Member of the Marine Board. 1836: First Member of the Board of Revenue. 1838: *At home on absentee allowance. (Annuitant on the Fund in* 1839.) *Died, 24th October* 1868, *in England.*

MACDOUALL, JOHN.—1792: Writer. 1794: Assistant under the Secretary to the Board of Revenue, and Assistant to the Accountant-General. 1796: Paymaster to the Expedition against Trincomallee. 1798: Paymaster to the Expedition at Columbo. 1799: Collector of Columbo; *Out of Employ.* 1802: *At home.* 1806: *Returned to India.* 1809: Civil Auditor. 1810: Dutch Translator to Government. *Died, 5th August* 1814, *at Madras.*

MACKAY, GEORGE.—1766: Appointed Senior Merchant and Member of Council of the Governor. 1777: *Recalled by the order of the General Court of Proprietors, 9th May.* 1780: *At home, and suspended from the service.*

MACKENZIE, ALEXANDER.—1789: Writer. 1790: Assistant under the Secretary in the Political and Revenue Department 1791: Assistant under the Board of Assumed Revenue. 1793:

Assistant to the Commercial Resident at Vizagapatam. 1796: Deputy Commercial Resident at Ganjam. 1798: *At home.* 1801: *Returned to India.* 1802: Secretary to the Board of Trade; Commercial Resident at Vizagapatam and Ganjam. 1805: Senior Judge of the Court of Circuit and Appeal, Southern Division. 1807: *At home.* 1811: *Out of the service.*

M'KERRELL, JOHN.—1804: Writer. 1806: Assistant under the Principal Collector in Canara; Register of the Zillah of the Northern Division of Canara. 1811: *At home.* 1812: *Returned to India;* Gentoo and Teloogoo Translator to Government. 1815: Reporter of External Commerce, and Sheriff of Madras. 1816: Superintendent of Police. 1817: Canarese Translator to Government. 1820: Mint-Master. (*Annuitant on the Fund, from 12th May 1830.*) *Died in November 1835.*

MACKLIN, JOHN CHARLES.—1769: Writer. *No trace after 1771.*

MACKONOCHIE, ROBERT.—1800: Writer. 1803: Assistant to the Collector of Ramnad and Tinnevelly; *At home for his health.* 1809: *Returned to India;* Deputy Mint-Master. 1811: Deputy Accountant in the Military Accounts Department. 1812: *Out of employ.* 1819: Mint-Master. 1820: *At home.* 1826: *Out of the service.* (*Annuitant on the Fund in 1842.*) *Died, 19th February 1858, in England.*

MACLEAN, ALEXANDER.—1817: Writer. 1821: Assistant to the Collector and Magistrate of Chingleput. 1825: Head Assistant to the Collector and Magistrate of Malabar. 1826: Acting Head Assistant to the Register of the Sudder Court, and Sanscrit Examiner to the College Board. 1828: Sub-Collector and Joint Magistrate of Malabar. 1830: Sub-Collector and Joint Magistrate of Canara; Judge and Criminal Judge of Combaconum. 1831: Judge and Criminal Judge of Malabar. 1833: Collector and Magistrate of Chingleput. 1835: Acting Malayalum Translator to Government. 1836: Malayalum Translator to Government. 1838: Acting Temporary Member of the Board of Revenue; Third Member of the Board of Revenue. 1839: Collector and Magistrate of Chingleput; Temporary Member of the Board of Revenue; and Malayalum Translator to Government. 1845: Collector and Magistrate, Cuddapah, and Malayalum Translator to Government. 1848: Third Member of the Board of Revenue, and Malayalum Translator to Government. 1850: *Retired from the service, 1st May, in India.* (*Annuitant on the Fund, 1850.*) *Died, 28th November 1872, in England.*

MACLEOD, Alexander.—1777: Writer. 1780: *At home.* 1782: Factor. 1790: Senior Merchant, and one of the Collectors of the Jaghire Revenue. 1792: Collector in the Madura and Nellore Districts, and Peishcash of the Marwars. 1795: Collector in the Dindigul Districts. 1800: Resident at Negapatam, and Revenue Assistant under the Resident at Nagore. 1801: *At home.* 1803: *Out of the service.*

MACLEOD, John M'Pherson.—1811: Writer. 1814: Second Assistant, afterwards First Assistant to Secretary to Government in the several Civil Departments. 1816: Member and Secretary of the Committee for Revising the Customs Laws. 1820: *At home on account of health.* 1823: *Returned to India;* Acting Secretary to Government in Financial and General Departments. 1824: Secretary to Government in Financial and General Departments. 1825: Tamil Translator to Government, Member of the College Board, of the Board of Public Instruction, and of the Mint Committee. 1826: Persian Translator to Government. 1827: Secretary in the Revenue and Judicial Departments. 1829: Temporary Member, afterwards Third Member of the Board of Revenue. 1832: Commissioner for the Government of Mysore. 1834: Deputed to Hyderabad on Special Duty by the Governor-General. 1835: Member of the Indian Law Commission. 1836: Member of the Committee for Revising the System of Prison Discipline throughout India. 1838: *At home on absentee allowance.* 1841: *Retired from the service.* (*Annuitant on the Fund,* 1841.) *Died,* 1*st March* 1881, *in England.*

MAIDMAN, George.—1793: Writer. 1796: Assistant under the Collector in the Jaghire. 1798: *Out of employ;* Assistant under the Commercial Resident at Ingeram. 1802: Deputy Commercial Resident at Ingeram. 1807: Commercial Resident in the Ceded Districts; Commercial Resident at Masulipatam. *Died, 8th April* 1810, *at Masulipatam.*

MAIDMAN, Charles.—1801: Writer. 1803: Assistant to the Commercial Resident at Ingeram. 1807: Deputy Commercial Resident at Ingeram. *Died,* 29*th August* 1824, *at Ingeram.*

MAINWARING, William.—1794: Writer. 1796: Assistant to the Secretary in Public, Commercial, and Revenue Department. 1797: Assistant to the Secretary in Military, Political, and Secret Department, and French Translator. 1798: Assistant to the Collector of the First Division of Masulipatam. 1800: Assistant to the Collector of Muglatore. 1802: Collector in the Zillah of Guntoor. 1803: *Out of employ.* 1804: Paymaster and Garrison Storekeeper at Trichinopoly. 1806: Paymaster and Garrison Storekeeper at Madura. 1810: *Out of employ. Died, 5th February* 1812, *at Tinnevelly.*

MAITLAND, WILLIAM.—1763: Writer. 1768: Factor and Assistant at Cuddalore. 1771: Junior Merchant and Fourth in Council at Cuddalore. 1774: Senior Merchant and Fourth in Council at Cuddalore. 1776: Third in Council at Cuddalore. *No trace after* 1782.

MAITLAND, ADAM.—1824: Writer. 1827: Employed in the Mahratta Country under the Bombay Government. *Died, 26th May* 1828, *at Dharwar.*

MAJENDIE, ANDREW.—1766: Writer. 1771: Factor. 1774: Junior Merchant. 1778: Senior Merchant. 1782: *At home. Died in* 1793, *in England.*

MALCOLM, ROBERT.—1781: Writer. 1783: Assistant at Masulipatam. 1796: Assistant to the Collector in the Fifth Division of Masulipatam District; Commercial Resident at Vizagapatam. 1802: Second Judge of the Court of Circuit and Appeal, Northern Division. 1808: *At home.* 1809: *Out of the service.*

MALTBY, EDWARD.—1828: Writer. 1831: Second Assistant to the Principal Collector, Canara. 1833: Acting Head Assistant, afterwards Head Assistant, to the Principal Collector and Magistrate, Canara. 1835: Acting Additional Sub-Collector and Joint Magistrate, Canara. 1837: Additional, and afterwards Sub-Collector and Joint Magistrate, Canara. 1839: Acting Principal Collector and Magistrate, Canara. 1841: *Proceeded on furlough to Europe.* 1844: Acting Deputy Collector, Madras; and Acting Sub-Collector and Joint Magistrate, Nellore. 1845: Sub-Collector and Joint Magistrate, Nellore; Acting Collector and Magistrate, Chingleput. 1848: Civil and Sessions Judge, Cuddapah. 1849: Collector and Magistrate, Trichinopoly. 1851: Collector and Magistrate, South Arcot. 1854: Third Member of the Board of Revenue; and Member of the Board of Examiners. 1857: Acting Chief Secretary to Government. 1858: Provincial Member of Council. 1859: Member of Council of the Governor, and President of the Revenue and Marine Boards. 1864: *Resigned the service,* 16*th December.* (*Annuitant.*)

MALTBY, FRANCIS NEWCOMBE.—1830: Writer. 1832: Register

to the Zillah Court of Canara. 1834: Acting Assistant Judge and Joint Criminal Judge, Malabar. 1835: Acting Assistant Judge and Joint Criminal Judge, Canara; Acting Head Assistant to Principal Collector and Magistrate, Canara. 1836: Register to the Zillah Court of Canara. 1837: Additional Sub-Collector and Joint Magistrate, Canara. 1841: Sub-Collector and Joint Magistrate, Canara; *Proceeded to Europe on furlough.* 1845: Acting Assistant Judge, Mangalore. 1846: Sub-Collector and Joint Magistrate, Salem. 1850: Agent to the Governor of Madras, at Kurnool; Collector and Magistrate, Canara. 1855: Acting Member of the Board of Revenue. 1856: Financial and Judicial Commissioner of the Hyderabad Assigned Territories. 1858: *On medical leave to Europe.* 1859: Resident at Travancore and Cochin. 1861: *On medical leave for* 6 *months.* 1862: *Resigned the service,* 1*st May.* (*Annuitant.*) *Died,* 27*th August* 1877, *in North Britain.*

MARRIOTT, WILLIAM.—1795: Writer. 1798: Assistant under the Collector of Burramehal. 1799: Head Assistant under the Collector of Kistnagherry. 1801: *At home for his health. Died,* 18*th February* 1805, *in England.*

MARTIN, GEORGE SULLIVAN.—1781: Writer. 1783: Assistant to the Secretary to the Select Committee in Bengal. 1784: Under the Resident at Tanjore. 1787: Assistant under the Resident at Negapatam. 1788: Under the Secretary, Secret Department; Deputy Postmaster-General; and Sheriff. 1789: Secretary to the Board of Trade. 1790: Paymaster at Palamcottah. 1794: Commercial Resident in the Southern Provinces. 1796: Commercial Resident at Ramnad and Tinnevelly. 1799: *At home. No trace after* 1799.

MARTINDALE, JOSEPH.—1779: Writer. *No trace after* 1782.

MASON, JOHN GEORGE.—1812: Writer. 1815: Second Assistant to the Collector of Tanjore. 1816: Head Assistant to the Collector of Ganjam; Assistant Magistrate of Ganjam. *Died,* 18*th December* 1817, *in camp, at Itchapore.*

MASON, WILLIAM.—1813: Writer. 1817: Second Assistant to the Collector of Malabar, and Assistant Magistrate. 1821: Head Assistant to the Collector of Malabar, and Magistrate of Malabar. 1825: Sub-Collector and Assistant Magistrate of Malabar. 1826: Sub-Collector and Assistant Magistrate of Bellary. 1831: Collector and Magistrate of Guntoor. 1832: Collector and Magistrate of Vizagapatam. *Died,* 2*d July* 1834, *at Vizagapatam.*

MASON, Wheeler Hood George. — 1832: Writer. 1834: Assistant to the Collector and Magistrate of Masulipatam. 1835: Assistant to the Collector and Magistrate of Chingleput. 1837: Acting Head Assistant Collector and Magistrate of Chingleput. 1838: Head Assistant to Collector and Magistrate of Chingleput. 1839: Assistant to Collector and Magistrate of Vizagapatam. 1840: Assistant to Agent of the Governor, Collector, and Magistrate, Vizagapatam. *Died, 2d August* 1842, *at Madras.*

MATHISON, Archibald Stirling.—1830: Writer. 1832: Assistant to the Collector and Magistrate of Rajahmundry. 1833: Head Assistant to the Collector and Magistrate of Guntoor. 1836: Officiating Joint Criminal Judge of Guntoor. 1838: Acting Sub-Collector and Joint Magistrate of Nellore. 1839: Sub-Collector and Joint Magistrate of Nellore. 1843: *Proceeded on furlough.* 1846: *Returned to India.* 1847: Principal Assistant to Agent of the Governor, Collector, and Magistrate, Vizagapatam. 1852: Civil and Sessions Judge, Chittoor. 1856: *Proceeded on furlough.* 1859: *Resigned the service,* 19*th February, in India.* (*Annuitant.*)

MAUNSELL, Robert.—1763: Writer. 1768: Factor. 1771: Junior Merchant and Paymaster at Itchapore. 1774: Senior Merchant, and Assistant at Ganjam. 1776: Senior Merchant, and Second in Council at Ganjam. 1790: *At home.* 1792: *Out of the service.*

MAXTONE, Charles. — 1769: Writer. 1774: Factor and Assistant at Vizagapatam. 1778: Junior Merchant. 1780: Senior Merchant. 1790: *At home.* 1793: Senior Merchant without Employ. 1800: Commercial Resident at Ingeram. 1803: Postmaster-General and Military Paymaster at the Presidency, and of Extraordinaries. 1806: First Judge of the Court of Circuit and Appeal, Centre Division. 1808: First Judge of the Court of Circuit and Appeal, Centre Division, and Acting Judge of the Sudder and Foujdarry Adawlut Courts. *Died,* 24*th February* 1809.

MAXWELL, Hugh.—1773: Writer. 1778: Factor. 1782: Junior Merchant. 1790: Senior Merchant, and Manager of the Ganjam Havelly. 1792: Member of the Revenue Board. *Died in* 1793.

MAYNAND, Josias.—1767: Writer. 1771: *At home.* 1774: Factor (*but still at home*). 1776: Junior Merchant; *At home; Resigned the service.*

MAYNE, Dawson.—1837: Writer. 1838: Assistant to the Principal Collector and Magistrate of Bellary. 1841: Head Assistant to Principal Collector and Magistrate, Cuddapah. 1850:

Subordinate Judge, Cuddapah. 1852: *Proceeded on furlough.* 1855: *Returned to India;* Subordinate Judge, Bellary. 1858: Civil and Sessions Judge, Madura. *Died, 23d November* 1858, *at Tutticorin.*

MEGGISON, Robert.—1804: Writer. 1808: Assistant under the Collector of Cuddapah. *Died, 20th May* 1808, *at Cuddapah.*

MELLOR, Abel.—1824: Writer. 1828: Head Assistant to the Principal Collector at Madura. 1832: Sub-Collector and Joint Magistrate of Tinnevelly. 1835: *At home on absentee allowance.* 1838: *Returned to India overland.* 1839: Acting Civil Auditor and Superintendent of Stamps. 1840: Collector and Magistrate, Bellary. 1850: *Resigned the service, 5th November, in India.* (*Annuitant on the Fund,* 1851.) *Died, 16th July* 1878, *England.*

MICHELL, William.—1773: Writer. 1778: Factor. 1782: Junior Merchant. 1790: Senior Merchant, and Assistant at Tanjore. 1792: Resident at Nagore. 1794: *At home.* 1800: *Out of the service.*

MICHELL, Henry Chickley.—1777: Writer. 1782: Factor. 1790: Senior Merchant, and Member of the Board of Trade; Rental General and Scavenger. 1792: Member of the Board of Trade and Export Warehouse-keeper. 1795: *In England.* 1796: *Dismissed by order of the Court of Directors, dated 30th March.*

MICROP, Isaac Van.—1776: Writer. 1782: Factor. *No trace after* 1782.

MITCHELL, John.—1829: Writer. 1831: Second Assistant to the Collector and Magistrate of Tinnevelly. 1833: Register of the Zillah of Combaconum. *Died, 1st March* 1834.

MITFORD, John.—1771: Writer. 1776: Factor. 1780: Junior Merchant. 1782: Senior Merchant and Export Warehouse-keeper. 1795: *At home.* 1801: Member of the Board of Trade. 1806: *At home.* 1809: *Out of the service.*

MOLE, Frederick.—1830: Writer. 1833: Assistant to the Principal Collector and Magistrate of Salem. 1834: Register of Salem. 1836: Acting Head Assistant to the Principal Collector and Magistrate of Salem. 1837: Register of the Zillah Court of Salem. *Died, 1st December* 1842, *at Salem.*

MOLLE, William Macquarie.—1832: Writer. 1833: Assistant to the Principal Collector of South Arcot. 1834: Assistant to the Collector of Tinnevelly. 1838: Head Assistant to the Collector and Magistrate of Tinnevelly. 1841: *Out of employ.* 1844: Head Assistant to Collector and Magistrate of Tanjore.

1845: Head Assistant to Collector and Magistrate of Trichinopoly. 1846: Sub-Collector and Joint Magistrate, Cuddapah. 1847: *Proceeded on furlough.* 1850: *Returned to India;* Sub-Collector and Joint Magistrate, Coimbatore. 1856: Civil and Sessions Judge, Honore. 1861: *Proceeded on furlough; Resigned the service, 8th June, in England.* (*Annuitant in* 1861.)

MONCKTON, EDWARD.—1762: Writer. 1768: Factor. 1771: Junior Merchant. 1774: Senior Merchant. 1780: *Out of the service.*

MONCKTON, GEORGE PACKENHAM.—1837: Writer. 1839: Assistant to the Collector and Magistrate of Malabar. 1844: Assistant to Collector and Magistrate, Northern Division of Arcot. 1845: *Proceeded on furlough.* 1848: *Pensioned, 30th August.*

MONEY, SEPTIMUS.—1802: Writer. 1805: Assistant to the Secretary in the Revenue and Judicial Department. 1806: Register of the Zillah of Chittoor. 1813: Judge and Magistrate of Cochin. 1817: Judge and Criminal Judge of Dharapooram, afterwards of Coimbatore. 1821: Judge and Criminal Judge of Cuddapah. 1824: *At home.* 1826: *Returned to India;* Acting Additional Judge of Provincial Court, Northern Division. 1828: Third Judge of Provincial Court, Northern Division. *Died, 14th August* 1830, *at Masulipatam.*

MONK, WILLIAM GARROW.—1804: Writer. 1805: Assistant under the Principal Collector of Coimbatore. 1806: Register of the Zillah of Coimbatore. 1811: *At home.* 1814: *Returned to India;* Register of the Zillah of Coimbatore. 1820: Judge and Criminal Judge of Tinnevelly. 1822: Judge and Criminal Judge of Chicacole. 1827: *At home on absentee allowance.* (*Annuitant on the Fund from 1st January* 1829.) *Died, 3d March* 1859, *in England.*

MONTGOMERIE, WILLIAM.—1804: Writer. 1806: Assistant under the Register of the Sudder and Foujdarry Adawlut. 1807: Assistant to the Register of the Zillah of Vizagapatam. 1809: Register of the Zillah of Ganjam. 1811: Deputy Commercial Resident at Vizagapatam. 1818: Deputy Commercial Resident at Maddepollam and Masulipatam. 1823: Assistant to the Commercial Resident at the General Factory at Ingeram. 1824: Deputy Commercial Resident at the General Factory at Ingeram. 1826: Commercial Resident at Tinnevelly. 1831: *Out of employ.* 1832: *At home on absentee allowance.* (*Annuitant on the Fund from 1st May* 1834.) *Died, 23d October* 1852, *in England.*

MONTGOMERIE, HUGH.—1812: Writer. 1816: Head Assistant to the Collector and Magistrate of Vizagapatam; Assistant Magistrate at Vizagapatam. 1826: Deputy Commercial Resident at the Factory of Ingeram. 1830: Sub-Collector and Joint Magistrate of Tinnevelly. 1832: Judge and Criminal Judge of Nellore. 1833: *At home on absentee allowance.* 1835: *Returned to India, per "Mary Ann."* 1836: Acting Third Judge of the Provincial Court, Northern Division; Acting Judge and Criminal Judge of Rajahmundry. 1838: Acting Second Judge of the Provincial Court, Northern Division; Judge and Criminal Judge of Cuddapah; Third Judge of the Provincial Court, Northern Division. 1840: Second Judge of the Provincial Court of Appeal and Circuit, Northern Division. 1841: First Judge of the Provincial Court of Appeal and Circuit, Northern Division. 1842: *Resigned the service, 12th May. (Annuitant on the Fund, 1842.) Died, 24th February 1864, in England.*

MONTGOMERY, Sir HENRY CONYNGHAM, Bart.—1825: Writer. 1827: Assistant to the Principal Collector and Magistrate of Nellore. 1828: Head Assistant to the Principal Collector of Nellore; Head Assistant to the Principal Collector of Tanjore. 1830: Acting Additional Sub-Collector of Salem; Additional Sub-Collector and Joint Magistrate of Tanjore. 1832: Sub-Collector and Joint Magistrate of Tanjore. 1836: *At home for his health.* 1838: *Returned to India, per "Windsor."* 1839: Acting Principal Collector and Magistrate of Bellary. 1840: Sub-Collector and Joint Magistrate, Tanjore. 1841: Principal Collector and Magistrate of Tinnevelly. 1843: Collector and Magistrate of Tanjore. 1847: Secretary to Government in Revenue and Judicial Department. 1850: Chief Secretary to Government. 1855: Chief Secretary to Government; Provisional Member of Council; afterwards Member of Council, and Chief Judge of the Sudder Dewannee and Sudder Foujdarry Adawluts. 1857: *Resigned the service, 29th October, in India. (Annuitant on the Fund, 1859.) Died, 24th June 1878, in England.*

MOORE, GEORGE.—1796: Writer. 1799: Assistant in the Military, Secret, and Political Department. 1802: Register of Passports. 1804: Head Assistant to the Secretary in the Revenue and Judicial Department, and Postmaster-General. 1806: Deputy Accountant-General and Commercial. 1812: Superintendent of Stamps. 1814: Civil Auditor. *Died, 12th December 1834, at Madras.*

MOORE, THOMAS PERRING.—1806: Writer. 1808: Assistant

to the Secretary to the Board of Revenue. *Lost on his passage home, 14th March 1809, in the ship "Jane Duchess of Gordon."*

MOORE, MARK.—1831: Writer. 1834: Assistant to the Principal Collector and Magistrate of Salem. *Died, 26th November 1835, at Madras.*

MORDAUNT, CHARLES.—1765: Writer and Assistant at Cuddalore. 1771: Factor and Assistant at Cuddalore. 1774: Junior Merchant. 1776: Senior Merchant. 1778: *At home; Returned to India. Died, April 1780.*

MOREHEAD, WILLIAM AMBROSE.—1824: Writer. 1828: Assistant to the Principal Collector, North Arcot; subsequently appointed Register of the Zillah of Chingleput. 1830: Head Assistant to the Principal Collector and Magistrate, Chingleput. 1832: Sub-Collector and Joint Magistrate, Cuddapah; afterwards Acting Judge and Criminal Judge, Cuddapah. 1833: Acting Assistant Judge and Joint Criminal Judge, Chingleput. 1834: Acting Sub-Collector and Joint Magistrate, North Arcot; Officiating Sub-Collector and Magistrate, South Arcot; Acting Assistant Judge and Joint Criminal Judge, Chingleput. 1836: Assistant Judge and Joint Criminal Judge, Chingleput; *(Proceeded to Europe on private affairs.)* 1840: Acting Deputy Collector, Madras; Acting Secretary to the College Board; and Acting Judge and Criminal Judge at Chingleput. 1841: Acting Judge and Criminal Judge, Canara; Acting Judge and Criminal Judge at Madura; and Judge and Criminal Judge, Chingleput. 1843: Acting Principal Collector and Magistrate, Madura; and Civil and Sessions Judge, Chingleput. 1846: Officiating Puisne Judge of the Court of Sudder and Foujdarry Adawlut. 1847: Third Puisne Judge of the Court of Sudder and Foujdarry Adawlut; also Member of the College Board. 1851: *Absent on medical leave.* 1854: President of the Board of Examiners. 1855: Provisional Member of Council. 1856: *Proceeded to Europe on medical leave.* 1857: Member of Council, and Chief Judge of the Court of Sudder and Foujdarry Adawlut. 1859: Commissioner for Inquiring into the System of Judicature in the Presidency. 1860: Governor and President in Council. 1862: *Resigned the service, 29th October. (Annuitant.)*

MORRIS, JOHN CARNAC.—1818: Writer. 1820: Assistant to the Chief Secretary to Government. 1821: Head Assistant to the Collector and Magistrate of Masulipatam. 1822: Senior Deputy Secretary to the Board of Revenue. 1823: Deputy

Teloogoo Translator to Government. 1824: Secretary to the College Board; Secretary to the Civil Fund. 1825: Assistant to the Collector of Sea Customs at the Presidency. 1829: *At home on absentee allowance.* 1831: *Returned to India, per "Duke of Buccleuch;"* Acting Secretary to the Board of Revenue. 1832: Secretary to the Board of Revenue and Teloogoo Translator to Government; Acting Register of the Sudder and Foujdarry Adawlut; Trustee to St. George's Church. 1833: Register to the Sudder and Foujdarry Adawlut. 1834: Acting Secretary and Treasurer to the Government Bank; Acting Sub-Treasurer. 1835: Superintendent and Treasurer of the Government Bank, and Sub-Treasurer. 1837: Member of the Mint Committee. 1838: Acting Temporary Member of the Board of Revenue. 1839: Civil Auditor and Superintendent of Stamps, Member of the College Board and Mint Committee, also Teloogoo Translator to Government. 1843: Civil Auditor and Superintendent of Stamps, Member of the College Board, and Teloogoo Translator to Government. 1846: *Resigned the service,* 1st *July.* (*Annuitant on the Fund,* 1846.) *Died,* 2d *August* 1858, *in England.*

MORRIS, HENRY.—1823: Writer. 1825: Assistant to the Collector and Magistrate of Nellore. 1826: Head Assistant to the Principal Collector and Magistrate of Northern Division of Arcot. 1828: Head Assistant to the Principal Collector and Magistrate of South Arcot. 1829: Sub-Collector and Joint Magistrate of Madura. 1830: Sub-Collector and Joint Magistrate of Coimbatore. 1835: Acting Assistant Judge of Salem; Acting Deputy Collector of Madras. 1836: Commissioner for Drawing Lotteries; Officiating Police Magistrate. 1837: *At home on absentee allowance.* 1841: *Returned to India.* 1842: Third Judge of the Provincial Court of Appeal and Circuit, Western Division. 1844: Civil and Sessions Judge, Calicut. 1852: *Resigned the service,* 30*th July.* (*Annuitant on the Fund,* 1852.)

MORTLOCK, HENRY.—1808: Writer. 1810: Assistant to the Register of the Sudder and Foujdarry Adawlut; Fixed Examiner to the Sudder and Foujdarry Adawlut. 1811: Deputy Persian Translator to Government; First Assistant to the Sudder Adawlut. 1813: Deputy Register to the Sudder and Foujdarry Adawlut. 1816: *At home.* 1818: *Returned to India;* Cashier to the Government Bank. 1819: Deputy Persian Translator to Government. 1820: Deputy Register of the Sudder Adawlut; Secretary to the

College Board. 1823: *At home.* 1824: *Resigned, 1st September, in England.* (*Accepted an Annuity from the Civil Fund from 1st January* 1828.) *Died, 13th February* 1837, *in England.*

MOWBRAY, GEORGE.—1771: Senior Merchant, with fixed Appointment as Accountant. 1791: Member of the Board of Revenue. 1793: *At home; Retired from service.*

MUNRO, ROBERT DUNCAN.—1765: Writer. 1771: Factor. 1774: Junior Merchant. 1776: Senior Merchant; Paymaster at Chingleput. 1791: Second in Council at Ganjam. 1792: *At home. Died,* 1795, *in India.*

MUNRO, JAMES A.—1806: Writer. 1807: Assistant to the Collector of the Northern Division of Arcot. 1808: *Out of employ;* Acting Register of the Zillah of Salem. 1809: Register of the Zillah of Salem. 1812: Register of the Zillah of Coimbatore. 1821: Sub-Collector and Magistrate of Coimbatore. 1823: Collector and Magistrate of Tinnevelly. *Died, 23d May* 1827, *at Palamcottah.*

MUNRO, JOHN COLLINS.—1817: Writer. 1819: Employed in the late Peishwah's Dominions. *Died, 11th December* 1824, *at Kittoor.*

MURRAY, The HON. LEVESTON GRANVILLE KEITH.—1792: Writer. 1793: Assistant under the Secretary in the Public, Revenue, and Commercial Department. 1796: Deputy Commercial Resident at Salem. 1797: Assistant under the Collector in the First Division of Masulipatam. 1798: Paymaster and Garrison Storekeeper at Innacondah and its Dependencies. 1799: Paymaster and Garrison Storekeeper at Vizagapatam and its Dependencies. 1803: Collector of the Zillah of Vizagapatam. 1805: *Out of Employ.* 1806: Collector of Madras. 1807: General Agent for the Monopoly of Salt. 1809: Military Paymaster-General. 1810: Collector of Rajahmundry. 1812: *Out of employ.* 1814: Superintendent of Investments and in Charge of the Import Warehouse. 1819: Second Member of the Board of Trade. 1820: Collector of Madras. 1828: Superintendent of Stationery. 1830: Collector of Sea Customs at Madras. (*Annuitant on the Fund, 9th May* 1831.) *Died, 6th January* 1837.

MURRAY, MACKENZIE.—1832: Writer. 1833: Assistant under the Principal Collector and Magistrate of Salem. 1836: Acting Register of the Zillah of Canara; Register of the Zillah of Cuddapah. 1838: Acting Head Assistant to the Principal Collector and Magistrate of Nellore. 1839: Register of the Zillah

Court of Cuddapah. 1840: Sub-Collector and Joint Magistrate, Southern Division of Arcot. 1844: *Proceeded on furlough.* 1846: *Returned to India.* 1847: Sub-Collector and Joint Magistrate, Cuddapah. 1854: Collector and Magistrate, Cuddapah. 1860: *Proceeded on furlough.* 1861: *Resigned the service in England.* (*Annuitant on the Fund,* 1861.) *Died,* 14*th February* 1876, *in England.*

NAPIER, FRANCIS.—1796: Writer. 1797: Assistant under the Secretary to the Board of Trade. *Died,* 19*th July* 1797.

NEAVE, WILLIAM AUGUSTUS.—1821: Writer. 1825: Assistant to the Principal Collector and Magistrate of the Northern Division of Arcot. 1826: Head Assistant to the Collector and Magistrate of Salem. 1827: Head Assistant to the Collector and Magistrate of Chingleput. 1828: Head Assistant to the Principal Collector of Coimbatore. 1830: Sub-Collector and Joint Magistrate of Malabar. 1832: Deputy Accountant-General; Acting Mint-Master; Assistant Judge and Joint Criminal Judge of Chingleput. 1836: *At home on absentee allowance.* 1839: *Returned to India;* Acting Judge and Criminal Judge of Salem. 1840: Judge and Joint Criminal Judge of Salem. 1842: Third Judge of the Provincial Court of Appeal and Circuit, Southern Division. 1844: Civil and Sessions Judge, Rajahmundry. *Died on his passage to Europe,* 3*d October* 1844, *on board the "Samarang."*

NELSON, ROBERT.—1816: Writer. 1818: Second Assistant to the Collector and Magistrate of Salem. 1821: Head Assistant to the Collector and Magistrate of Salem; *Leave to St. Helena, and eventually to England.* 1824: *Returned to India;* Head Assistant to the Collector and Magistrate of Madura. 1827: Sub-Collector and Joint Magistrate of Tanjore. 1831: Acting Collector and Magistrate of Trichinopoly. 1832: Acting Collector and Magistrate of Masulipatam; Acting Zillah Judge of Salem; Acting Third Judge of Provincial Court, Centre Division. 1833: Judge and Criminal Judge of Malabar. 1836: Acting Third Judge of the Provincial Court, Southern Division. 1837: *At home on absentee allowance.* 1842: *Absent five years from India.*

NEWBERY, EDWARD.—1829: Writer. 1831: Second Assistant to the Collector of Masulipatam. 1833: Register of the Zillah of Chicacole. 1834: Assistant Judge of Rajahmundry. 1837: Acting Assistant Judge and Joint Criminal Judge of Guntoor. 1838: Assistant Judge and Joint Criminal Judge of Guntoor. 1839:

Acting Judge and Criminal Judge of Cuddapah. 1840: Assistant Judge and Joint Criminal Judge of Guntoor. 1841: *Proceeded on furlough. Died, 27th August 1842, in England.*

NEWBOLT, JOHN DIGBY.—1814: Writer. 1816: Assistant to the Collector of Chingleput; Register of the Zillah of Chittoor. 1818: *At home.* 1822: *Returned to India;* Head Assistant to the Collector and Magistrate of Masulipatam. 1824: Head Assistant to the Collector and Magistrate of Ganjam. *Died, 12th September 1826.*

NEWNHAM, THOMAS.—1799: Writer. 1800: Assistant under the Secretary in the Revenue and Judicial Department. 1803: Register of the Zillah Court of Ramnad. 1805: Officiating Judge and Magistrate of Ramnad. 1806: Judge and Magistrate of the Zillah of Arnee. 1808: British Agent for Captured Property at Tranquebar; Commissioner at Tranquebar; Judge, Magistrate, and Collector of Seringapatam. 1809: Register of the Sudder and Foujdarry Adawlut; Commissioner to Receive Depositions at Madras; Judge and Magistrate of the Zillah of Cuddapah. 1816: Judge and Criminal Judge of Cuddapah. 1821: Acting Judge in Circuit, Centre Division; Judge and Criminal Judge of Cuddapah; Third Judge of Provincial Court of Appeal and Circuit, Northern Division, and Acting Third Judge of Provincial Court of Appeal, Centre Division. 1822: Third Judge of Provincial Court, Centre Division, and Acting in Northern Division. 1824: Second Judge of Provincial Court, Centre Division. 1828: Acting Judge, afterwards Senior Judge of Provincial Court, Western Division, and Acting in Centre Division. 1830: Acting First Judge of Provincial Court, Centre Division; Permitted as First Judge, Western Division, to leave Chittoor for Madras. 1831: Resumed at Tellicherry the Duties of First Judge of Provincial Court, Western Division. 1833: *Resigned the service; Annuitant from 1st May. Died, 29th September 1861, in England.*

NICHOLLS, SOLOMON.—1806: Writer. 1807: Assistant under the Chief Secretary in the Foreign, Political, and Secret Department; Assistant to the Collector of Tinnevelly. 1808: Deputy Commercial Resident at Tinnevelly. 1811: Deputy Commercial Resident at Salem. 1812: *At home.* 1817: *Returned to India;* Deputy Accountant-General in the Military Department. 1822: Deputy Accountant-General in the Military Department, Commercial Accountant, and Auditor. 1826: Judge and Criminal Judge of Madura. 1830: Third Judge, Provincial Court, Southern Division.

1831: *At home on absentee allowance.* 1833: *Returned to India, per "Orient."* 1834: Second Judge of Provincial Court, Northern Division. 1836: *Retired from service. (Annuitant on the Fund.)*

NISBET, JOSIAH.—1807: Writer. 1810: Assistant to the Chief Secretary in the Secret, Political, and Foreign Department. 1811: Assistant to the Collector of Bellary. 1814: Head Assistant to the Collector of Bellary. 1816: Assistant Magistrate of Bellary. 1819: Employed in the late Peishwah's Dominions. 1822: *At home.* 1824: *Returned to India.* 1825: Principal Collector and Magistrate of the Northern Division of Arcot. 1827: Principal Collector and Political Agent at Dharwar, under the Bombay Government. *Died, 5th August 1834, at Dharwar.*

NORMAN, MARTIN.—1852: Writer. 1853: Assistant to Collector and Magistrate, Madura. 1857: Deputy Secretary to Government, Revenue Department. *Died, 16th October 1859, at Chiselhurst.*

NORRIS, HENRY.—1769: Writer. 1774: Factor and Assistant at Vizagapatam. 1778: Junior Merchant. 1780: Senior Merchant. *No trace after 1782.*

OAKELEY, CHARLES.—1767: Writer. 1774: Factor. 1776: Junior Merchant. 1778: Senior Merchant. 1790: *Created a Baronet, 5th June;* Appointed Member of Council of the Governor. 1792: Succeeded as Governor of Madras; *Assumed charge of office, 1st August.* 1794: *Embarked for England, 29th September.*

OAKES, THOMAS.—1770: Writer. 1776: Factor and Assistant at Ganjam. 1778: Junior Merchant. 1782: Senior Merchant. 1792: Senior Merchant and Member of the Board of Revenue. 1795: *At home.* 1802: *In India without employ.* 1803: Second Member of the Board of Revenue. 1804: Senior Member of the Board of Revenue. 1806: *Out of the service.*

OAKES, THOMAS ALEXANDER.—1802: Writer; Assistant to the Secretary in the Revenue and Judicial Department, and Acting Assistant to the Special Commission. 1805: Assistant to the Register in the Zillah of Vizagapatam. 1806: Register of the Zillah of the Eastern Division of the Ceded District. 1808: Subordinate Collector at Coimbatore; First Assistant to the Collector of Nellore. 1811: Collector of Vizagapatam. 1812: Collector and Magistrate of Guntoor. 1823: *At home.* 1828: *Returned to India;* Second Judge of the Provincial Court, Centre Division. 1830: First Judge of the Provincial Court, Centre Division. 1832: Officiating Third Judge of the Sudder and Foujdarry Adawlut. 1838: Officiating Second Judge of the Sudder and Foujdarry Adawlut. 1839: First Judge of the Provincial Court of Appeal and Circuit, Centre Division. 1840: *Proceeded on furlough. Died, 12th September 1840, in London.*

OAKES, HENRY ROBERT.—1804: Writer; Assistant under the Secretary to the Board of Revenue. 1806: Register of the Zillah of Manar Goody. 1808: Acting Register of the Zillah of Madura; Register of the Zillah of Madura. 1809: Register of the Zillah of Vizagapatam. 1811: Assistant Judge of Combaconum. 1813: Collector of Rajahmundry. 1817: *At home.* 1819: *Returned to India;* Commercial Resident at the Ceded Districts. 1820: *Dismissed the service, 25th October, in England.*

OAKES, CHARLES E.—1822: Writer. 1825: Assistant to the Collector and Magistrate of Tinnevelly. 1828: Register of the Zillah of Nellore; Register to the Provincial Court, Northern Division. 1831: *At home on absentee allowance.* 1833: *Returned to India, per "Vansittart;"* Acting Judge and Criminal Judge of Chittoor. 1836: Assistant Judge and Criminal Judge of Guntoor. *Died, 20th August 1837, at Ootacamund.*

OGILVIE, THOMAS.—1771: Writer. 1776: Factor. 1780: Junior Merchant. 1782: Senior Merchant. 1790: *Out of the service.*

OGILVIE, JOHN HUGH DONALD.—1789: Writer. 1790: Assistant under the Secretary in the Military, Political, and Secret Department. 1793: Assistant under the Resident at Ingeram and Maddepollam. 1796: Deputy Commercial Resident at Ingeram. 1798: Deputy Commercial Resident at Ganjam. 1802: Head Assistant to the Manager for the Supply of Beetle, and Collector of Revenue derived from the Sale of Arrack, &c.; Collector of Madras, and Superintendent of Revenue of Home Farm Villages, Arrack and Toddy Quit Rent, and Company's Lands in Black Town. 1806: Second Judge of the Provincial Court, Centre Division. 1807: Collector of Madras. 1809: Mint-Master. 1819: Third Judge of the Sudder and Foujdarry Adawlut. 1820: Fourth Member of Council and President of the Sudder Adawlut. 1821: Senior Member of the Board of Trade. 1824: Member of Council. 1830: *At home on absentee allowance. (Annuitant on the Fund from 1st May 1831.) Died, 10th March, 1851, in England.*

OGILVIE, GEORGE MACARTNEY.—1812: Writer. 1816: Second Assistant to the Collector and Magistrate of the Southern Division of Arcot. 1818: Head Assistant to the Collector and Magistrate of Tanjore. 1823: Sub-Collector and Assistant Magistrate of Cuddapah. 1828: *At home on absentee allowance.* 1832: *Returned to India;* Collector and Magistrate of Ganjam. 1835: Principal Collector and Magistrate of Canara; Third Judge of the Provincial Court, Southern Division. 1836: Acting Principal Collector and Magistrate of the Northern Division of Arcot. 1837: Principal Collector and Magistrate of North Arcot. 1842: *Resigned the service. (Annuitant on the Fund,* 1842.) *Died,* 5*th February* 1878, *in England.*

OGILVIE, William Cecil.—1825: Writer. 1827: Assistant to the Collector and Magistrate of Masulipatam. 1828: Head Assistant to the Collector and Magistrate of Masulipatam; Secretary to the Board of College and for Public Instruction; and Deputy Teloogoo Translator to Government. 1829: Head Assistant to the Secretary in the Revenue Department. 1831: Additional Sub-Collector and Joint Magistrate of Canara. 1832: Additional Sub-Collector and Joint Magistrate of Salem. 1833: Sub-Collector and Joint Magistrate of Salem. 1838: Acting Collector and Magistrate of Trichinopoly. 1839: Acting Judge and Criminal Judge of Combaconum. 1842: Judge and Criminal Judge, Bellary. 1844: Civil and Sessions Judge, Bellary. 1845: *Proceeded on furlough; Resigned the service,* 17*th September, in England. (Annuitant on the Fund,* 1849.) *Died,* 24*th April* 1868, *in England.*

OGILVIE, Alexander.—1845: Writer. 1848: Assistant to Collector and Magistrate, Chingleput. 1851: *Proceeded on furlough.* 1856: *Absent from India five years.*

OLIVER, William.—1800: Writer. 1805: Second Assistant, afterwards First Assistant, to the Register of the Sudder and Foujdarry Adawlut. 1807: Deputy Persian Translator to Government. 1811: Secretary to the Board of Revenue; Persian Translator to Government. 1813: Register of the Sudder and Foujdarry Adawlut. 1824: Second Judge, afterwards First Judge, of the Provincial Court, Southern Division. 1826: Third Puisne Judge of the Sudder and Foujdarry Adawlut. 1830: Second Puisne Judge of the Sudder and Foujdarry Adawlut. 1831: Member of Council, and President of the Sudder Court. 1836: *Retired from service. (Annuitant on the Fund.)*

ONSLOW, Arthur Pooley.—1822: Writer. 1826: Assistant to the Principal Collector and Magistrate of Coimbatore. 1828: *Leave to sea for his health.* 1830: Head Assistant to the Collector of Masulipatam. 1831: Head Assistant to the Collector and Magistrate of Bellary. 1832: Acting as Cashier to the Government Bank; Acting Judge and Joint Criminal Judge of Chingleput. 1833: Sub-Collector and Joint Magistrate of Bellary. 1835: Secretary to the Board of Revenue. 1839: Collector and Magistrate of Trichinopoly. 1850: Collector, Magistrate, and Agent to the Governor, Ganjam. 1854: *Proceeded on furlough.* 1855: *Resigned the service, 1st January, in India. (Annuitant on the Fund,* 1856.)

ONSLOW, THOMAS.—1831: Writer. 1833: Assistant to Principal Collector and Magistrate, Bellary. 1834: Acting Register to the Zillah Court of Cuddapah. 1835: At first Acting, and afterwards Register to the Zillah Court of Chittoor. 1840: Acting Deputy Collector of Land Customs, Madras. 1841: Acting Assistant Judge and Joint Criminal Judge, Rajahmundry. 1842: *Proceeded on furlough.* 1845: Acting Assistant Judge of the Zillah of Calicut. 1846: Acting Sub-Judge of the Zillah of Calicut. 1847: Sub-Judge of the Zillah of Cuddapah, and Acting Civil and Sessions Judge of Cuddapah. 1850: Sub-Judge of the Zillah of Calicut. 1852: *Proceeded to England.* 1856: Acting Civil and Sessions Judge, Guntoor. 1857: Civil and Sessions Judge, Guntoor. 1862: *On medical leave for* 15 *months;* Civil and Sessions Judge, Masulipatam. 1863: Civil and Sessions Judge of Nundial, and of Chittoor; also Collector and Magistrate of South Canara. 1864: *Resigned the service, 1st April. (Annuitant.) Died, 2d July* 1882, *at Ootacamund.*

ORAM, WILLIAM.—1772: Writer. 1778: Factor. 1780: Junior Merchant. 1790: Senior Merchant, and Manager of Part of the Havally, Masulipatam. 1792: Member of the Revenue Board. 1793: *At home.* 1800: *Out of the service.*

ORPIN, RICHARD THOMAS.—1778: Writer. *No trace after* 1782.

ORR, JOHN.—1815: Writer. 1818: Second Assistant to the Collector and Magistrate of Coimbatore. 1820: Assistant to the Collector and Magistrate of Malabar; *At home.* 1824: *Returned to India;* Head Assistant to the Collector and Magistrate of Nellore. 1826: Sub-Collector and Assistant Magistrate of Nellore. 1829: Acting Secretary in the Public, Commercial, and Revenue Department; Collector and Magistrate of Salem. 1832: Principal Collector and Magistrate of Salem. 1838: Principal Collector and Magistrate of Cuddapah; Acting Civil Auditor and Superintendent of Stamps; Civil Auditor and Superintendent of Stamps.

1839: *At home on private affairs.* 1842: *Returned to India.* 1843: Accountant-General. 1844: Accountant-General, and Member of the Mint Committee. 1845: *Resigned the service, 30th April.*

OSWELL, W. F.—1827: Writer. 1829: Assistant to the Head Collector of South Arcot. 1831: *At home on absentee allowance. No trace after this date.*

OSWELL, WILLIAM COTTON.—1837: Writer. 1840: Assistant to Principal Collector and Magistrate, Southern Division of Arcot. 1842: Head Assistant to Principal Collector and Magistrate, Southern Division of Arcot. 1844: Head Assistant to Principal Collector and Magistrate, Coimbatore. 1848: *Proceeded on furlough.* 1851: *Resigned the service, 19th March, in England.*

OWEN, ARTHUR MOSTYN.—1832: Writer. 1833: Assistant under the Principal Collector of South Arcot. 1834: Assistant to the Principal Collector of Malabar. 1839: Acting Head Assistant to the Principal Collector and Magistrate of Bellary; Acting Second Assistant to the Accountant-General; Commissioner for Drawing Government Lotteries. 1840: Assistant to Collector and Magistrate, Malabar. 1841: Head Assistant to Collector and Magistrate, Madura. 1844: *Proceeded on furlough.* 1848: *Absent from India five years.*

PALK, THOMAS.—1769: Writer. 1774: Factor. 1778: Junior Merchant. 1780: Senior Merchant. 1790: *At home.* 1793: *Out of the service.*

PALMER, ARCHDALE.—1755: Writer. 1768: Senior Merchant. 1771: Paymaster at Madura. 1774: Second in Council at Masulipatam. 1776: Member of Council of the Governor. 1777: *Recalled by order of the General Court of Proprietors, 9th May.* 1780: *Suspended from the service.*

PARISH, GEORGE.—1796: Writer. 1799: Assistant in the Public, Revenue, and Commercial Department. 1800: Assistant to the Collector of Canara; Head Assistant under the Collector of the Polygar Peishcush. 1803: Subordinate Collector in the Ceded Districts; Collector of the Zillah of Ramnad, and of the Provinces of Dindigul and Madura. 1812: *At home.* 1817: *Out of the service.*

PARKER, ROBERT DEANE.—1829: Writer; Assistant to the Secretary in the Revenue Department. 1831: Head Assistant to the Collector of Trichinopoly. 1832: Acting Deputy Persian Translator to Government; Head Assistant to the Register of the Sudder and

Foujdarry Adawlut; Deputy Persian Translator to Government. 1833: Junior Deputy Secretary to the Board of Revenue. 1835: Acting Sub-Collector of Cuddapah. 1836: Acting Sub-Collector and Joint Magistrate of Nellore. 1837: Sub-Collector and Joint Magistrate of Nellore; Officiating Senior Deputy Secretary to the Board of Revenue. 1838: Acting Sub-Secretary to the Board of Revenue; Acting Principal Collector and Magistrate of Nellore. 1839: Sub-Secretary to the Board of Revenue. 1842: *Proceeded on furlough.* 1844: *Returned to India;* Additional Sub-Collector and Joint Magistrate, Canara. 1845: Sub-Collector and Joint Magistrate, Canara. 1848: Collector and Magistrate, Madura. 1858: Collector and Magistrate, Malabar. 1859: *Resigned the service, 1st May, in India. (Annuitant on the Fund,* 1859.)

PARRY, GEORGE.—1789: Writer. 1790: Acting Deputy Secretary in the Military, Political, and Secret Department. 1793: Examiner and Head Assistant under the Secretary in the Military, Political, and Secret Department; Land Customer and Choultry Register. 1796: Civil Paymaster-General. 1797: Deputy Secretary in the Military, Political, and Secret Department. 1798: *At home for his health.* 1801: *Returned to India;* Special Agent for Conducting the Department of Provision. *Died, 6th September* 1801, *in Bengal.*

PARRY, WILLIAM HENRY.—1816: Writer. 1819: Second Assistant to the Secretary to Government. 1820: Assistant to the Secretary in the Military Department; Register of the Zillah of Nellore. 1828: *At home on absentee allowance. Died, 11th April* 1832, *at Brighton.*

PARSONS, WILLIAM.—1779: Writer. 1790: Senior Merchant; Assistant at Ingeram. 1793: *At home.* 1800: *Out of the service.*

PASKE, GEORGE.—1797: Writer. 1798: Assistant under the Political, Revenue, and Commercial Department. 1799: Assistant under the Collector of Vizagapatam. 1800: Assistant to the Collector of the Third Division of Vizagapatam; Assistant under the Collector of Ganjam. 1802: Assistant to the Collector of Nellore. 1805: Register under the Collector of Nellore and Ongole. 1806: Judge and Magistrate of the Zillah of Masulipatam. 1821: Third Judge of the Provincial Court, Centre Division. *Died on his passage home, April* 1822, *on board the "Cambridge."*

PASKE, JOHN BENSLEY GRESHAM PAGE.—1806: Writer. 1807: Assistant to the Register of the Zillah of Vizagapatam. 1811:

Register of the Zillah of Vizagapatam. 1814: *At home.* 1817: *Returned to India;* Register to the Provincial Court, Northern Division. 1824: Judge and Criminal Judge of Chingleput. 1830: Third Judge of the Provincial Court, Centre Division. 1832: First Judge of the Provincial Court, Northern Division. 1840: *Retired from the service.* (*Annuitant on the Fund,* 1840.) *Died, 3d August* 1859, *in England.*

PATERNOSTER, JOHN. — 1815: Writer. 1818: Second Assistant to the Collector and Magistrate of Vizagapatam. 1820: Register of the Zillah of Ganjam. 1821: Register of the Zillah of Bellary. 1824: Register of the Zillah of Masulipatam. 1827: Register to the Zillah of Salem. 1828: Register of the Zillah of Combaconum. 1831: Register of the Zillah of Chingleput. 1833: Register to the Provincial Court, Northern Division. 1834: *At home on absentee allowance.* 1837: *Returned to India, per "Sophia;"* Judge and Criminal Judge of Cuddapah. 1838: Judge and Criminal Judge of Bellary. 1843: *Out of employ.* 1844: *Proceeded on furlough.* 1846: *Resigned the service, 30th April.* (*Annuitant on the Fund,* 1846.)

PATERNOSTER, RICHARD.—1821: Writer. 1824: Assistant to the Collector and Magistrate of Bellary. 1825: Assistant to the Principal Collector and Magistrate of Malabar. 1827: *At home on absentee allowance. Pensioned, 6th January* 1830, *in England.*

PEARCE, THOMAS.—1783: Writer; Assistant in the Select Office. 1785: Clerk to the Court of Requests. 1786: Assistant to the Secretary in the Revenue Department, and Deputy Import Warehouse-keeper. 1789: Assistant to the Accountant-General; Accountant-General in the Mayor's Court; and Deputy Postmaster-General. 1790: Deputy Accountant and Accountant-General in the Mayor's Office. 1792: Provisional Paymaster at Tanjore. *Died, February* 1794.

PEILE, JOHN HENRY.—1796: Writer. 1798: Assistant in the Military, Political, and Secret Department. 1799: Head Assistant under the Resident at Mysore. 1800: Postmaster at Mysore. 1803: Secretary to the Resident at Mysore. 1806: Judge and Magistrate of Cuddapah. 1809: Secretary to Government in Military Department, and Superintendent of Stamps. 1811: Persian Translator to Government; Third Judge of the Provincial Court, Southern Division. 1818: *At home.* 1823: *Out of the service.*

PELLY, CHARLES.—1830: Writer. 1832: Second Assistant to Principal Collector and Magistrate, Bellary. 1834: Acting Head

Assistant to Principal Collector and Magistrate, Bellary. 1835: Head Assistant to Principal Collector and Magistrate, Bellary. 1837: Acting Sub-Collector and Joint Magistrate, Bellary. 1838: Sub-Collector and Joint Magistrate, Bellary. 1841: Acting Judge and Criminal Judge, Bellary. 1844: *Proceeded to Europe on furlough.* 1848: Acting Collector and Magistrate, Bellary. 1850: Collector and Magistrate, Bellary. 1859: Member of the Board of Revenue, and Acting President of the Board of Examiners. 1862: Government Director of the Bank of Madras. 1863: Acting President of Income Tax Commission, and Commissioner for the Uncovenanted Civil Service Examination. 1867: *Resigned the service, 15th January.* (*Annuitant.*)

PERRING, PETER.—1759: Writer. 1768: Junior Merchant. 1771: Senior Merchant, and Second in Council at Vizagapatam. 1778: Member of the Council of the Governor. 1781: *Dismissed the service.*

PERRING, RICHARD.—1779: Writer. *No trace after* 1780.

PETER, ROUS.—1801: Writer. 1804: Assistant under the Collector of Trichinopoly. 1805: Register under the Principal Collector of Tanjore. 1806: Register of the Zillah of Trichinopoly. 1807: Assistant to the Collector of Dindigul and Madura. 1812: Collector and Magistrate of Dindigul and Madura. 1825: Principal Collector and Magistrate of Madura. *Died, 6th August* 1828, *at Madura.*

PETERS, EDWARD.—1837: Writer. 1838: Assistant to the Principal Collector and Magistrate of Tanjore. 1839: Acting Head Assistant to the Collector and Magistrate of Masulipatam. 1840: Second Assistant to Accountant-General. 1841: Assistant to Collector and Magistrate of Chingleput. 1843: Head Assistant to Collector and Magistrate of Coimbatore; *Proceeded on furlough.* 1846: *Returned to India.* 1847: *Proceeded on furlough.* 1851: *Absent from India five years.*

PETRIE, WILLIAM.—1765: Writer. 1771: Factor. 1774: Junior Merchant. 1776: Senior Merchant; *At home.* 1778: *In India.* 1782: *At home.* 1790: Member of the Council of the Governor. 1793: *At home.* 1800: President of the Board of Revenue, and Member of the Council of the Governor. 1809: Appointed Governor of the Prince of Wales Island. *Died, 27th October* 1816, *at Prince of Wales Island.*

PHILLIPS, GEORGE.—1812: Writer. 1815: Assistant to the Register of the Provincial Court, Centre Division. 1816: Head Assistant to the Collector of Trichinopoly; Assistant Magistrate of

Trichinopoly. 1823: Sub-Collector and Assistant Magistrate of Coimbatore. *Died, 5th April 1825, at Coimbatore.*

PHILLIPS, HENRY DOMINIC.—1830: Writer. 1832: Acting Second Assistant to Principal Collector and Magistrate, Nellore; Register of the Zillah of Nellore. 1835: Acting Head Assistant to Principal Collector and Magistrate, Nellore; and Register to the Zillah Court there. 1836: Acting Assistant Judge and Joint Criminal Judge, Guntoor. 1837: Junior Deputy Secretary to the Board of Revenue; Officiating Senior Deputy Secretary to the Board of Revenue; Acting Assistant Judge and Joint Criminal Judge, Salem; Acting Assistant Judge and Joint Criminal Judge at Madura. 1838: Assistant Judge and Joint Criminal Judge, Madura; Acting Second Assistant to the Accountant-General; Acting Sub-Secretary to the Board of Revenue; Acting Deputy Register of the Sudder and Foujdarry Adawlut. 1839: Assistant Judge and Joint Criminal Judge of the Auxiliary Court, Trichinopoly; Acting Senior Deputy Register to the Sudder and Foujdarry Adawlut; and Commissioner for Government Lotteries. 1842: Acting Register to the Sudder and Foujdarry Adawlut. 1843: Acting Register to the Sudder and Foujdarry Adawlut, and Sub-Judge, Combaconum. 1846: Sub-Judge, Madura. 1847: Agent to the Governor of Madras at Kurnool and Bunganapilly. 1850: Collector and Magistrate, Salem. 1853: *Proceeded to England.* 1856: *In India, and without employ.* 1857: Acting Collector and Magistrate, and Resident Commissioner at Tanjore; also Civil and Session Judge at Mangalore, and at Madura; 1858: Collector and Magistrate, and Resident Commissioner at Tanjore; also Puisne Judge of the Court of Sudder and Foujdarry Adawlut. 1859: President of the Board of Examiners; Commissioner for the Affairs of the late Rajah of Tanjore. 1862: Judge of the High Court of Judicature, Madras. 1864: Provisional, afterwards Member of Council of the Governor of Fort St. George. 1869: *Resigned the service, 12th November.* (*Annuitant.*)

PHILLIPS, ALEXANDER WILLIAM.—1839: Writer. 1841: Assistant to Collector and Magistrate, Tanjore. 1842: Acting Register of the Zillah Court of Combaconum. 1843: Acting Head Assistant to Collector and Magistrate, Trichinopoly. 1845: Acting Head Assistant to Collector and Magistrate, North Arcot; Acting Sub-Judge of the Zillah of Chittoor; Acting Head Assistant to Collector and Magistrate, North Arcot. 1846: Head Assistant to Collector and Magistrate, Salem, and at Chingleput.

1850: *Proceeded to Europe on furlough.* 1853: Special Assistant to Collector and Magistrate, Tanjore. 1854: Acting Sub-Judge, Madura. 1855: Acting Civil and Sessions Judge, and Sub-Judge, at Madura. 1856: Acting Civil and Sessions Judge, Madura. 1859: Acting Civil and Sessions Judge, Tinnevelly, and at Salem. 1861: Civil and Sessions Judge of Chingleput. 1862: *On medical leave.* 1863: Collector and Magistrate of Godavery District. 1864: Acting Civil and Sessions Judge, Ootacamund. 1866: *On 3 months' special leave;* Civil and Sessions Judge, Ootacamund. 1867: *On medical leave to Europe for 27 months.* 1869: *Resigned the service, 27th April, in England.* (*Annuitant.*) *Died, 25th February* 1883, *at Southsea.*

PHIPPS, CONSTANTINE.—1791: Writer. 1792: Assistant under the Secretary in the Public, Commercial, and Revenue Department. 1793: Assistant under the Secretary to the Revenue Board. 1794: Assistant to the Accountant to the Revenue Board. *Died, 15th April* 1794.

PINDER, JAMES ROSE.—1790: Writer. 1791: Assistant under the Secretary to the Board of Trade. *Died, 21st February* 1793.

PLACE, LIONEL.—1783: Writer. 1785: Assistant to the Secretary to the Select Committee. 1786: Assistant to the Secretary in the Military Department, and Clerk to the Committee of Stores; Assistant at Cuddalore. 1788: Assistant to the Accountant to the Board of Revenue. 1789: Deputy to the Accountant to the Board of Revenue. 1790: Accountant to the Board of Assumed Revenue. 1791: Accountant to the Board of Revenue. 1796: Collector in the Jaghire. 1799: *At home.* 1802: *Returned to India;* Acting Second Member of the Board of Revenue. 1803: *At home.* 1807: *Out of the service.*

PLUMER, HALL.—1769: Writer. 1774: Factor. 1778: Junior Merchant. 1780: Senior Merchant. *No trace after* 1782.

POPHAM, STRACHAN IRVINE.—1828: Writer. 1829: Assistant to the Collector of Tinnevelly. 1830: Assistant to the Collector of Salem. 1831: Second Assistant to the Collector and Magistrate of Tinnevelly. 1832: Acting Assistant Judge and Joint Criminal Judge of Salem; Head Assistant to the Principal Collector of Salem. 1834: Superintendent of a Division in Mysore. 1839: *At home on absentee allowance.* 1844: *Absent from India five years.*

PORCHER, JOSIAS DU PRÉ.—1778: Writer. 1790: Senior Merchant, Member of the Board of Trade, and Clerk to the Committee of Works. 1792: Member of the Board of Trade, Mayor of Madras, and Military Storekeeper. 1800: *At home, and retired from the service.*

PORTER, RICHARD TINDAL.—1825: Writer. 1827: Assistant to the Principal Collector and Magistrate of Coimbatore. 1828: Head Assistant to the Principal Collector and Magistrate of Coimbatore; Head Assistant to the Principal Collector of Chingleput. 1829: Deputy Tamil Translator to Government. 1830: Junior Deputy Secretary to the Board of Revenue. 1831: Senior Deputy Secretary to the Board of Revenue. 1837: *At home on absentee allowance.* 1840: *Returned to India.* 1841: Sub-Secretary to the Board of Revenue. 1843: Collector and Magistrate, Masulipatam. 1852: *Out of employ.* 1854: Civil Auditor and Superintendent of Stamps. 1855: *Resigned the service, 1st May, in India. (Annuitant on the Fund,* 1856.) *Died, 9th December* 1879, *in England.*

PORTIS, GEORGE.—1781: Writer. 1783: Assistant to the Secretary to the Select Committee; *At home. No trace after* 1783.

POWNEY, GEORGE.—1779: Writer. 1790: Senior Merchant. 1791: Resident at Travancore, and Paymaster of Troops there. 1800: *At home, and retired from the service.*

POWNEY, HENRY SAVERNE.—1781: Writer. 1783: Assistant at Vizagapatam. *No trace after* 1785.

POWNEY, EDWARD.—1797: Writer. 1799: Assistant under the Secretary in the Military, Political, and Secret Department. 1800: Assistant Collector of Tanjore. 1803: Register to the Adawlut of the Zillah of Salem. 1806: Register to the Court of Appeal and Circuit, Southern Division. 1810: Judge and Magistrate of the Zillah of Combaconum. 1823: *At home. (Retired on the Annuity Fund, 8th January* 1828.) *Died, 3d January* 1855, *in England.*

PRENDERGAST, THOMAS.—1826: Writer. 1828: Assistant to the Principal Collector of Tanjore. 1829: Acting Head Assistant to the Principal Collector of Nellore. 1830: Head Assistant to the Principal Collector of Nellore. 1831: Acting Sub-Collector and Joint Magistrate of Nellore. 1833: Acting Assistant Judge and Joint Criminal Judge at Guntoor. 1834: Assistant Judge and Joint Criminal Judge of Tinnevelly. 1838: *At home on absentee allowance.* 1841: *Returned to India.* 1842: Sub-Collector and Joint Magistrate, Salem. 1844: Collector and Magistrate, Rajahmundry. 1855: Collector and Magistrate, and Agent to Governor, in Ganjam; *Proceeded on furlough.* 1858: *Retired from the service, 27th March, in India. (Annuitant on the Fund,* 1859.)

PRENDERGAST, GUY LUSHINGTON.—1827: Writer. 1829:

Assistant to the Secretary in the Revenue Department. 1830: Assistant to the Resident at Mysore; Senior Assistant to the Register of the Sudder and Foujdarry Adawlut; Superintendent of Government Lotteries. 1832: Senior Deputy Register of the Sudder and Foujdarry Adawlut. 1838: *At home on absentee allowance.* 1839: *Returned to India per "General Kyd."* 1840: Assistant Judge and Joint Criminal Judge, Malabar; Deputy Accountant-General. 1857: Accountant-General and Member of the Mint Committee. 1859: *Dismissed the service, 3d September, in India.*

PRINGLE, Alexander. — 1766: Writer. 1771: Factor. 1774: Junior Merchant, and Assistant at Masulipatam. 1778: Senior Merchant. 1790: *Out of the service.*

PRINGLE, John Robert.—1835: Writer. 1837: Doing Duty as an Assistant under the Collector of Chingleput. 1838: Assistant to the Collector and Magistrate of Tinnevelly. 1841: Head Assistant to the Collector and Magistrate of Tinnevelly. 1846: Head Assistant to the Collector and Magistrate of Madura. 1847: Head Assistant to the Collector and Magistrate of Nellore. *Died, 5th September* 1847, *on board the "Mary Ann."*

PROCTOR, George.—1767: Writer. 1774: Factor. 1776: Junior Merchant. 1778: Senior Merchant. 1790: *At home.* 1795: *Out of the service.*

PURVIS, Arthur.—1831: Writer. 1834: Assistant to Principal Collector, Nellore. 1835: Assistant to Principal Collector and Magistrate, Nellore. 1837: Acting Assistant to Collector and Magistrate, Cuddapah, and Acting Head Assistant to Principal Collector and Magistrate, Nellore. 1838: Head Assistant to Principal Collector and Magistrate, Masulipatam. 1839: Head Assistant to Principal Collector and Magistrate, Nellore. 1840: Acting Register of the Zillah Court of Nellore. 1842: Acting Sub-Collector and Joint Magistrate, Nellore. 1843: Sub-Collector and Joint Magistrate, Nellore. 1845: *Proceeded to Europe on furlough.* 1848: Acting Sub-Collector and Joint Magistrate, Nellore. 1849: Sub-Collector and Joint Magistrate, Nellore. 1851: Acting Collector and Magistrate, Guntoor. 1854: Collector and Magistrate, Rajahmundry. 1859: Collector and Magistrate, Godavari. 1863: *Resigned the service, 1st June.* (*Annuitant.*) *Died, 1st June* 1877, *in England.*

PYBUS, John.—1742: Writer. 1768: Member of Council of the Governor. 1768: *Arrived in England, in the "Hector."*

PYBUS, John Bryan.—1807: Writer. 1810: Assistant to the Secretary in the Revenue and Judicial Department; Assistant to the Superintendent of Stamps. 1811: Fixed Examiner in the Office of Secretary to the Board of Revenue. 1814: Deputy Secretary to the Board of Revenue; Head Assistant to the Superintendent of Stamps. *Died, 27th January 1820, at Madras.*

PYCROFT, Thomas.—1828: Writer. 1831: Second Assistant to Principal Collector, South Arcot. 1832: Acting Assistant Judge and Joint Criminal Judge, Chingleput; Acting Head Assistant to Principal Collector and Magistrate, South Arcot. 1833: Head Assistant to Principal Collector and Magistrate, South Arcot. 1837: Acting Sub-Collector and Joint Magistrate, and Sub-Collector and Joint Magistrate, South Arcot. 1839: *Proceeded to Europe on furlough.* 1843: Acting Sub-Secretary to the Board of Revenue; Commissioner for Government Lotteries; and Deputy Collector, Madras. 1845: Assistant Judge, Calicut; Secretary to the Board of Revenue; and Acting Tamil Translator. 1850: Secretary to Government in Revenue and Judicial Departments. 1855: Chief Secretary to Government. 1857: *Proceeded to Europe on private affairs.* 1862: Additional, afterwards Provisional, and then Member of Council of the Governor of Fort St. George. 1866: *Knight Commander of the Star of India, 25th May* 1867: *Resigned the service, 29th October.* (*Annuitant.*)

PYNE, George.—1753: Writer. 1768: Senior Merchant. 1771: Resident at Bandermallee. 1774: *Out of the service.*

RADDAN, Edward.—1755: Writer. 1768: Senior Merchant, and Third in Council at Masulipatam. 1774: *Out of the service.*

RAITT, Charles.—1763: Writer. 1768: Factor. *No trace after* 1768.

RAM, George Andrew.—1767: Writer. 1774: Factor. 1776: Junior Merchant. 1778: Senior Merchant. 1791: Resident at Tanjore. 1795: Collector of Guntoor. 1801: *At home.* 1802: *Out of the service.*

RANDAL, Benjamin.—1797: Writer. 1798: Assistant in the Public, Revenue, and Commercial Department. 1799: Second Assistant under the Collector of Dindigul. 1800: Assistant under the Commercial Resident at Cuddalore. 1802: Assistant to the Commercial Resident at Nagore. 1804: Deputy Commercial Resident at Nagore. 1811: Commercial Resident in the Ceded Districts. *Died, 10th July 1819, at Cuddapah.*

RATLIFF, John.—1839: Writer. 1840: Assistant to Collector and Magistrate, Bellary. 1841: Register of the Zillah Court of Bellary. 1843: Assistant to Collector and Magistrate, North Arcot. 1844: Acting Head Assistant to Principal Collector and Magistrate, Nellore. 1845: Assistant to Collector and Magistrate, and Agent to the Governor of Madras, in Vizagapatam; afterwards Head Assistant to Principal Collector and Magistrate, Madura. 1846: Assistant to the Collector and Magistrate, afterwards Head Assistant to Collector and Magistrate, Cuddapah. 1847: Acting Sub-Judge of the Zillah of Cuddapah. 1848: Head Assistant to Collector and Magistrate, Madura. 1849: Acting Sub-Judge, Madura. 1850: *Proceeded to Europe on furlough.* 1853: Acting Sub-Collector and Joint Magistrate, Nellore. 1854: Additional Sub-Collector and Magistrate, Canara; Acting Collector and Magistrate, Nellore. 1855: At first Acting, afterwards Sub-Judge, Cuddapah. 1857: Acting Civil and Sessions Judge, and Acting Sub-Judge, Rajahmundry. 1858: Acting Collector and Magistrate, South Arcot. 1859: Acting Civil and Sessions Judge, Nellore. 1860: Civil and Sessions Judge, Cuddapah. 1861: Officiating Civil and Sessions Judge, Honore. 1862: Civil and Sessions Judge, Bellary. 1864: Civil and Sessions Judge, Nundial. 1865: *On medical leave to Europe for* 15 *months.* 1866: *Resigned the service,* 14*th October.* (*Annuitant.*) *Died,* 18*th May* 1877, *in England.*

RAVENSHAW, John Goldsborough.—1796: Writer. 1797: Assistant under the Secretary to the Board of Trade. 1798: Assistant under the Secretary to the Board of Revenue, and Assistant to the Accountant-General. 1799: Head Assistant to the Collector of Dindigul. 1800: Collector in the Southern Division of the Canara Districts. 1805: Principal Collector of the Southern Division of Arcot. 1809: In Charge of the Revenues of Cuddalore and Pondicherry. 1813: *At home.* 1818: *Out of the service. Elected a Director of the East India Company,* 14*th July* 1819. *Died,* 6*th June* 1840, *at Crawley, Sussex.*

READ, John.—1789: Writer. 1790: Assistant under the Military Secretary. 1791: Acting Deputy Secretary to the Board of Revenue. 1793: Deputy Secretary to the Board of Revenue. 1796: *At home.* 1797: *Returned to India;* Head Assistant to the Collector of the Fourth Division of Masulipatam. 1799: Collector of the Fourth Division of Masulipatam. 1802: Collector of the Third Division of Masulipatam; Second Judge of the Court of Circuit and Appeal, Southern Division. 1809: Acting Puisne Judge of the Sudder and Foujdarry Adawlut. 1811: First Judge of the Court of Appeal and Circuit, Southern Division. 1815: *At home.* 1820: *Out of the service.*

READ, George.—1790: Writer. 1791: Assistant under the Secretary to the Military and Political Department. 1792: Assistant under the Secretary to the Board of Trade. 1793: Assistant under the Accountant to the Board of Revenue. 1796: Deputy Accountant and Malabar Translator to the Board of Revenue. 1798: Accountant to the Board of Revenue. 1800: Deputy Accountant in the Revenue and Commercial Department, and Malabar Translator. 1801: Subordinate Collector under Major M'Leod's Authority. 1802: Third Judge of the Provincial Court, Centre Division. 1809: Second Judge of the Provincial Court, Centre Division. 1812: *At home.* 1816: *Out of the service.*

READ, ALEXANDER.—1796: Writer. 1797: Assistant under the Secretary to the Board of Trade. 1798: Assistant under the Board of Revenue, Assistant under the Collector in Burramehal. 1799: Head Assistant under the Collector in the Canara District. 1800: Collector in the Northern Division of Canara and Soondah. 1805: Principal Collector in Canara. 1816: *At home.* 1820: *Out of the service.*

READE, CHARLES WILLIAM.—1835: Writer. 1836: Under Principal Collector of Canara. 1837: Doing Duty as Assistant to Principal Collector of Canara. 1838: Assistant to Principal Collector and Magistrate, Canara. 1839: Acting Head Assistant to Principal Collector and Magistrate, Canara; and Acting Register to the Zillah Court of Chittoor. 1841: Register to the Zillah Court of Bellary; and Acting Head Assistant, subsequently Head Assistant to Principal Collector and Magistrate, Canara. 1842: Acting Register to the Zillah Court of Canara. 1846: Acting additional Sub-Collector and Joint Magistrate of Canara. 1848: *Proceeded to Europe on furlough.* 1852: Acting Civil and Sessions Judge, Chingleput. 1853: Sub-Judge at Salem. 1856: Acting Civil and Sessions Judge, Salem. 1857: Acting Civil and Sessions Judge, Cuddalore; Collector, Magistrate, and Agent to the Governor of Madras, in Vizagapatam. 1859: *Without employ. On private affairs to England for 6 months.* 1861: Acting Collector and Magistrate of Madras. 1862: Collector and Magistrate of South Arcot. 1871: *Resigned the service, 26th March. (Annuitant.) Died, 27th April* 1884, *in England.*

RENTON, JOHN.—1763: Junior Merchant, with Fixed Appointment as Sub-Accountant. *No trace after* 1774.

RENTON, WILLIAM.—1771: Junior Merchant, with Fixed Appointment as Sub-Accountant. *Died, 8th November* 1775.

REVELL, JOSEPH.—1769: Writer. 1774: Factor. 1778: Junior Merchant. 1780: Senior Merchant. 1791: Manager of the Muglatore Zemindary. 1793: *At home.* 1800: *Out of the service.*

RICE, John Adamson.—1796: Writer. 1799: Second Assistant under the Collector of Canara. *Died, 21st October* 1799.

RICHARDSON, William.—1777: Writer. *No trace after* 1780.

RICHARDSON, John.—1779: Writer. *No trace after* 1782.

RICHARDSON, Francis.—1793: Writer. 1796: Assistant under the Resident at the Presidency. 1797: *At home for his health.* 1799: *Returned to India;* Assistant under the Commercial Resident at Nagore; Deputy Commercial Resident at Nagore. 1801: Commercial Resident at Nagore. 1817: *At home.* 1822: *Out of the service.*

RICKARDS, Richard.—1827: Writer. 1829: Assistant to the Principal Collector of South Arcot. 1830: Head Assistant to the Collector of Vizagapatam. 1832: Head Assistant to the Collector and Magistrate of Trichinopoly. 1833: Register of the Zillah of Salem. *Died, 26th November* 1834, *at Amboorpatt.*

RIDDLE, John.—1797: Writer. 1799: Assistant under the Secretary to the Board of Revenue. 1801: Assistant under the Collector of Salem. 1803: Assistant to the Collector of Coimbatore. 1805: Subordinate Collector of Coimbatore. 1808: Head Assistant to the Collector of Coimbatore. 1811: Acting Judge and Magistrate of the Zillah of Dharapooram; Judge, Magistrate, and Collector of Seringapatam. 1813: Judge and Magistrate of the Zillah of Madura. *Died, on his passage to England, 7th February* 1815, *on board the "Europe."*

ROBERTS, Charles.—1807: Writer; Assistant to the Collector of the Northern Division of Arcot. 1810: Head Assistant to the Collector of Chittoor. 1816: Assistant Magistrate of Chittoor. 1821: Sub-Collector and Assistant Magistrate of Tanjore. 1822: Sub-Collector and Assistant Magistrate of Madura. 1824: Collector and Magistrate of Masulipatam, and in Charge of the Treasury there. 1827: Principal Collector and Magistrate of the Northern Division of Arcot. 1832: Acting Second Member of the Board of Revenue; Third Member of the Board of Revenue. 1837: *At home on absentee allowance. (Retired on Annuity Fund from 8th May* 1838.) *Died, 31st July* 1850, *in London.*

ROBERTSON, Francis William.—1806: Writer. 1807: Assistant under the Secretary to the Board of Revenue. 1808: Deputy Commercial Resident at Masulipatam; Assistant under the Collector of Masulipatam. 1811: Register of the Zillah of Canara. 1812: Assistant to the Collector of Guntoor. 1814: Head Assistant to the Collector of Masulipatam. 1816: Assistant

Magistrate of Masulipatam. 1819: Collector and Magistrate of Rajahmundry. 1824: Collector and Magistrate of Bellary. 1826: Principal Collector and Magistrate of Bellary. *Died, 16th December 1838, at Anantapoor.*

ROBERTSON, ANDREW.—1817: Writer. 1819: Assistant to the Collector and Magistrate of Chittoor. 1820: *At home.* 1825: *Returned to India;* Junior Deputy Secretary to the Board of Revenue. 1826: Tamil Translator to Government. 1827: Senior Deputy Secretary to the Board of Trade. 1830: Secretary and Treasurer to the Government Bank. 1833: Collector of Madras, Tamil Translator, and Member of the College Board. 1844: Second Member of the Board of Revenue; Member of the College Board; and Tamil Translator to Government. 1847: *Proceeded on furlough.* 1850: *Returned to India.* 1851: Collector, Magistrate, and Agent to the Governor, Vizagapatam. 1855: *Resigned the service, 1st May, in India. (Annuitant on the Fund,* 1856.) *Died, 11th January* 1868, *in England.*

ROBINSON, THOMAS.—1796: Writer. 1799: Assistant under the Deputy Commercial Resident at Ganjam. 1802: Head Assistant under the Secretary to the Board of Trade; Assistant to the Collector in the Second Division of Masulipatam. 1805: *At home for his health.* 1808: *Returned to India.* 1811: Deputy Commercial Resident at Ramnad; Deputy Commercial Resident at Nagore. 1814: Deputy Commercial Resident at Ramnad. *Died in* 1816, *in Madras.*

ROBSON, FRANCIS AUGUSTUS.—1795: Writer. 1797: Assistant under the Collector of Vizagapatam. 1799: Assistant under the Collector of Ganjam. 1800: Assistant under the Collector, Second Division of Vizagapatam. 1802: Assistant to the Collector of Ganjam, &c. 1804: Collector of Ganjam, &c. 1807: Paymaster and Garrison Storekeeper in the Ceded Districts. 1812: Commercial Resident at Ganjam. 1818: *Out of employ.* 1821: Deputy Collector of Madras; Superintendent of Stationery. 1823: Treasurer and Secretary to the Government Bank. 1828: Judge and Criminal Judge of Guntoor. 1831: *Out of employ.* 1832: Acting as Judge and Criminal Judge of Rajahmundry. *Died, 3d September* 1833, *at Rajahmundry.*

ROEBUCK, BENJAMIN.—1776: Writer. 1782: Factor. 1790: Senior Merchant. 1791: Land Customer, and Deputy Military Storekeeper. 1792: Civil and Military Paymaster-General; A Member of the Committee for Investigating the King's Army Accounts, and Assay Master. 1801: Assay Master. 1802: Assay

Master, and Military Paymaster-General. 1809: Mint Master. *Died, 13th August 1809, at Vizagapatam.*

ROGERS, Reginald.—1806: Writer. 1809: Assistant to the Chief Secretary in the Secret and Political Department. 1810: Assistant under the Collector of the Zillah of Chingleput. 1812: Deputy Commercial Resident at Tinnevelly. 1821: Register and Assistant to the Collector of Seringapatam. 1822: *At home.* 1825: *Returned to India;* Register of the Provincial Court, Southern Division. 1827: Assistant Judge and Joint Criminal Judge of Salem. (*Retired on the Annuity Fund from 1st January 1828.*) *Died, 23d December 1855, in England.*

ROHDE, John.—1829: Writer. 1832: Second Assistant to Collector and Magistrate, Ganjam. 1835: Acting Register of the Zillah of Rajahmundry, and Acting Assistant Judge and Joint Criminal Judge, Chicacole. 1836: Officiating Assistant Judge, &c., at Chicacole. 1837: Register of the Zillah of Rajahmundry. 1838: Acting Assistant Judge and Joint Criminal Judge, Rajahmundry. 1839: Head Assistant to Collector and Magistrate, Masulipatam. 1840: Assistant Judge and Joint Criminal Judge, Rajahmundry. 1843: Sub-Judge at Rajahmundry. 1844: Acting Civil and Sessions Judge, Masulipatam, and at Rajahmundry. 1847: *Proceeded to Europe on furlough.* 1850: *In India, and without employ for 7 months;* Acting Civil and Sessions Judge, Trichinopoly. 1851: Acting Civil and Sessions Judge at Guntoor, Appointment subsequently confirmed. 1855: Inspector-General of Jails. 1866: *Resigned the service, 21st February.* (*Annuitant.*)

ROOKE, Harry.—1808: Writer. *Died in 1813.*

ROSS, John.—1765: Writer. 1771: Factor and Assistant at Cuddalore. 1774: Junior Merchant. *No trace after 1774.*

ROSS, James.—1770: Writer. *No trace after 1771.*

ROSS, William.—1770: Writer. 1776: Factor. 1778: Junior Merchant. 1782: Senior Merchant. *No trace after 1782.*

ROSS, Robert Charles.—1800: Writer. 1804: Register of the Southern Division of Arcot. 1805: Sub-Collector in the Southern Division of Arcot. 1808: Head Assistant to the Collector in Arcot. 1810: Collector of Cuddapah. *Died, 26th November 1816, at Masulipatam.*

ROUPELL, Thomas Boone.—1830: Writer. 1832: Assistant to the Principal Collector and Magistrate of Coimbatore. 1835: Head Assistant to the Principal Collector and Magistrate of Coimbatore. 1836: *At home on absentee allowance.* 1841: *Returned to India.* 1842: *Out of employ.* 1843: Sub-Secretary to the

Board of Revenue. 1850: Civil and Sessions Judge, Coimbatore. 1857: Civil and Sessions Judge, Cuddalore. 1858: *Proceeded on furlough.* 1859: *Resigned the service, 13th June, in India. (Annuitant on the Fund,* 1859.)

ROWLEY, JOHN.—1777: Writer. 1782: Factor. 1790: Senior Merchant. 1791: Muster-Master in Masulipatam, and Assistant at Maddepollam. 1795: Resident at Maddepollam. 1800: Postmaster-General. 1801: Postmaster-General and Military Paymaster-General. 1803: First Judge of the Court of Circuit and of Appeal for the Southern Division. *Died, 14th September* 1805, *at Pondicherry.*

RUSSEL, DANIEL.—1776: Writer. 1782: Factor. *No trace after* 1782.

RUSSELL, CLAUD.—1752: Writer. 1771: Member of Council of the Governor. 1777: *Recalled by order of the General Court of Proprietors, 9th May.* 1780: *At home.* 1782: Chief of Vizagapatam. *No trace after* 1782.

RUSSELL, GEORGE EDWARD.—1802: Writer. 1803: Assistant to the Secretary in the Revenue and Judicial Department. 1804: Assistant under the Register of the Zillah of Chingleput. 1805: Register of the Zillah of Chingleput. 1812: Collector and Magistrate of Masulipatam. 1815: In Charge of the General Treasury at Masulipatam. 1822: Second Member of the Board of Revenue. 1824: At first Acting, then Senior Member of the Board of Revenue. 1832: Officiating as Resident at the Court of H. H. the Rajah of Mysore; Commissioner to Inquire into the State of Affairs at Ganjam and Vizagapatam. 1834: Member of Council of the Governor, and President of the Revenue and Marine Boards. 1836: Chief Judge of the Sudder and Foujdarry Adawlut. (*Retired on the Annuity Fund in* 1838.) *Died, 20th October* 1863, *in England.*

RUSSELL, JOHN WILLIAM.—1807: Writer. 1809: Assistant to the Collector of the Southern Division of Arcot. 1813: Assistant to the Secretary to the Board of Revenue; Secretary to the Native Fund, and to the Civil Fund Committee. 1817: Deputy Secretary to the Board of Revenue. 1819: *Leave to the Cape of Good Hope, and eventually to Europe.* 1822: *Returned to India;* Private Secretary to the Governor. 1824: Third Judge of Provincial Court, Centre Division. 1826: Principal Collector and Magistrate of Cuddapah. 1828: *At home on absentee allowance.* 1830: *Returned to India, per "Lord Hungerford." Died, 21st August* 1831, *on board the "Claudine."*

RUTHERFORD, ROBERT.—1769: Writer. 1774: Factor and Assistant at Vizagapatam. 1778: Junior Merchant. 1780: Senior Merchant. *No trace after* 1782.

SADLEIR, ANTHONY.—1760: Writer. 1768: Factor. 1771: Senior Merchant. 1774: Resident at Madura. 1776: Resident at Ingeram. 1782: *Out of the service.*

SANDEMAN, ALEXANDER STUART.—1845: Writer. 1848: Assistant to Collector and Magistrate, Guntoor. 1850: *Proceeded on furlough.* 1852: *Returned to India;* Assistant to Collector and Magistrate, Malabar. 1855: Head Assistant to Collector and Magistrate, Malabar. *Died, 29th January* 1855, *at Cannanore.*

SAUNDERS, EDWARD.—1762: Writer. 1768: Factor. 1771: Junior Merchant and Paymaster, Chingleput and Wandi. 1774: Senior Merchant. 1776: Second in Council at Cuddalore. 1791: Member of the Board of Revenue. 1792: *At home.* 1795: *Out of the service.*

SAUNDERS, WILLIAM.—1800: Writer. 1805: Assistant to the Collector of Tinnevelly. 1806: Register of the Zillah of Ramnad. 1808: Acting Assistant to the Collector of Government Customs; Assistant to the Collector of Land Customs. 1810: Gentoo Translator to Government; Assistant to the Collector of Madras. *Died, 22d May* 1811, *on his passage to the Mauritius.*

SAUNDERS, GEORGE WILLIAM.—1806: Writer. 1807: Assistant to the Secretary in the Revenue and Judicial Department; Register of the Zillah of Nellore. 1817: Assistant to the Accountant-General. 1818: Register to the Provincial Court, Southern Division. 1822: Sub-Collector and Assistant Magistrate of Canara. 1823: Collector and Magistrate of Trichinopoly. 1826: Judge and Criminal Judge of Nellore. 1828: Third Judge of the Provincial Court, Centre Division. *Died, 31st July* 1830, *at Cuddapah.*

SAVAGE, GEORGE.—1765: Writer. 1771: Factor. 1774: Junior Merchant. 1776: *At home.* 1780: *In India. No trace after* 1782.

SAVAGE, FRANCIS ARCHIBALD.—1790: Writer; Assistant under the Secretary in the Revenue and Judicial Department, and Under Searcher of the Sea Gate. 1792: Assistant under the Collector of Muglatore. 1796: Assistant to the Collector in the Second Division of Masulipatam. 1800: Assistant to the Collector in the Third Division of Masulipatam; Paymaster and Garrison Storekeeper in the Ceded Districts. 1803: Deputy Postmaster at Bellary. 1807: Commercial Resident at Maddepollam;

Paymaster and Garrison Storekeeper at Masulipatam. 1812: Commercial Resident at Ingeram. 1820: Commercial Resident at the General Factory at Ingeram. 1830: *Out of employ. Died, 23d June 1831, at Madras.*

SAVORY, JAMES SCOTT.—1796: Writer. 1798: Assistant under the Secretary to the Board of Revenue. 1799: Second Assistant under the Collector of Kistnagherry. 1801: Assistant under the Collector of Arcot, South of the River Palar. 1802: Register to the Court of Circuit and Appeal, Centre Division. 1806: Judge and Magistrate of Dharapooran in Coimbatore. 1817: *At home.* 1821: *Resigned the service, 24th October, in England.*

SCOTNEY, BRYAN.—1777: Appointed Military Storekeeper on the First Vacancy. *No trace after* 1782.

SCOTT, ANDREW.—1773: Writer. 1778: Factor. 1782: Junior Merchant. 1790: Senior Merchant, and Manager of the Southern Division of the Masulipatam Havelly, and Assistant there. 1795: Second in Council at Masulipatam, and Collector in Southern Division of Masulipatam Havelly. 1800: Collector of the Third Division of Vizagapatam District. 1801: Collector of Guntoor and of the Palnaud. 1803: First Judge of the Court of Circuit and of Appeal for the Northern Division. 1808: First Judge of the Court of Sudder and Foujdarry Adawlut. 1822: *Without employ. Died, 21st January* 1825, *at Fort St George.*

SCOTT, JOHN CORSE.—1822: Writer. 1825: Assistant to the Principal Collector and Magistrate of Malabar. 1826: Register of the Zillah of Canara. 1828: *At home on absentee allowance.* 1832: *Returned to India;* Acting Assistant, afterwards Assistant Judge and Joint Criminal Judge of Madura. 1834: Assistant Judge and Joint Criminal Judge of Canara. 1835: Acting Zillah Judge of Madura; Assistant Judge and Joint Criminal Judge of Chicacole. 1837: Acting Judge and Criminal Judge of Malabar. 1839: *At home for his health.* 1844: *Resigned the service, 3d January, in England.* (*Annuitant on the Fund,* 1849.) *Died, 17th January* 1870, *in England.*

SCOTT, SEPTIMUS.—1829: Writer. 1830: Assistant under the Principal Collector of Coimbatore. 1832: Acting Assistant Judge and Joint Criminal Judge of Salem; Head Assistant to the Principal Collector and Magistrate of Tanjore. 1836: Acting, afterwards Sub-Collector and Joint Magistrate of Tanjore. 1840: *Proceeded on furlough.* 1842: *Returned to India.* 1844: Agent to the Governor of Fort St. George at Kurnool and Bunganapilly. 1848: Civil and Sessions Judge, Combaconum. 1855: *Proceeded* *on furlough.* 1857: *Resigned the service, 12th August, in England.* (*Annuitant on the Fund,* 1859.)

SEDGLEY, WILLIAM.—1770: Writer. 1776: Factor, and Assistant at Masulipatam. 1778: Junior Merchant. 1782: Senior Merchant. *Died in* 1782.

SEWELL, HENRY.—1807: Writer; Assistant to the Collector of Rajahmundry. 1816: Assistant to the Magistrate of Rajahmundry. *Died, 6th June* 1823, *at Rajahmundry.*

SEWELL, ROBERT BROWNRIGG.—1831: Writer. 1834: Assistant to the Collector of Chingleput. 1836: Acting Secretary to the Board of College and for Public Instruction; Acting Deputy Secretary in the Chief Secretary's Department. 1837: Deputy Secretary in the Chief Secretary's Department; Commissioner for Drawing Government Lotteries; Acting Secretary to the College Board. 1838: *At home on absentee allowance. Died, 4th June* 1840, *at Carlsbad, Germany.*

SHAKESPEAR, WILLIAM OLIVER.—1800: Writer. 1803: Assistant to the Commercial Resident at Vizagapatam and Ganjam. 1806: Assistant to the Register of the Zillah of Masulipatam. 1807: Register of the Zillah of Trichinopoly. 1810: Assistant Judge of Madura. 1815: Judge and Magistrate of Madura. 1826: Third Judge of the Provincial Court, Western Division. 1830: Second Judge of the Provincial Court, Western Division. 1832: First Judge of the Provincial Court, Western Division. *Died, 10th August* 1838, *at Cannanore.*

SHAW, THOMAS.—1778: Writer. *Dead in* 1780.

SHAW, JOSEPH.—1781: Writer. 1783: Assistant to the Secretary to the Select Committee. 1784: Assistant to the Secretary in the Civil Department. 1785: Register of the Choultry Court and Deputy Land Customer. 1786: Assistant in the Military Department; Assistant to the Sea Customer. 1787: Assistant in the Secret Department. 1788: One of the Contractors for Repairs. 1789: Examiner in the Mayor's Court. 1792: *At home. No trace after* 1795.

SHAW, HECTOR.—1801: Writer. 1803: Assistant to the Principal Collector in the Ceded Districts. 1807: Subordinate Collector in the Ceded Districts. *Died, 11th February* 1808, *at Bellary.*

SHEFFIELD, WILLIAM.—1800: Writer on the Bencoolen Establishment. 1804: *Transferred to the Madras Presidency.* 1805: Assistant to the Principal Collector of the Southern Division of Arcot. 1806: Register of the Zillah of Combaconum. 1814: Assistant Judge of the Zillah of South Malabar. 1817: Head Assistant to the Collector and Magistrate of Malabar. 1820: Judge and Criminal Judge of Malabar. 1826: Principal Collector and Magistrate of Malabar. 1831: *At home on absentee allowance.* (*Retired on the Annuity Fund from 1st May 1832.*) *Died, 24th February 1859, in England.*

SHERIDAN, RICHARD BRINSLEY.—1825: Writer. 1828: Head Assistant to the Secretary to the Board of Revenue. 1830: Superintendent of Government Lotteries; Temporary Additional Sub-Collector and Joint Magistrate of Salem. 1831: Assistant to the Commissioners for the Government of Mysore. 1832: *At home on absentee allowance.* 1837: *Out of the service.*

SHERSON, ROBERT.—1793: Writer. 1795: Assistant under the Secretary in the Public, Commercial, and Revenue Department. 1796: Assistant to the Sea Customer. 1798: Deputy Sea Customer. 1800: *At home.* 1801: *Returned to India;* Deputy Collector of Government Customs. 1802: Reporter of External Commerce of Madras Territories. 1807: Joint Assay Master. 1808: *Under temporary suspension from his different employments; At home.* 1816: *Returned to India;* Third Member of the Board of Trade. 1818: Collector and Magistrate of Chittoor. 1819: Postmaster-General. 1821: Treasurer and Secretary to the Government Bank. 1824: *At home.* 1827: *Out of the service.*

SHUBRICK, CHARLES JOHN.—1831: Writer. 1834: Assistant to Principal Collector and Magistrate, Bellary. 1838: *Proceeded to Europe on absentee allowance.* 1841: Acting Register to the Zillah Court of Canara. 1842: Acting Additional Sub-Collector and Joint Magistrate; and Acting Head Assistant to Sub-Collector and Joint Magistrate, Canara. 1843: Register to the Zillah Court of Salem; Acting Sub-Collector and Joint Magistrate, North Arcot; and Extra Assistant to Principal Collector and Magistrate, Salem. 1844: Acting Principal Assistant to Collector and Magistrate, and Agent to the Governor of Madras, in Vizagapatam. 1845: Principal Assistant to Collector and Magistrate, and Agent to the Governor of Madras, in Ganjam. 1847: Acting Collector and Magistrate, and Agent to the Governor in Ganjam. 1849: *Proceeded to Europe on furlough.* 1853: Acting Civil and Sessions Judge, Chingleput. 1855: At first Acting, afterwards Collector and Magistrate, Chingleput. 1859: *On medical leave to Europe for 15 months.* 1860: Civil and Sessions Judge of Chingleput; *On* *medical certificate to Europe for 21 months.* 1861: Collector of Sea Customs, Madras. 1862: Member and Commissioner for the Presidency Town, for Income Tax Acts for 1862–63. 1863: *Resigned the service, 27th July.* (*Annuitant.*)

SILVER, James.—1832: Writer. 1834: Assistant to Principal Collector and Magistrate, Madura. 1836: Assistant to Collector and Magistrate, Tinnevelly. 1838: Officiating Assistant Judge and Joint Criminal Judge, Madura; Acting Head Assistant to Principal Collector and Magistrate, Malabar. 1839: Head Assistant to Principal Collector and Magistrate, Malabar; Acting Assistant Judge and Joint Criminal Judge, Cochin. 1843: Special Assistant to Collector, Tinnevelly. 1844: *Proceeded to Europe on furlough.* 1848: *Without employ for* 10 *months, after which* Additional Sub-Collector and Joint Magistrate, Canara. 1849: Acting Sub-Collector and Joint Magistrate, Canara. 1851: Acting Civil and Sessions Judge, Honore. 1854: At first Sub-Judge, then Acting Civil and Sessions Judge, Combaconum. 1855: Acting Collector and Magistrate, Tinnevelly. 1856: Collector and Magistrate, Tinnevelly. 1858: *On medical certificate to Europe for* 21 *months.* 1859: Resumed Charge of the Collectorate of Tinnevelly. 1865: *Permitted to retire from the service, 31st January.* (*Annuitant.*) *Died, 8th July* 1870, *in England.*

SIMPSON, James.—1778: Writer. *No trace after* 1782.

SINCLAIR, Alexander.—1812: Writer. 1816: Assistant under the Chief Secretary in the Secret, Political, and Foreign Department. 1817: Register of the Zillah of Cuddapah. 1820: *At home.* 1824: *Returned to India;* Sub-Collector and Assistant Magistrate of Tanjore. 1827: *At home on absentee allowance.* 1832: *Out of the service.*

SKARDON, John Humphrey.—1771: Writer. 1776: Factor, and Assistant at Cuddalore. 1780: Junior Merchant. 1782: Senior Merchant. 1791: Secretary to the Military Board, and Inspector of the Jaghire Accounts. 1792: At Permacoil. 1795: Paymaster at Pondicherry. 1800: Paymaster and Garrison Storekeeper at Nellore and its Dependencies. 1803: *At home.* 1806: *Out of the service.*

SKELTON, George Hougham.—1829: Writer. 1832: Acting Register of the Zillah of Cuddapah; *At home on absentee allowance.* 1836: *Returned to India.* 1837: Register of the Zillah of Nellore. 1838: Acting Assistant Judge and Joint Criminal Judge of Cochin. 1841: Sub-Collector and Joint Magistrate, Cuddapah. 1842: *Out of employ.* 1843: *Proceeded on furlough.* 1845: *Resigned the service, 9th July, in England.*

SKELTON, Charles Pitman.—1830: Writer. 1833: Register to the Zillah of Cuddapah. *Died, 21st February 1836, at Sydney.*

SKINNER, Samuel.—1791: Writer. 1792: Assistant under the Secretary in the Public, Commercial, and Revenue Department. 1794: Assistant under the Superintendent of the Noozeed Zemindary. 1796: Assistant Collector of the Third Division of Masulipatam. 1799: Assistant Collector of the Second Division of Masulipatam. 1803: Judge of the Zillah of Rajahmundry. 1806: Judge of the Zillah of Ganjam. 1808: Acting Judge of the Centre Circuit Court. 1809: Third Judge of the Centre Circuit Court. 1812: Second Judge of the Centre Circuit Court. 1820: *At home.* 1825: *Out of the service.*

SLINGSBY, Andrew.—1793: Writer. 1795: Assistant under the Secretary to the Board of Trade. 1796: Assistant under the Secretary in the Public, Commercial, and Revenue Department. 1797: Assistant under the Commercial Resident at Masulipatam. 1804: Assistant to the Commercial Resident at Cuddalore. 1806: *Out of employ. Died, 6th October 1809, at Vepery.*

SMALLEY, Edward.—1806: Writer. 1808: Assistant under the Collector of Tanjore. 1812: Head Assistant to the Collector of Coimbatore; Assistant to the Secretary in the Political, Revenue, and Judicial Department. 1815: Secretary to the Board of Trade; Assistant Judge of Combaconum. 1817: Acting Collector and Magistrate of Rajahmundry. 1818: Acting Collector of Bellary. 1820: Collector and Magistrate of Chingleput. 1823: Collector and Magistrate of Nellore. 1826: Principal Collector and Magistrate of Nellore. 1830: Collector of Madras. 1832: Acting Senior Member of the Board of Revenue; Temporary Member, afterwards Member, of the Board of Revenue. 1833: *At home on absentee allowance.* (*Annuitant on the Fund,* 1836.) *Died, 4th April 1873, in England.*

SMITH, John Lewin.—1752: Writer. 1768: Senior Merchant, and First in Council at Masulipatam; also Member of the Council of the Governor. 1771: *Out of the service.*

SMITH, John.—1752: Writer. 1768: Senior Merchant, and First in Council at Vizagapatam; also Member of Council of the Governor. 1776: *Out of the service.*

SMITH, Charles.—1753: Writer. 1768: Senior Merchant.

1774: Member of the Council of the Governor. 1782: *Out of the service.*

SMITH, CECIL.—1789: Writer. 1790: Assistant under the Accountant and Assistant to the Import Warehouse-keeper. 1793: Examiner and Head Assistant under the Accountant. 1794: Deputy Accountant-General. 1796: Superintendent of the Company's Lands. 1798: Deputy Accountant-General. 1799: Secretary to the Committee of Reform, and Secretary and Accountant to the Commissioners of the Sinking Fund. 1800: Deputy Accountant-General and Civil Auditor. 1801: Accountant-General to the Supreme Court of Judicature. 1802: Accountant-General and Civil Auditor. 1809: Third Judge of the Northern Provincial Court; *At home.* 1812: *Returned to India.* 1813: Senior Member of the Board of Trade. *Died,* 8*th December* 1813, *at the Cape of Good Hope.*

SMITH, JOHN STUART.—1789: Writer. 1790: Assistant under the Secretary in the Public and Revenue Department. 1791: Assistant under the Collector in the Northern Division of Arcot. 1793: Assistant under the Secretary in the Military, Political, and Secret Department. 1796: Assistant under the Military Paymaster-General and Choultry Register. 1797: Register of Native Alienations. 1799: Deputy Commercial Resident at Cuddalore. 1804: Paymaster and Garrison Storekeeper at Vellore and its Dependencies. *Died,* 10*th July* 1806, *at Vellore.*

SMITH, HENRY.—1793: Writer. 1794: Assistant under the Secretary to the Board of Revenue. *No trace after* 1796.

SMITH, JOHN.—1795: Writer on the Bencoolen Establishment. 1803: *Transferred to the Madras Presidency;* Assistant to the Chief Secretary to Government. 1804: Secretary to the Committee of Audit for Captured Dutch Settlements. 1806: Paymaster and Garrison Storekeeper at Seringapatam. 1813: Collector of Vizagapatam. *Died,* 20*th June* 1824, *at Vizagapatam.*

SMITH, HOTHAM PITCHES.—1797: Writer. 1798: Assistant under the Military, Political, and Secret Department. 1799: Deputy Secretary to the Board of Trade. 1800: *Resigned the service,* 7*th February.*

SMITH, FRANCIS CURWEN.—1805: Writer. 1807: *Removed to the Bengal Establishment,* 7*th April.*

SMITH, CHARLES M.—1805: Writer. 1809: Assistant under the Judge and Collector of Seringapatam. 1812: *At home.* 1815: *Out of the service.*

SMITH, SAMUEL.—1812: Writer. 1814: Head Assistant to the Collector of Salem. 1816: Assistant Magistrate of Salem. 1821: Head Assistant to the Principal Collector and Magistrate of Coimbatore. 1822: *At home.* 1827: *Returned to India;* Sub-Collector and Assistant Magistrate of Ganjam. 1830: Judge and Criminal Judge of Malabar. *Died, 1st June* 1831, *at Calicut.*

SMITH, GEORGE ANTHONY.—1820: Writer. 1822: Assistant to the Collector and Magistrate of Rajahmundry. 1824: Head Assistant to the Collector and Magistrate of Masulipatam. 1826: Head Assistant to the Collector and Magistrate of Rajahmundry. 1832: Acting Collector and Magistrate of Vizagapatam. 1833: *At home on absentee allowance.* 1836: *Returned to India, per "Royal William;"* Acting Judge and Criminal Judge of Rajahmundry. 1837: Acting Collector and Register of Rajahmundry. 1838: Collector and Magistrate of Rajahmundry. 1845: *Proceeded on furlough.* 1846: *Returned to India.* 1847: Collector and Magistrate, Nellore. *Died, 1st June* 1849, *at Nellore.*

SMITH, EDMUND.—1827: Writer. 1829: Assistant to the Chief Secretary to Government, and Deputy Persian Translator. 1831: Assistant to the Commissioners for the Government of Mysore. 1832: Junior Deputy Secretary to the Board of Revenue, and Secretary to the Board for the College, and for Public Instruction; Sub-Collector and Joint Magistrate of Malabar; Acting Private Secretary to the Governor. 1838: Acting Deputy Register to the Sudder and Foujdarry Adawlut. 1839: *At home on absentee allowance.* 1847: *Not traced after being on furlough. Died, 16th August* 1873, *in England.*

SMOLLET, PATRICK BOYLE.—1825: Writer. 1828: Head Assistant to the Collector of Guntoor. 1830: Head Assistant to the Secretary to the Board of Revenue. 1832: Assistant to the Commissioners for the Government of Mysore. 1833: Acting Assistant to the Chief Secretary in the Public and Secret Department. 1834: Assistant Judge and Joint Criminal Judge of Madura; Head Assistant to the Principal Collector and Magistrate of Nellore. 1835: Acting Junior Deputy Secretary to the Board of Revenue. 1836: Commissioner for Drawing Lotteries. 1837: Assistant to the Judge and Criminal Judge of Chicacole; Acting Senior Deputy Secretary to the Board of Revenue; Officiating Secretary to the Board of Revenue. 1838: Assistant Judge and Joint Criminal Judge of Rajahmundry; Sub-Secretary to the Board of Revenue, and Acting Secretary. 1839: Secretary to the Board of

Revenue. 1843: Register to the Courts of Sudder and Sudder Foujdarry Adawlut. 1845: Principal Assistant to Collector, Magistrate, and Agent to Governor, Vizagapatam. 1847: Collector, Magistrate, and Agent to Governor, Vizagapatam. 1851: *Proceeded on furlough.* 1854: *Returned to India.* 1855: Collector and Magistrate, Chingleput. 1856: Collector, Magistrate, and Agent to Governor, Vizagapatam. 1857: *Proceeded on furlough; Resigned the service, from 28th December.* (*Annuitant on the Fund,* 1859.)

SMYTH, JAMES.—1801: Writer. *No trace after this date.*

SNEYD, GEORGE.—1789: Writer. 1790: Assistant under the Secretary in the Public and Revenue Department, and Under Searcher at the Sea Gate. 1791: *At home for his health. No trace after* 1791.

SNODGRASS, THOMAS.—1777: Writer. 1782: Factor. 1790: Senior Merchant and Assistant at Ganjam. 1795: Resident at Ganjam. 1800: Collector at Ganjam. 1801: *Without employ.* 1804: *Out of the service.*

SNOW, JOHN.—1776: Writer. 1782: Factor. 1790: Senior Merchant. 1791: Third in Council at Vizagapatam. 1795: Second in Council at Vizagapatam, and Collector of the Vizianagram Zemindary. 1800: *At home.* 1805: *Out of the service.*

SPALDING, JOHN.—1781: Writer. 1783: Assistant to the Secretary to the Select Committee; Assistant to the Auditor of Accounts. 1785: Assistant to the Secretary in the Revenue Department. 1787: Agent for Half-mounting and Clothing the Revenue Battalions. 1789: *At home for his health. No trace after* 1789.

SPARKES, GEORGE.—1828: Writer. 1829: Register of the Zillah of Canara. 1832: Head Assistant to the Principal Collector and Magistrate of Malabar; Acting Sub-Collector and Joint Magistrate of Malabar. 1834: Acting Assistant Judge of Malabar. 1836: Additional Sub-Collector and Joint Magistrate of Canara. 1837: *At home on absentee allowance.* 1840: *Resigned the service, 29th January.*

SPOTTISWOODE, HUGH.—1801: Writer. 1804: Acting Register of the Zillah of Vizagapatam. 1806: Register of the Zillah of Ganjam. 1809: Collector of Ganjam. 1819: Collector and Magistrate of the Northern Division of Arcot; Collector of Madras; Superintendent of Stationery. *Died, 4th April* 1820, *on his passage to the Cape.*

STATHAM, SAMUEL.—1771: Writer. 1776: Factor, and

Assistant at Masulipatam. 1780: Junior Merchant. 1782: Senior Merchant. 1791: Supernumerary Councillor at Masulipatam, and Resident at Nezampatam. *Dead in* 1793.

STEPHENS, PHILIP.—1780: Writer. *No trace after* 1782.

STEVENSON, JAMES ARTHUR ROBERT.—1819: Writer. 1823: Employed under the Commissioners in the Deccan. 1831: *At home on absentee allowance.* 1833: *Returned to India, per "Eliza."* 1834: Acting Mint Master. 1835: Collector and Magistrate of Ganjam. 1837: Acting Commissioner in Goomsur and Sooradah, under the Provisions of the Act of No. 23 of 1836. *Died, 20th June* 1837, *at Chatterpore.*

STODART, ALEXANDER.—1789: Writer. 1790: Assistant under the Secretary in the Public and Revenue Department. 1792: Assistant under the Commercial Resident at Vizagapatam. 1796: Assistant under the Collector of Dindigul. 1797: *Out of employ.* 1798: Assistant to the Collector in the Third Division of Vizagapatam. 1800: Subordinate Collector in the Ceded Districts. 1801: *Out of employ.* 1803: *At home for his health.* 1807: *Returned to India;* Deputy Commercial Resident at Ganjam. *Died, 16th May* 1807, *at Madras.*

STOKES, JOHN.—1807: Writer. 1809: Assistant to the Register of the Sudder and Foujdarry Adawlut. 1811: Assistant to the Collector of Trichinopoly. 1812: Fixed Examiner to the Secretary to the Board of Revenue, and Assistant to the Superintendent of Stamps; Assistant to the Secretary in the Military and Political Department. 1813: French Translator to Government. 1815: Deputy Collector of Sea Customs in Malabar and Canara. 1823: Sub-Collector of Canara. 1824: Secretary in the Revenue and Judicial Department. 1827: Third Member of the Board of Revenue. 1832: Employed as Commissioner in Canara. 1833: *At home on absentee allowance.* (*Annuitant on the Fund from 1st May* 1835.) *Died, 17th June* 1876, *in England.*

STOKES, HUDLESTON.—1826: Writer. 1828: Assistant to the Collector of Tinnevelly. 1830: Head Assistant to the Collector of Tinnevelly. 1831: Head Assistant to the Principal Collector and Magistrate of Canara. 1832: Under the Orders of the Commissioners for the Government of Mysore. 1834: Superintendent of a Division in Mysore. 1838: *At home on absentee allowance.* 1841: *Returned to India.* 1842: Assistant to Commissioner, Kurnool. 1843: Collector and Magistrate, Guntoor. 1854: Collector and Magistrate, Guntoor, and Member of the College Board.

1855: Collector and Magistrate, Guntoor. 1856: Collector of Land Customs, Madras. 1856: *Resigned the service, 15th February, in India.* (*Annuitant on the Fund*, 1857.)

STONE, JOHN MAXWELL.—1755: Writer. 1768: Senior Merchant. 1774: Member of Council of the Governor. 1777: *Recalled by order of the General Court of Proprietors, 9th May* 1782: Chief at Ganjam. *No trace after* 1782.

STONE, JOHN TROTTER.—1779: Writer. *No trace after* 1782.

STONEHOUSE, TIMOTHY VANSITTART.—1816: Writer. 1819: Assistant to the Secretary to the Board of Revenue. 1820: Assistant to the Collector and Magistrate of Nellore. 1826: Head Assistant to the Principal Collector and Magistrate of Nellore. 1828: *At home on absentee allowance.* 1830: *Returned to India, per "Duke of Bedford."* 1831: Acting Collector and Magistrate of Masulipatam. 1832: Collector and Magistrate of Masulipatam, and in Charge of Treasury there; Acting Collector and Magistrate of Tinnevelly; Acting Secretary in the Revenue and Judicial Department; Member of the Mint Committee; Acting Mint Master. 1833: Mint Master and Malyalum Translator to Government. 1835: Principal Collector and Magistrate of Nellore. 1845: Accountant-General and Member of the Mint Committee. 1847: Accountant-General and Member of the College Board. 1850: Accountant-General and Member of the Mint Committee. 1851: Accountant-General and Provisional Member of Council. 1855: Accountant-General and Member of the Mint Committee. 1856: *Resigned the service, 20th December, in India.* (*Annuitant on the Fund*, 1858.) *Died*, 29*th January* 1866, *in England.*

STORY, EDMUND.—1829: Writer. 1833: Assistant under Principal Collector, Nellore. 1834: Second Assistant to Principal Collector and Magistrate, Cuddapah. 1835: Acting Register to the Zillah Courts of Cuddapah, and of Bellary. 1836: Acting Register to the Zillah Court, Chicacole. 1838: Register to the Zillah Court, Chicacole. 1839: Acting Assistant Judge and Joint Criminal Judge, Chicacole; Register to the Zillah Court, Vizagapatam. 1840: Acting Register to the Northern Provincial Court; Assistant Judge and Joint Criminal Judge, Guntoor. 1843: Sub-Judge, Cuddapah; Acting Sub-Judge at Salem. 1845: *Proceeded to Europe on furlough.* 1847: Acting Civil and Sessions Judge, Trichinopoly. 1849: Acting Civil and Sessions Judge, Salem; Sub-Judge at Bellary. 1850: Acting Civil and Sessions Judge, Cuddapah. 1851: Acting Civil and Sessions Judge,

Bellary. 1856: Civil and Sessions Judge, at Guntoor and at Tinnevelly. 1859: *On medical certificate to England.* 1860: Civil and Sessions Judge, Nellore. 1865: *Permitted to retire from the service, 1st February. (Annuitant.) Died, 17th April 1874, in England.*

STRACEY, EDWARD.—1758: Writer. 1768: Junior Merchant. 1771: Senior Merchant. 1774: Member of Council of the Governor. 1776: *Resigned the service.*

STRACHAN, FRANCIS. — 1796: Writer on the Bencoolen Establishment. 1804: *Transferred to the Madras Presidency;* Assistant to the Commercial Resident at Salem. 1806: Register of the Zillah of Nellore; Register of the Zillah of Salem. *Died, on his passage to the Cape of Good Hope, 20th April 1808, on the "Brunswick" transport.*

STRACHEY, GEORGE.—1796: Writer. 1798: Assistant in the Military, Secret, and Political Department. 1800: Secretary and Accountant to the Commissioners of the Sinking Fund. 1803: Secretary in the Military Department. 1805: Secretary to the Finance Committee. 1807: Joint Assay Master. 1808: Private Secretary to the Governor. 1809: Judge and Magistrate of the Zillah of Cuddapah. 1810: *Out of employ.* 1811: Secretary in the Military Department. 1812: Junior Secretary to Government. 1813: Chief Secretary to Government. 1821: *At home.* 1824: *Out of the service.*

STRANGE, JAMES.—1773: Writer. 1778: Factor. 1782: Junior Merchant. 1790: Senior Merchant. 1791: Paymaster at Tanjore. 1795: *At home.* 1800: *Out of the service.*

STRANGE, THOMAS LUMSDEN.—1825: Writer. 1829: Register of the Zillah of Malabar. 1831: Assistant Judge and Joint Criminal Judge, Malabar. 1839: *Proceeded to Europe on furlough.* 1842: Acting Judge and Criminal Judge, Malabar. 1843: Sub-Judge at Calicut, and Acting Civil and Sessions Judge, Tellicherry. 1845: Civil and Sessions Judge, Tellicherry; Civil and Sessions Judge, Bellary. 1851: Acting Judge, subsequently Puisne Judge of the Court of Sudder and Foujdarry Adawlut. 1852: Special Commissioner for Inquiring into the Moplah Disturbances in Malabar. 1856: *Proceeded on medical certificate to Europe.* 1859: Commissioner for Inquiring into the System of Judicature in the Presidency. 1862: Judge of the High Court of Judicature. 1863: *Resigned the service, 2d May. (Annuitant.) Died, 3d September 1884, in England.*

STRATTON, GEORGE.—1751: Writer. 1768: Member of Council of the Governor. 1777: *Recalled by order of the General Court of Proprietors, 9th May.* 1780: *Suspended from the service.*

STRATTON, GEORGE.—1793: Writer. 1796: Assistant to the Beetle and Tobacco Manager, and to the Secretary to the Board of Revenue. 1797: Assistant to the Superintendent of the Court of Cutcherry. 1799: Head Assistant under the Collector of Salem. 1800: *Out of employ;* Collector of the Western Polygar Peishcush. 1801: Collector of Arcot, North of the River Palar. 1803: Judge of the Zillah of Carangooly. 1806: Judge of the Zillah of Tinnevelly. 1810: *At home.* 1815: *Returned to India;* Second Commissioner for the Revision of the Judicial System; Third Judge of the Sudder Adawlut Court. 1819: Third Member of the Board of Revenue. 1820: Member of Council, and President of the Sudder Court and Board of Trade. 1824: *At home.* 1829: *Out of the service.*

STROMBOM, PETER HENRY.—1816: Writer. 1818: Secretary to the Commissioner for Conducting the Restitution of the Dutch Settlements; French Translator to Government. 1820: Register of the Zillah of Vizagapatam. 1821: Assistant to the Collector and Magistrate of Cuddapah. 1830: Register of the Zillah of Rajahmundry. 1832: Judge and Criminal Judge of Cuddapah. 1837: Judge and Criminal Judge of Chicacole. 1838: Acting, afterwards Judge and Criminal Judge of Cuddapah. 1839: Judge and Criminal Judge of Chittoor. 1840: Third Judge of the Provincial Court of Appeal and Circuit, Northern Division. *Died, 28th August* 1841, *at Guntoor.*

STUART, CHARLES EDWARD.—1804: Writer. 1807: Assistant under the Principal Collector in the Ceded Districts; Assistant to the Principal Collector in the Ceded Districts, Malabar. *Died on his passage home, 3d April* 1809, *on board the "Huddart."*

SULIVAN, JOHN.—1765: Writer. 1771: Factor. 1774: Junior Merchant, and Fifth in Council at Masulipatam. 1776: Senior Merchant, and Fourth in Council at Masulipatam. 1778: *At home.* 1782: *In India. No trace after* 1782.

SULIVAN, RICHARD JOSEPH.—1770: Writer. 1776: Factor; *At home.* 1778: Junior Merchant (*still at home*). 1782: Senior Merchant. *No trace after* 1782.

SULIVAN, STEPHEN.—1778: Persian Translator and Secretary. 1780: Resident at Tanjore. *No trace after* 1780.

SULIVAN, JOHN STEWART.—1795: Writer. 1798: Assistant

under the Secretary in the Public, Commercial, and Revenue Department. 1799: Assistant under the Commercial Resident at Tinnevelly. 1800: Deputy Commercial Resident at Tinnevelly. 1801: Deputy Commercial Resident at Ramnad. 1809: Commercial Resident at Ramnad. 1814: Commercial Resident at Tinnevelly. 1821: *Out of employ.* 1823: Commercial Resident at Tinnevelly. 1826: *At home.* (*Annuitant on the Fund from 9th May 1826.*) *Died, 14th December 1837, in England.*

SULLIVAN, John.—1804: Writer. 1805: Assistant under the Secretary in the Revenue and Judicial Department. 1806: Register of the Zillah of Chittaput. 1807: Assistant to the Chief Secretary in the Secret, Political, and Foreign Department. 1809: Acting Assistant to the Resident at Mysore. 1811: *At home.* 1814: *Returned to India;* Collector of Chingleput. 1815: Collector of Coimbatore. 1821: Principal Collector and Magistrate of Coimbatore. 1830: *At home on absentee allowance.* 1835: *Returned to India;* Senior Member of the Board of Revenue. 1836: President of the Revenue, Marine, and College Boards. 1839: Member of Council of the Governor, and President of the Revenue, Marine, and College Boards. (*Annuitant on the Fund, 1841.*) *Died, 16th January 1858, in England.*

SULLIVAN, Edward R.—1806: Writer. 1809: Assistant under the Collector of Malabar. 1811: Acting Assistant to the Resident at Mysore. 1813: Head Assistant to the Resident at Mysore. 1815: Postmaster-General and Superintendent of Government Lotteries. 1819: *At home.* 1822: *Returned to India;* Assistant to the Chief Secretary to Government; Secretary and Treasurer of the Government Bank. 1824: *Out of the service.*

SULLIVAN, Richard James.—1838: Writer. 1840: Assistant to Collector and Magistrate, Trichinopoly. 1843: *Proceeded on furlough.* 1845: *Returned to India;* Assistant to Collector and Magistrate, Trichinopoly. 1846: Head Assistant to Collector and Magistrate, Trichinopoly. 1847: Head Assistant to Collector and Magistrate, Coimbatore. 1850: Head Assistant to Collector and Magistrate, Northern Division of Arcot. 1851: Head Assistant to Collector and Magistrate, Coimbatore. 1852: *Proceeded on furlough.* 1854: *Returned to India.* 1855: *Out of employ.* 1856: Subordinate Judge, Mangalore. *Died, 5th February 1858, at Ryde, Isle of Wight.*

SUTHERLAN, Alexander Milford.—1837: Writer. 1838: Assistant to the Principal Collector and Magistrate of Nellore.

1839: Acting Head Assistant to the Collector and Magistrate of Rajahmundry. 1840: Assistant to Collector, Magistrate, and Agent to Governor, Ganjam. 1844: *Proceeded on furlough.* 1847: *Returned to India.* 1848: Head Assistant to Collector and Magistrate, Nellore. 1850: Head Assistant to Accountant-General. 1851: *Proceeded on furlough.* 1853: *Returned to India.* 1854: *Proceeded on furlough.* 1857: *Resigned the service, 26th August, in England.*

SWINTON, George Melville.—1833: Writer. 1835: Assistant to the Principal Collector and Magistrate of Cuddapah. 1837: Acting, afterwards Assistant to the Collector and Magistrate of Chingleput. 1838: Acting, afterwards Head Assistant to the Collector and Magistrate of Chingleput. 1841: Second Assistant to Accountant-General. 1842: Head Assistant to Accountant-General. 1848: *Proceeded on furlough.* 1850: *Returned to India;* Assistant Judge, Mangalore. 1852: Assistant Judge, Combaconum. *Died, 24th October* 1853, *at the Cape of Good Hope.*

TANNER, Theodore Ivey.—1769: Writer. 1774: Factor. 1778: Junior Merchant. 1780: Senior Merchant. *No trace after* 1782.

TASWELL, William.—1794: Writer. 1796: Assistant under the Secretary in the Military, Political, and Secret Department. 1798: Assistant to the Import Warehouse-keeper. 1799: Deputy Sea Customer. 1800: *Resigned the service, 12th April.*

TAYLOR, James.—1764: Writer. 1771: Factor. 1774: Junior Merchant. 1776: Senior Merchant. 1790: *Suspended from the service.* 1792: *At home.* 1800: *Out of the service.*

TAYLOR, Harry.—1777: Writer. 1782: Factor. 1790: Senior Merchant. 1791: Senior Merchant and Paymaster at Ellore. 1800: Collector of the Cuddalore and Pondicherry Revenues. 1801: *At home.* 1805: *In India, without employ. Died, on his way to England, 5th December* 1806, *on board the ship "Glory."*

TAYLOR, James.—1794: Writer. 1796: Assistant under the Secretary in the Military, Political, and Secret Department. 1797: Assistant under the Accountant-General. 1798: Deputy Secretary, afterwards Secretary to the Board of Trade. 1800: In Charge of the Import Warehouse. 1802: Superintendent of the Quality of Investment. 1814: Third Member of the Board of Trade. 1816: Second Member of the Board of Trade. 1825: Acting Third Judge of the Provincial Court, Northern Division.

1826: First Judge of the Provincial Court, Southern Division. 1828: Member of Council of the Governor, and President of the Revenue and Marine Boards. 1831: *At home on absentee allowance.* (*Annuitant on the Fund from 1st May* 1833.) *Died, 9th September* 1852.

TAYLOR, HENRY.—1796: Writer. 1799: Assistant under the Secretary to the Board of Trade. 1800: Assistant under the Commercial Resident at Vizagapatam. 1805: Deputy Commercial Resident at Vizagapatam and Ganjam. 1810: Commercial Resident at Vizagapatam. 1819: Commercial Resident at Maddepollam and Masulipatam. 1821: *Out of employ.* 1823: *At home.* 1827: *Returned to India;* Commercial Resident at Vizagapatam. 1830: *Out of employ. Died, 2d October* 1832, *at Vizagapatam.*

TAYLOR, WILLIAM RAYNSFORD.—1814: Writer; Assistant Commercial Resident at Vizagapatam. 1815: *At home.* 1819: *Returned to India;* Assistant to the Secretary to the Board of Trade; Assistant to the Superintendent of the Import Warehouse; Assistant to the Superintendent of Stamps. 1820: Register of the Zillah of Trichinopoly. 1823: Second Assistant to the Accountant-General. 1825: *At home.* 1827: *Returned to India;* Assistant Judge and Joint Criminal Judge of the Zillah of Madura. 1829: Judge and Criminal Judge of Combaconum. 1830: Judge and Criminal Judge of Chingleput. 1832: Third Judge of the Provincial Court, Southern Division. 1833: *At home on absentee allowance.* 1836: *Returned to India;* Acting Judge and Criminal Judge of Nellore; Acting Judge and Criminal Judge of Chingleput. 1837: Acting Second Judge of the Provincial Court, Southern Division; Acting, afterwards Postmaster-General. 1838: Second Judge of the Provincial Court, Southern Division. 1841: First Judge of the Provincial Court of Appeal and Circuit, Centre Division. 1844: Civil and Session Judge, Chittoor; *Resigned the service, 3d December, in India.* (*Annuitant on the Fund,* 1845.) *Died, 10th January* 1864, *in England.*

TAYLOR, JAMES CORBETT.—1831: Writer. 1832: Assistant to the Collector and Magistrate of Nellore. 1833: Assistant to the Principal Collector and Magistrate of Nellore. 1835: Acting Register of the Zillah of Nellore. 1837: Head Assistant to the Principal Collector and Magistrate of Nellore. 1838: Acting Sub-Collector and Joint Magistrate of Salem. 1839: Acting Head Assistant to the Principal Collector and Magistrate of Salem. *Died, 4th February* 1839, *at Salem.*

TEMPLE, Grenville Temple.—1818: Writer. 1820: *Resigned, 14th June, in England.*

TERRY, Edward.—1796: Writer. 1799: Assistant in the Public Revenue and Commercial Department. 1800: Assistant to the Accountant to the Board of Revenue. 1801: Assistant to the Commercial Resident at Tinnevelly. *Lost on his passage home, December 1801, in the ship "Generous."*

THACKERAY, William.—1793: Writer. 1797: Assistant under the Secretary in the Public, Commercial, and Revenue Department. 1798: Assistant under the Commercial Resident at Vizagapatam. 1799: Assistant under the Collector of Peddapore. 1800: Gentoo Translator to Government; Subordinate Collector in the Ceded Districts. 1803; Judge of the Adawlut in the Zillah of Masulipatam. 1806: Junior Member of the Board of Revenue. 1810: Chief Secretary to Government. 1813: *At home.* 1817: *Returned to India;* Acting Collector of Coimbatore. 1818: Collector and Magistrate of Bellary. 1820: Third Judge of the Sudder Adawlut Court; Member of Council of the Governor, and President of the Board of Revenue. *Died on his passage to the Cape of Good Hope, 11th January 1823, on board the "Nancy."*

THACKERAY, Webb.—1806: Writer. 1807: Assistant to the Judge and Magistrate of the Zillah of Bellary. *Died, 1st September 1807, at Gundloor.*

THACKERAY, St. John.—1806: Writer. 1809: Assistant under the Secretary to the Board of Revenue. 1812: Head Assistant to the Collector of Trichinopoly. 1814: Head Assistant to the Collector of Tanjore. 1816: Assistant Magistrate of Tanjore. 1819: Employed in the late Peishwah's Dominions. *Killed, 23d October 1824, at Kittoo.*

THOMAS, James.—1812: Writer. 1817: Second Assistant to the Collector of Tinnevelly. 1819: Head Assistant to the Collector and Magistrate of Tinnevelly. 1821: *At home.* 1825: *Returned to India;* Junior Assistant to the Accountant-General. 1826: Senior Deputy Accountant-General, Commercial Accountant, and Auditor. 1828: Sub-Collector and Joint Magistrate of Coimbatore. 1830: Principal Collector and Magistrate of Coimbatore. 1832: Third Judge of the Provincial Court, Centre Division. 1833: *At home on absentee allowance.* 1836: *Returned to India.* 1837: Acting Deputy Accountant-General; Judge and Criminal Judge of Rajahmundry. *Died, 6th January 1840, at Madras.*

THOMAS, John Fryer.—1816: Writer. 1818: Assistant to

the Register of the Sudder and Foujdarry Adawlut. 1819: Sanscrit Examiner to the College; Head Assistant to the Register of the Sudder Adawlut. 1824: Senior Deputy to the Register of the Sudder Adawlut. 1827: *At home on absentee allowance.* 1831: *Returned to India;* Judge and Criminal Judge of Combaconum. 1832: Acting Principal Collector and Magistrate of Coimbatore. 1834: Register of the Sudder and Foujdarry Adawlut. 1835: Additional Government Commissioner for Carnatic Claims. 1836: Acting Third Judge of the Provincial Court, Northern Division. 1837: Additional Government Commissioner for Carnatic Claims. 1838: Sole Commissioner for Final Adjustments of Small Claims drawn from the Carnatic Fund. 1839: Sole Government Commissioner for Small Claims withdrawn from the Carnatic Fund, and Member of the College Board. 1842: *Proceeded on furlough.* 1843: *Returned to India;* Secretary to Government, Civil Department. 1844: Secretary to Government, Civil Department, and Member of the Mint Committee. 1845: Chief Secretary to Government. 1849: Chief Secretary to Government, and Provisional Member of Council. 1850: Member of Council, and Chief Judge of the Sudder Dewannee and Sudder Foujdarry Adawlut. 1855: *Proceeded on furlough; Resigned the service, 31st December, in India.* (*Annuitant on the Fund,* 1857.) *Died, 7th April* 1877, *in England.*

THOMAS, THOMAS J. W.—1824: Writer. 1826: *At home on absentee allowance.* 1830: *Returned to India, per "Alfred;"* Register of the Zillah of Chicacole. 1832: Acting Head Assistant to the Collector and Magistrate of Masulipatam. 1833: Head Assistant to the Collector of Masulipatam. 1838: Acting Deputy Collector of Sea Customs at Madras; Assistant Judge and Joint Criminal Judge of Rajahmundry. 1841: Assistant Judge and Joint Criminal Judge, Vizagapatam. 1844: Subordinate Judge, Madura. *Died, 17th March* 1845, *at Madras.*

THOMAS, EDWARD BROWN.—1824: Writer. 1827: Assistant to the Principal Collector and Magistrate, North Arcot. 1828: Head Assistant to the Collector and Magistrate, Trichinopoly. 1830: Head Assistant to the Principal Collector, Coimbatore. 1833: Acting Sub-Collector and Joint Magistrate, Coimbatore. 1834: Acting Assistant Judge and Joint Criminal Judge at Salem; Acting Sub-Collector and Joint Magistrate, South Arcot. 1835: Sub-Collector and Joint Magistrate, South Arcot. 1837: *At home.* 1840: Acting Judge and Criminal Judge, Malabar. 1841: Judge and Criminal Judge, Malabar. 1842: Acting Collector and Magistrate, Tinnevelly. 1843: Collector and Magistrate, Tinnevelly. 1848: Officiating Secretary to Government. 1849: Acting Principal Collector and Magistrate, Coimbatore. 1851: Collector and Magistrate, Coimbatore. 1858: *Proceeded to Europe in April, on medical certificate.* 1862: *Resigned the service, 1st May.* (*Annuitant.*)

THOMPSON, George.—1776: Writer. 1782: Factor. 1790: Senior Merchant. 1791: Senior Merchant and Assistant at Nagore. 1800: Resident at Negapatam, and Revenue Assistant under the Resident at Nagore. 1802 to 1804: *Without employ.* 1805: *Out of the service.*

THOMPSON, Christopher Anstey.—1816: Writer. 1819: Register of the Zillah of Bellary. 1820: Register of the Zillah of Combaconum. 1824: Junior Deputy Register of the Sudder and Foujdarry Adawlut. 1828: Secretary in the Public, Revenue, and Commercial Department; Collector of Chingleput. 1829: Principal Collector and Magistrate of Nellore. *Died, 11th June* 1831, *at Madras.*

THOMPSON, Edward Penton.—1822: Writer. 1826: Assistant to the Collector and Magistrate of Vizagapatam. 1827: Head Assistant to the Principal Collector of Cuddapah. 1828: Acting Assistant to the Resident at Mysore. 1830: Sub-Collector and Assistant Magistrate of Salem; Assistant Judge and Joint Criminal Judge of Salem. 1832: Acting, afterwards Judge and Criminal Judge of Canara. 1835: Acting Zillah Judge of Canara. 1836: Acting Judge and Criminal Judge of Malabar; Acting Judge and Criminal Judge of Madura. 1837: Acting Collector and Criminal Magistrate of Tinnevelly. 1838: Assistant Judge and Joint Criminal Judge of Salem. 1840: Principal Collector and Magistrate of Tinnevelly. 1841: *Proceeded on furlough.* 1844: *Returned to India.* 1845: Secretary to Government, Civil Department. 1846: Secretary to Government, Revenue, and Judicial Department. 1847: Second Puisne Judge of the Sudder Dewannee and Sudder Foujdarry Adawlut. 1852: *Resigned the service, 1st January, in India.* (*Annuitant on the Fund,* 1852.)

THORP, Samuel.—1789: Writer. *Died, 15th July* 1791.

THURESBY, John William.—1789: Writer. 1790: Assistant under the Secretary to the Board of Trade. 1791: Assistant under the Collector of the Southern Division of Arcot. 1793: Assistant to the Resident at Cuddapah. 1794: Assistant under the Accountant at Cuddalore and Pondicherry. 1797: Assistant under the Collector of Cuddalore and Pondicherry. 1800: *Out of employ.* 1801: Paymaster and Garrison Storekeeper at Madura. *No trace after* 1801.

TIMBRELL, JAMES.—1823: Writer. *Died, 25th January* 1825, *on his passage to England.*

TOD, JAMES OGILVIE.—1798: Writer on the Bencoolen Establishment. 1805: *Transferred to the Madras Presidency;* Assistant under the Chief Secretary in Secret, Political, and Foreign Department: Assistant under the Subordinate Collector of Trichinopoly. 1806: Register of the Zillah of Masulipatam. 1809: Judge and Criminal Judge of Masulipatam. 1822: Third Judge of the Provincial Court, Northern Division. 1825: Acting Judge of the Provincial Court, Northern Division. 1828: Second Judge of the Provincial Court, Northern Division. (*Annuitant on the Fund from 9th May* 1831.) *Died, 6th January* 1837, *in England.*

TORIN, BENJAMIN.—1779: Writer. 1790: Senior Merchant. 1791: Paymaster at Pallamcottah. 1792: Collector in the Tinnevelly Districts. 1795: *At home.* 1800: Resident at Tanjore. 1803: *At home.* 1805: *Out of the service.*

TORIN, CHARLES BEAUVOIR.—1794: Writer. 1796: Assistant under the Secretary in the Public, Commercial, and Revenue Department. 1798: Assistant to the Commercial Resident at Tanjore. 1799: *At home for his health.* 1801: *Returned to India, and out of employ. No trace after* 1811.

TORRIANO, WILLIAM HARCOURT. — 1766: Writer. 1771: Factor. 1774: Junior Merchant. 1778: Senior Merchant. 1791: Paymaster at Vellore. 1795: Resident at Nagore. 1800: Sea Customer and Boat Master. 1801: *At home.* 1803: *In India, and without employ.* 1808: *Out of the service.*

TORRIANO, LIONEL AUGUSTUS.—1769: Writer. 1774: Factor and Assistant at Cuddalore. *Dead in* 1776.

TOWNSEND, THOMAS. — 1792: Writer. 1793: Assistant under the Secretary in the Political, Military, and Secret Department. 1794: Assistant to the Commercial Resident at Salem. 1796: Assistant under the Collector of the Southern Division of the Vizianagram Zemindary. 1800: Assistant under the Collector in the First Division of Vizagapatam. 1801: Assistant under the Collector of Nellore and Ongole. 1802: Judge of the Zillah of Guntoor. 1806: Judge and Magistrate of the Zillah of Manargoody. 1808: *Out of employ.* 1809: Judge and Magistrate of the Zillah of Masulipatam; Third Judge of the Provincial

Court, Northern Division. 1815: *At home.* 1817: *Out of the service.*

TRACEY, HON. WILLIAM HANBURY.—1829: Writer. 1831: Assistant under the Principal Collector of Coimbatore. 1832: Register to the Zillah of Combaconum. 1833: Register of the Zillah of Chittoor. 1834: Register of the Zillah of Combaconum. 1838: *At home.* 1839: *Returned to India.* 1840: *Out of employ.* 1841: Assistant Judge and Joint Criminal Judge, Cochin. 1843: *Proceeded on furlough.* 1846: *Name removed, 19th August, in England.*

TRAVERS, JOHN BENWARD.—1792: Writer. 1793: Assistant under the Accountant-General. 1794: Assistant to the Collector in the Northern Division of Jaghire. 1796: Assistant under the Collector in the Southern Division of the Vizianagram Zemindary. 1797: Deputy Secretary to the Board of Revenue. 1799: Secretary to the Board of Revenue. 1801: Collector of Nellore and Ongole. 1809: Acting Judge, afterwards Second Judge of the Provincial Court, Northern Division. 1816: *At home.* 1817: *Returned to India.* 1819: Third Judge of the Provincial Court, Northern Division. 1820: Second Judge of the Provincial Court, Centre Division. *Died in 1820, in Madras.*

TRAVERS, GEORGE FRANCIS.—1794: Writer. 1797: Assistant under the Secretary in the Military, Political, and Secret Department. 1798: Assistant to the Commercial Resident at Vizagapatam. 1799: Assistant under the Accountant-General. 1801: Deputy Accountant in the Commercial and Revenue Departments. 1802: Deputy General and Commercial Accountant. 1803: Subordinate Collector in the Ceded Districts. 1806: Judge and Magistrate of Kodicondah. 1808: Collector of the Zillah of Kodicondah; Collector of the Zillah of Ganjam. 1809: Collector of the Zillah of Trichinopoly. 1815: Judge and Magistrate of the Zillah of Guntoor; Third Judge of the Provincial Court, Northern Division. 1819: *At home.* 1822: *Out of the service.*

TRAVERS, OCTAVIUS.—1851: Writer. 1853: *Proceeded on furlough.* 1855: *Resigned the service 18th April, in England.*

TREMAMONDO, ANTHONY EDWARD A.—*See* ANGELO, ANTHONY EDWARD.

TUDOR, MATTHEW.—1770: Writer. 1776: Factor. 1778: Junior Merchant. 1782: Senior Merchant. 1791: Paymaster at Aska. 1792: Collector of the Northern and Centre Divisions of the Masulipatam Havelly. *Dead in 1795.*

TULLOH, ROBERT HENRY.—1804: Writer. 1807: Assistant

to the Register of the Sudder and Foujdarry Adawlut; *Removed to the Bengal Establishment*, 30*th July* 1807.

TURING, JOHN.—1762: Writer. 1768: Factor. 1771: Junior Merchant. 1774: Senior Merchant, and Third in Council at Cuddalore. 1791: Civil and Military Paymaster-General, and Garrison Storekeeper. 1792: *At home.* 1795: *Out of the service.*

TURING, WILLIAM.—1769: Writer. 1774: Factor. 1778: Junior Merchant. 1780: Senior Merchant. 1790: *Out of the service.*

TURING, JOHN.—1795: Writer. 1798: Assistant in the Military, Political, and Secret Department. 1799: *At home for his health.* 1800: *Returned to India;* Assistant to the Secretary in the Public, Revenue, and Commercial Department; Head Assistant in the Military Department; Deputy Postmaster-General. 1802: *At home.* 1808: *Out of the service.*

TURNBULL, JOHN GEORGE.—1804: Writer. 1807: Assistant under the Principal Collector of Tanjore and Trichinopoly. 1808: Assistant under the Collector of Salem. 1810: Register of the Zillah of Northern Malabar. 1812: Register of the Zillah of Tinnevelly; Deputy Accountant in the Military Department. 1814: Deputy Accountant-General. 1815: Commercial Accountant and Auditor. 1822: Accountant-General. (*Retired upon Annuity Fund*, 1840.) *Died*, 2*d January* 1872, *in England.*

TWEEDIE, ALEXANDER GEORGE.—1842: Writer. 1845: Assistant to Collector and Magistrate, Bellary. 1852: Head Assistant to Collector and Magistrate, Guntoor; Head Assistant to Collector and Magistrate, Masulipatam. 1854: *Proceeded on furlough. Died*, 27*th August* 1855, *at Dover.*

TYLER, GEORGE.—1777: Writer. 1782: Factor. 1790: Senior Merchant. 1791: *In Bengal, and continued there till* 1822; *employment not specified, though stated to be in the service.* 1823: *At home.* 1827: *In Madras without employ.* 1830: Cashier of the Government Bank. *Died*, 18*th October* 1834, *at Fort St. George.*

UNDERWOOD, WILLIAM ELPHINSTONE.—1823: Writer. 1826: Assistant to the Collector and Magistrate of Guntoor. 1828: Register of the Zillah of Chingleput; Register to the Provincial Court, Centre Division. 1830: Secretary to the Marine Board; Acting Boat Paymaster. 1831: Acting Magistrate on the Beach. 1832: Deputy Collector of Sea Customs at Madras; Secretary to the Marine Board. 1837: Commissioner for Drawing

Government Lotteries. 1838: Acting Deputy Secretary to Government in the Chief Secretary's Department. 1839: Acting Principal Collector and Magistrate of Malabar; Deputy Collector of Sea Customs, Madras. 1841: Collector of Sea Customs, Madras. 1860: *Resigned the service in India. (Annuitant on the Fund, May* 1860.) *Died,* 19*th January* 1874, *in England.*

UTHOFF, EDWARD.—1812: Writer. 1806: Assistant to the Register of the Provincial Court, Southern Division; Assistant Magistrate of Tinnevelly. 1817: Head Assistant to the Collector of Tinnevelly. 1819: Deputy Malabar and Tamul Translator to Government; Junior Deputy Secretary to the Board of Revenue. *Died,* 21*st August* 1822, *at Madras.*

VANSITTART, GEORGE. — 1777: Writer. *No trace after* 1778.

VAUGHAN, HUGH.—1771: Writer. 1776: Factor. 1780: Junior Merchant. 1782: Senior Merchant. 1791: Senior Merchant, and Paymaster at Madura. 1800: *At home.* 1801: *Out of the service.*

VAUGHAN, JAMES.—1802: Writer. 1803: Assistant to the Collector of Nellore. 1806: Register of the Zillah of the Northern Division of Malabar. 1808: Register of the Zillah of the Augadeeporam. 1811; Deputy Collector of Sea Customs at Malabar and Canara. 1815: Head Assistant to the Collector of Malabar. 1816: Collector and Magistrate of Malabar. 1822: Principal Collector and Magistrate of Malabar. 1826: Second Judge of the Provincial Court, Western Division. 1830: *At home on absentee allowance. (Annuitant on the Fund from* 1*st May* 1830.) *Died,* 4*th January* 1833, *in England.*

VAUGHAN, JOHN.—1808: Writer. 1814: Register of the Zillah of Bellary. 1816: Register of the Zillah of Guntoor. 1817: Head Assistant to the Collector, and Assistant to the Magistrate of Nellore. 1822: Sub-Collector and Assistant Magistrate of Cochin. 1823: Sub-Collector and Assistant Magistrate of Malabar. 1826: Judge and Criminal Judge of Canara. 1830: Third Judge of the Provincial Court, Western Division. 1832: Second Judge of the Provincial Court, Western Division. 1838: First Judge of the Provincial Court, Western Division. 1842: *Proceeded on furlough. Died,* 5*th October* 1842, *in Shropshire, England.*

VIBART, HENRY.—1804: Writer. 1807: Assistant to the Secretary to the Board of Revenue; Assistant to the Collector of the Zillah of Ganjam. 1811: Register of the Zillah of Rajahmundry. 1822: Register and Assistant Collector of the Zillah of Seringapatam. 1824: Judge and Criminal Judge of the Zillah of Masulipatam. (*Annuitant on the Fund from December* 1832.) *Died,* 5*th November* 1839, *in England.*

VINES, GOODSON.—1792: Writer. 1793: Assistant under the Secretary to the Board of Revenue. 1796: Assistant under the Commercial Resident at Masulipatam. 1797: Assistant under the Commercial Resident at Palamcottah. 1800: *Out of employ.* 1803: *Suspended the service and ordered home.* 1806: *Out of the service.*

VIVEASH, HARRY (now BASKERVILLE)—1811: Writer. 1815: Head Assistant to the Collector of Madras. 1817: Mahratta Translator to Government. 1822: Sub-Collector and Assistant Magistrate of Bellary. 1826: Collector and Magistrate of Chingleput. 1828: Principal Collector and Magistrate of Madura. 1833: Principal Collector and Magistrate of Canara. 1835: Third Member of the Board of Revenue. 1836: Second Member of the Board of Revenue. 1838: *At home on absentee allowance.* (*Annuitant on the Fund from* 30*th April* 1838.) *Died,* 6*th February* 1877, *in Englnad.*

WALKER, JOHN.—1823: Writer. 1826: Assistant to the Collector of Tinnevelly; Register of the Zillah of Madura. 1828: Junior Deputy Register of the Sudder Adawlut; Assistant Judge of the Zillah of Canara. 1834: *At home on absentee allowance.* 1837: *Returned to India, per "General Kyd;"* Police Magistrate. 1838: Acting Deputy Collector of Madras, and Superintendent of Stationery; Canarese Translator to Government. 1839: Assistant Judge and Joint Criminal Judge of Madura, and Acting Judge and Criminal Judge of Malabar. 1840: Judge and Criminal Judge of Cuddapah. 1844: Civil and Session Judge, Nellore. 1853: *Resigned the service,* 1*st May, in India.* (*Annuitant on the Fund.*) *Died,* 24*th July* 1862, *in England.*

WALLACE, JOHN, sen.—1789: Writer. 1790: Assistant under the Accountant. 1794: Assistant at Masulipatam. 1796: Deputy Commercial Resident at Nagore. 1799: Commercial Resident at Nagore. 1800: *Leave to the Cape of Good Hope, and eventually to Europe.* 1805: *Returned to India;* Commercial Resident at Ingeram. 1808: *At home for his health.* 1811: *Out of the service.*

WALLACE, THOMAS.—1790: Writer. 1791: Assistant under

the Secretary in the Military Department. 1792: Assistant at Ganjam. 1796: Deputy Secretary in the Military Department. 1797: *At home for his health. No trace after* 1797.

WALLACE, JOHN, jun.—1792: Writer. 1794: Assistant under the Secretary in the Military, Political, and Secret Department, and Assistant to the Accountant to the Board of Revenue. 1795: Assistant to the Accountant to the Board of Trade. 1796: Assistant under the Secretary to the Board of Trade, and to the Import Warehouse-keeper and Deputy Postmaster-General. 1798: Assistant under the Resident at Nagore. 1799: Assistant to the Collector of Nagore. 1800: Head Assistant to the Collector of Tanjore. 1801: Collector of Trichinopoly and its Dependent Polygars. 1805: Principal Collector of Tanjore and Trichinopoly. 1813: Second Member of the Board of Revenue. *Died, 7th August* 1814, *at Madras.*

WARD, SAMUEL NEVILL.—1831: Writer. 1833: Assistant to Collector and Magistrate, Trichinopoly. 1834: Acting Register to the Zillah Courts of Combaconum and of Chittoor. 1837: Acting Head Assistant to Collector and Magistrate, Ganjam; and Register of the Zillah Court of Canara. 1842: Acting Assistant Judge and Joint Criminal Judge, Cochin; Acting Register of the Zillah Court of Malabar; Acting Assistant Judge and Joint Criminal Judge, Malabar; and Acting Assistant Judge of the Zillah Court of Canara. 1843: Extra Assistant to Principal Collector and Magistrate, and Acting Sub-Collector and Joint Magistrate, Canara. 1844: Acting Additional Sub-Collector and Sub-Judge, Mangalore. 1845: Additional Sub-Collector and Joint Magistrate, Canara. 1847: *Proceeded to Europe on furlough.* 1850: Acting Civil and Sessions Judge, Madura; Acting Civil and Sessions Judge, Cuddapah; and Acting Collector and Magistrate, South Arcot. 1851: Sub-Collector and Joint Magistrate, Salem. 1852: At first Acting, then Civil and Sessions Judge, Calicut. 1853: Civil and Sessions Judge, Cuddalore. 1855: Acting Civil Auditor and Superintendent of Stamps. 1857: Civil and Sessions Judge, Coimbatore. *Resigned the service, 27th October* 1863. (*Annuitant.*)

WARD, EDWARD EYRE.—1834: Writer. 1836: Assistant to the Principal Collector and Magistrate of Salem. 1837: Assistant to the Principal Collector and Magistrate of Canara. 1838: Assistant to the Principal Collector and Magistrate of Coimbatore; Assistant to the Principal Collector and Magistrate of South Arcot. 1841: Head Assistant to Collector and Magistrate, Masulipatam.

1843: Head Assistant to Collector and Magistrate, Coimbatore. *Died, 5th March 1843, at Ootacamund.*

WARE, THOMAS STEPHEN.—1793: Writer. 1796: Assistant under the Secretary to the Board of Revenue. 1797: Assistant under the Accountant to the Board of Revenue. 1798: Deputy Accountant to the Board of Revenue. 1799: Acting Persian Translator to the Board of Revenue. *Died, 5th November 1799.*

WARRICKER, JOHN.—1777: Writer. 1782: Factor. 1790: Senior Merchant and Assistant at Vizagapatam. 1800: Assistant to the Collector at Ganjam. *No trace after 1800.*

WASEY, WILLIAM GEORGE.—1778: Writer. *No trace after 1782.*

WATERS, GEORGE JENKINS.—1808: Writer. 1814: Register of the Zillah of Canara. 1821: *At home.* 1823: *Returned to India;* Acting Judge and Criminal Judge of Chittoor. 1825: Acting Judge of the Zillah of Cuddapah. 1826: Judge and Criminal Judge of the Zillah of Chittoor. 1832: Officiating Mint-Master; Third Judge of the Provincial Court, Northern Division. 1836: *At home on absentee allowance.* 1837: *Returned to India, per "Barretto Junior."* 1838: Acting First Judge of the Provincial Court, Centre Division. 1839: Acting Civil Auditor and Superintendent of Stamps; Acting First Judge, Provincial Court, Southern Division. 1840: Judge and Criminal Judge of Cuddapah; First Judge of the Provincial Court of Appeal and Circuit for the Southern Division. 1842: First Judge of the Provincial Court of Appeal and Circuit for the Western Division. 1844: Civil and Session Judge, Second Class, Tellicherry. 1845: Puisne Judge of the Sudder Dewannee and Sudder Foujdarry Adawlut. 1846: First Puisne Judge of the Sudder Dewannee and Sudder Foujdarry Adawlut. 1847: Civil and Session Judge, Coimbatore. *Resigned the service, 4th December. (Annuitant on the Fund, 1848.) Died, 12th February 1882, in England.*

WATTS, JOHN NICHOLSON.—1796: Writer. 1799: Assistant under the Secretary in Public, Revenue, and Commercial Department. 1800: Head Assistant in the Revenue and Judicial Department. 1801: Assistant under the Commercial Resident at Tinnevelly; Deputy Commercial Resident at Tinnevelly. 1802: Head Assistant to the Collector of Dindigul. 1804: Register of Tanjore. 1805: Subordinate Collector of Tanjore. 1808: *At home.* 1814: *Returned to India. Died, 28th July 1815, at Fort St George.*

WATTS, Thomas.—1806: Writer; Assistant to the Secretary to the Board of Revenue. 1807: Assistant to the Principal Collector of Tanjore, &c. 1808: Second Assistant to the Collector of Trichinopoly. 1811: Register of the Zillah of Dharapooram. *Died, May* 1811, *at Dharapooram.*

WAYTE, William.—1797: Writer. 1800: Assistant under the Secretary in the Military, Political, and Secret Department. 1802: Deputy Secretary to the Board of Revenue. 1806: Secretary to the Board of Revenue. 1810: Third Member of the Board of Revenue. 1819: Second Member of the Board of Revenue. 1822: *At home.* 1827: *Out of the service.* (*Annuitant on the Fund from 1st January* 1827.) *Died, 17th December* 1860, *in England.*

WEBB, William.—1770: Writer. 1776: Factor. 1778: Junior Merchant. 1782: Senior Merchant. 1791: Import Warehouse-keeper at Cutwal, and Member of the Committee of Regulations. 1795: Member of the Board of Trade, and Import Warehouse-keeper. 1800: Agent for Supplies. 1801: *Without employ. Died, 14th August* 1807, *in Madras.*

WEBB, Nathaniel.—1778: Writer. 1790: Senior Merchant. 1791: Collector of the Guntoor Circar. 1792: Manager of the Ganjam Havelly. 1800: Collector in the Second Division of the Vizagapatam Districts. 1803: Second Judge of the Court of Circuit and of Appeal for the Centre Division. 1808: Senior Judge of the Court of Circuit and for Appeal for the Northern Division. 1829: Postmaster-General. (*Annuitant on the Fund in* 1838.) *Died, 5th August* 1838.

WEBBE, Josiah.—1783: Writer; Assistant to the Secretary to the Select Committee. 1786: Assistant to the Secretary in the Military Department, Mahratta Translator, and Deputy Commissary-General. 1787: Under the Secretary in the Public and Revenue Department. 1790: Secretary to the Board of Assumed Revenue. 1792: Temporary Member of the Board of Assumed Revenue. 1793: Deputy Secretary in the Public, Commercial, and Revenue Department. 1796: Secretary in the Public and Commercial Department, Clerk to the Court of Appeal, and to the Committee of Treasury. 1797: Secretary to Government, and Mahratta Translator. 1800: Chief Secretary to Government, and Mahratta Translator. 1801: Resident at the Durbar of the Rajah of Mysore. 1803: Resident at Nagpore. 1804: Resident at the Court of Dowlut Rao Scindia. *Died, 9th November* 1804, *at Mussingabad, on the banks of the Nerbudda.*

WEBSTER, George.—1778: Writer. 1790: Senior Merchant. 1791: Sepoy Paymaster. *Died, 3d July 1794, in Madras.*

WEDDERBURN, James A.—1848: Writer. 1852: Assistant to Collector and Magistrate, Coimbatore. 1853: Assistant to Collector and Magistrate, Chingleput. *Died, 19th May 1854, at Chingleput.*

WELCH, Thomas.—1771: Writer. 1776: Factor. 1780: Junior Merchant. 1782: Senior Merchant. 1790: *At home.* 1793: *Out of the service.*

WEST, Francis Alexander.—1826: Writer. 1829: Register of the Zillah of Bellary; Register of the Zillah of Cuddapah. *Died, 26th September 1832, at Arcot.*

WESTCOTT, George.—1764: Writer. 1771: Factor and Assistant at Masulipatam. 1774: Junior Merchant. 1776: Senior Merchant and Paymaster at Ellore. 1790: *At home*; *Returned to India.* 1801: Senior Member of the Board of Trade. *Died, 8th May 1809, at Fort St. George.*

WETHERELL, Charles.—1792: Writer. 1794: Assistant under the Secretary in the Public, Commercial, and Revenue Department. 1795: Assistant to the Collector in the Burramehal. 1797: Assistant under the Commercial Resident at Ingeram. 1799: *Out of employ*; Paymaster at Khistnagherry. 1802: Paymaster and Garrison Storekeeper at Madura. 1806: Paymaster and Garrison Storekeeper at Trichinopoly. 1811: *At home.* 1816: *Out of the service.*

WHEATLEY, Thomas Rundall.—1817: Writer. 1819: Assistant to the Register of the Zillah of Bellary; Head Assistant to the Collector and Magistrate of Cuddapah. 1826: Acting Deputy Accountant-General in the Military Department. 1827: Sub-Collector and Joint Magistrate of Malabar. 1828: *At home on absentee allowance.* 1832: *Returned to India*; Secretary in the Revenue and Judicial Department. 1835: *At home.* 1840: *Absent from India five years.*

WHISH, John Clinton.—1807: Writer. 1809: Assistant to the Chief Secretary in the General, Commercial, and Law Department. 1810: Assistant to the Superintendent of Stamps. 1811: Fixed Examiner in the Office of Sub-Secretary in the Commercial and Law Department. 1812: Head Assistant to the Collector of Coimbatore. 1816: Assistant Magistrate of Coimbatore. 1821: Sub-Collector and Assistant Magistrate of Coimbatore; Collector and Magistrate of Guntoor. 1831: Principal Collector and Magistrate of Nellore. 1835: *At home on absentee allowance.* (*Annuitant on the Fund, from 1st July 1837.*) *Died, 22d November 1837, at Mortimer House, near Reading.*

WHISH, Charles Matthew.—1813: Writer. 1815: Register of the Zillah of South Malabar. 1823: Register of the Zillah of Malabar. 1826: Sub-Collector and Joint Magistrate of Malabar. 1827: Assistant Judge and Joint Criminal Judge of Malabar. 1830: Assistant Judge and Joint Criminal Judge of Cuddapah. 1831: *Out of employ.* 1832: Acting Judge and Criminal Judge of Cuddapah. *Died, 14th April 1833, at Cuddapah.*

WHITE, Charles Nicholas.—1776: Writer. 1782: Factor. 1790: Senior Merchant. 1791: Secretary in Public and Revenue Department, and Clerk of Appeals, and to Treasury. 1795: Member of the Revenue Board. 1800: Senior Member of the Board of Revenue. 1801: *At home.* 1805: *Out of the service.*

WHITE, Evan Marsh.—1790: Writer. 1793: Assistant under the Secretary in the Military, Political, and Secret Department. 1794: Assistant to the Collector of Guntoor. 1796: Acting Paymaster at Ongole. *Died, 17th August 1796.*

WHITE, Daniel.—1829: Writer. 1831: Assistant to the Principal Collector of Malabar. 1832: Acting Head Assistant to the Principal Collector and Magistrate of Malabar. 1835: Assistant to the Principal Collector and Magistrate of Malabar; Acting Sub-Collector, Malabar. 1836: Head Assistant to the Principal Collector and Magistrate of Malabar. 1837: Acting Assistant Judge and Joint Criminal Judge of Salem; Acting Additional Sub-Collector and Joint Magistrate of Canara; Head Assistant to the Principal Collector and Magistrate of Malabar (Resumed); Acting Assistant Judge and Joint Criminal Judge of Malabar. 1838: Acting Assistant Judge and Joint Criminal Judge of Cochin; Acting Assistant Judge and Joint Criminal Judge of Malabar. 1839: Assistant Judge and Joint Criminal Judge of Malabar. 1840: *Proceeded on furlough.* 1843: *Returned to India;* Sub-Collector and Joint Magistrate, Southern Division of Arcot. 1850: Collector and Magistrate, Nellore. *Died, 31st March 1853, at Pointe de Galle, Ceylon.*

WHITEHILL, John.—1752: Writer. 1768: Senior Merchant and Member of the Council of the Governor. 1780: *Dismissed from Council and service.*

WHITTINGHAM, Charles.—1830: Writer. 1834: Assistant to Principal Collector and Magistrate, South Arcot. 1836: Acting Register to the Zillah Court of Combaconum; Acting Head Assistant to Principal Collector and Magistrate, South Arcot; Officiating Joint Criminal Judge, Chingleput. 1837: Head Assistant to Principal Collector and Magistrate, South Arcot; Officiating Junior Deputy Secretary to the Board of Revenue. 1838: Head Assistant to Collector and Magistrate, South Arcot. 1839: Acting Sub-Collector and Joint Magistrate, South Arcot. 1840: Acting Head Assistant to the Accountant-General; Commissioner for Government Lotteries. 1841: Acting, afterwards Sub-Collector and Joint Magistrate, Tinnevelly. 1845: *Proceeded to Europe on furlough.* 1848: Acting Sub-Collector and Joint Magistrate, Tinnevelly. 1849: Sub-Collector and Joint Magistrate, Tinnevelly. 1854: Collector and Magistrate, North Arcot. 1859: *On medical certificate to England for* 30 *months.* 1861: *Resigned the service,* 18*th December, in England.* (*Annuitant.*) *Died,* 10*th November* 1879, *in London.*

WHITTINGHAM, ANTHONY. — 1837: Writer. 1840: *Proceeded on furlough. Pensioned in England,* 2*d August* 1843.

WHITTINGTON, WILLIAM.—1804: Writer. *Died,* 17*th September* 1806, *in Madras.*

WILLIAMS, MORGAN.—1760: Writer. 1768: Junior Merchant. 1771: Senior Merchant, and Third in Council at Vizagapatam. 1782: Member of the Council of the Governor. *Died in* 1790.

WILLIAMS, HENRY.—1820: Writer; *At home.* 1826: *Returned to India;* Assistant to the Principal Collector and Magistrate of Canara; Head Assistant to the Collector and Magistrate of Chingleput. 1827: Head Assistant to the Collector and Magistrate of Salem. 1828: Head Assistant to the Collector and Magistrate of Cuddapah. *Died,* 29*th March* 1830, *at Cuddapah.*

WILLIAMSON, ROBERT HUDLESTON.—1828: Writer. 1832: Register of the Zillah of Madura; Acting Assistant to the Accountant-General. 1833: Register to the Zillah Court of Rajahmundry. 1834: Register to the Zillah Court of Madura. 1836: *Proceeded to Europe on furlough.* 1841: Acting Deputy Collector of Sea Customs, Madras. 1842: Deputy Collector of Sea Customs, Madras; Commissioner for Government Lotteries. 1845: Acting Collector of Sea Customs, Madras. 1853: Acting Postmaster-General. 1854: Postmaster-General. 1859: Officiating Director-

General of Post Offices in India. 1860: Resumed Charge of Office of Postmaster-General, Madras. 1862: *Proceeded to Europe on furlough; Resigned the service, 25th November* 1862. (*Annuitant.*)

WILLIS, RICHARD LEGGE.—1778: Writer. 1790: Senior Merchant. 1791: Paymaster in Guntoor Circar. 1792: *Suspended from service.*

WILLOCK, ARTHUR.—1817: Writer. 1823: Assistant to the Secretary to the Board of Revenue. *Died, 18th September* 1824, *at Madras.*

WILMOT, ARTHUR.—1824: Writer. 1827: Assistant to the Principal Collector and Magistrate of Bellary. *Died,* 1827, *at Anantapoor.*

WILSON, GEORGE.—1781: Writer. 1782: Assistant to the Secretary in the Civil Department. 1783: Assistant at Vizagapatam. 1790: Paymaster at Chicacole. 1798: Paymaster and Garrison Storekeeper at Vizagapatam and its Dependencies. *Died, 24th August* 1799, *at Vizagapatam.*

WILSON, HENRY.—1789: Writer; Assistant under the Secretary in the Secret Department, and Assistant to the Secretary to the Board of Revenue. 1791: Assistant to the Collector in the Northern and Central Division of Masulipatam Havelly. 1796: Assistant to the Collector in the First Division of the Masulipatam District. 1797: *At home for his health.* 1799: *Returned to India;* Paymaster and Garrison Storekeeper at Jumacondah and its Dependencies. 1800: Deputy Paymaster at Guntoor. 1802: *Out of employ.* 1803: Paymaster and Garrison Storekeeper at Vizagapatam. 1808: *At home.* 1810: *Out of the service.*

WILSON, ALEXANDER.—1797: Writer. 1799: Assistant under the Secretary to the Board of Revenue. 1801: Assistant under the Collector of the Northern Division of Canara. 1803: Register of the Zillah of Rajahmundry. 1805: Subordinate Collector of Canara. 1807: Judge and Magistrate of the Zillah of Honore. 1809: Judge and Magistrate of the Zillah of Canara. 1814: Judge and Magistrate of the Zillah of Malabar. 1823: Judge and Criminal Judge of the Zillah of Malabar. 1824: Third Judge of the Provincial Court, Western Division. 1826: *Annuitant from 1st May. Died, 28th November* 1863, *in England.*

WILSON, WILLIAM.—1830: Writer. 1832: Assistant to the Principal Collector and Magistrate of the Southern Division of

Arcot. 1833: Register of the Zillah of Chingleput. 1834: Register of the Zillah of Chittoor. 1835: *At home.* 1840: *Absent from India five years.*

WISSETT, Robert.—1793: Writer. 1795: Assistant under the Secretary to the Board of Trade. 1796: Assistant under the Resident at Vizagapatam. 1797: Assistant under the Resident at the Presidency. *Died at sea in* 1798.

WISSETT, Thomas.—1795: Writer. 1797: Assistant under the Secretary in the Military, Secret, and Political Department. 1798: Assistant under the Commercial Resident at Vizagapatam. 1800: Deputy Commercial Resident at Ganjam. *Died,* 11*th December* 1806, *at Ganjam.*

WOOD, John.—1772: Writer. 1778: Factor. *No trace after* 1778.

WOOD, Edward.—1800: Writer. 1803: Persian Translator to the Sudder and Foujdarry Adawlut. 1804: Deputy Register to the Sudder and Foujdarry Adawlut. 1806: Acting Register to the Sudder and Foujdarry Adawlut. 1807: Register to the Sudder and Foujdarry Adawlut. 1809: Judge and Magistrate of Seringapatam; Register to the Sudder and Foujdarry Adawlut. 1813: Senior Secretary to Government. 1815: Paymaster of Stipends at the Presidency. 1820: Chief Secretary to Government. *Died,* 28*th May* 1824, *at Madras.*

WOOD, Henry.—1832: Writer. 1834: Assistant to Principal Collector, Cuddapah. 1835: Assistant to Principal Collector, South Arcot. 1837: Assistant to Principal Collector and Magistrate, South Arcot. 1838: Acting Second Assistant to Accountant-General. 1839: *Proceeded to Europe on furlough.* 1841: Acting Register of the Provincial Court of the Northern Division, and Assistant Collector and Magistrate, Chingleput. 1842: Acting Assistant Judge and Joint Criminal Judge, Guntoor. 1843: Acting Head Assistant to Collector and Magistrate, Chingleput. 1844: Head Assistant to Collector and Magistrate, Chingleput. 1845: Acting Sub-Collector and Joint Magistrate, South Arcot. 1846: Head Assistant to Collector and Magistrate, Salem. 1847: Acting Sub-Collector and Joint Magistrate, South Arcot. 1849: Sub-Collector and Joint Magistrate, South Arcot. 1854: Acting Collector and Magistrate, Guntoor. 1855: Collector and Magistrate, Guntoor. 1859: *Leave to England, on private affairs, for* 6 *months;* Collector and Magistrate, South Arcot. 1862: *Proceeded to Europe on furlough.* 1865: *Extension of* 6 *months on* *private affairs; Resigned the service, 14th December, in England. (Annuitant.) Died, 10th October 1873, in England.*

WOODCOCK, CHARLES.—1796: Writer. 1798: Assistant under the Accountant to the Board of Revenue; Senior Assistant under the Accountant to the Board of Revenue; Deputy Postmaster-General. 1800: Deputy Accountant to the Board of Revenue, and Head Assistant to the Accountant-General in the Revenue and Commercial Department. 1801: *At home.* 1806: *Returned to India;* Register of the Zillah of Tinnevelly. 1807: Judge and Magistrate of the Zillah of Combaconum. 1810: Judge and Magistrate of the Zillah of Ganjam. 1818: Judge and Criminal Judge of the Zillah of Guntoor; *Out of employ.* 1820: *At home. (Annuitant on the Fund in 1834.) Died, 25th May 1852, in England.*

WOODCOCK, EDWARD H.—1806: Writer. 1807: Assistant to the Secretary in the Revenue and Judicial Department; Assistant to the Register to the Sudder and Foujdarry Adawlut. 1808: Fixed Examiner under the Secretary in the Revenue and Judicial Department. 1809: Register of the Zillah of Cuddapah. 1812: Register of the Zillah of Tinnevelly. 1816: Register of the Zillah of Salem. 1822: Sub-Collector of Tanjore. 1824: Judge and Criminal Judge of the Zillah of Cuddapah. 1825: Judge and Criminal Judge of the Zillah of Salem. 1828: Third Judge of the Provincial Court, Southern Division. 1830: Second Judge of the Provincial Court, Southern Division. 1831: *At home on absentee allowance. (Annuitant on the Fund from 1st May 1834.) Died, 30th October 1870, in England.*

WOODGATE, CHARLES HENRY.—1832: Writer. 1833: Assistant to the Principal Collector and Magistrate of North Arcot. 1835: Acting Head Assistant to the Collector and Magistrate of Trichinopoly. 1836: Acting Head Assistant to the Collector and Magistrate of Coimbatore. 1838: Head Assistant to the Collector and Magistrate of Trichinopoly. 1844: *Proceeded on furlough.* 1847: *Returned to India.* 1848: Subordinate Judge, Madura. 1855: Civil and Sessions Judge, Tinnevelly. *Died, 30th October 1856, on board the "Alma."*

WOOLF, ROBERT.—1779: Writer. 1790: Senior Merchant. 1791: Auditor of Civil Accounts, Deputy Accountant, and Contractor for Repairs. 1795: Accountant-General. 1803: *At home.* 1805: *Out of the service.*

WORDSWORTH, FAVEL.—1777: Writer. 1782: Factor. *No trace after 1782.*

WRANGHAM, JOHN. — 1783: Writer. 1785: *In Bengal.* 1787: Assistant to the Secretary in the Public Department. 1788: Assistant at Tanjore. 1790: Deputy Paymaster and Deputy Import Warehouse-keeper, and Member of the Committee for Investigating the King's Army Accounts. 1791: Assistant to the Collector of Madura and Dindigul. 1793: Member of the Committee of Investigation at Noozeed. 1796: Collector of the Fourth Division of the Masulipatam Districts. 1798: *Out of employ.* 1800: *At home. Died, 4th November* 1804, *at Tunbridge Wells.*

WREY, EDWARD BOURCHIER.—1811: Writer. 1815: Assistant to the Accountant-General. 1819: Secretary to the Native Pension Fund Committee. 1822: Assistant to the Accountant-General. 1825: Register to the Provincial Court, Northern Division. 1827: Assistant Judge and Joint Criminal Judge of Masulipatam. 1830: *At home on absentee allowance.* 1833: *Returned to India.* 1834: Judge and Criminal Judge of Nellore; Judge and Criminal Judge of Rajahmundry. (*Annuitant on the Fund in* 1839.) *Died,* 30*th May* 1840, *in England.*

WRIGHT, WILLIAM EVATT.—1794: Writer. 1797: Assistant under the Secretary to the Board of Revenue. 1799: Acting Deputy Secretary to the Board of Revenue. 1800: *At home.* 1803: *Returned to India;* Deputy Secretary to the Board of Trade. 1805: Malabar Translator to Government. 1806: Judge and Magistrate of Chittoor. 1808: Third Judge of the Provincial Court, Centre Division. 1821: *At home.* 1824: *Out of the service.*

WROUGHTON, JOHN CHARDIN.—1817: Writer. 1823: Assistant to the Collector and Magistrate of Bellary. 1824: Assistant to the Collector and Magistrate of Cuddapah; *At home.* 1827: *Returned to India;* Head Assistant to the Principal Collector and Magistrate of Madura. 1828: Sub-Collector and Joint Magistrate of Cuddapah. 1829: Sub-Collector and Joint Magistrate of Tinnevelly. 1830: Sub-Collector and Joint Magistrate of Madura. 1835: Collector and Magistrate of Masulipatam, and in Charge of the Treasury there. 1836: Acting Collector of Sea Customs at Madras, and Member of the Marine Board. 1838: Collector of Sea Customs at Madras, and Member of the Marine Board. 1841: Principal Collector and Magistrate of Coimbatore. 1851: *Proceeded on furlough.* 1852: *Resigned the service, 30th April, in India.* (*Annuitant on the Fund,* 1852.) *Died,* 30*th November* 1854, *in England.*

WYLIE, George.—1849: Writer. 1851: Assistant to Collector and Magistrate, Chingleput. 1853: *Proceeded on furlough.* 1854: *Returned to India;* Assistant to Collector and Magistrate, Guntoor. 1855: Head Assistant to Collector and Magistrate, Guntoor. 1857: Head Assistant to Collector and Magistrate, Rajahmundry; *Proceeded on furlough.* 1859: *Resigned the service, 12th April, in England.*

WYNCH, William.—1767: Writer. 1774: Factor and Assistant at Masulipatam. 1776: Junior Merchant and Paymaster at Trichinopoly. 1778: *At home. Returned to India after 1782, became Senior Merchant, and was at home in 1790.* 1793: *Out of the service.*

WYNCH, Alexander.—1768: Member of the Council of the Governor. 1774: Governor of the Presidency. *Resigned before 1775.*

WYNCH, George.—1772: Writer. 1778: Factor. 1780: Junior Merchant. 1790: Senior Merchant. 1791: Third in Council at Ganjam. 1792: Collector at Caroor. 1795: *Without employ. Suspended from the service, and at home in 1800.* 1805: *Out of the service.*

WYNCH, John.—1777: Writer. 1782: Factor; *At home.* 1790: Senior Merchant. 1791: Deputy Export Warehouse-keeper. 1792: Paymaster to the Western Army. 1795: Paymaster at Walajabad and at Arnee. *Died in 1795.*

WYNOX, Charles.—1789: Writer. 1790: Assistant to the Secretary to the Board of Revenue. 1793: Assistant under the Resident at Ingeram. 1794: *Out of employ.* 1796: Collector in the Fourth Division of the Masulipatam District. 1798: *Out of employ.* 1803: Secretary to the Board of Trade. 1807: Acting Member of the Board of Trade. 1811: *At home.* 1815: *Returned to India. Died, January 1818.*

YEATES, Matthew.—1767: Writer. 1774: Factor. 1776: Junior Merchant and Assistant at Ingeram. 1778: Senior Merchant. 1791: Senior Merchant and Resident at Ingeram. 1800: *Without employ. Died, 13th November 1808, at St. Thomé, Madras.*

YOUNG, Samuel.—1781: Writer. 1783: Assistant to the Secretary to the Select Committee in Bengal; Assistant to the Secretary in the Civil Department. 1786: Assistant at Masulipatam. 1787: Paymaster at Ongole and at the Palnaud. 1793: *At home.* 1801: *Returned to India.* 1802: Paymaster and Garrison Storekeeper at Masulipatam and its Dependencies. 1808: *At home.* 1812: *Out of the service.*

YOUNG, Robert Herries.—1797: Writer on the Bencoolen Establishment. 1803: *Transferred to the Madras Presidency;* Acting Assistant to the Secretary in the Military Department; Assistant to the Collector in the Southern Division of Arcot. 1805: Subordinate Collector of Trichinopoly. 1808: Head Assistant to the Collector of Trichinopoly. 1810: Judge and Criminal Judge of Tinnevelly. 1820: Collector and Magistrate of Tinnevelly. *Died, 9th May* 1820, *at Trichindoor.*

YOUNG, Stuart Johnson.—1833: Writer. 1835: Assistant to the Collector and Magistrate of Chingleput. 1837: Assistant to the Principal Collector and Magistrate at Canara. 1838: Acting Head Assistant to the Collector and Magistrate of Tinnevelly. 1840: Head Assistant to Collector and Magistrate, Tinnevelly. *Died, 2d June* 1840, *at Satoor.*

SUPPLEMENTARY LIST

OF

MADRAS CIVIL SERVANTS.

AGNEW, GEORGE VANS.—1852: Writer and Student at the College. 1854: Assistant to Collector and Magistrate, Tanjore. 1856: Acting Assistant to Collector and Magistrate, Trichinopoly; Acting Special Assistant, afterwards Special Assistant at Tanjore. 1859: Acting Sub-Judge, Combaconum; Acting Principal Assistant to Collector and Magistrate, and Agent to the Governor of Fort St. George, in Vizagapatam; Acting Sub-Collector and Joint Magistrate, Godavari. 1860: Sub-Collector and Joint Magistrate, Godavari. 1861: *On medical leave to Europe for 15 months;* Sub-Collector and Joint Magistrate, Tinnevelly. 1863: Sub-Collector and Joint Magistrate, Madura. 1864: *On special leave to Europe for 5 months.* 1866: Acting Collector and Magistrate, Trichinopoly; Sub-Collector and Joint Magistrate, Tanjore. 1867: Acting Collector and Magistrate, Trichinopoly. 1868: Acting Collector and Magistrate, North Arcot; also of Cuddapah. 1869: Collector and Magistrate, Cuddapah. 1870: Collector and Magistrate, Nellore. 1876: *On furlough to Europe.* 1877: *Retired from service, 15th January.* (*Annuitant on the Fund.*)

ALDERSEY, WILLIAM.—1754: Arrived on the Coromandel Coast 8th June as Writer and under the Secretary to the Secret Committee at Fort St. George. 1759: Factor; and Secretary in the Secret Department and Translator. 1761: Secretary, Solicitor, and Clerk of Appeals. 1762: Junior Merchant, and Secretary, Solicitor, and Clerk of Appeals. 1766: *Services transferred to Bengal.* 1767: Senior Merchant, appointed Eighth Member of Council of the Governor of Fort William in Bengal: Import Warehouse-keeper and Buxey. (*See Bengal Volume.*)

AMES, CHARLES HERBERT.—1851: Writer and Student at the

College. 1854: Assistant to Collector and Magistrate, Tinnevelly. 1856: *On medical leave for* 15 *months.* 1857: Assistant and Acting Head Assistant to Collector and Magistrate, Tinnevelly. 1858: Acting Sub-Collector and Magistrate, and Head Assistant to the Collector and Magistrate, Tinnevelly. 1859: Acting Sub-Collector and Magistrate, Canara, afterwards at Madura. 1860: Sub-Collector and Magistrate, Madura. 1862: *On furlough to Europe.* 1864: *Retired from service, 8th February.* (*Invalid Annuitant.*) 1878: *Died, 19th January, at Henley-on-Thames.*

ARBUTHNOTT, HON. DAVID.—1841: Writer. 1843: Assistant to Collector and Magistrate, Bellary. 1845: Acting Head Assistant to Collector and Magistrate, Bellary. 1847: Head Assistant to Collector and Magistrate, Bellary. 1848: Acting Sub-Collector and Joint Magistrate, Bellary. 1849: Acting Sub-Judge, Bellary. 1854: Sub-Collector and Joint Magistrate, Bellary. 1858: Collector and Magistrate of the District of Kurnool. 1860: *On medical leave to Europe for* 24 *months.* 1862: Assumed Charge of Office of Collector and Magistrate, Kurnool; afterwards Collector and Magistrate, Salem. 1867: Acting Collector and Magistrate, afterwards Collector and Magistrate, Madura. 1869: *On furlough to Europe for* 18 *months.* 1871: Acting Collector and Magistrate of Sea Customs and of the Madras District, and Acting Protector of Emigrants, Madras. 1873: Acting Collector and Magistrate, and Agent, Tanjore. 1874: Acting Third Member of the Revenue Board. 1875: Acting Second Member, afterwards Acting First Member of the Revenue Board. 1878: *Retired from service, 1st January.* (*Annuitant on the Fund.*)

ARBUTHNOT, SIR ALEXANDER JOHN, K.C.S.I., C.I.E.—1842: Writer. 1843: Acting Assistant to the Collector and Magistrate, Chingleput. 1844: Assistant to the Principal Collector and Magistrate, Nellore. 1845: Head Assistant to the Register to the Court of Sudder and Foujdarry Adawlut. 1846: Officiating Secretary to the College Board and University, Madras. 1848: Acting Head Assistant to Collector and Magistrate, Cuddapah; afterwards Acting Malayum Translator to Government. 1849: Malayum Translator to Government. 1851: Acting Secretary, afterwards Secretary to the College and University Boards, Madras. 1852: Acting, afterwards Deputy Register to the Court of Sudder and Foujdarry Adawlut. 1853: Acting Register to the aforesaid Court. 1854: Member of, and Secretary to, the Board of Examiners. 1855: Director of Public Instruction. 1861: Commissioner for the Uncovenanted Civil Service Examination. 1862: Acting Chief Secretary, afterwards Chief Secretary to Government; Fellow of the University of Madras. 1864: Additional Member of Council of Fort St. George, for the purpose of making Law and Regulations. 1867: Member of Council. 1872: *On furlough to Europe for 2 years.* 1873: *Made a K.C.S.I. 24th January.* 1874: *Retired from service, 29th October.* 1878: *Made a Companion of the Order of the Indian Empire 1st January.* (*Annuitant on the Fund.*)

ARBUTHNOT, William Henry.—1855: Writer and Student at the College. 1856: Assistant to Collector and Magistrate, North Arcot; afterwards Acting Head Assistant at Tinnevelly. 1857: Acting Second Assistant to the Accountant-General, Madras. 1858: Officiating Second Assistant to the Accountant-General; *On medical leave to Europe for 3 years and 9 months.* 1862: *On medical leave to Europe, forfeiting appointment.* 1865: *Retired from service, 16th February.* (*Invalid Annuitant.*)

ARBUTHNOTT, John Robert.—1857: Writer and Student at the College. 1859: Assistant to Collector and Magistrate, Kurnool. 1861: Officiating Head Assistant, Kurnool. 1862: Head Assistant at Kurnool. 1863: Acting Civil and Sessions Judge, Nundyal. 1865: *On furlough to Europe for 16 months.* 1866: Acting Sub-Collector, Malabar; also Head Assistant Collector, Tinnevelly, Sub-Collector, Bellary, and Sub-Collector, Madura. 1868: Acting Collector and Magistrate, Madura; also in South Arcot. 1869: Acting Collector and Magistrate, Madura. 1870: Acting Collector and Magistrate, Tinnevelly. 1871: *On furlough to Europe for 12 months.* 1872: *Died, 30th April, in England.*

BALLARD, George Alexander.—1845: Writer. 1847: Assistant to Collector and Magistrate, Tinnevelly. 1851: Acting Head Assistant to Collector and Magistrate, Tinnevelly. 1853: In the same capacity at Madura; afterwards Special Assistant to Collector and Magistrate, Masulipatam. 1854: Acting Principal Assistant to Collector and Magistrate, and Agent to the Governor of Fort St. George, in Vizagapatam. 1855: Head Assistant to Collector and Magistrate, Madura; Acting Sub-Collector and Joint Magistrate, Masulipatam; Sub-Collector and Joint Magistrate, Madura; *On furlough to Europe for 3 years.* 1857: Acting Sub-Judge, Chittoor. 1858: Additional Sub-Collector and Joint Magistrate, Bellary; Deputy Director of Revenue Settlement. 1860: *On furlough for the un-*

expired portion of leave granted in 1855, *with* 3 *months in addition for time occupied on his passage to and from India.* 1861: *Returned to Madras.* 1862: Acting Collector and Magistrate, Tanjore; Sub-Collector of Madura; Collector and Magistrate, Malabar. 1869: At first Acting, afterwards Resident in Travancore and Cochin. 1870: *On furlough to Europe for* 14 *months.* 1871: Resumed Office as Resident in Travancore and Cochin. 1875: Acting Second Member, afterwards Acting Third Member, of the Revenue Board. 1876: Third Member of the Revenue Board; *On furlough to Europe for* 1 *year and* 4 *months.* 1877: Acting Second Member of the Revenue Board. 1878: First Member of the Revenue Board; Services placed at the Disposal of the Government of India on Appointment as Member of the Famine Commission. 1879: *Retired from service, 28th January.* (*Annuitant on the Fund.*)

BANBURY, George.—1848: Writer. 1849: Student at the College. 1850: Assistant to Collector and Magistrate, South Arcot. 1853: Acting Head Assistant, South Arcot. 1855: Head Assistant, South Arcot. 1856: Acting Additional Sub-Collector and Joint Magistrate, North Arcot. 1858: Deputy Director of Revenue Settlement. 1859: *On furlough to Europe for* 3 *years and* 4 *months.* 1862: Acting Collector and Magistrate, Kurnool. 1863: Acting Sub-Collector and Joint Magistrate, North Arcot; Acting Civil and Sessions Judge, Cuddalore; Sub-Collector and Joint Magistrate, afterwards Acting Collector and Magistrate, Madras District. 1864: Acting Collector and Magistrate, North Arcot. 1865: Acting Collector and Magistrate, Tinnevelly, afterwards of South Arcot; Acting Civil and Sessions Judge, Rajahmundry; Acting Sub-Secretary to the Revenue Board. 1866: Collector and Magistrate, Trichinopoly, afterwards Acting at Tanjore. 1867: *On medical leave for* 19 *months.* 1870: Acting Director of Revenue Settlement. 1872: Director of Revenue Settlement. 1873: Second Member of the Revenue Board. 1874: *On furlough to Europe for* 15 *months.* 1876: *Retired from service, 21st March.* (*Annuitant on the Fund.*)

BARLOW, Richard Wellesley.—1855: Writer and Student at the College. 1857: Assistant to Collector and Magistrate, Guntoor. 1858: Assistant at South Arcot; *On medical leave to Europe for* 21 *months.* 1860: Assistant to Collector and Magistrate, Nellore. 1861: Officiating Head Assistant, Nellore; Acting Head Assistant, North Arcot. 1862: Head Assistant, North Arcot; Acting Sub-Collector there, with full Powers of a Magistrate.

1864: Justice of the Peace; Acting Sub-Collector, North Arcot; *On special leave for 6 months;* Acting Sub-Collector and Joint Magistrate, North Arcot. 1865: Sub-Collector and Joint Magistrate, North Arcot. 1866: In Charge of the Collector's Office, North Arcot. 1867: Sub-Collector, North Arcot; *On medical leave to Europe for 2 years and 6 months.* 1869: Acting Judge of Small Cause Court, Tellicherry. 1870: Acting Civil and Sessions Judge, Chingleput. 1871: Acting Collector and Magistrate, Chingleput. 1872: Collector and Magistrate, Kistna. 1873: Collector and Magistrate, Godavari; also at Chingleput. 1875: *On furlough to Europe for 12 months.* 1876: Collector, Chingleput. 1878: Acting Commissioner, Nilgiri Hills; Government Member of the Lawrence Asylum Committee; appointed Commissioner, Nilgiri Hills. 1880: Acting Third Member of the Revenue Board; Acting Collector of Sea Customs, and Protector of Emigrants, Madras. 1881: Acting Third Member of the Revenue Board, and in Charge of the Settlement Department; Acting Collector of Sea Customs, and Protector of Emigrants, Madras; Commissioner, Nilgiri Hills. 1882: Collector and Magistrate, and Additional Sessions Judge of the Nilgiri District. 1883: Collector of Sea Customs and Protector of Emigrants, Madras; *On furlough to Europe for 4 months, and 6 weeks in India.* 1884: Resumed Collector of Sea Customs, Madras District; Appointed Acting Resident in Travancore and Cochin; Returned to Madras as Collector of Sea Customs, and Protector of Emigrants.

BIRD, Edward Wheler.—1842: Writer. 1843: Assistant to the Collector and Magistrate, Masulipatam. 1845: Acting Head Assistant to the Collector and Magistrate, Masulipatam. 1846: *Proceeded to Europe.* 1847: Assistant to Collector and Magistrate, Chingleput; afterwards Officiating Government Agent at Chepauk, and Paymaster of Carnatic Stipends. 1848: Acting Head Assistant to the Register to the Court of Sudder and Foujdarry Adawlut; afterwards Assistant to Collector and Magistrate, and Agent to the Governor of Fort St. George, Vizagapatam. 1850: Acting Head Assistant to Collector and Magistrate, Nellore. 1851: Special Assistant to Collector and Magistrate, Masulipatam. 1853: Acting Assistant Judge, afterwards Assistant Judge, Combaconum. 1856: Acting Civil and Sessions Judge, Combaconum. 1857: Acting Sub-Judge, Combaconum. 1858: Sub-Judge, Octacamund. 1859: Acting Civil and Sessions Judge, Coimbatore. 1861: Officiating, afterwards Acting Civil and Sessions Judge, Negapatam;

Civil and Sessions Judge, Tanjore. 1866: *On medical leave to Europe.* 1868: *Retired from service, 28th September.* (*Annuitant on the Fund.*)

BLAIR, JOHN HUNTER.—1845: Writer. 1846: Under the Principal Collector of Coimbatore. 1847: Assistant to Collector and Magistrate, Madura. 1848: In the same capacity at Tinnevelly. 1851: Acting Head Assistant to Collector and Magistrate, Tinnevelly. 1852: *Absent in England.* 1853: Assistant to Collector and Magistrate, Rajahmundry; Acting Assistant, afterwards Assistant to Collector and Magistrate, and Agent to the Governor of Fort St. George, in Vizagapatam. 1855: Acting Principal Assistant, and Agent to the Governor, in Vizagapatam. 1856: Acting Sub-Collector and Joint Magistrate, Masulipatam; Acting Sub-Judge, afterwards Sub-Judge, Rajahmundry. 1859: Acting Civil and Sessions Judge, Masulipatam; *Proceeded on furlough to Europe for* 3 *years.* 1863: Acting Civil and Sessions Judge, Cuddalore; afterwards at Tinnevelly; Sub-Collector and Joint Magistate, Tinnevelly, but Acting Collector of Sea Customs, Madras. 1864: Collector of Sea Customs, Madras. 1865: Member of the Income-Tax Commission. 1866: On Special Duty at Calcutta. 1868: Protector of Emigrants, Madras. 1869: On Special Duty at Bangalore. 1870: Collector of the Town of Madras. 1871: Acting Third Member of the Revenue Board; *On furlough to Europe for* 2 *years.* 1873: Resumed Acting Third Member of the Revenue Board. 1876: *On furlough to Europe for* 6 *months.* 1877: *Retired from service, 14th March.* (*Annuitant on the Fund.*) *Died, 27th March* 1885, *in England.*

BLAIR, WILLIAM THOMAS.—1848: Writer. 1849: Assistant to Collector and Magistrate, North Arcot. 1850: Acting Head Assistant, North Arcot. 1851: Acting Head Assistant to Collector and Magistrate, Cuddapah. 1852: Acting Sub-Judge, Cuddapah. 1853: Head Assistant to Collector and Magistrate, Cuddapah. 1856: Acting Sub-Judge, Cuddapah. 1857: Sub-Collector and Magistrate, Cuddapah. 1858: *On medical leave to Europe for* 24 *months.* 1860: Sub-Collector and Joint Magistrate, North Arcot. 1862: Acting Inam Commissioner. 1863: Acting Civil and Sessions Judge, Chittoor; Acting Civil and Sessions Judge, Rajahmundry, but continuing to Act as Inam Commissioner at Madras. 1865: Acting Civil and Sessions Judge, Coimbatore. 1866: Civil and Sessions Judge, Cuddapah, but still Acting as Inam Commissioner; Civil and Sessions Judge, Chingleput, and continuing to

Act as Inam Commissioner. 1868: Civil and Sessions Judge, Berhampore, and Inam Commissioner; Member of the Committee for the Examination of Assistants. 1869: Civil and Sessions Judge, Vizagapatam; Acting Collector, Madras District. 1870: Secretary to the Revenue Board, with Previous Office; Acting Collector and Magistrate, Chingleput. 1871: *On furlough to Europe for 2 years.* 1872: Civil and Sessions Judge, Mangalore. 1873: *Retired from service, 15th January, in England. (Annuitant on the Fund.)* 1877: *Died, 21st December, in England.*

BOSWELL, John Alexander Corrie.—1855: Writer and Student at the College. 1856: Assistant, afterwards Acting Head Assistant, to Collector and Magistrate, Coimbatore. 1858: Assistant to Collector and Magistrate, and Agent to the Governor of Fort St. George, in Vizagapatam; Acting Head Assistant to Collector and Magistrate, Coimbatore. 1859: Head Assistant to Collector and Magistrate, Salem; officiating Subordinate Judge, Combaconum. 1860: *On medical leave to Europe for 3 years and 9 months.* 1863: Acting Sub-Collector and Joint Magistrate, Madras. 1864: Acting Principal Assistant to Collector and Magistrate, and Agent to the Governor, in Vizagapatam; also Head Assistant at Nellore. 1865: Principal Assistant at Vizagapatam; Sub-Collector and Joint Magistrate, Nellore. 1867: Acting Collector and Magistrate, Nellore. 1868: Acting Collector and Magistrate, South Canara. 1869: In the same capacity at Kistna. 1870: Collector and Magistrate, Kistna. 1871: *On furlough to Europe for 12 months.* 1872: *Died, 6th January, in England.*

BREEKS, James Williamson.—1849: Writer and Student at the College. 1852: Assistant to Collector and Magistrate, Bellary. 1855: Acting Third Assistant to the Accountant-General, Madras. 1856: Second Assistant, afterwards Acting First Assistant to the Accountant-General. 1857: Canarese Translator to Government. 1858: Civil Auditor for the Punjab Government. 1859: Officiating Sub-Judge, Madura; Sub-Collector and Joint Magistrate, afterwards Acting Subordinate Judge, Bellary; *Proceeded to Europe on furlough for 3 years.* 1861: Private Secretary to the Governor of Fort St. George. 1864: Judge of Small Cause Court, Combaconum, continuing to Act as Private Secretary to the Governor; *On medical leave to Europe for 3 years.* 1868: Acting Civil and Sessions Judge, Chittoor; Acting Commissioner, afterwards Commissioner, Nilgiri Hills. 1872: *Died, 6th June, in India.*

CADELL, William Molle.—1840: Writer. 1841: Assistant

to the Principal Collector and Magistrate, Canara. 1842: Acting Register of the Zillah Court of Canara; afterwards Assistant to the Collector and Magistrate, Chingleput. 1845: Assistant, afterwards Acting Head Assistant to the Collector and Magistrate, Chingleput. 1846: Acting Head Assistant to the Collector and Magistrate, Masulipatam; afterwards Head Assistant to Collector and Magistrate, Trichinopoly. 1847: *On furlough to Europe.* 1850: *Returned to Madras;* Assistant to Collector and Magistrate, Nellore; and Acting Head Assistant of that District; *Proceeded to Europe.* 1851: *Without employ on return.* 1852: Acting Sub-Judge, Combaconum. 1853: Head Assistant to Collector and Magistrate, afterwards Acting Sub-Collector and Joint Magistrate, then Sub-Collector and Joint Magistrate, Tanjore. 1858: Collector and Magistrate, Tanjore. 1862: *On medical leave for* 15 *months.* 1865: Collector and Magistrate, South Canara. 1867: Acting Civil and Sessions Judge, Cuddapah; afterwards at Trichinopoly. 1870: Acting Collector and Magistrate, Trichinopoly; Civil and Sessions Judge, Tellicherry, continuing to Act as before; Acting Collector and Magistrate and Political Agent at Tanjore. 1872: Civil and Sessions Judge, Nellore, but continuing to Act as before at Tanjore; also Civil and Sessions Judge, Madura, continuing to Act at Tanjore. 1873: *Retired from service,* 31*st March.* (*Annuitant on the Fund.*)

CARMICHAEL, DAVID FREEMANTLE (SMYTH).—1851: Writer and Student at the College; Assistant to Collector and Magistrate, North Arcot. 1852: Justice of the Peace. 1854: Acting Head Assistant and Register to the Court of Sudder and Foujdarry Adawlut. 1855: Head Assistant and Register to the aforesaid Court; *On medical leave to Europe for* 20 *months.* 1856: Deputy Secretary to Government in Chief Secretary's Departments, and Secretary to the Board of Examiners. 1859: Private Secretary to Sir C. E. Trevelyan, K.C.B., Governor of Fort St. George. 1860: *On medical leave to Europe for* 17 *months.* 1861: Acting Sub-Judge, Chicacole; Principal Assistant to Collector and Magistrate, and Agent to the Governor of Fort St. George, in Ganjam. 1862: Acting Collector and Magistrate, and Agent to the Governor, in Vizagapatam. 1863: Collector and Magistrate, and Agent, Vizagapatam. 1867: Acting, afterwards Collector and Magistrate, and Agent to the Governor, Ganjam. 1869: Acting Judge of the High Court of Judicature; *On furlough to Europe for* 23 *months.* 1871: Acting Secretary to Government, Revenue Department;

Acting Third Member of the Revenue Board; President of the Committee for Examination of Assistants; Inam Commissioner. 1872: Acting Secretary to Government, Revenue Department; Acting Second Member of the Revenue Board; on Special Duty as President of the Committee inquiring into the Action of Officials during the Cyclone; Acting Third Member, afterwards Second Member, and again Third Member of the Revenue Board: Assistant Secretary, afterwards Secretary, to Government, Revenue Department. 1873: *On furlough to Europe for* 8 *months;* resumed Secretary to Government, Revenue Department. 1874: Acting Chief Secretary to Government; additional Member of Council for making Laws and Regulations. 1876: On special duty with Government at the Imperial Assemblage at Delhi. 1877: Chief Secretary to Government. 1878: At first Temporary, afterwards Ordinary Member of Council, *took his seat* 10*th December.* 1883: Vacated Seat in Council; *On furlough to Europe for* 18 *months.*

CARR-GOMM, Francis Culling (*Barrister-at-Law*).—1855: Writer and Student at the College. 1857: Assistant to Collector and Magistrate, Salem. 1858: Acting Head Assistant at Salem. 1859: Acting Head Assistant, afterwards Head Assistant to Collector and Magistrate, Coimbatore; officiating Subordinate Judge, Salem. 1860: Acting Sub-Collector and Joint Magistrate, Salem. 1861: Officiating Sub-Collector and Joint Magistrate, Coimbatore. 1865: Judge of Small Cause Court, Cuddalore. 1866: *On furlough to Europe for* 3 *years and* 3 *months.* 1870: Acting Civil and Sessions Judge, Calicut; Acting Civil and Sessions Judge, Vizagapatam. 1871: Acting Collector and Magistrate, and Agent to the Governor, Ganjam; Acting Civil and Sessions Judge, Tinnevelly. 1872: District and Sessions Judge, Tinnevelly. 1874: *On special leave to Europe for* 6 *months;* Resumed his Previous Duties on Return to Madras. 1878: *On furlough to Europe for* 2 *years and* 7 *months.* (*Took the name of Gomm on marriage.*) 1880: District and Sessions Judge, Coimbatore. 1882: *Retired from the service* 10*th June.* (*Annuitant on the Fund.*)

CHAMIER, Charles Frederic.—1843: Writer. 1844: Assistant to the Principal Collector and Magistrate, Coimbatore. 1847: Acting Head Assistant to the Register to the Court of Sudder and Foujdarry Adawlut, and Acting Secretary to the Madras University and to the College Board; afterwards Acting Head Assistant to Collector and Magistrate, Trichinopoly. 1850: Acting Head Assistant to Collector and Magistrate, Canara. 1852: Head Assistant to Collector and Magistrate, Canara; afterwards Acting Sub-Judge, Mangalore. 1855: Officiating Special Assistant to the Collector, Madras; afterwards Deputy Register to the Court of Sudder and Foujdarry Adawlut, and Tamil Translator to Government. 1857: Acting Register to the Court of Sudder and Foujdarry Adawlut. 1859: Register to the High Court of Judicature, Appellate side. 1864: *On medical leave to Europe for 16 months.* 1865: Civil and Sessions Judge, Salem. 1869: *Died, 20th April, in India.*

CHASE, MORGAN CHARLES.—1847: Writer. 1848: Assistant to Collector and Magistrate, Canara. 1854: Acting Head Assistant to Collector and Magistrate, Canara; afterwards Head Assistant at Bellary. 1856: Acting Sub-Judge, Cuddapah; afterwards at Chittoor; also Sub-Collector and Joint Magistrate, Masulipatam. 1857: Assistant to Collector and Magistrate, and Agent to the Governor of Fort St. George, in Vizagapatam. 1858: Senior Assistant to Collector and Magistrate, and Agent to the Governor in Ganjam; Acting Sub-Collector and Joint Magistrate, Masulipatam; *Proceeded on furlough to Europe for 12 months.* 1863: *Retired from service, 5th January, in England. (Annuitant on the Fund.)* 1874: *Died, 21st December, in England.*

CHASE, THOMAS ALEXANDER NICHOLLS.—1850: Writer and Student at the College. 1851: Assistant to Collector and Magistrate, Masulipatam. 1855: Acting Head Assistant at Masulipatam; afterwards Head Assistant to Collector and Magistrate, Rajahmundry; then Head Assistant at Masulipatam. 1859: Acting Sub-Collector and Magistrate, Masulipatam; afterwards Head Assistant and Acting Sub-Collector and Magistrate, Kistna. 1860: *On furlough to Europe for 2 years.* 1862: Acting Sub-Collector and Joint Magistrate, Godavari. 1863: Sub-Collector and Joint Magistrate, Kistna, but continuing to Act as before; Acting Civil and Sessions Judge, Rajahmundry. 1865: Sub-Collector and Joint Magistrate, Godavari; Acting Collector and Magistrate, Kistna. 1866: Acting Civil and Sessions Judge, Cuddapah; Acting Collector and Magistrate, Kistna, afterwards at Nellore, then at Kurnool. 1867: Collector and Magistrate, Kurnool. 1873: *On furlough to Europe for 2 years.* 1875: *Retired from service, 8th April. (Annuitant on the Fund.)*

CHILD, FREDERICK SAMUEL.—1844: Writer. 1846: Assistant to Collector and Magistrate, South Arcot. 1847: Assistant to

Collector and Magistrate, Tinnevelly. 1849: Assistant to Collector and Magistrate, Nellore; afterwards at Tinnevelly. 1851: Acting Head Assistant, afterwards Head Assistant, to Collector and Magistrate, Tinnevelly. 1855: Acting Sub-Judge, Madura; afterwards Sub-Collector and Joint Magistrate, Madura. 1855: *On furlough to Europe.* 1857: Resumed Acting Sub-Judge at Madura. 1858: Sub-Collector and Joint Magistrate, Malabar. 1859: *On furlough to Europe for the unexpired portion of his leave obtained in* 1855; *Granted* 12 *months' extension on medical certificate in* 1859 *and* 1861. 1861: *Returned to Madras, 25th October.* 1862: Acting Sub-Collector and Joint Magistrate, afterwards Sub-Collector, South Arcot; Acting Civil and Sessions Judge, afterwards Civil Judge, Guntoor; Civil and Sessions Judge, Cuddapah. 1865: Civil and Sessions Judge, Tinnevelly. 1867: *On medical leave for* 4 *months.* 1869: *On furlough to Europe for* 12 *months.* 1871: *Retired from service, 22d July.* (*Annuitant on the Fund.*) 1873: *Died, 1st October, in England.*

COCKERELL, John Rennie.—1850: Writer and Student at the College. 1852: Assistant to Collector and Magistrate, Madura. 1855: Acting Head Assistant, afterwards Head Assistant at Madura. 1856: Acting Sub-Judge, Madura; Acting Sub-Collector and Joint Magistrate, Madura. 1859: Acting Sub-Judge, Combaconum; Sub-Collector and Joint Magistrate, Tinnevelly. 1860: Acting Sub-Collector and Joint Magistrate, South Arcot. 1861: Officiating Collector and Magistrate, South Arcot; *On furlough for* 3 *years.* 1865: Acting Sub-Collector and Joint Magistrate, Kistna; Acting Collector of Sea Customs, Madras; Acting Collector and Magistrate, Cuddapah; Acting Sub-Collector and Joint Magistrate, Madras. 1866: Sub-Collector and Joint Magistrate, afterwards Acting Collector and Magistrate, Madras. 1867: Sub-Secretary, afterwards Acting Secretary of the Revenue Board; Civil and Sessions Judge, Nellore. 1872: Commissioner, Nilgiri Hills. 1878: *Retired from service, 30th September.* (*Annuitant on the Fund.*)

COLLETT, Charles.—1845: Writer. 1846: Assistant to the Collector and Magistrate, Nellore. 1847: Assistant to Collector and Magistrate, Malabar. 1851: Acting Head Assistant to Collector and Magistrate, Malabar. 1855: Acting Sub-Judge, Calicut; afterwards Sub-Collector and Joint Magistrate, Malabar. 1856: Acting Deputy Collector of Sea Customs, Madras; *Proceeded to Europe on furlough.* 1857: Resumed Acting Deputy Collectorship of Sea

Customs, Madras; afterwards Additional Sub-Collector and Joint Magistrate, Bellary. 1858: Sub-Collector and Joint Magistrate, Bellary. 1859: *On furlough to Europe for the unexpired portion of his leave granted in 1856.* 1861: *Permitted extension of 2 months and 6 days on account of time occupied on his passage to and from India;* Officiating Collector of Sea Customs, Madras; afterwards Member of Central Committee at Madras for the London Exhibition of 1862; also Commissioner for the Assessment of Income-Tax; and Sub-Judge, Calicut. 1862: Acting Civil and Sessions Judge, Chittoor; Judge of the Small Cause Court, Cuddalore. 1863: Acting Civil and Sessions Judge, Nundyal; Civil and Sessions Judge, Vizagapatam. 1866: Judge of the High Court of Judicature, Madras. 1871: *Retired from service, 30th July. (Annuitant on the Fund.)*

DALYELL, ROBERT ANSTRUTHER, C.S.I.—1850: Writer and Student at the College. 1853: Assistant to Collector and Magistrate, Salem. 1855: *On medical leave to Europe for 39 months.* 1859: Assistant Collector and Magistrate, South Arcot; Senior Assistant to Collector and Magistrate, and Agent to the Governor of Fort St. George, in Vizagapatam; Acting Sub-Collector, South Arcot. 1860: Principal Assistant to Collector and Magistrate, and Agent to the Governor, in Vizagapatam; to Act as Sub-Collector, South Arcot; Acting Subordinate Judge at Chicacole. 1861: Officiating Sub-Secretary, afterwards Sub-Secretary to the Revenue Board; Commissioner for the Assessment of Income-Tax. 1862: *On special leave for 6 months.* 1864: Member of the Income-Tax Commission. 1865: Acting Secretary to the Revenue Board; Officiating President of the Income-Tax Commission; Acting Secretary to the Board of Examiners. 1866: Secretary to the Board of Examiners; Acting Secretary to the Revenue Board; Acting Inam Commissioner; Acting Collector of Sea Customs, Madras. 1867: Secretary, Board of Revenue; and Acting Collector of Sea Customs. 1868: Acting Secretary to Government, Revenue Department. 1870: Collector and Magistrate, Madras District, as well as Secretary to Government; Collector and Magistrate, Chingleput; *On furlough to Europe for 12 months.* 1872: Acting Third Member of the Revenue Board; On Special Duty in Mysore. 1873: Additional Member of the Governor-General's Council for Making Laws and Regulations; Acting Secretary to Government, Revenue Department; Acting Chief Secretary to Government; Third Member of the Revenue

Board. 1875: Officiating Chief Commissioner of Mysore and Coorg. 1876: Second Member of the Revenue Board. 1877: *Proceeded on furlough to Europe;* appointed Member of Council of the Secretary of State for India, and took his seat 6th November, with permission to be considered still in the service of the Madras Government. 1879: *Retired from the service, 12th March; made a C.S.I., 29th July* 1879. (*Annuitant on the Fund.*)

DAVIDSON, ROBERT, C.S.I.—1852: Writer and Student at the College. 1853: Assistant to Collector and Magistrate, Salem. 1854: Acting Assistant, afterwards Assistant, to Collector and Magistrate, and Agent to the Governor of Fort St. George, in Ganjam. 1856: Acting Principal Assistant, and Agent to the Governor, in Ganjam. 1857: *On medical leave to Europe for* 21 *months.* 1858: Head Assistant to Collector and Magistrate, Malabar. 1859: Acting Sub-Judge, Rajahmundry; Head Assistant to Collector and Magistrate, Trichinopoly; afterwards Head Assistant at Malabar; Acting Principal Assistant to Collector and Magistrate, and Agent to the Governor of Fort St. George, in Vizagapatam. 1860: Officiating Collector and Magistrate, and Agent to the Governor, Ganjam; Subordinate Judge, Cuddapah. 1861: Acting Civil and Sessions Judge, Cuddapah. 1862: Sub-Judge, Cuddapah; Judge of the Court of Small Causes, Chittoor; Acting Civil and Sessions Judge, Madura; Acting Judge of Small Cause Court, Madura. 1863: Judge of Small Cause Court, Chittoor; Acting Civil and Sessions Judge, Nundyal. 1864: Justice of the Peace; Acting Civil and Sessions Judge, Bellary. 1866: Judge of Small Cause Court, Chittoor; Acting Civil and Sessions Judge, Tanjore. 1867: Civil and Sessions Judge, Trichinopoly. 1868: *On furlough to Europe for* 15 *months.* 1869: Resumed Civil and Sessions Judge, Trichinopoly. 1870: Acting Commissioner, Nilgiri Hills. 1873: *On special leave to Europe for* 6 *months.* 1874: District and Sessions Judge, Cuddapah; Acting Collector and Magistrate, and Agent to the Governor, in Ganjam. 1876: District and Sessions Judge, Chingleput; Acting Collector and Magistrate, Kurnool. 1878: *On furlough to Europe for* 22 *months;* appointed while on furlough Third Member of the Revenue Board; *Made a C.S.I.* 25*th May,* 1878. 1880: Chief Secretary to Government; Additional Member of the Legislative Council. 1881: Provisional Member of Council; Chief Secretary to Government. 1882: Acting First Member of the Revenue Board; In Charge of the Settlement Department; First Member of the Revenue Board; In Charge of the Inam Department. 1883: *On furlough to Europe for 9 months and 12 days.* 1884: *Retired from service 1st July.* (*Annuitant on the Fund.*)

DYKES, JAMES WILLIAM BALLANTYNE.—1842: Writer. 1844: Assistant to the Principal Collector and Magistrate, Salem. 1847: Acting Head Assistant to the Collector and Magistrate, Salem. 1849: Head Assistant to Collector and Magistrate, Salem. 1851: Acting Sub-Judge of the Zillah of Madura. 1852: Acting Sub-Judge of the Zillah of Chittoor; *On furlough to Europe.* 1857: Acting, afterwards Sub-Collector and Joint Magistrate, Salem. 1858: On Special Duty in Rajahmundry and Masulipatam; Acting Sub-Collector and Joint Magistrate, Cuddapah; afterwards Sub-Collector and Joint Magistrate, Rajahmundry. 1859: Acting Collector and Magistrate, Guntoor; afterwards at Nellore; then Sub-Collector and Joint Magistrate, Godavari. 1860: Collector and Magistrate, Nellore. 1867: *On medical leave to Europe for 18 months.* 1869: *Resigned the service, 4th September, in India.* (*Annuitant on the Fund.*)

ELLIOT, EDWARD FREDERICK.—1854: Writer and Student at the College. 1855: Assistant to Collector and Magistrate, Cuddapah; afterwards at North Arcot. 1856: Acting Head Assistant at South Arcot. 1857: Returned to North Arcot as Acting Head Assistant. 1859: Head Assistant to Collector and Magistrate, North Arcot; Acting Subordinate Judge, Chittoor; Officiating Sub-Collector and Joint Magistrate, Bellary, and at North Arcot. 1860: Officiating Sub-Collector and Joint Magistrate, Madras. 1862: Sub-Collector of Nellore; Acting Civil and Sessions Judge, Nellore. 1864: *On furlough to Europe for 3 years.* 1867: Sub-Collector and Joint Magistrate, Kistna; Acting Civil and Sessions Judge, Tranquebar. 1868: Acting Civil and Sessions Judge, Chittoor. 1869: Sub-Collector and Joint Magistrate, Tanjore, with Duties as before; Civil and Sessions Judge, Salem. 1873: *Died, 27th October, in India.*

ELLIS, ROBERT STAUNTON, C.B.—1844: Writer. 1846: Under the Principal Collector, Coimbatore; afterwards Assistant to Collector and Magistrate, Tanjore. 1848: *On furlough to Europe.* 1851: Assistant to the Collector of Land Customs, Madras. 1852: Head Assistant to the Register to the Court of Sudder and Foujdarry Adawlut. 1853: Acting Deputy Register to the aforesaid Court. 1854: Deputy Commissioner of the Second Class, Nagpore Commission. 1858: *On medical leave to Europe for 21 months.* 1860: Officiating Collector and Magistrate, Chingleput; afterwards

Sub-Collector, Madras, and Joint Magistrate, Chingleput; *Made a C.B. 19th May;* Special Commissioner for the Assessment of Income-Tax. 1862: Acting Superintendent of Stamps; Acting Deputy Secretary to Government in Chief Secretary's Departments; Member and Commissioner for the Assessment of Income-Tax; Services placed temporarily at the Disposal of the Government of India; Additional Member of Governor-General's Council for Making Laws and Regulations. 1863: Acting Collector and Magistrate, afterwards Collector and Magistrate, Madras District; on Special Duty as Member of Governor-General's Council. 1864: President of the Sanitary Commission. 1865: *On special leave to Europe for 12 months.* 1867: Chief Secretary to Government. 1869: Officiating Member of Council. 1872: Appointed Member of Council. 1873: *On furlough to Europe for 12 months.* 1875: Member of Council. 1877: *Retired from service,* 12*th March; Appointed Member of Council of the Secretary of State for India; Died, 9th October* 1877, *in London.*

FLOYER, Charles.—1755: Arrived on the Coromandel Coast 9th June; Writer and under the Secretary to the Secret Committee at Fort St. George. 1759: Commissary to the Troops in the Field. 1760: Factor, and under the Military Paymaster. 1761: Resident at Tranquebar; afterwards under the Import Warehouse-keeper. 1764: Junior Merchant, and Paymaster at Trichinopoly. 1766: *Services transferred to Bengal.* 1767: Senior Merchant; appointed Tenth Member of Council of the Governor of Fort William in Bengal, and Military Storekeeper. (*See Bengal Volume.*)

FOORD, Edward Bromley.—1844: Writer. 1846: Assistant to Collector and Magistrate, Masulipatam. 1851: Acting Senior Assistant to Collector and Magistrate, and Agent to the Governor of Fort St. George in Vizagapatam. 1853: Assistant to Collector and Magistrate, and Agent to the Governor, in Vizagapatam. 1854: Acting Principal Assistant to Collector and Magistrate, and Agent to the Governor, in Ganjam. 1856: Sub-Judge, Rajahmundry; *Proceeded to Europe on furlough.* 1859: Acting Subordinate Judge, Chittoor. 1860: Sub-Collector and Joint Magistrate, Bellary. 1861: Officiating Civil and Sessions Judge, Chingleput; *On medical leave for* 10 *months.* 1862: Acting Collector and Magistrate, Bellary; afterwards at Kistna. 1864: Acting Civil and Sessions Judge, Chicacole; Acting Collector and Magistrate, and Agent to the Governor, in Ganjam. 1865: Civil and Sessions Judge, Bellary; afterwards at Berhampore. 1868:

District and Sessions Judge, Chingleput. 1870: *On furlough to Europe for* 12 *months.* 1871: Resumed District and Sessions Judge, Chingleput. 1874: *On furlough to Europe for* 13 *months.* 1876: *Retired from service,* 15*th July.* (*Annuitant on the Fund.*)

FORBES, Louis.—1850: Writer and Student at the College. 1853: Assistant to Collector and Magistrate, Nellore. 1854: Acting Head Assistant at Nellore. 1855: Acting Head Assistant to the Register to the Court of Sudder and Foujdarry Adawlut. 1856: Acting Assistant Judge, Combaconum; Head Assistant to Collector and Magistrate, Nellore; Acting Sub-Secretary to the Revenue Board. 1858: Acting Additional Sub-Collector, Bellary; afterwards Acting Deputy Collector of Sea Customs, Madras. 1859: Deputy Secretary to Government in Chief-Secretary's Departments, and Secretary to the Board of Examiners. 1861: *On furlough for* 3 *years and* 8 *months.* 1865: Acting Civil and Sessions Judge, Nundyal; Sub-Collector and Joint Magistrate, Bellary. 1866: Judge of the Small Cause Court, Madura; and Civil and Sessions Judge, Nundyal. 1869: *On furlough to Europe for* 12 *months.* 1871: Acting Civil and Sessions Judge, Bellary. 1872: *On special leave to Europe for* 6 *months.* 1873: Resumed Acting Civil and Sessions Judge, Bellary. 1874: District and Sessions Judge, Coimbatore, continuing to Act as before mentioned. 1875: Acting Judge of the High Court of Judicature, Madras. 1877: District and Sessions Judge, Bellary. 1878: Again Acting Judge of the High Court, Madras. 1880: *On furlough to Europe for* 12 *months.* 1881: Additional Member of the Governor-General's Legislative Council. 1882: *Retired from service,* 4*th April.* (*Annuitant on the Fund.*)

FRASER, James.—1840: Writer. 1841: Assistant to the Collector and Magistrate, Bellary; afterwards at Rajahmundry. 1842: In the same Capacity at Masulipatam. 1843: Acting Assistant to the Collector and Magistrate, and Agent to the Governor of Fort St. George, in Ganjam. 1845: Acting Principal Assistant to the Collector and Magistrate, and Agent to the Governor, in Ganjam. 1854: Sub-Collector and Joint Magistrate, Masulipatam. 1855: Acting Collector and Joint Magistrate, Masulipatam. 1856: Acting Collector and Magistrate, Masulipatam. 1857: *On medical leave to Europe for* 15 *months.* 1859: Acting Collector and Magistrate, Cuddapah; afterwards Sub-Collector and Joint Magistrate, Kistna. 1860: Collector and Magistrate, South Canara. 1861: *On medical leave for* 3 *months.* 1862: Acting Collector and Magistrate, North

Arcot. 1863: Collector and Magistrate, Trichinopoly, but to continue to act as before. 1864: Acting Collector and Magistrate, Godavari. 1868: *On special leave for* 6 *months.* 1869: Collector and Magistrate, Godavari. 1871: *On furlough to Europe for* 2 *years.* 1873: *Retired from service, 1st August.* (*Annuitant on the Fund.*)

GARSTIN, John Henry, C.S.I.—1857: Writer and Student at the College. 1859: *Leave on private affairs to Calcutta for* 6 *months;* Assistant to the Collector and Magistrate, Tinnevelly. 1860: Officiating Head Assistant, afterwards Head Assistant at Tinnevelly. 1863: Acting Sub-Collector and Joint Magistrate, Malabar; Justice of the Peace. 1864: Head Assistant, Malabar; Acting Sub-Collector there. 1866: Private Secretary to H. E. Lord Napier. 1871: Acting Collector of Sea Customs, and Protector of Emigrants, Madras; Acting Collector and Magistrate, South Arcot; afterwards Collector and Magistrate, and Special Agent of the French Settlement and Political Agent for Pondicherry. 1872: *On furlough to Europe for* 21 *months.* 1874: Collector, South Arcot. 1875: On Special Duty at Madras. 1876: Collector, South Arcot; Acting Secretary to Government, Revenue Department. 1877: Temporary Additional Secretary to Government, Revenue Department. 1878: Collector, District Magistrate, and Agent to the Governor, in Vizagapatam; *Made a C.S.I.* 25*th May.* 1879: Acting Secretary to Government, Revenue Department. 1880: On Duty in the Government Secretariat; Collector, Magistrate, and Agent to the Governor, in Vizagapatam. 1881: Collector, Vizagapatam. *On furlough to Europe for* 20 *months.* 1882: Appointed Third Member of the Revenue Board. 1883: Acting Second Member, afterwards Acting First Member, of the Revenue Board; Also intrusted with the Duty of Revising the Establishments of Collectors and Divisional Officers in the Presidency. 1884: Second Member, afterwards Acting First Member, of the Revenue Board; Also Magistrate of the First Class with ordinary and special Powers, in Tinnevelly District.

GOLDINGHAM, John Dalrymple.—1853: Writer and Student at the College. 1855: Assistant to Collector and Magistrate, Salem. 1856: Acting Head Assistant at Cuddapah; afterwards at Bellary. 1857: Head Assistant to Collector and Magistrate, Bellary. 1858: Officiating Sub-Judge, Bellary. 1859: Officiating Sub-Judge, Madura. 1861: Head Assistant Collector and Magistrate, South Canara; Sub-Judge, Madura; Officiating Civil and Sessions Judge, Tinnevelly; Officiating Sub-Collector and Joint Magistrate, Madura. 1862: Sub-Judge, Madura; *On special leave to Europe for 6 months.* 1862: Judge of the Court of Small Causes, Madura. 1864: Justice of the Peace; Acting Civil and Sessions Judge, afterwards Judge of the Small Cause Court, Madura. 1865: *On furlough to Europe for 3 years.* 1868: Resumed Acting Civil and Sessions Judge, Madura. 1869: Civil and Sessions Judge, Madura. 1872: District and Sessions Judge, Nellore. 1874: *On furlough to Europe for 2 years.* 1876: District Judge, Nellore. 1880: *On furlough to Europe for 8 months;* Resumed District Judge, Nellore. 1881: Acting District and Sessions Judge, Bellary. 1882: District and Sessions Judge, Bellary.

GRÆME, Henry Munro Showers.—1848: Writer and Student at the College. 1851: Assistant to Collector and Magistrate, Salem; afterwards at Cuddapah. 1854: Acting Head Assistant to Collector and Magistrate, Salem. 1856: Acting Sub-Judge, Salem; Head Assistant to Collector and Magistrate, Trichinopoly. 1857: Acting Additional Sub-Collector and Joint Magistrate, Canara. 1859: *On furlough to Europe for 3 years and 9 months.* 1863: Acting Civil and Sessions Judge, Salem; Acting Sub-Collector and Joint Magistrate, South Arcot, also at Kistna; Sub-Collector and Joint Magistrate, Tinnevelly. 1864: *On medical leave to Europe.* 1868: *Resigned the service, 2d February, in England.* (*Invalid Annuitant.*) 1884: *Died, 28th August, in England.*

GRANT, Patrick.—1842: Writer. 1844: Assistant to the Collector and Magistrate, Tinnevelly. 1845: Assistant to Collector and Magistrate, Tanjore. 1846: Special Assistant to Collector and Magistrate, Tanjore. 1852: Acting Sub-Collector and Joint Magistrate, Tanjore. 1853: *Proceeded to Europe.* 1856: *Without employ.* 1857: Additional Sub-Collector and Joint Magistrate, South Arcot; afterwards Sub-Collector and Joint Magistrate, Salem. 1858: Acting Collector and Magistrate, Malabar. 1859: Collector and Magistrate, Malabar. 1862: Collector and Magistrate, Coimbatore. 1862: *Resigned the service, 21st March, in India.* (*Annuitant on the Fund.*)

HANNYNGTON, John Child.—1857: Writer and Student at the College. 1859: *On leave to Bengal for 6 months;* Assistant to Collector and Magistrate, Trichinopoly. 1861: Officiating Head Assistant at Malabar; Justice of the Peace. 1862: Invested with Full Powers of a Magistrate. 1863: Special Assistant to Collector and Magistrate, and Acting Head Assistant, Malabar;

Special Assistant to Collector and Magistrate, Coimbatore. 1866: Acting Judge of Small Cause Court, Tellicherry. 1867: Sub-Collector, Bellary; Acting Collector and Magistrate, Malabar; Judge of Small Cause Court, Tellichery. 1868: Acting Civil and Sessions Judge, Tellicherry; afterwards at Calicut. 1869: *On furlough to Europe for 2 years.* 1871: Resumed Judge of Small Cause Court, Tellicherry; Acting Collector and Magistrate, Malabar; also at Kistna. 1872: Acting Civil and Sessions Judge, Guntoor. 1873: Judge of Small Cause Court, Vellore; District and Sessions Judge, Guntoor; afterwards at Salem. 1876: *On furlough to Europe for 2 years.* 1878: Acting Resident, Travancore and Cochin. 1879: District and Sessions Judge, Salem. 1880: On Special Duty as Arbitrator of Boundary Disputes between Travancore and Cochin. 1881: Acting Resident, Travancore and Cochin. 1882: Resident at Travancore and Cochin. 1883: *On furlough to Europe for 15 months.* 1884: Resumed Resident at Travancore and Cochin.

HATHAWAY, WILLIAM FREDERICK.—1858: Writer and Student at the College. 1859: Assistant to Collector and Magistrate, Salem. 1860: Acting Head Assistant at Salem. 1862: Head Assistant at Salem. 1864: Acting Sub-Collector and Joint Magistrate, Madras; afterwards at North Arcot. 1865: *On furlough to Europe for 16 months.* 1866: Acting Sub-Collector, North Arcot; also Head Assistant to Collector and Magistrate, Kurnool. 1867: Acting Sub-Collector, South Arcot; Sub-Collector, Tinnevelly; Sub-Collector and Joint Magistrate, South Arcot. 1868: Sub-Collector and Joint Magistrate, Tanjore. 1870: Acting Collector and Magistrate, Tanjore; *On furlough to Europe for 18 months.* 1871: *Retired from service, 15th November.*

HODGSON, WILLIAM.—1840: Writer. 1841: Under the Principal Collector of Malabar. 1843: Assistant to the Principal Collector and Magistrate, Nellore. 1844: *Absent in Europe.* 1848: Assistant to Collector and Magistrate, Rajahmundry; *Proceeded to Europe.* 1851: Assistant to Collector and Magistrate, South Arcot. 1852: Acting Head Assistant to Collector and Magistrate, South Arcot; afterwards Head Assistant at Salem. 1853: Acting Sub-Judge, Salem. 1855: Acting Sub-Judge, Mangalore; *Proceeded to Europe.* 1857: Acting Sub-Judge, Salem. 1859: Sub-Judge, Bellary; afterwards at Salem. 1861: Acting Civil and Sessions Judge, Chittoor; afterwards at Salem. 1862: Assistant to Collector and Magistrate, Coimbatore. 1863:

Acting Civil and Sessions Judge, Tinnevelly. 1864: Sub-Collector and Joint Magistrate, Nellore; Acting Sub-Collector and Joint Magistrate, Tinnevelly. 1865: Civil and Sessions Judge, Guntoor. 1867: *On medical leave to Europe for* 10 *months.* 1868: Civil and Sessions Judge, Cuddapah; Acting Civil and Sessions Judge, Cuddalore. 1870: District and Sessions Judge, South Arcot. 1872: *On furlough to Europe for* 2 *years.* 1874: *Retired from service,* 19*th February.* (*Annuitant on the Fund.*)

HODGSON, Arthur Pemberton.—1844: Writer. 1845: Permitted to Pursue his Studies under the Collector of Salem. 1847: Assistant to Collector and Magistrate, Madura. 1847: Acting Head Assistant to Collector and Magistrate, Madura. 1851: Head Assistant to Collector and Magistrate, Madura. 1855: Acting Sub-Judge, Madura; *Proceeded to Europe.* 1857: *Without employ for* 5 *months.* 1858: Acting Sub-Collector and Joint Magistrate, afterwards Sub-Collector and Joint Magistrate, Madura. 1859: *On medical leave to Europe for* 2 *years.* 1861: Sub-Collector and Joint Magistrate, Cuddapah; Acting Collector and Magistrate, South Canara. 1862: Sub-Collector and Joint Magistrate, Kistna. 1863: Acting Sub-Collector and Joint Magistrate, Coimbatore; *on furlough to Europe.* 1866: *Resigned the service,* 16*th February, in England.* (*Invalid Annuitant.*)

HOLLOWAY, William, C.S.I.—1848: Writer. 1849: Student at the College. 1851: Assistant to Collector and Magistrate, Tanjore. 1852: Acting Head Assistant to Collector and Magistrate, Tanjore. 1853: Acting Deputy Register, afterwards Acting Head Assistant to the Register to the Court of Sudder and Foujdarry Adawlut. 1854: Head Assistant to Collector and Magistrate, Masulipatam. 1855: Acting Sub-Judge; Head Assistant to Collector and Magistrate, Rajahmundry: afterwards Acting Sub-Judge, Calicut. 1856: Head Assistant to Collector and Magistrate, Trichinopoly; Special Assistant to Collector and Magistrate, Tanjore; and Assistant to Collector and Magistrate, and Agent to the Governor of Fort St. George, in Vizagapatam. 1857: Sub-Judge, Calicut. 1859: Secretary to the Commission for Inquiring into the System of Judicature in the Madras Presidency; afterwards Acting Civil and Sessions Judge, Tellicherry. 1861: Civil and Sessions Judge, Tellicherry. 1863: Acting Puisne Judge, afterwards Judge of the High Court of Judicature, Madras. 1868: *On medical leave to Europe for* 1 *year and* 8 *months.* 1870: Resumed Judge of the High Court. 1873: Acting Chief

Justice, Madras. 1875: *On furlough to Europe; made a C.S.I., 31st December.* 1877: *Retired from service, 29th January. (Annuitant on the Fund.)*

HOOPER, William Stanley.—1855: Writer and Student at the College. 1857: Assistant to Collector and Magistrate, Nellore. 1858: Acting Head Assistant at Nellore. 1859: Acting Head Assistant at Tanjore. 1860: Senior Assistant to Collector and Magistrate, and Agent to the Governor of Fort St. George, in Ganjam; afterwards Principal Assistant, Ganjam. 1862: Acting Sub-Collector, Madras. 1863: *On medical leave to Europe for 15 months.* 1864: Principal Assistant to Collector and Magistrate, and Agent to the Governor of Fort St. George, in Ganjam. 1865: *Died, 24th February, in India.*

HORSLEY, William Dowdeswell.—1855: Writer and Student at the College. 1856: Assistant to Collector and Magistrate, Rajahmundry. 1859: Assistant at Godavari. 1860: Acting Head Assistant at Godavari. 1862: Invested with Full Powers of a Magistrate; Head Assistant to Collector and Magistrate, Cuddapah, also at Godavari, at Kurnool, and at Madura; Acting Sub-Collector, afterwards Acting Sub-Collector and Joint Magistrate, Kistna. 1864: Justice of the Peace; *On special leave in India for 4 months.* 1865: Acting Sub-Collector, Kistna; Sub-Collector and Joint Magistrate, Cuddapah. 1866; Acting Civil and Sessions Judge, afterwards Sub-Collector, Cuddapah. 1870: *On furlough in India for 8 months.* 1871: Acting Collector and Magistrate, Cuddapah. 1872: Collector and Magistrate, Cuddapah. 1876: *On furlough to Europe for 2 years.* 1878: Collector at Cuddapah; Acting Third Member of the Revenue Board. 1879: Acting Collector, District Magistrate, and Agent to the Governor in Ganjam. 1881: Acting Collector and Magistrate, Godavari; Acting Third Member, afterwards Acting Second Member of the Revenue Board. 1882: Collector and Magistrate, Cuddapah. 1883: *On furlough to Europe for 2 years.* 1884: *Retired from service, 31st December.*

HUDDLESTON, William, C.S.I. — 1845: Writer. 1847: Assistant to Collector and Magistrate, Canara. 1852: Acting Head Assistant to Collector and Magistrate, Canara. 1854: Acting Head Assistant to the Register to the Court of Sudder and Foujdarry Adawlut; Head Assistant to Collector and Magistrate, Chingleput; Acting Deputy Register to the Court of Sudder and Foujdarry Adawlut; Acting Deputy Secretary to Government in the Departments under the Chief Secretary. 1855: Deputy Secretary to Government under the Chief Secretary; afterwards Secretary to the Board of Examiners. 1856: *On furlough to Europe.* 1857: Acting Deputy Secretary to Government in the Revenue and Public Works Departments. 1858: Acting Deputy Collector of Sea Customs, Madras; afterwards Sub-Secretary to the Revenue Board. 1860: Acting Secretary to the Revenue Board. 1861: Secretary to the Revenue Board. 1865: Acting Secretary to Government, Revenue Department. 1867: Secretary to Government, Revenue Department. 1868: *On furlough to Europe for 23 months.* 1871: Acting Chief Secretary to Government. 1872: Chief Secretary to Government. 1873: Temporary Member of Council. 1874: *On furlough to Europe for 12 months.* 1875: Resumed Temporary Member of Council. 1877: Appointed Member of Council. 1881: Acting Governor of Fort St. George and President in Council. 1882: *Made a C.S.I. 23d May; Retired from service, 12th June.* (*Annuitant on the Fund.*)

HUTCHINS, ARTHUR ROBERT.—1857: Writer and Student at the College. 1858: Assistant to Collector and Magistrate, Trichinopoly. 1859: *On medical leave to Europe for 15 months.* 1861: Assistant to Collector and Magistrate, South Arcot. 1862: Acting Head Assistant, Tanjore. 1864: Head Assistant at Tanjore, and at Madura; Acting Judge of Small Cause Court, Madura; Acting Sub-Collector, South Arcot; Acting Sub-Collector and Joint Magistrate, Madura. 1865: Acting Sub-Collector and Joint Magistrate, Kistna. 1866: Acting Sub-Collector, Tanjore; Head Assistant to Collector and Joint Magistrate, South Arcot; Sub-Collector, Tanjore; *On furlough to Europe for 14 months.* 1867: Assistant and Acting Head Assistant to Collector and Magistrate, Tanjore. 1868: Acting Principal Assistant to Collector and Magistrate, and Agent to the Governor, in Vizagapatam; Junior Assistant, afterwards Senior Assistant, in Ganjam; Sub-Collector and Magistrate, Godavari. 1869: *On furlough to Europe for 12 months.* 1870: *Retired from service, 6th October.* (*Invalid Annuitant.*)

HUTCHINS, PHILIP PERCIVAL.—1858: Writer and Student at the College. 1859: Assistant to Collector and Magistrate, South Arcot. 1860: Head Assistant, South Arcot. 1862: Acting Sub-Collector and Joint Magistrate, South Arcot; Acting Deputy Secretary to Government, Revenue Department, afterwards under the Chief Secretary. 1863: Acting Secretary to the Board of Examiners, also Acting Deputy Secretary to Government, Revenue Department; Acting Judge of Small Cause Court, Chittoor; Acting

Sub-Collector and Joint Magistrate, Madras; Private Secretary to H.E. the Governor, the Hon. E. Maltby. 1864: Head Assistant to Collector and Magistrate, South Arcot, and Acting Sub-Collector and Joint Magistrate, Madras; Acting Registrar to the High Court, Appellate Side. 1865: Registrar to the High Court, Appellate Side. 1867: *On medical leave to Europe for 19 months.* 1868: Resumed Registrar, High Court. 1869: Acting Civil and Sessions Judge, Nundyal. 1870: Acting Civil and Sessions Judge, Tanjore. 1871: Acting Civil and Sessions Judge, Cuddapah. 1872: Acting Civil and Sessions Judge, Bellary, afterwards at Madura. 1873: District and Sessions Judge, Madura. 1874: *On furlough to Europe for 20 months.* 1875: District Judge, Madura. 1881: Acting Judge of the High Court, Madras; *On special leave to Europe, urgent private affairs, for 6 months.* 1882: District and Sessions Judge, Madura; Member of the Rent Law Committee; Acting Secretary to Government, Revenue Department. 1883: On Special Duty connected with Reorganisation of Judicial Establishments; Member of the Board of Examiners; Acting Judge of the High Court, Madras; appointed Judge of the High Court, Madras. 1884: Fellow of the Madras University.

INNES, Lewis Charles.—1844: Writer. 1846: Assistant to Collector and Magistrate, Canara. 1847: Assistant to Collector and Magistrate, Trichinopoly; afterwards Assistant to Collector and Magistrate, Salem. 1849: *On furlough to Europe.* 1852: Assistant and Acting Head Assistant to Collector and Magistrate, Salem. 1853: Acting Head Assistant, afterwards Head Assistant to Collector and Magistrate, Tanjore. 1855: Acting Sub-Judge, Combaconum. 1856: Sub-Judge, Combaconum. 1858: Civil and Sessions Judge at Nundyal. 1862: Civil and Sessions Judge, Rajahmundry. 1863: Civil and Sessions Judge, Coimbatore, afterwards at Ootacamund. 1865: Judge of the High Court of Judicature, Madras. 1867: *On medical leave to Europe for 21 months.* 1869: Resumed Judge of the High Court, Madras. 1875: *On medical leave to Europe for 5 months.* 1877: Acting Chief Justice, Madras. 1880: *On furlough to Europe for 8 months.* 1882: Acting Chief Justice, Madras. 1883: *Retired from service, 9th September.* (*Annuitant on the Fund.*)

IRVINE, Octavius Butler.—1856: Writer. 1857: Student at the College. 1858: Assistant to Collector and Magistrate, Coimbatore. 1861: Officiating Head Assistant at Coimbatore; Head Assistant, Kistna. 1862: *On medical leave for 2 years and*

6 *months.* 1865: Assistant, afterwards Acting Head Assistant to Collector and Magistrate, South Arcot. 1866: Head Assistant, North Arcot, and at South Arcot; Acting Sub-Collector, South Arcot; Sub-Collector, Bellary. 1867: Acting Judge of Small Cause Court, afterwards Sub-Judge, Vellore; Acting Civil and Sessions Judge, Chittoor. 1868: Acting Civil and Sessions Judge, Bellary. 1871: *On furlough to Europe for* 18 *months.* 1873: District and Sessions Judge, Godavari, also of North Arcot. 1874: Acting District and Sessions Judge, Chittoor; District and Sessions Judge, South Arcot. 1879: Acting Collector and Magistrate, and Agent to the Governor of Fort St. George, Vizagapatam. 1880: *Died,* 14*th May, at Vizagapatam.*

KELSALL, THOMAS.—1755: Arrived on the Coromandel Coast 9th June, as Writer, and placed under the Secretary at Fort St. George. 1756: Under the Accountant at Fort St. David. 1759: Under the Secretary in the Secret Department at Fort St. George. 1760: Factor and Paymaster at Arcot. 1761: Secretary in the Secret Department, and Translator at Fort St. George. 1762: Clerk to the Committee of Treasury and Accounts. 1764: Register of the Sea Gate, and Clerk to the Committee of Treasury and Accounts. 1765: Junior Merchant and Assistant at Masulipatam. 1766: *Services transferred to Bengal.* 1767: Appointed Ninth Member of Council of the Governor of Fort William in Bengal; Military Paymaster-General and Custom Master. *(See Bengal Volume.)*

KERR, WILLIAM HOBART.—1856: Writer and Student at the College. 1857: Assistant to Collector and Magistrate, Tanjore. 1859: Acting Special Assistant at Tanjore. 1860: Head Assistant at Madura. 1861: Head Assistant at Tanjore; Deputy Secretary to Government in Chief Secretary's Departments; *On medical leave to Europe for* 2 *years.* 1864: Superintendent of Coorg. 1865: *On special leave to Europe for* 6 *months;* resumed Superintendentship of Coorg. 1866: *On medical leave to Europe for* 12 *months.* 1867: *Retired from service,* 11*th March.* *(Invalid Annuitant.)*

KINDERSLEY, JOHN ROBERT.—1847: Writer. 1849: Assistant to Collector and Magistrate, Salem. 1851: Acting Head Assistant at Salem. 1852: Assistant to Collector and Magistrate, Masulipatam; *On medical leave to Europe.* 1855: Assistant to Collector and Magistrate, Chingleput; afterwards Acting Head Assistant at Trichinopoly; then Head Assistant at Malabar; and Acting Sub-Judge, Mangalore. 1856: Head Assistant to Collector and Magistrate, Chingleput. 1857: Assistant Judge, afterwards Acting Civil and Sessions Judge, Mangalore. 1858: Acting Sub-Judge, Bellary. 1859: Senior Assistant to Collector and Magistrate, and Agent to the Governor of Fort St. George, in Ganjam; Acting Civil and Sessions Judge, Nundyal. 1860: Officiating Civil and Sessions Judge, Bellary; *Proceeded on furlough to Europe for 3 years.* 1864: Acting Civil and Sessions Judge, Rajahmundry. 1865: Civil and Sessions Judge, Rajahmundry. 1866: Civil and Sessions Judge, Bellary; Officiating Judicial Commissioner, Mysore. 1870: Acting Judge of the High Court of Judicature, Madras; Officiating Judicial Commissioner, Mysore; Resumed Acting Judge of the High Court, Madras. 1877: Appointed Judge of the High Court, Madras; Fellow of the Madras University. 1878: *On furlough to Europe for 15 months.* 1879: Resumed Judge of the High Court, Madras. 1884: *Retired from service, 6th January.* (*Annuitant on the Fund.*)

KINDERSLEY, Francis Marten.—1855: Writer and Student at the College. 1857: Assistant to Collector and Magistrate, South Arcot. 1859: Acting Head Assistant, South Arcot. 1860: Head Assistant at Tanjore; Officiating Sub-Collector and Joint Magistrate, Tinnevelly. 1863: Acting Civil and Sessions Judge, Tinnevelly. 1864: Acting Judge of Small Cause Court, Tanjore. 1865: Sub-Collector and Joint Magistrate, Tanjore. 1866: Judge of Small Cause Court, Combaconum. 1867: Acting Civil and Sessions Judge, Trichinopoly; *On furlough to Europe for 2 years.* 1869: Acting Civil and Sessions Judge, Coimbatore. 1871: District and Sessions Judge, Tanjore. 1872: *On furlough for 7 months.* 1874: Acting District and Sessions Judge, Coimbatore. 1877: District and Sessions Judge, Coimbatore. 1878: *On furlough to Europe for 1 year.* 1880: *Retired from service, 24th December, in India.* (*Annuitant on the Fund.*)

LEMAN, George Downton.—1857: Writer and Student at the College. 1859: Assistant to Collector and Magistrate, North Arcot. 1861: *On medical leave for 3 months;* Officiating Head Assistant, North Arcot; *On medical leave to Europe for 21 months.* 1863: Assistant Collector, North Arcot; Acting Head Assistant to Collector and Magistrate; Invested with Full Powers of a Magistrate. 1864: Justice of the Peace; Acting Head Assistant, Trichinopoly; Senior Assistant to Collector and Magistrate, and Agent to the Governor in Ganjam. 1865: Acting Principal Assistant, and Agent, in Ganjam. 1866: Principal Assistant and

Agent, Ganjam. 1867: Acting Collector and Magistrate, Kistna. 1868: Acting Civil and Sessions Judge, Guntoor; Acting Collector of Sea Customs, and Protector of Emigrants, Madras; Acting Civil and Sessions Judge, Tellicherry. 1869: Acting Inam Commissioner; on Special Duty connected with the Quit Rent Department, Madras. 1870: *On furlough to Europe for 21 months.* 1872: Acting Collector and Magistrate, Kistna. 1873: Collector and Magistrate, Kistna. 1875: On Special Duty at Madras; Acting Collector of Sea Customs, and Protector of Emigrants, Madras. 1877: Collector and Magistrate, Kistna; Collector, Magistrate, and Agent to the Governor in Ganjam. 1879: *On furlough to Europe for 15 months.* 1880: Resumed Collector, Magistrate, and Agent, Ganjam. 1881: Acting Collector and Magistrate, Coimbatore; Acting Collector of Sea Customs, and Protector of Emigrants, Madras. 1882: Collector and Magistrate, Coimbatore. 1884: *Special leave to Europe on urgent private affairs for 6 months;* resumed Collector and Magistrate, Coimbatore.

LONGLEY, Charles Thomas.—1853: Writer and Student at the College. 1855: Assistant to Collector and Magistrate, Madura. 1856: Acting Head Assistant at Madura. 1858: Head Assistant to Collector and Magistrate, Kurnool; *On medical leave to Europe for 24 months.* 1860: Officiating Sub-Judge, Chicacole; Senior Assistant to Collector and Magistrate, and Agent to the Governor of Fort St. George, in Vizagapatam. 1861: Principal Assistant at Vizagapatam. 1862: Acting Collector and Magistrate, Ganjam. 1864: Acting Judge of Small Cause Court, Chittoor. 1866: *On furlough to Europe for 23 months and 11 days.* 1867: Acting Collector and Magistrate, Trichinopoly. 1868: Acting Collector and Magistrate, Tinnevelly. 1869: Collector and Magistrate, Nellore. 1870: Collector and Magistrate, Salem. 1873: *On furlough to Europe for 15 months.* 1874: Resumed Duties at Salem. 1878: Acting Second Member of the Revenue Board. 1879: Acting First Member of the Board of Revenue, and Commissioner for Examinations of Uncovenanted Civil Servants; Acting Third Member of the Revenue Board. 1880: Acting Second Member, afterwards Third Member, and again Second Member, of the Revenue Board; In Charge of the Inam Department. 1881: Acting Second Member, appointed Third Member, and Acting First Member, of the Revenue Board; *On furlough to Europe for 9 months and 14 days.* 1882: *Retired from service, 15th July, in England.* (*Annuitant on the Fund.*)

LUSHINGTON, James Law.—1841: Writer. 1843: Assistant to Principal Collector and Magistrate, Tanjore. 1844: In the same Capacity at Nellore. 1845: Acting Head Assistant to Collector and Magistrate, Nellore. 1847: Head Assistant to Collector and Magistrate, Trichinopoly; afterwards Second Assistant to the Accountant-General, Madras. 1848: Acting Head Assistant to the Accountant-General. 1850: Head Assistant to the Accountant-General, and Canarese Translator to Government. 1854: Acting First Assistant to the Accountant-General. 1856: First Assistant to the Accountant-General; afterwards Acting Sub-Treasurer, Secretary to the Savings Bank, Member of the Mint Committee, and Director of the Incorporated Bank of Madras. 1858: Acting Civil Auditor and Superintendent of Stamps. 1859: Civil Auditor; afterwards Accountant, North-Western Provinces. 1861: *On medical leave to Europe for* 15 *months.* 1863: Acting Deputy at Madras, afterwards Deputy Auditor and Accountant-General, Bengal, and officiating Auditor-General and Accountant-General to the Government of India. 1864: Acting Deputy Auditor and Accountant-General, Madras. 1865: Accountant-General, Bombay. 1868: *On private affairs to Europe for* 6 *months;* on duty in England. 1869: *On furlough to Europe for* 2 *years.* 1871: Resumed Accountant-General, Bombay. 1876: *Retired from service, 24th December, in India. (Annuitant on the Fund.)*

MACGREGOR, Atholl.—1855: Writer and Student at the College. 1857: Assistant to Collector and Magistrate, Madura. 1859: Acting Head Assistant at Tinnevelly. 1860: Special Assistant to Collector and Magistrate, Malabar. 1861: Acting Sub-Collector, Malabar. 1863: *On furlough to Europe for* 20 *months.* 1865: Acting Sub-Collector and Joint Magistrate, Tinnevelly; Head Assistant at Coimbatore; Sub-Collector, Nellore. 1866: Principal Assistant to Collector, and Agent to the Governor of Fort St. George, Ganjam; also Sub-Collector, Tinnevelly; Acting Collector and Magistrate, Coimbatore. 1867: Sub-Collector and Joint Magistrate, Madras District; Acting Resident, Travancore; *Leave on private affairs for* 6 *months.* 1868: Resumed Sub-Collector and Joint Magistrate, Madras District; Acting Secretary to the Revenue Board. 1869: Acting Collector of Sea Customs, and Protector of Emigrants, Madras. 1870: Secretary to the Revenue Board; Collector and Magistrate, Malabar; Agent for French Settlement of Mahé. 1875: Acting Secretary to Government, Revenue

Department; Acting Resident of Travancore and Cochin. 1876: Resident of Travancore and Cochin. 1877: *On furlough to Europe for 2 years, with extension for another year.* 1882: *Retired from service, 13th April, in England.* (*Annuitant on the Fund.*)

MASTER, Robert Edward.—1845: Writer. 1846: Assistant to Collector and Magistrate, Rajahmundry. 1849: Acting Head Assistant to Collector and Magistrate, Rajahmundry. 1850: Acting Sub-Judge, Rajahmundry. 1853: Head Assistant to Collector and Magistrate, Rajahmundry. 1855: Sub-Judge, Rajahmundry. 1856: *On furlough to Europe.* 1857: Acting Second Assistant to the Accountant-General. 1858: Deputy Director of Revenue Settlement. 1861: Acting Sub-Collector and Joint Magistrate, Godavari, without prejudice to previous Appointment; Acting Director of Revenue Settlement. 1862: Officiating Director. 1868: Director of Revenue Settlement. 1870: *On furlough to Europe for 2 years.* 1872: *Retired from service, 30th April.* (*Annuitant on the Fund.*)

MASTER, John Henry.—1852: Writer and Student at the College. 1853: Assistant to Collector and Magistrate, Rajahmundry. 1854: Assistant Commissioner, Third Class, Nagpur Commission. 1858: Officiating Deputy Commissioner, Chindwara, Central Provinces. 1859: Deputy Secretary to Government in the Revenue and Public Works Departments. 1860: Deputy Commissioner, Third Class, Chindwara. 1862: Deputy Commissioner, Second Class, Bhundara. 1864: *On furlough to Europe for 3 years.* 1867: Sub-Collector, Bellary; Acting Collector and Magistrate, and Agent to the Governor, in Vizagapatam. 1868: Acting Collector and Magistrate, afterwards Sub-Collector and Joint Magistrate, Godavari; Acting Civil and Sessions Judge, Berhampore; Civil and Sessions Judge, Tellicherry. 1869: Acting Civil and Sessions Judge, Vizagapatam; Acting Collector and Magistrate, Bellary. 1870: Civil and Sessions Judge, Cuddapah. 1873: Collector and Magistrate, Bellary; Political Agent at Sundur. 1878: *On furlough to Europe.* 1880: *Retired from service, 30th April, in England.* (*Annuitant on the Fund.*)

MASTER, Charles Gilbert.—1854: Writer and Student at the College. 1855: Assistant to Collector and Magistrate, Masulipatam. 1856: Acting Head Assistant at Guntoor. 1859: Head Assistant to the Collector, Guntoor; afterwards Head Assistant to Collector and Magistrate, North Canara; Deputy Secretary to

Government in the Revenue and Public Works Departments. 1860: Commissioner for the Assessment of Income-Tax. 1861: Officiating Secretary, afterwards Secretary, to the Board of Examiners. 1862: Acting Sub-Secretary to the Revenue Board. 1866: *On furlough to Europe for 3 years.* 1869: Acting Civil and Sessions Judge, Calicut; Justice of the Peace; on Special Duty on Irrigation Works, Godavari and Kistna; Acting Collector and Magistrate, Nellore. 1870: Collector and Magistrate, Kistna, afterwards at Cuddapah. 1871: Acting Collector and Magistrate, Ganjam. 1872: Collector and Magistrate, Vizagapatam. 1873: Collector and Magistrate, Ganjam. 1874: Acting Secretary to Government, Revenue Department. 1875: *On furlough to Europe for 14 months.* 1876: Collector and Magistrate, Ganjam. 1877; Acting Secretary, afterwards Secretary, to Government, Revenue Department. 1878: Acting Chief Secretary to Government. 1881: Chief Secretary to Government. 1882: Additional Member of the Legislative Council. 1883: Temporary Member of Council. 1884: Ordinary Member of Council; *took his seat 8th January.*

M'DONELL, Æneas Ranald.—1843: Writer. 1844: *Absent in Europe.* 1846: Assistant to the Collector and Magistrate, Chingleput; afterwards Head Assistant to the Accountant-General, Madras. 1847: Acting Head Assistant to Collector and Magistrate, South Arcot. 1849: Head Assistant to Collector and Magistrate, South Arcot. 1852: Acting Sub-Judge, Salem. 1853: Acting Additional Sub-Collector and Joint Magistrate, South Arcot. 1854: Acting Sub-Judge, Combaconum; Acting Additional Sub-Collector and Joint Magistrate, South Arcot. 1855: Sub-Judge, Cuddapah; Acting, afterwards Sub-Collector and Joint Magistrate, South Arcot. 1859: Acting Collector and Magistrate, South Arcot; Officiating Civil and Sessions Judge, Combaconum. 1860: Collector and Magistrate, Trichinopoly. 1863: *On medical leave to Europe for 10 months;* Collector and Magistrate, South Canara; Civil and Sessions Judge, Rajahmundry. 1864: Acting Collector and Magistrate, Madura, also at Trichinopoly. 1865: Collector and Magistrate, Trichinopoly. 1866: Civil and Sessions Judge, Trichinopoly. 1867: *Died, 2d February, in India.*

M'QUHAE, William.—1857: Writer and Student at the College. 1858: Assistant to Collector and Magistrate, Salem. 1859: Acting Head Assistant at Cuddapah. 1861: Head Assistant to

Collector and Magistrate, Kurnool. 1862: Head Assistant, Cuddapah. 1864: Acting Sub-Collector and Joint Magistrate, Coimbatore. 1866: Acting Sub-Collector, Coimbatore, and at Salem; Acting Sub-Secretary, Revenue Board; Sub-Collector, Coimbatore. 1867: Acting Civil and Sessions Judge, Trichinopoly. 1868: Acting Collector and Magistrate, Kistna; *On furlough to Europe for* 1 *year and* 11 *months.* 1870: Acting Collector and Magistrate, Trichinopoly. 1871: Acting Collector and Magistrate, Madura. 1873: Collector and Magistrate, Madura. 1875: *On furlough to Europe for* 13 *months.* 1876: Resumed Duties at Madura. 1878: *On furlough to Europe for* 1 *year.* 1879: *Retired from service, 28th July.* (*Invalid Annuitant.*)

MELVILLE, ROBERTSON JOHN.—1856: Writer. 1857: Student at the College. 1858: Assistant to Collector and Magistrate, Masulipatam. 1859: Acting Head Assistant at Masulipatam; afterwards Assistant and Acting Head Assistant to the Collector and Magistrate, Kistna. 1862: Acting Judge of Small Cause Court, Madura, also at Chittoor; Head Assistant to Collector and Magistrate, Madura. 1863: Acting Judge of Small Cause Court, Chittoor; Head Assistant to Collector and Magistrate, Godavari. 1864: Officiating Director of Revenue Settlement. 1866: Principal Assistant to Collector and Magistrate, and Agent to the Governor, Ganjam; Deputy Director of Revenue Settlement; Sub-Collector, Malabar. 1867: *On furlough to Europe for* 2 *years.* 1869: Acting Judge of Small Cause Court, Vellore; Acting Collector and Magistrate, Nellore; Sub-Collector, Nellore. 1870: Acting Collector and Magistrate, and Agent to the Governor, Vizagapatam. 1873: *On furlough to Europe for* 18 *months.* 1875: Acting Collector and Magistrate, Chingleput. 1876: Acting Collector of Sea Customs and of Madras Town, and Protector of Emigrants. 1880: *On furlough to Europe for* 14 *months.* 1882: *Retired from service, 31st December, in India.* (*Annuitant on the Fund.*)

MINCHIN, JAMES INNES.—1844: Writer. 1845: Assistant to Collector and Magistrate, Tanjore. 1847: Acting Head Assistant to Collector and Magistrate, Tanjore. 1849: Acting Special Assistant to Collector and Magistrate, Tanjore. 1850: Acting Head Assistant to Collector and Magistrate, Tanjore. 1851: Head Assistant to Collector and Magistrate, Tanjore. 1853: Head Assistant to Collector and Magistrate, Nellore. 1854: Acting Sub-Judge, Cuddapah; afterwards Acting Sub-Collector and Joint Magistrate, Nellore. 1856: Sub-Collector and Joint Magistrate,

Nellore. 1859: Officiating Civil and Sessions Judge, Masulipatam. 1860: Officiating Collector and Magistrate, Kurnool. 1862: Collector and Magistrate, Kurnool. 1866: *On medical leave to Europe for* 19 *months.* 1867: On Special Duty at Calcutta; Collector and Magistrate, and Agent to the Governor of Fort St. George, Vizagapatam. 1869: Acting Chief Secretary to Government. 1870: Acting Third Member of the Revenue Board; Acting Resident in Travancore and Cochin. 1871: *On furlough to Europe for* 2 *years.* 1873: *Retired from service,* 1st *April.* (*Annuitant on the Fund.*)

MOLONY, Frederick Beresford. — 1853: Writer. 1854: Student at the College. 1855: Assistant to Collector and Magistrate, Rajahmundry. 1856: Acting Head Assistant, Rajahmundry. 1857: Head Assistant to Collector and Magistrate, Cuddapah. *On medical leave to Europe for* 15 *months.* 1858: Acting Sub-Collector and Joint Magistrate, Cuddapah. 1862: Sub-Collector and Joint Magistrate, Kistna, but continuing to act as Sub-Collector at Cuddapah. 1865: *On furlough to Europe for* 3 *years.* 1868: *Died, in India,* 13*th November.*

MORRIS, George Lee.—1847: Writer. 1848: Under the Collector of Malabar. 1850: Assistant to Collector and Magistrate, Tanjore. 1852: Acting Special Assistant to Collector and Magistrate, Tanjore. 1855: Special Assistant at Tanjore; Officiating Special Assistant to Collector and Magistrate, Coimbatore. 1856: Acting Sub-Collector and Joint Magistrate, afterwards Sub-Collector and Joint Magistrate, Malabar. 1857: *On medical leave to Europe for* 24 *months.* 1858: Sub-Collector and Joint Magistrate, Madura; afterwards at Tanjore. 1862: Acting Collector at Tanjore. 1863: Acting Collector and Magistrate, South Canara. 1864: Collector and Magistrate, South Canara. 1865: Collector and Magistrate, and Political Agent at Tanjore. 1866: *On special leave for* 6 *months.* 1870: Acting Third Member of the Revenue Board. 1871: Acting Second Member of the Revenue Board; *On furlough to Europe.* 1873: *Retired from service,* 15*th May.* (*Annuitant on the Fund.*)

MORRIS, Henry.—1848: Writer and Student at the College. 1850: Assistant to Collector and Magistrate, Nellore. 1855: Acting Head Assistant at Nellore. 1856: Head Assistant at Nellore; Inspector of Schools, Madras. 1857: Acting Sub-Collector and Joint Magistrate, Rajahmundry; Head Assistant to Collector and Magistrate, Guntoor. 1859: *On* *furlough to Europe for 3 years and 7 months.* 1863: Acting Judge of the Small Cause Court, Chittoor; Acting Civil and Sessions Judge, Nundyal; Acting Collector and Magistrate, Godavari. 1864: Acting Sub-Collector and Joint Magistrate, Nellore; Sub-Collector and Joint Magistrate, Tanjore, with Duties as before; Acting Civil and Sessions Judge, Chicacole. 1865: Sub-Collector and Joint Magistrate, Nellore; Principal Assistant to Collector and Magistrate, and Agent to the Governor of Fort St. George in Ganjam; Acting Civil and Sessions Judge, Rajahmundry. 1866: District and Sessions Judge, Godavari. 1873: *On furlough to Europe for 2 years.* 1875: *Retired from service, 20th July.* (*Annuitant on the Fund.*)

MORRIS, Frederick William.—1854: Writer and Student at the College. 1856: Assistant to Collector and Magistrate, afterwards Acting Head Assistant, at Nellore. 1858: Acting Assistant to Collector and Magistrate, and Agent to the Governor of Fort St. George, in Ganjam. 1859: Senior Assistant and Agent to the Governor, afterwards Officiating Principal Assistant, Ganjam. 1860: Deputy Director of Revenue Settlement. 1863: *Died, 15th October, in India.*

NESBITT, William Smith.—1845: Writer. 1848: Assistant to Collector and Magistrate, Guntoor. 1851: Acting Head Assistant to Collector and Magistrate, Masulipatam; *On medical leave to Europe.* 1857: Acting Sub-Judge, Cuddapah. 1858: Acting Deputy Collector of Sea Customs, Madras; Acting Subordinate Judge, Chittoor. 1859: Acting Sub-Judge, Ootacamund; Assistant to Collector and Magistrate, Coimbatore. 1861: Acting Sub-Judge, Ootacamund. 1862: Sub-Judge, Ootacamund. 1866: *On furlough to Europe.* 1869: *Resigned the service, 1st February, in England.* (*Invalid Annuitant.*)

NEWILL, Henry.—1840: Writer. 1841: Assistant to the Collector and Magistrate, Guntoor. 1842: Acting Register to the Zillah Court of Cuddapah. 1843: Acting Head Assistant to the Collector and Magistrate, Guntoor. 1845: Head Assistant to the Collector and Magistrate, Guntoor. 1850: Acting Collector and Magistrate, Guntoor. 1851: *Proceeded on furlough to Europe.* 1853: *Returned to Madras.* 1854: Assistant to the Commissioner for the Northern Circars. 1855: Acting Collector and Magistrate, Guntoor. 1857: Director of Revenue Settlement. 1862: *On medical leave for 1 year.* 1863: Collector and Magistrate, Godavari. 1864: Acting Resident, and in 1865 Resident of Travancore and Cochin. 1869: *Died, 25th April, in India.*

NISBET, Walter.—1855: Writer and Student at the College. 1856: Assistant to Collector and Magistrate, Tanjore. 1857: *On medical leave to Europe for 30 months.* 1859: Assistant to Collector and Magistrate, Chingleput. 1860: Head Assistant at Trichinopoly. 1862: Acting Sub-Collector, Madura. 1864: *On medical leave to Europe, forfeiting appointment.* 1865: *Retired from service 24th August.* (*Invalid Annuitant.*)

PAUNCEFOTE, Bernard.—1845: Writer. 1847: Assistant to Collector and Magistrate, South Arcot. 1851: Acting Head Assistant to Collector and Magistrate, Nellore. 1853: Acting Assistant to the Accountant-General, Madras. 1854: Head Assistant to Collector and Magistrate, Trichinopoly; afterwards at Chingleput. 1855: Acting Sub-Collector and Joint Magistrate, Madura. 1856: Additional Sub-Collector and Joint Magistrate, North Arcot; *Proceeded to Europe on medical certificate for 27 months.* 1861: Officiating Civil and Sessions Judge, Chingleput; Acting Sub-Collector, South Arcot. 1862: Sub-Collector, South Arcot; *On furlough for 3 years.* 1865: *Retired from service, 27th January.* (*Invalid Annuitant.*)

PELLY, Charles Raymond.—1847: Writer. 1848: Assistant to Collector and Magistrate, Bellary. 1850: Acting Head Assistant at Bellary. 1854: Acting Head Assistant to Collector and Magistrate, Canara. 1855: Head Assistant to Collector and Magistrate, Malabar, and again at Canara; Acting Sub-Judge, Mangalore. 1856: Acting Sub-Collector and Joint Magistrate, Rajahmundry. 1857: Acting Principal Assistant to Collector and Magistrate, and Agent to the Governor of Fort St. George, in Vizagapatam. 1858: Senior Assistant, and Acting Principal Assistant to Collector and Magistrate, and Agent to the Governor, Vizagapatam. 1859: Sub-Judge, Chicacole. 1860: Acting Civil and Sessions Judge, Masulipatam. 1863: Judge of the Small Cause Court, Cuddalore; but acting as Civil and Sessions Judge, Nundyal; *On special leave for 6 months.* 1864: Acting Civil and Sessions Judge, Madura. 1865: Civil and Sessions Judge, Nellore. 1867: *On furlough to Europe for 1 year and 11 months.* 1869: Civil and Sessions Judge, Calicut. 1870: Civil and Sessions Judge, Tanjore, but acting at Tranquebar. 1871: Civil and Sessions Judge, Tranquebar. 1872: *On furlough to Europe for 12 months.* 1873: *Retired from service, 6th June.* (*Annuitant on the Fund.*)

PLUMER, Charles George.—1856: Writer and Student at

the College. 1857: Assistant to Collector and Magistrate, Tinnevelly. 1858: Acting Head Assistant Collector, Tinnevelly. 1859: Acting Head Assistant to Collector and Magistrate, Chingleput; *On medical leave to Europe for 25 months.* 1861: Acting Head Assistant, Tanjore; Assistant to Collector, Madura. 1862: Head Assistant to Collector, Salem, and at Tanjore; Sub-Collector at Tanjore; Head Assistant at Malabar. 1863: Head Assistant, Madura; Sub-Collector and Joint Magistrate, Tanjore. 1864: Justice of the Peace; Head Assistant to Collector, Trichinopoly, and Sub-Collector, Tanjore. 1866: Sub-Collector and Joint Magistrate, Nellore; Acting Judge of Small Cause Court, Vellore; Sub-Collector and Joint Magistrate, Kistna. 1867: *On furlough to Europe for 2 years.* 1869: Acting Civil and Sessions Judge, Calicut; also at Salem and at Chittoor. 1872: District and Sessions Judge, North Arcot. 1874: *On furlough to Europe for 12 months.* 1875: Resumed District and Sessions Judge, North Arcot; In Charge of Small Cause Court, Vellore. 1882: Member of the Board of Examiners; District and Sessions Judge, North Arcot; Officiating Chief Judge and Inspector-General of Prisons, Mysore; Judicial Commissioner of Coorg. 1884: *Retired from service, 1st June.* (*Annuitant on the Fund.*)

POCHIN, Charles Norman.—1848: Writer and Student at the College. 1850: Assistant to Collector and Magistrate, Madura; 1852: Officiating Head Assistant to the Register to the Court of Sudder and Foujdarry Adawlut; afterwards Assistant to Collector and Magistrate, Coimbatore. 1854: Acting Head Assistant to Collector and Magistrate, Tanjore. 1856: Head Assistant to Collector and Magistrate, North Arcot. 1857: Acting Additional Sub-Collector and Joint Magistrate, Canara. 1859: Additional Sub-Collector and Joint Magistrate, Canara; afterwards Acting Collector and Magistrate, North Canara. 1860: Acting Civil and Sessions Judge, afterwards Subordinate Judge, Mangalore; Officiating Collector and Magistrate, North Canara. 1861: *On furlough to Europe for 3 years.* 1864: Acting Sub-Collector and Joint Magistrate, Madras. 1865: Sub-Collector and Joint Magistrate, Tanjore, but acting as Collector of Salem; Acting Civil and Sessions Judge, Madura; Judge of the Small Cause Court, Madura. 1866: Acting Collector and Magistrate, Trichinopoly; Civil and Sessions Judge, Calicut; Acting Collector and Magistrate, Kurnool. 1867: Acting Collector and Magistrate, Salem, afterwards Collector and Magistrate there. 1870: *Died, 26th August, in India.*

PUCKLE, RICHARD KAYE, C.I.E.—1851: Writer and Student at the College. 1853: Assistant to Collector and Magistrate, South Arcot. 1855: Acting Head Assistant to Collector and Magistrate, Chingleput. 1856: Head Assistant to Collector and Magistrate, Malabar. 1857: Acting Assistant to the Agent to the Governor of Fort St. George, Vizagapatam; afterwards Acting Head Assistant to Collector and Magistrate, South Arcot. 1858: Head Assistant at South Arcot. 1859: Acting Deputy Director of Revenue Settlement; afterwards Deputy Director. 1860: *On medical leave to Europe for* 15 *months.* 1862: Deputy Director of Revenue Settlement; Special Assistant to Collector and Magistrate, Trichinopoly; Deputy Director of Revenue Settlement, Tinnevelly; and at Salem in 1863. 1866: Collector and Magistrate, Tinnevelly. 1869: On Special Duty at the Office of the Board of Revenue; *On furlough to Europe for* 16 *months.* 1874: Acting Director of Revenue Settlement. 1875: Director of Revenue Settlement; *On furlough to Europe for* 12 *months.* 1876: Acting Additional Member of the Revenue Board. 1877: Acting Third Member of the Revenue Board. 1878: *Made C.I.E. 1st January; On furlough to Europe.* 1881: *Retired from service, 16th June, in England.* (*Annuitant on the Fund.*)

REID, JOHN WILLIAM (*Barrister-at-Law*).—1855: Writer and Student at the College. 1856: Assistant, afterwards Acting Head Assistant, to Collector and Magistrate, Cuddapah. 1859: Head Assistant at Rajahmundry, and Acting Subordinate Judge, Cuddapah; Head Assistant to Collector and Magistrate, Godavari. 1860: Acting Sub-Collector and Joint Magistrate, Bellary; Acting Sub-Collector and Joint Magistrate, Kistna. 1861: Acting Sub-Collector, Bellary. 1863: Head Assistant Collector, Malabar; Acting Sub-Collector and Joint Magistrate, Bellary; Justice of the Peace. 1864: Head Assistant, Tinnevelly; Sub-Collector, Bellary. 1866: Sub-Collector, Kistna; Acting Sub-Collector, Bellary; *On furlough to Europe for* 3 *years.* 1869: Acting Civil and Sessions Judge, Calicut; afterwards at Tellicherry. 1872: District and Sessions Judge, North Malabar. 1873: *On special leave to Europe for* 6 *months;* District and Sessions Judge, Tellicherry. 1877: Additional Sessions Judge at Nellore, and at Coimbatore. 1878: *On furlough to Europe for* 12 *months.* 1879: District and Sessions Judge, North Malabar. 1882: *On furlough to Europe for* 18 *months.* 1884: Resumed District and Sessions Judge, North Malabar; afterwards at Coimbatore.

ROBERTS, CLARENCE ARMSTRONG.—1844: Writer and Student at the College. 1845: Permitted to Pursue his Studies under the Collector of Salem. 1847: Assistant to Collector and Magistrate, South Arcot. 1848: Acting Second Assistant to the Accountant-General, Madras. 1849: Acting Head Assistant to Collector and Magistrate, Tanjore. 1850: Second Assistant to the Accountant-General. 1852: Secretary to the Mint Committee. 1853: Acting Head Assistant to the Accountant-General, and Acting Canarese Translator to Government. 1854: Member of the Board of Examiners; Acting First Assistant to the Accountant-General. 1855: *Proceeded to Europe on furlough.* 1858: *Without employ for 3 months;* Secretary to the Mint Committee; Acting First Assistant to the Accountant-General; Acting Collector of Sea Customs, Madras; Acting Sub-Collector and Joint Magistrate, Tinnevelly. 1859: Sub-Collector and Joint Magistrate, Coimbatore; Officiating Postmaster-General, Madras. 1861: *On medical leave to Europe for 20 months.* 1863: Acting Collector and Magistrate, Madras District; Acting Collector of Sea Customs, Madras; Acting Civil and Sessions Judge, afterwards Civil and Sessions Judge, Chittoor. 1867: Commissioner for the Debts of H.H. Prince Azeem Jah, Bahadur. 1871: *On furlough to Europe for 16 months.* 1872: *Retired from service, 12th July.* (*Annuitant on the Fund.*)

ROBINSON, JAMES DOUGLAS.—1840: Writer. 1842: Assistant to the Collector and Magistrate, Bellary. 1844: Acting Head Assistant to the Collector and Magistrate, Bellary. 1845: In the same capacity at Coimbatore. 1846: Head Assistant to the Principal Collector and Magistrate, Madura. 1847: Acting Sub-Judge of the Zillah of Madura. 1848: *Proceeded to Europe on furlough.* 1851: *Returned to Madras.* 1852: Acting Additional Sub-Collector and Joint Magistrate, Canara; Acting Sub-Collector and Joint Magistrate, Malabar; Head Assistant to the Collector and Magistrate, Malabar. 1854: Acting Sub-Judge of the Zillah of Mangalore; Additional Sub-Collector and Joint Magistrate, Canara. 1856: Sub-Collector and Joint Magistrate, Canara. 1857: Acting Collector and Magistrate, Canara. 1858: On Special Duty in Connection with the Disturbances on the Frontier of Canara District. 1859: Acting Collector and Magistrate, North Arcot. 1860: Sub-Collector and Joint Magistrate, Kistna. 1861: Collector and Magistrate, North Arcot. 1862: *On medical leave for 10 months.* 1864: *On special leave for 12 months.* 1866: Resumed Collector and Magistrate, North Arcot. 1868: *On medical leave to Europe for 6 months.* 1869: Resumed his previous duties. 1870: *On furlough to Europe.* 1873: *Resigned the service, 3d March, in England.* (*Annuitant on the Fund.*)

ROBINSON, Sir WILLIAM ROSE, K.C.S.I.—1842: Writer. 1843: Assistant to the Collector and Magistrate, Canara. 1847: Acting Head Assistant to Collector and Magistrate, Malabar. 1848: Head Assistant to Collector and Magistrate, Malabar. 1849: Officiating Sub-Judge, Calicut. 1851: Acting Sub-Collector and Joint Magistrate, Malabar. 1852: *On furlough to Europe.* 1856: Sub-Collector and Joint Magistrate, Madura; Acting Sub-Collector and Joint Magistrate, Rajahmundry; Acting Collector and Magistrate, Malabar. 1858: Inspector-General of Police for the Madras Presidency. 1866: *Made a C.S.I.* 1867: Acting Third Member of the Revenue Board. 1868: *On special leave to Europe for 6 months;* resumed Acting Third Member of the Revenue Board. 1869: Third Member and Acting Second Member of the Revenue Board; afterwards Acting First Member; Inam Commissioner. 1870: Second Member, and Acting First Member of the Revenue Board; Additional Member of Council of the Governor-General for making Laws and Regulations. 1872: *On furlough to Europe for 9 months.* 1873: Member of Council. 1875: Acting Governor of Fort St. George for 7 months; *made a K.C.S.I. 31st December.* 1878: *Retired from service, 5th December.* (*Annuitant on the Fund.*)

RUSSELL, CLAUD.—1752: Arrived on the Coromandel Coast 17th June; Writer and under the Secretary at Fort St. George. 1754: Sub-Secretary and Accountant-General of the Mayor's Court. 1759: Factor and Sub-Import Warehouse-keeper. 1760: Junior Merchant and Commissary at Camp. 1762: Senior Merchant and Under Searcher at the Sea Gate and Assistant to Mint Master. 1764: Under Searcher and Assay Master. 1765: *Absent by desire of the Select Committee at Fort William in Bengal.* 1767: Appointed Sixth Member of Council of the Governor of Fort William; Accountant and Collector-General. (*See Bengal Volume.*)

SHARPE, GEORGE ROBINSON.—1855: Writer and Student at the College. 1856: Assistant to Collector and Magistrate, South Arcot. 1857: Acting Head Assistant at Salem; afterwards at Malabar. 1859 : Head Assistant at Malabar; Acting Subordinate Judge, Calicut. 1862 : Judge of the Small Cause Court, Tellicherry. 1864 : *On special leave to Europe for 6 months.* 1866 : Acting Civil and Sessions Judge, Calicut. 1867 : Civil and Sessions Judge, Calicut. 1868 : Civil and Sessions Judge, Madura; *On furlough to Europe for 2 years.* 1870 : District and Sessions Judge, Malabar. 1874 : *On furlough to Europe.* 1876 : *Forfeited appointment.* 1877 : *Retired from service, 24th October. (Invalid Annuitant.)*

SIM, James Duncan, C.S.I.—1842 : Writer. 1843 : Acting Head Assistant to the Register to the Court of Sudder and Foujdarry Adawlut. 1844 : *Proceeded to Europe.* 1849 : Assistant, afterwards Head Assistant, to Collector and Magistrate, Nellore. 1850 : Acting Deputy Secretary to Government. 1851 : Acting, afterwards Deputy Secretary under the Chief Secretary to Government. 1853 : Acting Teloogoo Translator to Government. 1854 : Teloogoo Translator to Government; Member of the Board of Examiners; Acting Sub-Secretary to the Revenue Board. 1855 : Sub-Secretary to the Revenue Board. 1856 : Acting Secretary to the Revenue Board. 1858 : Secretary to the Revenue Board. 1860 : Acting Secretary to Government, Revenue, and Public Works Department. 1861 : Secretary to Government, Revenue, and Public Works Department. 1865 : *On special leave to Europe for 6 months.* 1866 : Acting Chief Secretary to Government. 1867 : Third Member of the Revenue Board; Commissioner for the Examination of Uncovenanted Civil Servants. 1867 : Director of the Incorporated Bank of Madras; Second Member of the Revenue Board. 1868 : *Made a C.S.I. 22d December.* 1869 : *On furlough to Europe for 10 months.* 1870 : Member of Council. 1875 : *Retired from service, 7th March. (Annuitant on the Fund.)*

SIM, William Clulow.—1852 : Writer. 1853 : Student at the College. 1854 : Acting Third Assistant to the Accountant-General, Madras. 1855 : Assistant to Collector and Magistrate, North Arcot; *Medical leave to Europe for 16 months.* 1857 : Acting Head Assistant to Collector and Magistrate, Trichinopoly. 1858 : Acting Head Assistant at Chingleput. 1859 : Head Assistant to Collector and Magistrate, Salem; Acting Deputy Secretary to Government in the Revenue and Judicial Departments; Head Assistant at South Arcot; Acting Canarese Translator to Government. 1861 : *On furlough to Europe for 3 years.* 1864 : *Retired from service, 5th May, in England. (Invalid Annuitant.)*

SMITH, Henry George.—1844: Writer. 1846: Assistant to the Collector and Magistrate, Cuddapah. 1850: Acting Head Assistant to Collector and Magistrate, Trichinopoly. 1851: Head Assistant to Collector and Magistrate, Trichinopoly. 1852: Acting Assistant Judge, Combaconum. 1854: *On furlough to Europe.* 1857: Acting Sub-Collector and Joint Magistrate, Malabar. 1858: Acting Sub-Collector and Joint Magistrate, Salem. 1859: Sub-Collector and Joint Magistrate, Salem. 1862: Acting Collector and Magistrate, South Arcot. 1863: Acting Collector and Magistrate, Cuddapah; Civil and Sessions Judge, Nundyal, but continuing to act as before at Cuddapah. 1864: Civil and Sessions Judge, Bellary. 1865: Collector and Magistrate, Cuddapah. 1868: *On medical leave to Europe.* 1869: *Died, in India, 27th April.*

ST. CLAIR, Hon. James Chisholme.—1856: Writer. 1857: Student at the College. 1858: Assistant to Collector and Magistrate, Bellary. 1859: Acting Head Assistant at Bellary. 1861: Head Assistant at Bellary. 1862: Acting Sub-Collector, Coimbatore. 1864: Acting Sub-Collector and Joint Magistrate, Nellore. 1866: Sub-Collector and Joint Magistrate, Nellore. 1867: Sub-Collector and Joint Magistrate, North Arcot; Acting Civil and Sessions Judge, Mangalore. 1869: *On furlough to Europe for 2 years.* 1871: Acting Collector and Magistrate, Bellary: Sub-Collector and Joint Magistrate, Chingleput; Acting Civil and Sessions Judge, Nundyal. 1873: District and Sessions Judge, South Canara; and at Kurnool. 1874: District and Sessions Judge, Kurnool. 1880: *On furlough to Europe for 2 years.* 1882: *Retired from service, 25th March.* (*Annuitant on the Fund.*)

SULLIVAN, Augustus William.—1844: Writer. 1845: Assistant to Collector and Magistrate, Trichinopoly; Second Assistant to the Accountant-General, Madras. 1846: Assistant to Collector and Magistrate, North Arcot. 1847: Acting Head Assistant to Collector and Magistrate, North Arcot. 1850: Head Assistant to Collector and Magistrate, North Arcot. 1853: Acting Sub-Collector and Joint Magistrate, North Arcot. 1856: Sub-Collector and Joint Magistrate, North Arcot. 1859: Officiating Collector, Madras. 1860: *Without employ for 11 months.* 1861: Officiating Civil and Sessions Judge, Rajahmundry; Sub-Collector and Joint Magistrate, Kistna. 1862: Civil and Sessions Judge, Nundyal. 1863: Acting Civil and Sessions Judge, afterwards Civil and Sessions Judge, Tellicherry. 1868: *Died, 31st August, in India.*

SULLIVAN, Henry Edward.—1850: Writer and Student at the College. 1852: Assistant to Collector and Magistrate, Trichinopoly; Justice of the Peace. 1855: Head Assistant to Collector and Magistrate, Malabar; and at Coimbatore. 1856: Acting Sub-Collector and Joint Magistrate, Coimbatore. 1857: Acting Sub-Judge, Madura; Head Assistant, Coimbatore; Acting Sub-Collector and Joint Magistrate, Coimbatore; and at Malabar. 1859: Sub-Collector and Joint Magistrate, Malabar. 1861: *On medical leave to Europe for 23 months.* 1863: Sub-Collector, Malabar; Acting Civil and Sessions Judge, Bellary; Acting Judge of Small Cause Court, Tellicherry; Acting Sub-Collector and Joint Magistrate, Coimbatore; Sub-Collector, Coimbatore. 1865: Acting Civil and Sessions Judge, Salem; Sub-Collector, Coimbatore. 1866: Acting Collector and Magistrate, Kurnool; Judge of Small Cause Court, Cuddalore; afterwards at Madura; Acting Civil and Sessions Judge, Bellary; Civil and Sessions Judge, Cuddapah. 1868: Acting Collector and Magistrate, afterwards Collector and Magistrate, Bellary. 1869: Acting Collector and Magistrate, Coimbatore. 1870: On Special Duty at Bangalore; Collector at Bellary. 1871: *Special leave to Europe for 6 months.* 1872: Acting Collector and Magistrate, Godavari; and at South Arcot. 1873: Collector and Magistrate, Trichinopoly. 1874: Acting Collector, South Arcot; Officiating Director of Revenue Settlement; *On furlough to Europe for 18 months.* 1876: Acting Third Member of the Revenue Board; President of the Committee for Examination of Assistants; In Charge of the Inam Department. 1877: Acting Resident of Travancore and Cochin. 1878: Resumed Third Member, afterwards Second Member of the Revenue Board; In Charge of the Inam Department; Acting First Member of the Revenue Board. 1879: Member of the Famine Commission; First Member of the Revenue Board; Commissioner of Uncovenanted Civil Service Examinations; On Special Duty in Godavari District in Connection with the Rumpa Disturbances; Member of the Famine Commission in England. 1880: *Privilege leave in England for 3 months, including voyage to India;* resumed First Member of the Revenue Board. 1881: Additional Member of the Legislative Council; In Charge of Settlement Department; Provisional Member of Council. 1882: Ordinary Member of Council, *took his seat 12th June.*

SWINTON, Robert Blair.—1849: Writer and Student at the College. 1851: Assistant to Collector and Magistrate, Tinnevelly. 1855: Acting Head Assistant, afterwards Head Assistant at Tinnevelly. 1856: Acting Sub-Collector and Joint Magistrate, Tinnevelly; Acting Head Assistant to Collector and Magistrate, Trichinopoly. 1857: *On medical leave to Europe for 15 months.* 1858: Acting Head Assistant, afterwards Head Assistant to Collector and Magistrate, Rajahmundry; Acting Subordinate Judge, Cuddapah. 1859: Sub-Collector and Joint Magistrate, Bellary; Acting Sub-Judge, Madura, and at Ootacamund; Subordinate Judge, Mangalore. 1860: Subordinate Judge, Combaconum. 1862: Judge of Small Cause Court, Tanjore. 1863: Acting Civil and Sessions Judge, Tanjore; and at Negapatam. 1864: *On furlough to Europe for 3 years.* 1867: *Out of employ for six months;* Acting Judge of Small Cause Court, Madura; Acting Civil and Sessions Judge, Tinnevelly. 1868: District and Sessions Judge, Kistna. 1872: Acting District and Sessions Judge, South Arcot. 1874: *Retired from service, 23d June.* (*Annuitant on the Fund.*)

TAYLOR, George Noble.—1840: Writer. 1841: Assistant to the Collector and Magistrate, Masulipatam. 1842: Assistant to the Principal Collector and Magistrate, Cuddapah; Acting Assistant to the Collector and Magistrate, and Agent to the Governor of Fort St. George, in Ganjam. 1843: In the same capacity at Vizagapatam. 1845: Assistant to the Collector and Magistrate, and Agent to the Governor of Fort St. George, in Vizagapatam; *Proceeded to Europe on furlough.* 1848: *Returned to Madras.* 1849: Assistant to the Collector and Magistrate, Chingleput; Acting Secretary to the College and University Boards; Assistant to the Collector of Land Customs, Madras. 1851: Secretary to the College Board and to Madras University; at first Acting, then Sub-Collector and Joint Magistrate, Rajahmundry. 1856: Acting Deputy Secretary to Government, and Secretary to the Board of Examiners; *Proceeded to Europe on furlough for 6 months.* 1857: Acting Deputy Collector of Sea Customs, Madras; Acting Collector and Magistrate, Nellore; and at South Arcot. 1858: Inam Commissioner for the Presidency. 1863: Services placed temporarily at the Disposal of the Government of India. 1864: Provisional Member of the Council of the Governor-General of India. 1865: Member of Council of the Viceroy and Governor-General of India. 1869: *On medical leave to Europe for 6 months.*

1870: *Retired from service, 11th March.* (*Annuitant on the Fund.*)

THOMAS, Edward Croft Greenway.—1851: Writer and Student at the College. 1853: Assistant to Collector and Magistrate, Coimbatore. 1855: Acting Head Assistant to Collector and Magistrate, Malabar. 1856: Special Assistant to Collector and Magistrate, Malabar. 1858: Acting Sub-Judge, Calicut. 1859: Deputy Director of Revenue Settlement for the Wynaad Talook in Malabar. 1860: *On medical leave for* 4 *months;* Deputy Director of Revenue Settlement with the Salem Party. 1862: *On furlough to Europe for* 9 *months.* 1865: Sub-Collector and Joint Magistrate, Malabar; but to act as Civil and Sessions Judge, Cuddapah; Acting Collector and Magistrate, Kurnool. 1866: Acting Civil and Sessions Judge at Chingleput, and at Cuddalore, also Civil and Sessions Judge at the latter place; Judge of Small Cause Court, Madura. 1867: Civil and Sessions Judge, Madura. 1868: Civil and Sessions Judge, Calicut; *On medical leave for* 6 *months.* 1869: Acting Collector and Magistrate, afterwards Collector and Magistrate, Malabar; District and Sessions Judge, Vizagapatam. 1870: *On special leave for* 6 *months.* 1871: Resumed District and Sessions Judge, Vizagapatam. 1878: *On furlough to Europe for* 16 *months, with extension for another year.* 1882: *Retired from service,* 21*st January, in England.* (*Annuitant on the Fund.*)

THOMAS, Henry Sullivan.—1855: Writer and Student at the College. 1857: Assistant to Collector and Magistrate, Canara. 1858: *On medical leave to the Nilgiri Hills for* 9 *months.* 1859: Assistant to Collector and Magistrate, Madura. 1860: Acting Head Assistant, Madura. 1861: Head Assistant, Collector, and Magistrate, Madura; Officiating Sub-Collector and Joint Magistrate, Nellore. 1862: Sub-Collector and Joint Magistrate, Madura; Sub-Collector, Madras; Acting Sub-Collector, Salem. 1863: Sub-Collector, Madura; Acting Sub-Collector, Salem; Sub-Collector and Joint Magistrate, Salem. 1864: Justice of the Peace. 1866: Acting Collector of Sea Customs, Madras; Member of the Board of Examiners; Acting Civil and Sessions Judge, Ootacamund; and at Chingleput. 1867: Acting Collector and Magistrate, South Canara. 1870: *On furlough to Europe for* 2 *years.* 1872: Collector and Magistrate, South Canara. 1874: Acting Collector and Magistrate, and Agent to the Governor of Fort St. George, Tanjore, and Political Agent for French Settlement at Karikal. 1875: Collector and Magistrate, Kurnool. 1878: Acting Collector, Tanjore; Acting Third Member of the Revenue Board, afterwards Acting Second Member: Acting Secretary to Government, Revenue Department. 1879: Acting Second Member, afterwards Third Member of the Revenue Board; In Charge of the Inam Department. 1880: *On furlough to Europe for* 17 *months.* 1881: Second Member of the Revenue Board, and acting as First Member; President of the Board of Examiners. 1882: Member of the Local Self-Government Committee; proceeded to Calcutta as Additional Member of the Governor-General's Legislative Council. 1883: Acting First Member of the Revenue Board, Madras; again to Calcutta as Additional Member of the Governor-General's Legislative Council. 1884: On Special Duty connected with the "Pearl Fisheries," Tuticorin; on Deputation to Ceylon for the same purpose; Acting First Member of the Revenue Board, Madras, afterwards First Member. 1885: Additional Member of the Governor-General's Council for making Laws and Regulations.

THOMPSON, JOHN GEORGE.—1848: Writer. 1850: Assistant to the Principal Collector and Magistrate, Coimbatore. 1853: Acting Head Assistant at Coimbatore. 1855: Inspector of Schools. 1857: Acting Sub-Judge, Mangalore; Head Assistant to Collector and Magistrate, Salem. 1859: Sub-Judge, Mangalore; *Proceeded on furlough to Europe for* 3 *years and* 37 *days.* 1863: Acting Civil and Sessions Judge, Tellicherry; and at Mangalore; Sub-Collector and Joint Magistrate, Malabar. 1864: Acting Judge of Small Cause Court, Tellicherry. 1865: Civil and Sessions Judge, Cuddapah, but acting as such at Chingleput. 1866: Acting, afterwards, Civil and Sessions Judge, Vizagapatam. 1869: District and Sessions Judge, Ganjam. 1875: *On furlough to Europe for* 2 *years.* 1877: *Retired from service,* 30*th September.* (*Annuitant on the Fund.*)

THOMPSON, STEWART.—1855: Writer and Student at the College. 1857: *On medical leave to Europe for* 21 *months.* 1860: Assistant Collector, Bellary; *On medical leave for* 15 *months.* 1862: *Died,* 26*th December, in England.*

THORNHILL, GEORGE, C.S.I.—1842: Writer. 1844: Assistant to the Principal Collector and Magistrate, Coimbatore; Assistant to Collector and Magistrate, Rajahmundry. 1845: Acting Head Assistant to Collector and Magistrate, Rajahmundry, and at Cuddapah. 1846: In the same capacity at Masulipatam.

1847: Head Assistant to Collector and Magistrate, Masulipatam. 1852: Head Assistant to Collector and Magistrate, Guntoor. 1853: *On furlough to Europe.* 1856: Acting Principal Assistant to Collector and Magistrate, and Agent to the Governor of Fort St. George, in Ganjam. 1857: Principal Assistant, and Agent to the Governor, Ganjam. 1859: Acting Collector and Magistrate, and Agent to the Governor, in Vizagapatam; afterwards Acting Collector and Magistrate, Kurnool. 1860: Acting Civil and Sessions Judge, Masulipatam; Acting Collector and Magistrate, Kistna. 1861: Collector and Magistrate, Kistna. 1862: *On medical leave for 15 months.* 1865: Acting Collector and Magistrate, and Agent to the Governor, Ganjam. 1867: Acting Collector and Magistrate, Madras District. 1868: On Special Duty. 1869: Acting Third Member of the Revenue Board. 1870: Acting Second Member, afterwards Third Member of the Revenue Board. 1873: First Member of the Revenue Board. 1877: *Made a C.S.I., 1st January.* 1878: *Retired from service, 7th April, in India.* (*Annuitant on the Fund.*)

TOD, George Boulderson.—1852: Writer. 1853: Student at the College. 1854: Assistant to Collector and Magistrate, Malabar. 1856: Acting Head Assistant at Chingleput. 1857: Head Assistant at Chingleput. 1858: *On medical leave to Europe for 21 months.* 1860: Officiating Subordinate Judge, Cuddapah; Head Assistant to Collector and Magistrate, Trichinopoly; Acting Principal Assistant to Collector and Magistrate, and Agent to the Governor of Fort St. George, in Ganjam; Assistant to Collector and Magistrate, Kistna; Sub-Collector and Joint Magistrate, South Arcot. 1861: *Died, 14th November, at Madras.*

WALHOUSE, Moreton John.—1843: Writer. 1844: Assistant to the Principal Collector and Magistrate, Coimbatore. 1846: Acting Head Assistant to the Principal Collector and Magistrate, Coimbatore. 1851: Acting Sub-Judge, Salem. 1852: Head Assistant to Collector and Magistrate, Coimbatore. 1853: Acting Sub-Collector and Joint Magistrate, Madura. 1854: In the same capacity at Coimbatore. 1855: Sub-Collector and Joint Magistrate, Coimbatore. 1856: Acting Civil and Sessions Judge, Calicut; and at Honore. 1858: Acting Collector and Magistrate, Trichinopoly. 1859: *On furlough to Europe for 3 years.* 1862: Acting Civil and Sessions Judge, Tanjore. 1863: Acting Collector and Magistrate, Trichinopoly; Civil and Sessions Judge, Mangalore. 1864: Acting Collector and Magistrate, Malabar.

1867 : *On medical leave to Europe for 2 years.* 1870 : Civil and Sessions Judge, Mangalore. 1872 : *Resigned the service, 11th March, in India.* (*Annuitant on the Fund.*)

WEBSTER, ALEXANDER M'CALLUM.—1857 : Writer and Student at the College. 1859 : Assistant to Collector and Magistrate, Canara ; Assistant at North Canara. 1860 : Acting Head Assistant at North Canara, afterwards Head Assistant. 1862 : Head Assistant, South Canara. 1865 : Acting Sub-Collector and Joint Magistrate, Madras District. 1866 : *On medical leave for 20 months.* 1867 : Head Assistant to Collector and Magistrate, South Canara ; Sub-Collector and Joint Magistrate, Coimbatore ; Acting Principal Assistant to Collector and Magistrate, and Agent to the Governor, in Vizagapatam. 1868 : Acting Sub-Collector and Joint Magistrate, Coimbatore. 1869 : Sub-Collector and Joint Magistrate, Coimbatore ; Acting Collector and Magistrate, Coimbatore ; and at Malabar. 1870 : Acting Collector and Magistrate, South Canara. 1872 : Acting Collector and Magistrate, Trichinopoly ; Sub-Collector and Joint Magistrate, Chingleput ; *On furlough to Europe for 23 months.* 1873 : Collector and Magistrate, Godavari ; Acting Collector of Sea Customs, and Collector of Madras. 1874 : Acting Collector and Agent to the Governor of Fort St. George, Vizagapatam ; Acting Collector and Magistrate, South Canara. 1875 : Collector and Magistrate, South Canara ; *On special leave to Europe for 6 months.* 1876 : Acting Commissioner, Nilgiri Hills. 1877 : Collector, District Magistrate, and Agent to the Governor, Vizagapatam. 1879 : *Died, 27th September, at Coimbatore.*

WEBSTER, EDMUND FOSTER (*Barrister-at-Law*). — 1857 : Writer. 1858 : Student at the College. 1859 : Assistant to Collector and Magistrate, Tanjore. 1861 : Acting Head Assistant at Tanjore : *On medical leave to Europe for 2 years and 11 months.* 1864 : Assistant to Collector and Magistrate, Salem ; Acting Head Assistant at Salem, afterwards at Cuddapah. 1865 : Head Assistant at Kistna, and at Kurnool ; Acting Sub-Collector and Joint Magistrate, Bellary ; Head Assistant at Salem ; Acting Sub-Collector and Joint Magistrate, Godavari. 1866 : Justice of the Peace ; Head Assistant, afterwards Acting Sub-Collector, Godavari. 1867 : Sub-Collector, Godavari ; Acting First Judge of Small Cause Court, Madras ; Judge of Small Cause Court, Madura, also at Cuddalore in 1868, afterwards Acting Civil and Sessions Judge at Coimbatore. 1869 : Judge of Small Cause Court,

Cuddalore; Acting Civil and Sessions Judge, Tinnevelly. 1871: Judge of Small Cause Court, Cuddalore; *On furlough to Europe for 14 months.* 1873: Acting District and Sessions Judge, Cuddapah; Appointment confirmed; District and Sessions Judge, Trichinopoly. 1878: Collector and Magistrate, and Agent to the Governor of Fort St. George, in Tanjore; on Special Duty as a Member of the Famine Committee on Questions of Irrigation. 1879: Resumed Collector and Magistrate, and Agent, Tanjore; *On special leave to Europe for 5 months.* 1880: Collector and Magistrate, Tanjore. 1881: Acting Secretary to Government, Revenue Department; Secretary to Famine Code Committee. 1882: Resumed Acting Secretary, afterwards Secretary, to Government, Revenue Department; Member of the Forest Draft Bill Committee; Member of Local Self-Government Committee. 1883: Acting Chief Secretary to Government; Additional Member of Council for making Laws and Regulations. 1884: Chief Secretary to Government; Fellow of the Madras University.

WEDDERBURN, MAXWELL ANDREW.—1841: Writer. 1843: Assistant to Collector and Magistrate, South Arcot. 1845: Assistant to Collector and Magistrate, Malabar. 1846: Acting Head Assistant to Collector and Magistrate, North Arcot. 1847: *Proceeded to Europe.* 1848: Assistant to Collector and Magistrate, North Arcot; Acting Head Assistant to Collector and Magistrate, Cuddapah. 1850: Head Assistant to Collector and Magistrate, Cuddapah. 1851: Acting Sub-Collector and Joint Magistrate, Cuddapah. 1853: Sub-Collector and Magistrate, Cuddapah. 1857: *On furlough to Europe.* 1860: Acting Collector and Magistrate, Cuddapah. 1861: Collector and Magistrate, Cuddapah. 1863: Acting Collector and Magistrate, Bellary. 1864: *On medical leave to Europe for 16 months.* 1865: Collector and Magistrate, Tinnevelly. 1866: Collector and Magistrate, Bellary. 1868: Acting Collector and Magistrate, afterwards Collector and Magistrate, Coimbatore. 1869: *On furlough to Europe for 20 months.* 1872: Resumed Collector and Magistrate, Coimbatore. 1878: *Retired from service, 2d April, in India.* (*Annuitant on the Fund.*)

WHITESIDE, WILLIAM SOUTHEY.—1855: Writer and Student at the College. 1857: Assistant to Collector and Magistrate, North Arcot. 1858: Acting Head Assistant at Tanjore. 1859: Head Assistant to Collector and Magistrate, Nellore. 1860: Officiating Sub-Collector and Joint Magistrate, Nellore. 1861: Officiating Deputy Secretary to Government in Chief-Secretary's Departments. 1862: Sub-Collector and Joint Magistrate, South Arcot; Deputy Secretary to Government; Acting Civil and Sessions Judge, Chingleput; Sub-Collector, South Arcot. 1863: Justice of the Peace. 1864: *On special leave for 4 months.* 1866: Acting Judge, afterwards Judge, of Small Cause Court, Cuddalore. 1867: Acting Collector and Magistrate, South Canara; Acting Civil and Sessions Judge, Chingleput. 1868: Judge of Small Cause Court, Madura; Acting Civil and Sessions Judge, Tanjore. 1870: Acting Collector and Magistrate, North Arcot. 1871: Acting Collector and Magistrate, Trichinopoly. 1872: On Duty at Madras; Acting Collector and Magistrate, North Arcot; Collector of Trichinopoly. 1873: Collector and Magistrate, North Arcot. 1882: Acting Collector and Magistrate, and Agent to the Governor of Fort St. George, Tanjore; Collector and Magistrate, North Arcot; on Special Duty as Member of the Forest Draft Bill Committee, Ootacamund; Collector and Magistrate, and Agent, Tanjore; Acting Second Member of the Revenue Board; In Charge of the Inam Department; Acting President of the Board of Examiners. 1884: Acting Third Member of the Revenue Board; Director of Revenue Settlement and Agriculture; Acting Inam Commissioner; Third Member of the Revenue Board, and President of the Board of Examiners.

WILLIAMS, DERING.—1856: Writer and Student at the College. 1858: Assistant to Collector and Magistrate, Malabar. 1859: Acting Head Assistant, South Canara. 1861: Head Assistant, South Canara. 1862: Head Assistant at Nellore. 1864: *On furlough to Europe for 1 year and 8 months.* 1865: Assistant to Collector and Magistrate, Madras District; Acting Sub-Collector and Joint Magistrate, North Arcot. 1866: *Died, 4th April, in India.*

ADDENDUM.

Name	Status	Year		Date	PAGE
Anstey, Thomas	Annuitant,	1815.	Died	Oct. 25, 1843	3
Atkinson, Edward	„	1809.	„	Nov. 5, 1826	5
Aufrere, Thomas Norris	„	1815.	„	March 4, 1835	5
Babington, John	„	1833.	„	April 26, 1852	5
Baker, Charles	„	1808.	„	July 26, 1839	6
Balfour, James	„	1824.	„	April 19, 1845	6
Balfour, Walter	„	1815.	„	Aug. 12, 1837	7
Bayard, Robert	„	1833.	„	May 25, 1860	8
Binning, R. B. M.	Allowance from Fund, 1856–1879; disqualified on account of property				11
Blake, Ed. Parker	Annuitant,	1825.	Died	March 21, 1860	14
Boileau, Thos. E. J.	„	1851.	„	Feb. 8, 1853	15
Bourdillon, J. Dewar	„	1861.	„	May 21, 1883	15
Boutflower, Samuel	„	1824.	„	Sept. 7, 1830	16
Branfill, Benjamin	„	1805.	„	July 18, 1841	16
Buchan, George	„	1816.	„	Jan. 3, 1856	19
Casamaijor, J. A.	„	1837.	„	Oct. 25, 1865	22
Chamier (Deschamps), J.	„	1806.	„	Feb. 23, 1831	24
Chaplin, William	„	1826.	„	Sept. 6, 1843	24
Clarke, Richard	„	1828.	„	Aug. 3, 1848	28
Clerk, Robert (1st)	„	1805.	„	July 25, 1815	29
Clive, R. H.	„	1843.	„	Aug. 11, 1867	30
Cochrane, Hon. B.	„	1805.	„	Aug. 11, 1826	31
Cockburn, Thomas	„	1806.	„	Feb. 28, 1850	32
Cockburn, David	„	1828.	„	Feb. 10, 1836	32
Cole, Hon. A. H.	„	1829.	„	June 16, 1844	32
Coleman, Geo.	„	1817.	„	July 1, 1857	33
Cook, Wm.	„	1825.	„	Dec. 16, 1863	34

Name				PAGE
Cotton, J. J.	Annuitant, 1862.	Died	Dec. 20, 1867	36
Cunliffe, E. W.	„ 1836.	„	Dec. 20, 1866	39
Cunliffe, Brooke, Sen.	„ 1835.	„	Dec. 11, 1857	39
Dalzell, J. A.	„ 1839.	„	Dec. 30, 1877	40
Daniel, Thos.	„ 1837.	„	Aug. 25, 1842	41
Darvall, Roger	„ 1806.	„	Oct. 28, 1813	41
Dick, Mungo	„ 1809.	„	March 31, 1833	44
Dillon, Richard	„ 1807.	„	Aug. 21, 1818	45
Dodwell, Wm.	„ 1825.	„	Nov. 30, 1859	45
Elliott, Daniel (Sir)	„ 1859.	„	Oct. 30, 1872	49
Falconer, Alex.	„ 1812.	„	Dec. 10, 1847	51
Forbes, Michie	„ 1828.	„	Aug. 24, 1839	53
Forbes, Sir J.	„ 1827.	„	Feb. 16, 1846	54
Frere, Hatley	„ 1866.	„	Nov. 3, 1868	57
Gardiner, H.	„ 1836.	„	Aug. 8, 1843	59
Gordon, Wm.	„ 1806.	„	Oct. 13, 1833	62
Gowan, Geo.	„ 1826.	„	May 25, 1856	63
Græme, H. S.	„ 1837.	„	July 14, 1850	63
Grant, F. A.	„ 1832.	„	March 20, 1843	64
Gwatkin, J.	„ 1832.	„	July 10, 1855	66
Hankey, Thompson	„ 1827.	„	Oct. 26, 1855	69
Harris, Charles	„ 1835.	„	Jan. 12, 1840	71
Harris, T. J. P.	„ 1866.	„	June 28, 1867	72
Hawkins, W.	„ 1820.	„	July 31, 1836	73
Heath, J. M.	„ 1829.	„	Jan. 28, 1851	73
Hepburn, Jas.	„ 1824.	„	May 27, 1845	73
Hodgson, J.	„ 1820.	„	Dec. 29, 1857	75
Honeyman, R. B. J.	„ 1836.	„	Feb. 23, 1842	76
Hooper, G. S.	„ 1860.	„	May 21, 1867	76
Hudleston, J. A.	„ 1855.	„	Aug. 19, 1865	78
Hyde, Chas.	„ 1831.	„	Jan. 13, 1862	79
Ince, Daniel	„ 1807.	„	July 13, 1822	79
Inglis, W. A. D.	„ 1856.	„	Oct. 18, 1873	80
Jones, W.	„ 1806.	„	March 16, 1812	82
Keene, G. H.	„ 1836.	„	Jan. 29, 1864	83
Kelso (Hamilton), A. H.	„ 1834.	„	June 11, 1853	83
Kindersley, N. E.	„ 1806.	„	Feb. 16, 1831	84
Lacon, H.	„ 1835.	„	Feb. 1, 1864	85
Lascelles, F.	„ 1858.	„	July 15, 1882	86
Linley, W.	„ 1825.	„	May 6, 1839	89

			PAGE
Lushington, C. M. . .	Annuitant, 1843.	Died March 8, 1864 .	91
Macdonell, Æ. R. . .	„ 1839.	„ Oct. 24, 1866 .	92
Mackenzie, Alex. . .	„ 1810.	„ April 14, 1852 .	93
Mackonochie, R. . .	„ 1842.	„ Feb. 19, 1858 .	93
Malcolm, R. . . .	„ 1806.	„ Oct. 2, 1813 .	95
Mathison, A. S. . .	„ 1859.	„ April 18, 1882 .	97
Mitford, J. . . .	„ 1805.	„ Oct. 9, 1834 .	98
Monk, W. G. . . .	„ 1829.	„ March 3, 1859 .	99
Montgomerie, W. . .	„ 1834.	„ Oct. 23, 1852 .	99
Montgomery, Sir H. C. . Appointed Member of Council of the Secretary of State, September 2, 1858, on transfer of Government from the East India Company to the Crown. Retired from Council, November 13, 1876			100
Morehead, W. A. . .	Annuitant, 1862.	Died Dec. 1, 1863 .	101
Mortlock, H. . . .	„ 1828.	„ Feb. 13, 1837 .	103
Newnham, Thos. . .	„ 1833.	„ Sept. 29, 1861 .	105
Nicholls, Solomon . .	„ 1836.	„ Aug. 22, 1857 .	106
Oakes, Thos. . . .	„ 1815.	„ Dec. 29, 1834 .	106
Ogilvie, J. H. D. . .	„ 1831.	„ March 10, 1851 .	107
Oliver, W. . . .	„ 1836.	„ Aug. 2, 1846 .	108
Orr, John . . .	„ 1844.	„ in 1845 . .	110
Parish, G. . . .	„ 1828.	„ April 7, 1839 .	110
Parker, R. D. . . .	„ 1859.	„ Sept. 20, 1873 .	111
Read, John . . .	„ 1816.	„ July 7, 1843 .	119
Read, George . . .	„ 1815.	„ Sept. 28, 1825 .	120
Read, Alex. . . .	„ 1825.	„ Oct. 8, 1849 .	120
Reade, C. W. . . .	„ 1871.	„ April 27, 1884 .	120
Richardson, Francis .	„ 1821.	„ Sept. 25, 1856 .	121
Savory, J. S. . . .	„ 1821.	„ June 22, 1857 .	126
Sherson, Robt. . .	„ 1823.	„ March 23, 1843 .	128
Skardon, J. H. . .	„ 1803.	„ April 24, 1810 .	129
Skinner, Samuel . .	„ 1819.	„ May 21, 1854 .	130
Snodgrass, Thos. . .	„ 1805.	„ Aug. 28, 1834 .	133
Strachey, Geo. . .	„ 1820.	„ in 1849 . .	136
Strange, Jas. . . .	„ 1816.	„ Oct. 6, 1840 .	136
Stratton, Geo. . . .	„ 1824.	„ Aug. 30, 1853 .	137
Taswell, W. . . .	„ 1830.	„ Aug. 24, 1857 .	139
Thompson, G. . . .	„ ...	„ in 1804 (*India*) .	143
Torin, Benjamin . .	„ 1805.	„ May 11, 1839 .	144
Torriano, W. H. . .	„ 1808.	„ Nov. 16, 1828 .	144